Student Guide for Learning Economics

Fourth Edition

Student Guide for Learning Economics

Fourth Edition

Ralph T. Byrns
The University of Colorado at Boulder

Gerald W. Stone
Metropolitan State College

Scott, Foresman and Company
Glenview, Illinois   London, England

ISBN 0-673-38335-0

2   3   4   5   6—MKN—93   92   91   90   89

CONTENTS IN BRIEF

CONTENTS IN BRIEF
(cont.)

How to Study Economics

No doubt about it. Economics is among the most challenging topics that many of you will encounter during your college educations. This *Student Guide for Learning Economics* will help focus your study so that the time you devote to this fascinating subject is as productive as possible. Before you work on any chapter in this study guide, you should thoroughly read (and perhaps, reread) the corresponding material in our texts, *Economics*, *Microeconomics* or *Macroeconomics*. The "Contents in Brief" for this study guide provides cross-references so that you can discern which chapter here corresponds to a particular chapter from the text you are using.

Conscientious use of this study guide is the single factor that seems to differentiate students who do well in our courses from those who do poorly. This guide, instead of introducing new material, will aid you in learning and retaining the material in your text. You will find that time spent working through this study guide will pay huge dividends when you take examinations that test your mastery of economic concepts. More importantly, we hope that five years from now you remember and are able to apply economic reasoning to everyday problems. If you have any suggestions that you believe would make this guide more useful for other students, please send your comments to us, c/o Scott, Foresman & Company, 1900 East Lake Avenue, Glenview, Illinois 60025.

A Strategy for Studying Economics

Superficial cramming is very unlikely to succeed in an economics course. Keeping up is crucial. Research by educational psychologists indicates that learning is most effective when you are exposed to information and concepts in several ways over a period of time. You will learn more economics and retain it longer if you read, see, hear, communicate, and then apply economic concepts and information. This material is much more than a few facts and glib generalizations; understanding economics requires reflection. Here is one systematic study strategy that many students have found successful in economics, and have adapted for other classes.

Visual Information

Don't let the extensive graphs in economics frighten you. There is a brief review of graphical analysis at the end of Chapter 1 of your text; this *Student Guide for Learning Economics* also opens with a set of helpful exercises. Avoid the agony of trying to memorize each graph by taking the time to learn how graphs work. Proceed to Chapter 2 of your text only after you quell your anxiety a bit. (Be sure that you also understand simple algebra. The algebra in the text is elementary, and should prove no problem if you have learned the material from a basic course.) As you become familiar with graphs, you may be surprised to find yourself mentally graphing many noneconomic relationships, and even more amazed to find this process enjoyable.

Reading

Schedule ample time to read your assignments, and try to use the same quiet and cool (but not cold) room every day. Avoid drowsiness by sitting in a hard chair in front of a desk or table. Think about the material as you read. Many students spend hours highlighting important points for later study, for which they somehow never find time. Too frequently, busy work substitutes for thinking about economics. Try to skim a chapter; then go back and really focus on five or six pages. Don't touch a pen or pencil except to make margin notes cross-referencing related materials you already know.

Writing

After a healthy dose of serious reading, close your text and outline the important points with a half-page of notes. If you cannot briefly summarize what you just read, put your pen down and re-read the material. You have not yet digested the central ideas. Don't be surprised if some concepts require several readings. Be alert for graphs and tables that recapitulate important areas. When you finish each chapter, read its Chapter Review, work through all Problems, and outline good, but brief, answers to all Questions for Thought and Discussion.

Listening

Most lectures blend your instructor's own insights and examples with materials from the text, but few students conscientiously work through assignments before lectures. You will have a major advantage over most of your classmates if you do, and will be able to take notes selectively. Focus on topics that your instructor stresses but which are not covered in depth in the text. Notes from lectures should supplement, not duplicate, your text.

Teaching

Your instructors know that they learn their subject in greater depth every time they teach it. Teaching exposes you to previously unfamiliar aspects of a topic because you must conceptualize and verbalize ideas so that other people can understand them. Take turns with a classmate in reading the text's Key Points (in the Chapter Review) to each other. After one person reads a Key Point aloud, the other should explain it in his or her own words. Study groups work well in this way, but you may learn economics even more thoroughly if you simply explain economic concepts to a friend who has never studied it.

Applications

Working through the material from this *Student Guide* that parallels each chapter of the text will make it easier to comprehend the economic events regularly featured in the news. When this happens, you will be among the minority who truly understand economic and financial news. Use economic reasoning to interpret your day-to-day behavior, and that of your friends and relatives. This will provide unique insights into how people function and how the world works.

Examinations

Following the preceding suggestions should prepare you for minor tests and quizzes. To prepare for major exams and finals:

1. Read the Chapter Reviews for all chapters that will be covered on the examination. Keep a record of each Key Point that you could not explain to an intelligent friend who had never taken economics.

2. Return to each Key Point that you have not grasped adequately. Read the text material that covers it and rework the parallel parts of the accompanying chapter from your *Student Guide*.

3. Discuss any Key Point that is not clear to you with a friend.

4. Skim the Glossary at the end of the text for a last minute refresher before your final exam. See if this technique works for you.

We know that this is a tall order, but if you conscientiously follow these study tips, we guarantee you an enjoyable and enlightening course.

CHAPTER ONE
SCARCITY AND CHOICE

CHAPTER OBJECTIVES

You get your feet wet in this chapter. We focus on economic concepts that provide a general framework for understanding the remainder of this book. After you have read and studied this introduction you should be able to explain why scarcity is the basic economic problem; describe various kinds of productive resources and the payments to the owners of these resources; discuss a number of fundamental economic concepts, including the nature of economic prices, opportunity costs, and efficiency; discuss the nature of scientific theory, including its evolution into common sense, and the use of Occam's Razor; and distinguish normative from positive economics, and macroeconomics from microeconomics.

CHAPTER REVIEW: KEY POINTS

1. *Economics* is concerned with choices and their consequences; it is the study of how individuals and societies allocate their limited resources to satisfy relatively unlimited wants.

2. *Scarcity* occurs because our relatively unlimited wants cannot be completely met from the limited resources available. A good is scarce if people cannot freely get all they want, so that the good commands a positive price.

3. Production occurs when knowledge or technology is used to apply energy to materials to make them more valuable.

4. *Resources* (factors of production) include:

   a. *Labor.* Productive efforts made available by human beings. Payments for labor services are called *wages*.
   b. *Land.* All natural resources such as land, minerals, water, air. Payments for land are called *rents*.
   c. *Capital.* Improvements that increase the productive potential of other resources. Payments for the use of capital are called *interest*. When economists refer to capital, they mean physical capital rather than financial capital, which consists of paper claims to goods or resources.
   d. *Entrepreneurship.* The organizing, innovating, and risk-taking function that combines other resources to produce goods. Providers of this factor receive *profits*.

5. The *opportunity costs* of the consumption choices you make are measured by the subjective values of alternatives you sacrifice.

6. *Common sense* is theory that has been tested over a long period and found useful. In general, good theory accurately predicts how the real world operates. *Occam's Razor* suggests that the simplest workable theories are the most useful or "best."

7. *Positive economics* is scientifically testable and involves value-free descriptions of economic relationships, dealing with "what is." *Normative economics* involves value judgments about economic relationships and addresses "what should be." Normative theory can be neither scientifically verified nor proven false.

8. *Macroeconomics* is concerned with aggregate (the total levels of) economic phenomena, including such items as Gross National Product, unemployment, and inflation.

9. *Microeconomics* concentrates on individual decision making, resource allocation, and how prices and output are determined.

10. *Economic efficiency* occurs when a given amount of resources produces the most valuable combination of outputs possible. *Production (technical) efficiency* is obtained when a given output is produced at the lowest possible cost. Another way of looking at efficiency is that it occurs when the opportunity cost of obtaining some specific amount of a good is at its lowest. *Consumption efficiency* requires consumers to adjust their purchasing patterns to maximize their satisfactions from given budgets.

11. *Comparative advantage* is a guide to efficient specialization: You gain by specializing in producing things where your opportunity costs are lowest if you trade your production for things other people can produce at lower opportunity costs.

MATCHING KEY TERMS AND CONCEPTS

SET I

H 1. microeconomics

A 2. Occam's razor

B 3. positive economics

G 4. land

J 5. model

E 6. normative economics

I 7. macroeconomics

D 8. entrepreneurship

C 9. financial capital

F 10. production

a. The simplest workable theory is the best theory. *Occam's razor*

b. Economic theory free of personal bias or value judgments. *positive econ.*

c. Stocks, bonds, and other paper claims to goods or resources. *financial capital*

d. The organizing, risk-taking, and innovating resource. *ent.*

e. Untestable theories rife with value judgments. *normative econ.*

f. Using technology to apply energy to make materials more valuable. *production*

g. Nonhuman resources other than capital. *land*

h. The study of individual decisions made by consumers and firms. *econ (micro)*

i. Focuses on aggregate, or economy-wide, variables. *macro econ*

j. A representation of a theory. *model*

efficiency
given output maximum from given resources
given output maximum from given price
opportunity costs low

SET II

J	1.	technology	
B	2.	capital	
C	3.	*Homo economicus*	
D	4.	labor	
I	5.	rent	
A	6.	scarce good	
H	7.	profits	
F	8.	investment	
G	9.	depreciation	
E	10.	wages	

a. Desired amounts of a good exceed those freely available. *scarce good*

b. Improvements to natural resources that make them more productive. *capital*

c. The view that humans maximize their satisfaction or wealth.

d. The hours of human effort available for production. *labor*

e. Payments for labor services. *wages*

f. Physical capital accumulation. *interest / investment*

g. Decreases in capital because of wear-and-tear. *depreciation*

h. Entrepreneur's reward. *profits*

i. Payment for the use of land. *rent*

j. The "recipes" used to combine resources for production. *technology*

SET III

C	1.	interest
B	2.	free good
A	3.	opportunity cost
E	4.	division of labor
G	5.	comparative advantage
D	6.	economic efficiency
H	7.	specialization
J	8.	production efficiency
I	9.	equity
E	10.	consumption efficiency

a. The value foregone whenever people make choices. *opportunity cost*

b. Adds to human happiness, but is not scarce. *free good*

c. Payments to capital owners. *interest*

d. When this is reached, further gains in happiness to anyone require losses to someone else. *efficiency*

e. Achieving maximum satisfaction from given budgets. *consumption efficiency*

f. When each worker's simple tasks are combined into a complex good. *division of labor*

g. When your opportunity cost of producing some good is lowest, so that you gain by trading for something else for which your opportunity cost is relatively high. *Comparative adv.*

h. More can be produced by doing one or two things instead of many. *specialization*

i. Fairness *equity*

j. Getting maximum output from given resources. *production efficiency*

CHAPTER REVIEW (FILL-IN QUESTIONS)

1. Scarcity is a result of ___limited___ resources confronted by ___unlimited___ wants.

2. ___Production___ is the process of using knowledge to apply energy to materials so that they are more valuable. The knowledge used to combine resources for production is referred to as ___technology___.

3. ___Profit___ is the residual after all economic costs are paid out of a firm's revenues, and is received by ___entrepreneurs___ who organize the firm's activities, innovate new products and technologies, and take business risks.

4. People act rationally and purposefully to ___maximize___ their ___happiness___.

5. When economists say price or cost, they typically mean the value of the best ___alternative___ forgone when choices are made, rather than monetary prices. This is known as ___opportunity cost___, or alternative cost. These costs are implicit in all choices, even when it is not obvious that conventional "economics" is involved.

6. Theory is judged by how well it ___predicts___ how the world works. ___Occam's razor___ expresses a common preference among scientists for simple, rather than complex, workable theories.

7. ___Macroecon___ is the study of employment, inflation, money, the level of taxation, the relative prices of two or more countries' currencies, unemployment, national income, economic growth, and similarly aggregated variables. ___Microecon___ is a more localized study of the consequences of interactive decisionmaking by individual consumers and firms.

8. ___Production eff___ occurs when the opportunity cost of producing a given amount of goods is ___minimized___.

9. There is ___consumption___ efficiency if a consumer experiences maximum satisfaction from a given ___budget___.

10. Some self sufficiency is lost, but production and consumption rise when we use ___comparative___ advantage to guide us into areas of ___specialization___ in which our opportunity costs of production are relatively low.

STANDARD MULTIPLE CHOICE

THERE IS ONE BEST ANSWER FOR EACH QUESTION.

___ 1. Economics involves broadly studying how:
   a. political power is used unethically to make money.
   b. resources are allocated to satisfy human wants.
   c. proper nutrition and budgeting benefit your family.
   d. to get away with cheating the Internal Revenue Service.
   e. different species are environmentally interdependent.

___ 2. Scientific attempts to describe economic relationships are:
   a. factual and can never be wrong.
   b. accurate ways to predict political viewpoints.
   c. known as positive economics.
   d. directed at the fairness of social programs.
   e. intended to boost the egos of entrepreneurs.

_____ 3. Disagreements between economists arise most commonly in:
  a. microeconomic reasoning.
  (b.) normative economics.
  c. positive economics.
  d. practical applications of common sense.
  e. macroeconomic theories.

_____ 4. Economists:
  a. hardly ever agree on anything.
  (b.) agree on much of economic theory.
  c. never make normative value judgments.
  d. accurately predict the effects of all economic policies.
  e. disagree most about positive economics.

_____ 5. Macroeconomics is primarily concerned with aggregates. Which of the following is *not* a macroeconomic aggregate?
  (a.) Decisionmaking by a household.
  b. The unemployment rate, and inflation levels.
  c. National income.
  d. The supply of money.
  e. Fiscal policies of the federal government.

_____ 6. Which of the following *least* explains the widespread but erroneous view that economists seldom agree?
  a. The media focus on controversy, not agreement.
  b. More than economic logic, politics shapes policymaking.
  c. Economists who are political appointees often feel obligated to support the president even if they disagree privately.
  d. Economic policies embody controversial value judgments.
  (e.) Economic policy is more scientific than economic theory.

_____ 7. Unnecessary complexity in a theory is a violation of:
  a. common sense.
  b. the principle of nonsatiety.
  c. the law of supply and demand.
  (d.) Occam's razor.
  e. the anti-parsimony corollary.

_____ 8. Decisions made in households, firms, and government are the focus of:
  a. positive economics.
  b. environmental economics.
  (c.) microeconomics.
  d. normative economics.
  e. macroeconomics.

_____ 9. When less is freely available than people want, a good is:
  a. in short supply.
  b. a free good.
  c. a luxury good.
  (d.) scarce.
  e. a necessity.

_____ 10. Which of the following comes closest to being a free good?
  (a.) A wino's lunch, dug from the trash behind a restaurant.
  b. Hot lunches provided to needy students at school.
  c. Bacon and eggs bought with food stamps.
  d. A record you bought from money earned by picking up aluminum cans in your spare time.
  (e.) Free public education.

_____ 11. *TANSTAAFL* is an acronym suggesting that:
  a. tax agents never see the awful affects from levies.
  b. tenants and needy should take all assets from landlords.
  (c.) there ain't no such thing as a free lunch.
  d. temperance and non-satiety together are adequate for life.
  e. toffs and nabobs say that abstinence angers fun lovers.

_____ 12. People have a comparative advantage in a good if their:
  a. satisfaction from it exceeds that from other goods.
  (b.) opportunity cost of producing it is relatively low.
  c. production of all goods is faster than their neighbors.
  d. purchases of imports are cheaper than domestic goods.
  e. psychic enjoyment is greater than the market price.

___13. An economy suffers from production inefficiency if:
  a. water runs off lawns and down big city streets but is greatly needed by remote drought-stricken farmers.
  b. it operates in a region of diminishing returns.
  c. costs increase when production is expanded.
  d. a consumer could gain by buying different goods.
  (e.) costs could be reduced by using resources differently.

___14. Labor, land, capital, and entrepreneurship are all:
  a. examples of technology.
  b. allocative mechanisms.
  (c.) resources, or factors of production.
  d. tools of capitalistic exploitation.
  e. natural resources.

___15. Opportunity costs are the values of the:
  a. monetary costs of goods and services.
  (b.) best alternatives sacrificed when choices are made.
  c. minimal budgets of families on welfare.
  d. profits gained by successful entrepreneurs.
  e. freedom people enjoy in a socialist economy.

___16. Economic equity refers to the:
  a. financial settlements in civil court cases.
  b. balance of national trade.
  (c.) fairness of some economic arrangement.
  d. hidden costs passed on to consumers.
  e. gross value of any stocks or bonds you own.

___17. Economic efficiency for the entire economy requires that:
  a. potential gains to anyone necessitate losses to another.
  b. all goods be produced at their lowest possible opportunity costs.
  c. maximum-valued output is obtained from given resources.
  d. all benefits are obtained at the lowest possible cost.
  (e.) All of the above.

___18. When you specialize in that which you can do at relatively low cost and buy from others when their relative costs are low, all parties mutually gain by exploiting:
  a. the division of labor.
  (b.) comparative advantage.
  c. centralized coordination.
  d. diversified investment.
  e. diseconomies of scale.

___19. Knowledge used to combine resources productively is called:
  a. entrepreneurship.
  b. capitalism.
  c. investment.
  (d.) technology.
  e. comparative advantage.

___20. The process by which capital becomes worn out or obsolete is known as:
  a. capital attenuation.
  b. disinvestment.
  c. bankruptcy.
  d. disinflation.
  (e.) depreciation.

TRUE/FALSE

F 1. Economics resembles accounting or finance in being more relevant for business firms than individuals.

F 2. Complexity is desirable in a scientific theory.

? E 3. Unlike theory, common sense emphasizes practicality.

T 4. Normative economics is concerned with what should be, rather than what is.

T 5. Macroeconomics focuses on aggregate variables such as national income, employment, and inflation.

F 6. Occam's Razor is more relevant for other sciences than it is for economics.

T 7. Economic reasoning is involved anytime people choose one thing instead of another.

T 8. Models are less complicated and formal than theories.

T 9. Positive economic analysis can help in determining how to reach politically-set economic goals.

F 10. Positive economics specifies the value judgments used to draw inferences in economic analysis.

T 11. Successful entrepreneurs combine resources productively.

F 12. Financial capital refers to all improvements made to land, machinery, and equipment.

F 13. Payments for the use of capital services are called profit.

T 14. Deciding to take a nap is an economic decision.

T 15. Self sufficiency is an efficient goal for everyone.

F 16. Importing goods from foreigners because their production costs are below U.S. costs is a symptom of inefficiency.

F 17. It is invariably less costly to mow your own grass than to hire someone else to cut it.

T 18. Economic considerations shape even such decisions as selecting a spouse or determining how many children to have.

T 19. Opportunity costs are incurred while you study economics.

F 20. Most of the best things in life are free.

UNLIMITED MULTIPLE CHOICE

WARNING: EACH QUESTION HAS FROM ZERO TO FOUR CORRECT ANSWERS!

___ 1. Economics is a(n):
   a. study of decisionmaking and its consequences.
   b. mathematical and physical science, like chemistry.
   c. concern only for people who are miserly.
   d. "apparatus of the mind."

___ 2. A positive economic statement can be scientifically tested to see if it is false. Which of the following are positive economic statements?
   a. The economy will grow faster if tax rates are cut.
   b. A high tax on tobacco will severely cut cigarette smoking.
   c. People would have fewer children if their tax deductions for having them were increased.
   d. The federal budget should be balanced annually.

___ 3. Theories are:
   a. much more complicated than common sense.
   b. scientific only if based on normative value judgments.
   c. proven if only a few unimportant exceptions exist.
   (d.) developed when we collect data, try to explain how things work, and then test for validity.

___ 4. According to the characterization of humans as *Homo economicus*, all human behavior is:
   (a.) assumed to be self-interested, including charitable acts.
   b. intended to generate monetary profits.
   (c.) aimed at maximizing pleasure and minimizing pain.
   d. guided by an instinct to perpetuate the species.

___ 5. A comparative advantage in some good requires that you:
   (a.) are able to produce it at relatively low opportunity cost.
   b. can make it better and faster than any other producers.
   c. encounter minimal marketing costs in finding buyers for it.
   d. be self-sufficient in all goods.

PROBLEM

When Alferd and Zachariah, two pioneers, operate independently, their average daily production and consumption over the course of a year are as shown in Table 1:

Table 1

	DAILY WORK HOURS	AVERAGE DAILY PRODUCTION AND CONSUMPTION
Alferd	6	2 pounds of buffalo meat
	2	4 pounds of pinto beans
Zachariah	2	4 pounds of buffalo meat
	6	2 pounds of pinto beans

Who has the comparative advantage in hunting? In farming? Fill in Table 2 on the assumption that they begin to specialize and trade, and that their tastes are sufficiently similar that they end up eating identical diets.

Table 2: After Specialization

	DAILY WORK HOURS	AVERAGE DAILY PRODUCTION	AVERAGE DAILY CONSUMPTION
Hunter name *Alferd*	8	_16_ pounds of *meat*	_8_ pounds of *meat*
			_8_ pounds of *beans*
Farmer name *Zach*	8	_16_ pounds of *meat*	_8_ pounds of *meat*
			_8_ pounds of *beans*

8

ANSWERS

Matching Key Terms and Concepts

SET I

Answer	Reference
1. h	p. 11
2. a	p. 9
3. b	p. 10
4. g	p. 4
5. j	p. 9
6. e	p. 10
7. i	p. 11
8. d	p. 4
9. c	p. 4
10. f	p. 4

SET II

Answer	Reference
1. j	p. 4
2. b	p. 4
3. c	p. 5
4. d	p. 4
5. i	p. 4
6. a	p. 3
7. h	p. 4
8. f	p. 4
9. g	p. 4
10. e	p. 4

SET III

Answer	Reference
1. c	p. 4
2. b	p. 3
3. a	p. 6
4. f	p. 13
5. g	p. 13
6. d	p. 12
7. h	p. 13
8. j	p. 12
9. i	p. 10
10. e	p. 12

Chapter Review (Fill-in Questions)

1. scarce or limited, unlimited
2. Production, technology
3. Profit, entrepreneurs
4. maximize, satisfactions or happiness
5. alternative, opportunity cost
6. predicts, Occam's Razor
7. Macroeconomics, Microeconomics
8. Production efficiency, minimized
9. consumption, income or budget
10. comparative, specialization

Standard Multiple Choice Questions

Answer	Reference
1. b	p. 3
2. c	p. 10
3. b	p. 10
4. b	p. 10
5. a	p. 11
6. e	p. 10
7. d	p. 9
8. c	p. 11
9. d	p. 3
10. a	p. 3
11. c	p. 3
12. b	p. 13
13. e	p. 13
14. c	p. 4
15. b	p. 6
16. c	p. 10
17. e	p. 12
18. b	p. 13
19. d	p. 4
20. e	p. 4

True/False Questions

Answer	Reference
1. F	p. 3
2. F	p. 9
3. F	p. 8
4. T	p. 10
5. T	p. 11
6. F	p. 9
7. T	p. 3
8. F	p. 9
9. T	p. 10
10. F	p. 10
11. T	p. 4
12. F	p. 4
13. F	p. 4
14. T	p. 6
15. F	p. 12
16. F	p. 13
17. F	p. 14
18. T	p. 6
19. T	p. 6
20. F	p. 3

Unlimited Multiple Choice Questions

Answer	Reference
1. ad	p. 3, 8
2. abc	p. 10
3. d	p. 8, 9
4. ac	p. 5
5. a	p. 13

PROBLEM

Reference pp. 13-15

Table 3: After Specialization

	Daily Work Hours	Average Daily Production	Average Daily Consumption*
Hunter Zachariah	8	16 pounds of meat	8 pounds of meat
			8 pounds of beans
Farmer Alferd	8	16 pounds of beans	8 pounds of meat
			8 pounds of beans

*Note that each can now consume more of both meat and beans.

OPTIONAL MATERIAL:
GRAPHICAL TECHNIQUES IN ECONOMICS

CHAPTER OBJECTIVES

Be sure that graphical analysis is not a mystery when you launch into economics. Take the time now to work through "Graphical Techniques in Economics" at the end of Chapter 1 of your text. That done, carefully do the following exercises. The graphs that pervade economics will not appear as formidable to you as they do to the many students who suffer from "graphobia." After you have studied this material on Graphical Techniques you should be able to: (1) Plot data using the Cartesian Coordinate system. (2) Use descriptive graphs to answer questions, and (3) Measure and interpret the slopes and intercepts of lines.

CARTESIAN COORDINATES

Problem 1

Plot the following pairs of coordinates on Figure 1.

Figure 1

a. (1,1)

b. (-5,8)

c. (-8,-8)

d. (5,-7)

e. (3,8)

f. (9,-2)

g. (-9,2)

h. (-5,5)

i. (8,4)

j. (2,-2)

k. (-3,-4)

l. (-4,-9)

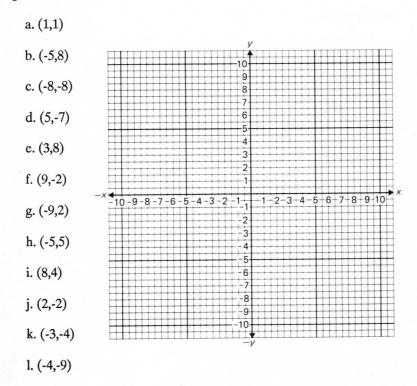

Problem 2

New "How-to-Get-Rich-Quick" books appear regularly, while old ones go out of print. Another employee at your firm (a publisher) used the letters *a* through *l* to plot monthly data for 1988 in Figure 2, showing changes in the number of "get rich" books in print and the percentage changes in worldwide sales per book. You want to see if these data are related, but first need to match the letters from the figure with their corresponding months.

Table 1	Corresponding Letter	Month	Change in Number of Books	Percentage Change in Sales per Book
	_____	1. Jan.	-3	+2
	_____	2. Feb.	-5	+8
	_____	3. Mar.	+4	-3
	_____	4. Apr.	0	+1
	_____	5. May.	-2	0
	_____	6. Jun.	+4	-2
	_____	7. Jul.	-3	+1
	_____	8. Aug.	+7	-4
	_____	9. Sep.	+9	-3
	_____	10. Oct.	+8	-2
	_____	11. Nov.	+3	0
	_____	12. Dec.	-4	+8

After you match the graphed points with their corresponding months, the company president wants to know if there is a relationship. Your opinion is that there is a (13) _____ (positive/negative/no) relationship. This means that as more "get rich" books are in print, sales per book (14) _____ (rise/fall/are unaffected).

Figure 2

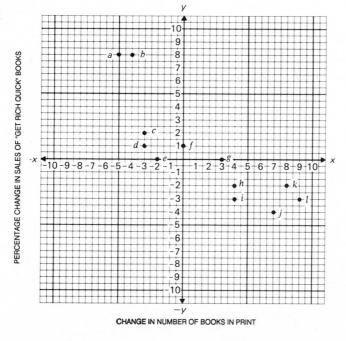

CHANGE IN NUMBER OF BOOKS IN PRINT

Problem 3

Wall Street gurus constantly search for variables that predict stock market movements. A stockbroker develops a theory that percentage increases in sales of new yellow cars indicate consumer optimism and, hence, suggest that the Dow Jones stock market index will rise by some percentage the next year. Plot the data from Table 2 into Figure 3 for the broker, using *a, b, c,* and so on.

Table 2

Point	Year	Percentage Change in Yellow Cars Sold	Next Year's Percentage Change in the Dow Jones Index
a.	1976	1	10
b.	1977	-5	10
c.	1978	-8	-8
d.	1979	6	-8
e.	1980	4	4
f.	1981	-5	-5
g.	1982	9	-3
h.	1983	5	-3
i.	1984	0	5
j.	1985	-7	-2

Looking at Figure 3, do you think the broker's theory is good or bad?

Figure 3

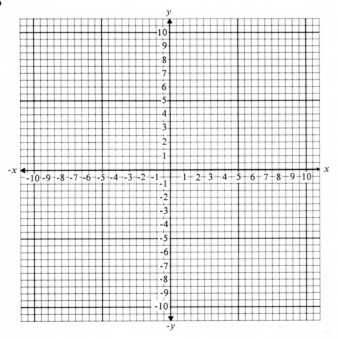

13

Problem 4

Using Figure 4, graph the relationships between *x* and *y* (based on the formula *y* = *a* + *bx*) if the intercept *a* and the slope *b* have the following values. You will need to set *x* equal to some arbitrarily selected values, and then calculate the corresponding values of *y*. Label each line with the corresponding letter, from *a* through *f*. Identify negative relationships with an asterisk.

Figure 4

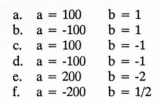

a.   a = 100   b = 1
b.   a = -100   b = 1
c.   a = 100   b = -1
d.   a = -100   b = -1
e.   a = 200   b = -2
f.   a = -200   b = 1/2

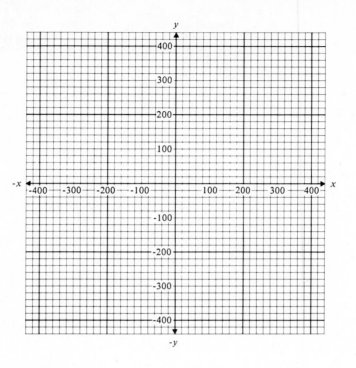

DESCRIPTIVE GRAPHICS

Problem 5

Panels A and B in Figure 5 depict the distribution of income in 1965 and 1977. Use these data to answer the following questions.

a.   How many families' annual incomes exceeded $9,999 in 1977? ____

b.   If 10 percent of the families in the annual income class $25,000 and over had incomes exceeding $35,000 in 1965, how many families had income from $25,000 to $34,999? _____

c.   In 1977 how many more white than black families earned over $25,000? _____ Is this a good measure of the comparative income positions of the two groups? What would be a better measure of their relative positions for higher familial income? _____.

d.   If black families had the same proportional income distribution as whites in 1977, how many more black families would have earned income greater than $9,999? _____

e.   What was the percentage increase from 1965 to 1977 in the number of families annually earning between $10,000 and $14,999? _____

Figure 5

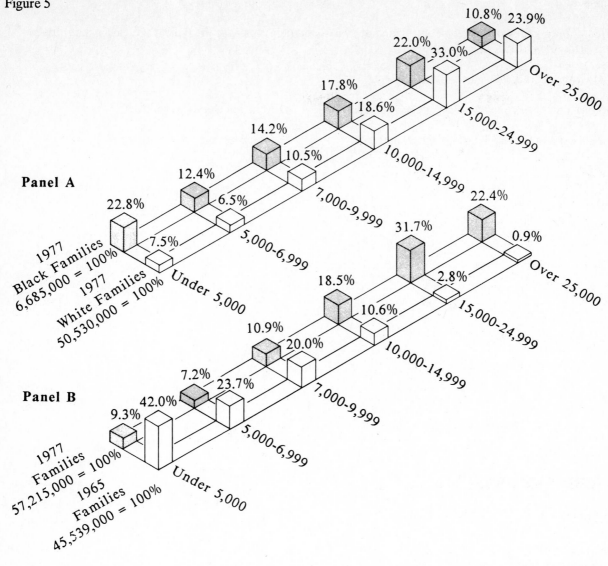

Panel A

Panel B

10.8% 23.9%

22.0% 33.0%

17.8% 18.6%

14.2% 10.5%

12.4% 6.5%

22.8% 7.5%

Over 25,000

15,000-24,999

10,000-14,999

7,000-9,999

5,000-6,999

Under 5,000

1977
Black Families
6,685,000 = 100%

1977
White Families
50,530,000 = 100%

22.4% 0.9%

31.7% 2.8%

18.5% 10.6%

10.9% 20.0%

7.2% 23.7%

9.3% 42.0%

Over 25,000

15,000-24,999

10,000-14,999

7,000-9,999

5,000-6,999

Under 5,000

1977
Families
57,215,000 = 100%

1965
Families
45,539,000 = 100%

Problem 6

Age/earnings profiles show how people's incomes vary with their ages. Use the typical age/earnings profile in Figure 6 to answer the following questions.

a.   On average, the peak earning age is _____ ?

b.   The slope of the line between age 20 and 50 is _____ ? How is that slope interpreted? _____

c.   The slope of the line between age 50 and 65 is_____ ? Between age 65 and 70, the slope is? _____

Figure 6

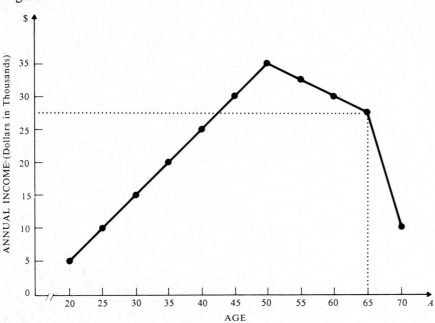

GRAPHICAL ANALYSIS OF AREAS

While in grade school you learned such formulas as: the area of a rectangle (*A*) equals the base (*b*) times the height (*h*), or $A = bh$. The following problems show how such calculations are useful in graphically analyzing individual expenditures or the costs of firms.

Problem 7

A world famous restaurant, *Les Gourmandes,* often features Quiche Lorraine as its luncheon special. Over the years, it has discovered how prices affect daily sales, as graphed in Figure 7. If you draw lines from the points we have identified to the vertical and horizontal axes, you can calculate the areas of the resultant rectangles to fill in the table and find out how quiche revenues are influenced by the price charged. (Why? Because *bh* is the same as price (*P*) times quantity (*Q*), and *PQ* equals total revenue.) Does the negative relationship between price and quantity seem reasonable? Why? (Answer this question for yourself at this point. We explore the reasons why such relationships are negative in Chapter 3.)

Figure 7

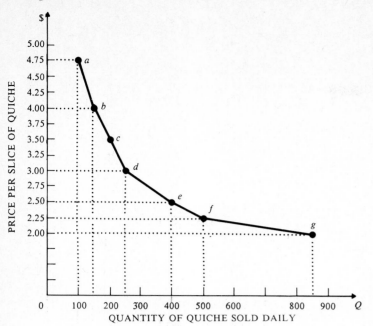

Point	Price (P)	Quantity (Q)	Total Revenues (P X Q)
a			
b			
c			
d			
e			
f			
g			

Table

Problem 8

Suppose that a U.S. Department of Agriculture study suggests the relationship shown in Figure 8 between the price (P) of kumquats and the quantities (Q) that farmers are willing to produce. Fill in the table to indicate how the total dollar revenues of kumquat farmers vary with the changes in market conditions that cause prices to vary. (**Hint**: You must compute the areas of rectangles much as you did in the preceding problem.) Shade the area representing farmers' total income (P x Q) when kumquats are 50 cents a pound. Use a different shading technique to show how much extra revenue they receive if they sell as much as they want to when the price is 60 cents per pound. Does the positive relationship we have shown between price and farmers' willingness to produce seem reasonable? Why? (Answer this question for yourself at this point. We explore reasons for such positive relationships in Chapter 3.)

Figure 8

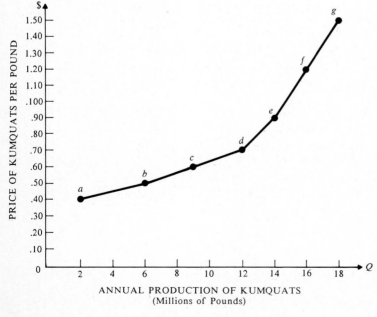

Table

Point	Price (P)	Quantity (Q)	Total Revenues (P X Q)
a			
b			
c			
d			
e			
f			
g			

17

ANSWERS

Problem 1
Reference p. 18
See Figure 9.

Figure 9

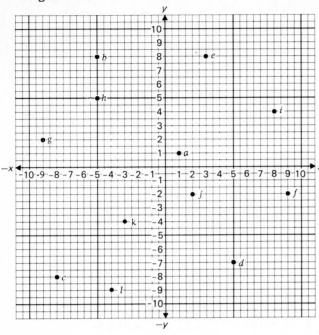

Figure 10

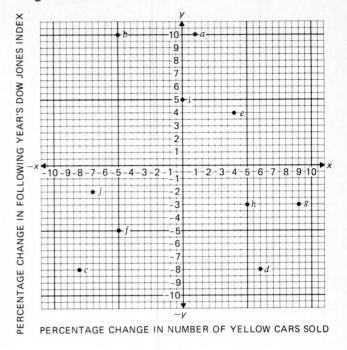

b. This theory does not appear to work very well.

Problem 2
Reference pp. 18-19, 22

1.	c	8.	j
2.	a	9.	l
3.	i	10.	k
4.	f	11.	g
5.	e	12.	b
6.	h	13.	negative
7.	dg	14.	fall

Problem 3
Reference pp. 22-24
See Figure 10.

Problem 4
Reference pp. 22-24
See Figure 11.

Figure 11

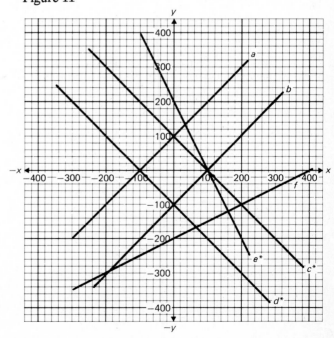

18

Problem 5
Reference pp. 19-24

a. 57,215,000 x .726 = 41,538,090.

b. (.009(45,539,000)) x .9 = 368,866.

c. White ($25,000) = .239 x 50,530,000 = 12,076,670; Black ($25,000) = .108 x 6,685,000 = 721,980; Difference = 11,354,690; No; The difference in percentages in the greater than $25,000 category (23.9 - 10.8 = 13.1) would be a better measure.

d. (1) 75.5 percent of whites earn more than $9,999.
.755 x 6,685,000 = 5,047,175 (blacks who would earn more than $9,999).

(2) 50.6 percent of blacks earn more than $9,999.
.506 x 6,685,000 = 3,382,610 (blacks earning more than $9,999 in 1977).

(3) 5,047,175 - 3,382,610 = 1,664,565.

e. 1965: .106 x 45,539,000 = 4,827,134.
1977: .185 x 57,215,000 = 10,584,775.
percentage change = (10,584,775 - 4,827,134)/4,827,134 = 1.19 (rounded) x 100 = 119

Problem 6
Reference pp. 22-23

a. 50

b. 1000; for each extra year in age, the typical individual in this age range earns $1000 more annually.

c. -7500/15 = -500; -17,500/5 = -3,500.

Problem 7
Reference pp. 18-24

Table 3

POINT	PRICE (P)	QUANTITY (Q)	TOTAL REVENUES (P X Q)=$MILLIONS)
a	$ .40	2	$ .8 million
b	$ .50	6	$ 3.0 million
c	$ .60	9	$ 5.4 million
d	$ .70	12	$ 8.4 million
e	$ .90	14	$12.6 million
f	$1.20	16	$19.2 million
g	$1.50	18	$27.0 million

Problem 8
Reference pp. 18-24

Table 4

POINT	PRICE (P)	QUANTITY (Q)	TOTAL REVENUES (P X Q)
a	$4.75	100	$ 475
b	$4.00	150	$ 600
c	$3.50	200	$ 700
d	$3.00	250	$ 750
e	$2.50	400	$ 1000
f	$2.25	500	$1,125
g	$2.00	850	$1,700

Figure 12

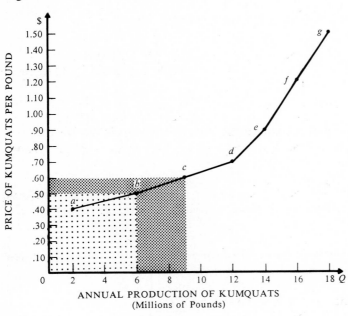

CHAPTER TWO
RESOLVING THE PROBLEM OF SCARCITY

(handwritten in top margin: a graph with P and Q axes, curve labeled; "As an activity increases costs more")

CHAPTER OBJECTIVES

After you have read and studied this chapter, you should be able to describe the four basic questions posed by scarcity; use production possibilities curves to describe scarcity, increasing opportunity costs, and choice; discuss how our answer to "When?" affects economic growth; explain how alternative allocative mechanisms work; and understand some basic differences between capitalism and socialism.

CHAPTER REVIEW: KEY POINTS

1. Every society must address four basic economic questions: (a) *What* goods will be produced? (b) *How* will productive resources be used? (c) *Who* will get the production? (d) *When* will production and consumption occur?

2. A *production-possibilities frontier (PPF)* shows the maximum combinations of goods that a society can produce. The PPF curve assumes that (a) resources are fixed; (b) technology is constant; and (c) all scarce resources are fully and efficiently employed. *(handwritten: RET)*

3. Opportunity costs are the values of outputs if resources were switched to their best alternative uses. Opportunity costs are not constant because resources are not equally suited for all types of production. Increasing a particular form of production ultimately leads to *diminishing returns* and *increasing opportunity costs*, so the production-possibilities curve is concave (bowed away) from its origin.

4. *Economic growth* occurs when technology advances or when the amounts of resources available for production increase. Economic growth can be shown as an outward shift of the production-possibilities curve; more of all goods can be produced.

5. When technology advances for one good in a PPF model, most of the curve will shift outward and to the right; fewer resources are needed to produce that good and thus are available for producing other goods.

6. The choices a society makes between consumption and investment goods affects its future production-possibilities curve. Lower saving and investment restricts economic growth and PPF expansion.

7. Alternative *allocative mechanisms* include: (a) the *market system,* (b) *brute force,* (c) *queuing,* (d) *random selection*, (e) *tradition,* and (f) *government.*

8. Many different economic systems are used in attempts to resolve the problem of scarcity. They can be classified by who makes the decisions (*centralized* or *decentralized*) and who owns the resources (*public* versus *private*).

9. Property is privately owned under pure *capitalism* and government follows *laissez-faire* (hands-off) policies. Thus, decisions are decentralized and rely on individual choices in a market system. Under *socialism,* government acts as a trustee over the nonhuman resources jointly owned by all citizens, with many socialist economies also relying heavily on centralized production and distribution decisions.

MATCHING KEY TERMS AND CONCEPTS

SET I

J 1. centralized decision making   a.   Capitalism's answer to "who owns?". *private property*

G 2. random selection   b.   When more goods can be produced with fewer resources. *increase in tech.*

H 3. *laissez-faire*   c.   "We do it this way because we always have." *tradition*

C 4. tradition   d.   Equal shares. *egalitarianism*

I 5. economic growth   e.   Might makes right, and right makes mine. *brute force*

F 6. queuing   f.   First-come/first-served. *queuing*

B 7. technological advance   g.   A selective service draft for the military is an example. *random sample*

E 8. brute force   h.   Minimal government. *laissez faire*

A 9. private property   i.   One path to this is to increase investment. *saving - econ growth*

D 10. egalitarianism   j.   Economic planning in the Soviet Union. *socialism centralized decision making*

SET II

E 1. socialism   a.   The broadest and least restrictive form of property rights. *fee simple*

I 2. increasing costs   b.   A society in which most major economic decisions are centralized. ~~socialism~~ *command economy*

J 3. mixed economy   c.   Any activity eventually becomes more difficult the further it is extended. *diminishing returns*

C 4. law of diminishing returns   d.   Basic economic questions. *what when How who*

E 5. production possibilities frontier   e.   Government acts as "trustee" over most nonhuman resources. *socialism*

G 6. concave from below   f.   Depicts limits to the amounts that given resources can produce. *PPF*

H 7. capitalism   g.   "Bowed away" from the origin of a graph.

B 8. command economy   h.   Emphasizes private property rights and *laissez faire* policies. *capitalism*

A 9. "fee simple"   i.   A logical extension of the law of diminishing returns. *increasing costs*

D 10. What? How? Who? When?   j.   Some property and decisions are private, others are governmental. *mixed economy*

CHAPTER REVIEW (FILL-IN QUESTIONS)

1-2. Four basic economic questions are posed by scarcity and must be resolved by all economic systems: _What_ economic goods will be produced, and how much of each? ~~when~~ _How_ will productive resources be utilized? _Who_ will get to use the economic goods produced? and ~~Where~~ _when_ will production occur?

3. If the current output combination is inside the production possibilities frontier, some resources are _unemployed_; points outside the PPF are _unattainable_.

4. A typical production possibilities curve is concave (bowed away) from its origin because of _high (increasing)_ opportunity costs. The costs of producing any good eventually rise as output is expanded because _diminishing_ returns are encountered.

5. One reason why diminishing returns are encountered along a PPF is that resources are somewhat _limited_, so that they tend to be relatively _suited (specialized)_ for different forms of production.

6-8. Several allocative mechanisms are available to any society to make choices between competing demands. They include _government_, _tradition_, _queuing_, _random sample_ _brute force_, and _market system_.

9. The United States largely relies on a _decentralized_ form of decision making. The opposite of this form, used in the Soviet Union and elsewhere, is _centralized_ decision making.

10. Government is minimal and follows _laissez-faire_ policies under pure capitalism. No society is either purely capitalistic or purely socialistic, so we all live in _mixed_ economies.

STANDARD MULTIPLE CHOICE

THERE IS ONE BEST ANSWER FOR EACH QUESTION.

resources fixed
tech constant
resources fully employed

___ 1. The basic economic questions are What? How? For Whom? and When? When we ask "For whom?", we want to know who will:
  a. produce the goods.
  (b.) consume the goods.
  c. get the profits.
  d. decide what to produce.
  e. decide when we use our valuable resources.

___ 2. Production possibilities curves can be used to illustrate:
  a. scarcity.
  b. full employment and efficiency.
  c. scarcity, opportunity costs, and choice.
  d. diminishing returns and increasing costs.
  (e.) All of the above.

scarcity
opportunity cost
choice

___ 3. Production possibilities frontiers depend on the assumption that:
  a. resources are variable in supply.
  b. there are unlimited goods.
  c. the economy is expanding.
  (d.) all resources are efficiently employed.
  e. technology advances quickly.

___ 4. Operating inside society's PPF is a:
  a. way to build reserves to stimulate economic growth.
  b. result whenever the capital stock depreciates rapidly.
  c. drawback of capitalism relative to socialism.
  d. sign that population is outstripping the food supply.
  (e.) symptom of inefficiency or idle resources.

23

___ 5. Production possibilities frontiers shift outward when:
   a. the economy approaches full employment.
   b. technology advances.
   c. the economy's demand for output increases.
   d. productive resources are efficiently utilized.
   e. capital depreciates rapidly.

___ 6. If more goods can be produced from given resources than was previously possible, there has been a/an:
   a. technological advance.
   b. expansion of the resource base.
   c. change in the convexity of the PPF.
   d. increased investment and growth of the capital stock.
   e. enhanced financial investment.

___ 7. If an economy is operating efficiently, economic growth will tend to be greater if:
   a. capital depreciates and becomes obsolete rapidly.
   b. threats of war divert resources to national defense.
   c. people's saving rises to allow greater investment.
   d. funds for research and development are reduced.
   e. the law of diminishing returns is fully operative.

___ 8. One important reason why production possibilities frontiers are concave from the origin is that:
   a. production costs fall because of diminishing returns.
   b. capitalistic economies tend to operate inefficiently.
   c. technology advances faster than it can be utilized.
   d. prosperity reduces people's work incentives.
   e. resources vary in suitability among types of production.

___ 9. A society in which your occupation is determined primarily by your parents' jobs bases many allocative decisions on:
   a. queuing.
   b. tradition.
   c. brute force.
   d. the market place.
   e. random selection.

___ 10. Allocation by queuing entails waste because some people:
   a. get unsuitable jobs when tradition rules.
   b. may gain while others lose when lotteries are used.
   c. inefficiently protect themselves from brute force.
   d. have their needs met last in this heartless system.
   e. spend long unproductive periods waiting in line.

___ 11. Rights to drill for oil on government property are often assigned by lottery. You submit your name and, if you are lucky, you win drilling rights. This is an example of:
   a. brute force.
   b. queuing.
   c. random selection.
   d. tradition.
   e. egalitarianism.

___ 12. Trying to distribute goods according to needs:
   a. is efficiently accomplished in most command economies.
   b. equitably answers the basic "What" and "How" questions.
   c. often ensures that judges of needs are viewed as needy.
   d. is the major goal of all mixed economic systems.
   e. explains why many poor people prefer pure capitalism.

___13. Consumer tastes tend to be efficiently met when decisions are made:
    (a.) individually.
    b. by democratic voting.
    c. in a command economy.
    d. to distribute income according to need.
    e. by queuing and random selection.

___14. John Locke thought that property rights derived from:
    a. a person's inheritance.
    b. the usefulness of goods and services.
    c. the reliability of the monetary system of the time.
    (d.) human labor.
    e. saving and investing.

___15. Most economists agree that property rights are determined primarily by:
    (a.) laws and regulations.
    b. the labor theory of value.
    c. brute force.
    d. supply and demand.
    e. central planning and licensing agencies.

___16. Fee simple property rights do not include the right to:
    a. destroy your property.
    b. sell your property.
    c. develop your property for your own benefit.
    (d.) use your property if your use harms another's property.
    e. give your property to whomever you choose.

___17. The U.S. economy is most accurately characterized by:
    (a.) decentralized decision making.
    b. public ownership of productive resources.
    c. egalitarian distributions of goods.
    d. persistent full employment.
    e. strict reliance on tradition to determine occupations.

___18. A government that follows *laissez-faire* policies:
    a. specifies production plans in detail.
    b. invariably aids the rich at the expense of the poor.
    (c.) keeps "hands off" of most economic decisions.
    d. stimulates investment through supply-side tax policies.
    e. monitors trends to keep pace with what consumers want.

___19. A command economy:
    a. uses *laissez-faire* government policies.
    b. bases decisions on *kolkhoz* roundtables.
    c. meets consumer wants most efficiently.
    d. encourages a private property system.
    (e.) requires detailed centralized decision making.

___20. Government acts as a trustee of nonhuman resources under:
    a. *laissez-faire* capitalism.
    b. traditional feudalism.
    c. fee simple property rights systems.
    (d.) socialism.
    e. mercantilist monarchies.

TRUE/FALSE QUESTIONS

T 1. Queuing allocates on a first-come, first-served basis and may be used to discourage the consumption of particular goods.

T 2. In the United States most economic decisions are made in markets in which prices and productivity are major factors determining what is produced and who gets what.

F 3. Economic planners try to encourage high unemployment rates so that the economy will have the reserves needed for growth.

F 4. The means of production are individually owned by citizens in socialist economies.

T 5. High rates of investment tend to raise labor productivity and stimulate the creation of new products and technologies.

F 6. Most people view random selection as inequitable, but it is an extremely efficient mechanism for distribution choices.

T 7. Brute force inefficiently diverts productive resources into protecting what we have or taking from others.

T 8. *Laissez-faire* policies mean that government does little.

T 9. The broadest of property rights are called fee simple property rights.

F 10. Tradition as a mechanism for resolving economic issues is used more today than at any previous time in history.

T 11. Resolutions to intertribal and international disputes have historically often relied on brute force.

F 12. Decreasing opportunity costs cause production possibilities frontiers to be concave from the origin.

F 13. If an economy operates inside its production possibilities frontier, additional output can be produced without costs.

T 14. Production possibilities curves can illustrate scarcity, opportunity costs, efficiency, and competitive choices.

F 15. A society can move along its production possibility frontier without incurring any opportunity costs.

UNLIMITED MULTIPLE CHOICE

WARNING: EACH QUESTION HAS FROM ZERO TO FOUR CORRECT ANSWERS!

___ 1. Production possibilities frontiers are concave from their origins because:
  a. identical proportions of capital, land, and labor are used to produce various goods.
  b. as more and more resources are devoted to any single output, production costs fall consistently.
  c. capital, land, and labor are used in different intensities to efficiently produce various goods.
  d. resources are not equally suited to all forms of production.

___ 2. Economic growth can result from:
  a. an increased resource base.
  b. advances in production technology.
  c. consumer saving that facilitates investment.
  d. job-training programs for the unskilled.

___ 3. Every social system confronts scarcity and must somehow resolve the following basic economic questions:
  a. What quantities of which goods should be produced?
  b. How will the chosen goods be produced?
  c. Who will use the goods that are produced?
  d. Where can free goods most effectively be distributed to the needy?

___ 4. In a command economy,
  a. the central government makes major economic decisions.
  b. most nonhuman factors of production are held by government as "trustee" for the populace.
  c. matching production choices to people's wants is a very difficult task.
  d. there is relatively little private property.

____ 5. The foundations of pure capitalism include:
  a. private rights to property.
  b. inheritance as the major pathway to a high income.
  c. *laissez-faire* government policies.
  d. exploitation of labor, the real source of all wealth.

PROBLEMS

Problem 1

Table 1 shows the menu of production possibilities confronting Atlantis, a newly rediscovered "lost" continent.

Table 1

COMBINATION	(PAIRS) ROLLER SKATES	CRUISE MISSILES	(CRUISE MISSILES IN TERMS OF ROLLER SKATES) OPPORTUNITY COSTS
A	7	0	_____
B	6	10	_____
C	5	19	_____
D	4	27	_____
E	3	34	_____
F	2	40	_____
G	1	45	_____
H	0	49	_____

a. Plot the eight bundles of goods and smoothly connect the points in Figure 1.

Figure 1

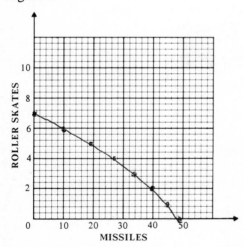

b. How is this production possibilities frontier shaped? _____concave_____

c. What conditions must be met for Atlantis to produce on its PPF? _full employment full use of all resources_

d. Fill in the opportunity cost column in Table 1.

e. Skates are transformed into missiles at (constant, diminishing, increasing) opportunity costs.

27

Problem 2

Use Figure 2 to answer the following True/False questions.

Figure 2

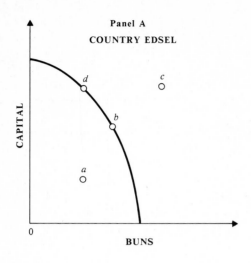

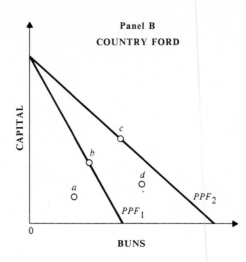

F a. The Edselian economy can move from point *d* to point *b* without incurring any opportunity costs.

F b. Fordic capital can be transformed into buns at constant opportunity costs along both production possibilities frontiers.

T c. Ever greater costs are incurred in producing buns as capital production is expanded in Edsel.

T d. Edselian capital is transformable into buns only at ever increasing opportunity costs.

F e. Increased demand could move Edsel from point *b* to point *c*.

F f. Edsel could move from point *a* to point *b* costlessly.

T g. Edsel's production possibilities frontier suggests increasing opportunity costs.

F h. Land, labor, and capital probably are used in a fixed ratio in producing both capital and buns in Ford.

T i. Opportunity costs are incurred when Ford moves from point *a* to point *b*.

T j. Point *a* is easily attained in both countries.

Problem 3

A map of Apabana, a Central American country divided into seven 1,000,000-acre sectors, is shown in Figure 3. The potential harvests of bushels of apples or bananas per acre are shown for each sector. Growing apples in a sector means that you lose bananas proportionally, and vice versa. For example, growing 60 million bushels of apples in sector X requires three-quarters of the land in X, leaving room for growth of only 25 million bushels of bananas.

Figure 3   Table 2

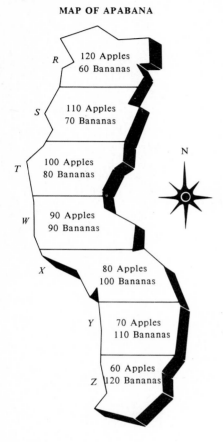

MAP OF APABANA

R 120 Apples
   60 Bananas

S 110 Apples
   70 Bananas

T 100 Apples
   80 Bananas

W 90 Apples
   90 Bananas

X 80 Apples
   100 Bananas

Y 70 Apples
   110 Bananas

Z 60 Apples
   120 Bananas

SECTOR	R	S	T	W	X	Y	Z
COSTS: APPLES IN TERMS OF BANANAS							
BANANAS IN TERMS OF APPLES							

a. Fill in Table 2 by computing the costs of apples in terms of bananas, and vice versa, for each sector.

b. Apple production costs the fewest bananas in sector ____.

c. Banana production costs the fewest apples in sector ____.

d. Suppose that only bananas were grown in all sectors except Z, which was reserved for apple production. Harvests, in millions of bushels, would be ____ bananas and ____ apples.

e. If only apples were grown in sector R, with all other sectors being used for bananas, output (in millions of bushels) would be ____ bananas and ____ apples.

f. Together, the results of answers d and e suggest that it would be ____ to ever grow ____ north of any ____ being produced.

g. Construct a production possibilities frontier for Apabana in Figure 4.

29

h. If you had to pay five apples for four bananas, where would only apples be produced? Only bananas? In which sector might both be produced?

i. Construct a curve in Figure 5 relating the cost of apples (in terms of bananas) to each possible output of apples in Figure 5. Put apple production on the horizontal axis, and the cost of extra apples on the vertical axis. (As you will learn in Chapter 3, this is a supply curve for apples.)

Figure 4

APABANA'S PRODUCTION POSSIBILITIES FRONTIER

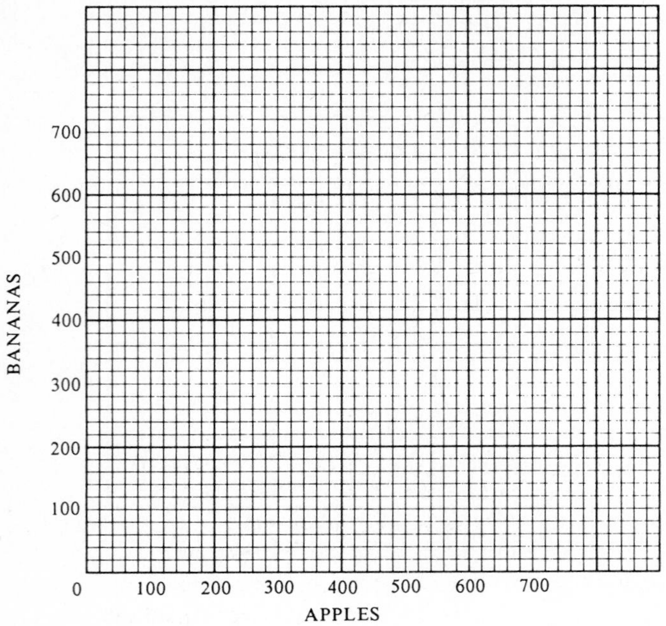

BANANAS

700
600
500
400
300
200
100

0   100 200 300 400 500 600 700

APPLES

Figure 5

APABANA'S SUPPLY OF APPLES

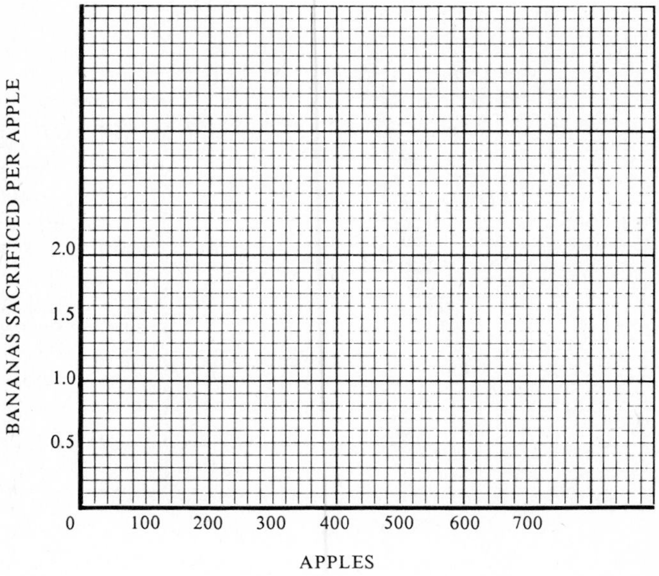

BANANAS SACRIFICED PER APPLE

2.0
1.5
1.0
0.5

0   100 200 300 400 500 600 700

APPLES

Problem 4

Use Figure 6 to answer the following True/False questions.

Figure 6

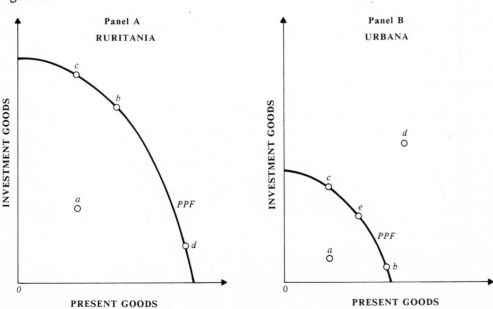

E a. If these countries have equal resources, Urbana is more technologically advanced than Ruritania.

I b. Both countries confront diminishing returns in producing both products.

F c. Ruritania invests more at point *d* than at point *c*.

I d. If Ruritania were at point *a*, it could move to point *d*.

T e. In both countries, point *a* implies underemployment of resources and inefficiency.

I f. Opportunity costs are constant along Urbana's production possibilities frontier. *raising any form of production leads to opp. cost.* ✗ *more resources + costs*

I g. Ruritanian consumption exceeds investment at point *d*.

F h. Each country can grow faster by moving along its PPF frontier towards the future goods axis.

F i. Urbana can move from point *e* to point *c* costlessly.

T j. If they share the same technologies, Ruritania possesses more resources than Urbana.

Problem 5*

Two dimensional graphs limit the tradeoffs we normally illustrate with a PPF. However, with a little ingenuity we can accommodate a third output. We do this by drawing a family of PPF curves rather than a single curve, with each curve reflecting a different assumed level of production for the third good. Consider three commodities apples (*a*), bananas (*b*), and coconuts (*c*). The family of curves shown in Figure 7 shows the tradeoff between apples and bananas, holding coconut production constant along each curve. We portray changes in coconut output possibilities by shifting among these curves. (a) How does this diagram represent the law of increasing cost (diminishing returns) for apples? _____. (b) For coconuts?_____.

Figure 7

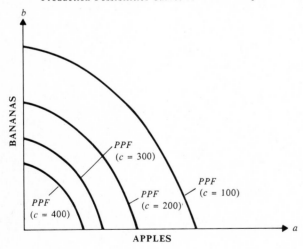

Production Possibilities Curves for Three Outputs

© 1989 Scott, Foresman and Company

Problem 6[*]

We suggest that you tackle this challenging production-possibilities problem only after solving all questions in Problem 3. **Hint:** Efficiency requires that **scarce** resources be fully employed. In this problem, full employment for labor in some instances may require that other (nonscarce?) resources be unemployed.

Suppose that an automobile may be produced by either (a) 5 workers and 1 robot, or (b) 3 workers and 2 robots; while a refrigerator requires either (c) 3 workers and 1 robot, or (d) 2 workers and 2 robots. Now suppose that an isolated factory has 60 workers and 15 robots employed. Filling in Table 3 requires ingenuity and some trial-and-error experimentation. Good luck!

Table 3

Autos	0	1	2	3	4	5	6	7	8	9	10	11	12
Refrigerators													
Idle Robots													
Unemployed Workers													

*Adapted with permission from Paul G. Coldagelli, author of "Production Possibilities Curves for Three Outputs", and "A Challenging Production Possibilities Problem" in *Great Ideas for Teaching Economics,* 4/e, edited by Ralph T. Byrns and Gerald W. Stone, Jr., Glenview, IL: Scott, Foresman and Company, 1989.

ANSWERS

Matching Key Terms and Concepts

SET I

Answer	Reference
1. j	p. 37
2. g	p. 35
3. h	p. 40
4. c	p. 35
5. i	p. 30
6. f	p. 35
7. b	p. 31
8. e	p. 34
9. a.	p.38
10. d	p. 35

SET II

Answer	Reference
1. e	p. 40
2. i	p. 29
3. j	p. 40
4. c	p. 29
5. f	p. 27
6. g	p. 29
7. h	p. 38
8. b	P. 37
9. a	p. 38
10. d	p. 26

Chapter Review (Fill-in Questions)

1. What, How
2. Who, When
3. unemployed or underemployed, unattainable
4. increasing, diminishing
5. specialized, suited
6-8. brute force, random selection, queuing, tradition, government, the market system
9. decentralized, centralized
10. *laissez-faire*, mixed

Standard Multiple Choice

Answer	Reference
1. b	p. 26
2. e	p. 27-30
3. d	p. 27
4. e	p. 28
5. b	p. 31
6. a	p. 31
7. c	p. 31
8. e	p. 29
9. b	p. 35
10. e	p. 35
11. c	p. 35
12. c	p. 35
13. a	p. 37
14. d	p. 38
15. a	p. 39
16. d	p. 38
17. a	p. 37
18. c	p. 40
19. e	p. 37
20. d	p. 40

True/False Questions

Answer	Reference
1. T	p. 35
2. T	p. 37
3. F	p. 31
4. F	p. 40
5. T	p. 31
6. F	p. 35
7. T	p. 34
8. T	p. 40
9. T	p. 38
10. F	p. 35
11. F	p. 34
12. F	p. 29
13. F	p. 29
14. T	p. 27-29
15. F	p. 29

Unlimited Multiple Choice

Answer	Reference
1. cd	p. 29
2. abcd	p. 30
3. abc	p. 26
4. abcd	p. 37
5. ac	p. 38

33

Problem 1
Reference pp. 27-29

a. See Figure 8.

Figure 8

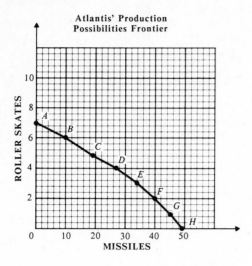

b. concave from the origin

c. full employment and efficient use of all scarce inputs

d. 1/10, 1/9, 1/8, 1/7, 1/6, 1/5, 1/4

e. increasing

Problem 2
Reference pp. 27-30

a. F
b. T
c. F
d. T
e. F
f. F
g. T
h. T
i. T
j. T

Problem 3
Reference pp. 27-30

a. See Table 4.

Table 4

SECTOR	R	S	T	W	X	Y	Z
COST OF AN APPLE IN TERMS OF BANANAS	1/2	7/11	4/5	1.0	5/4	11/7	2.0
COST OF A BANANA IN TERMS OF APPLES	2.0	11/7	5/4	1.0	4/5	7/11	1/2

b. *R*

c. *Z*

d. 10, 60

e. 570, 120

f. technically inefficient in production, bananas, apples

g. See Figure 9.

Figure 9

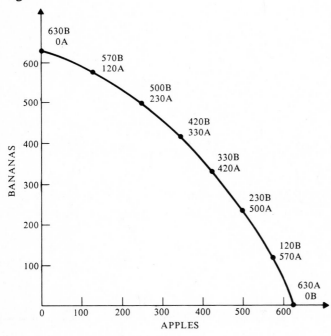

h. Sectors *R* and *S* would produce only apples, *T* might produce both, and *W, X, Y,* and *Z* would produce only bananas.

i. See Figure 10.

Figure 10

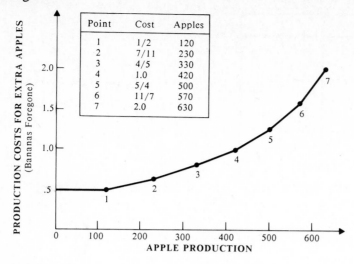

Point	Cost	Apples
1	1/2	120
2	7/11	230
3	4/5	330
4	1.0	420
5	5/4	500
6	11/7	570
7	2.0	630

PRODUCTION COSTS FOR EXTRA APPLES (Bananas Foregone)

APPLE PRODUCTION

Problem 4
Reference pp. 27-32

a. F
b. T
c. F
d. T
e. T
f. F
g. T
h. T
i. F
j. T

Problem 5
Reference pp. 27-30

a. The concavity (from the origin) of all these PPFs yields increasing costs for apples: As the number of apples produced grows, the number of bananas sacrificed per extra apple rises.

b. Widening the gap between PPF curves as more coconuts are produced (shrinking the apple/banana PPF towards the origin) illustrates the increasing costs of coconuts in terms of either apples or bananas.

Problem 6
Reference pp. 27-30

Table 5

Autos	0	1	2	3	4	5	6	7	8	9	10	11	12
Refrigerators	15	14	13	12	11	10	9	8	6	5	3	2	0
Idle Robots	0	0	0	0	0	0	0	0	1	1	2	0	3
Unemployed Workers	15	13	11	9	7	5	3	1	2	0	1	1	0

36

(handwritten annotations at top:)
influences on demand: MAKES CURVE SHIFT:
x) tastes + preference
x) income
} related goods
(# of buyers   x future goods/prices
                    x gov't. taxes

Gov't   Related goods
Income   no. of buyers
Future goods
Tastes

CHAPTER THREE

DEMAND AND SUPPLY

CHAPTER OBJECTIVES

After you have read and studied this chapter you should be able to explain the law of demand and the law of supply; describe the major determinants of demand and supply, and how they respectively cause demand and supply curves to shift; discuss the effects of time on demands and supplies; explain what market equilibrium is and how it is achieved; understand how transaction costs permit a range of prices for particular goods.

CHAPTER REVIEW: KEY POINTS

1. A *market* is a social institution that enables buyers and sellers to strike bargains and transact. *Absolute (monetary) prices* are far less important for consumer or business decisions than *relative prices*, of which consumers' *demand (subjective) prices* and *market prices* must be in accord before people will purchase goods.

2. The *law of demand.* All else constant, people buy less of a good per period at high prices than at low prices. *Demand curves* slope downward and to the right, and show the quantities demanded at various prices for a good. Changes in market prices cause changes in quantity demanded.   *Buy ↑ low P*

3. Consumers buy more of a product per period only at lower prices because consuming the additional units ultimately does not yield as much satisfaction as consuming previous units; *diminishing marginal utility* causes demand prices to fall as consumption rises. In addition, a lower price for one product means that the purchasing power of a given income rises (the *income effect*). Most importantly, the cheaper good will be used more ways as it is substituted for higher priced goods (the *substitution effect*).

4. In addition to the price of a good, demand depends on: (a) tastes and preferences; (b) income and its distribution; (c) prices of related goods; (d) numbers and ages of buyers; (e) expectations about prices, income, and availability; and (f) taxes, subsidies, and regulations. Changes in nonprice variables that influence demand cause shifts in demand curves. Taxes and subsidies shift demand curves from the perspectives of sellers, who are concerned with the price *received* when a good is sold, while buyers focus on the price *paid*. Taxes or subsidies make these two prices differ.   *P sell ↑*

5. The *law of supply.* All else constant, higher prices cause sellers to make more of a good available per period. The *supply* curve shows the positive relationship between the price of a good and the quantity supplied. *Supply curves* generally slope upward and to the right because: (a) diminishing returns cause opportunity costs to increase; (b) to expand output, firms must bid resources away from competing producers or use other methods (such as overtime) that increase cost; and (c) profit incentives are greater at higher prices.

6. In addition to the price paid to producers of a good, supply depends on: (a) the number of sellers; (b) technology; (c) resource costs; (d) prices of other producible goods; (e) producer's expectations; and (f) specific taxes, subsidies, and governmental regulations. Changes in prices cause *changes in quantities supplied*, while changes in other influences on production cause shifts in supply curves that are termed *changes in supply.*

(handwritten annotations at bottom:)
gov't   number of sellers
expectations
resource costs   37   price of other producic goods
tech.   number of sellers

7. When markets operate without government intervention, prices tend to move towards *market equilibrium* so that quantity supplied equals quantity demanded. At this point, the demand price equals the supply price.

8. When the market price of a good is below the intersection of the supply and demand curves, there will be *shortages* and pressures for increases in price. If price is above the intersection of the supply and demand curves, there will be *surpluses* and pressures for reduction in price.

9. *Transaction costs* arise because information and mobility are costly. This allows the price of a good to vary between markets.

10. Supply and demand are largely independent in the short run.

MATCHING KEY TERMS AND CONCEPTS

SET I

F   1.   market

H   2.   supply price

J   3.   relative price

E   4.   transaction costs

I   5.   market price

B   6.   complementary goods

D   7.   substitute goods

C   8.   inferior goods

A   9.   demand price

G   10.   absolute price

a.   A consumer's subjective gains from a bit more of a good.

b.   Right-hand gloves and left-hand gloves.

c.   Goods for which demands increase as income decreases.

d.   Coffee and tea.

e.   Emerge because mobility and information are costly.

f.   Mechanism that enables buyers and sellers to transact.

g.   Prices in dollars, dinars, marks, yen, pesos, francs, or pounds.

h.   The minimum payment that will induce a bit more production.

i.   Must be in accord with consumers' subjective evaluations before they will purchase a good.

j.   Monetary prices divided by one another.

D 1. substitution effect   a. Relationships between quantities demanded and price are negative.

A 2. law of demand   b. When neither shortages nor surpluses exist in a market.

I 3. change in quantity demanded   c. Extra units of a good add declining amounts of satisfaction.

G 4. income effect   d. Adjustments people make solely because relative prices change.

F 5. change in demand   e. Occurs when prices are below equilibrium.

H 6. law of supply   f. Effect on a demand curve when the price of a substitute changes.

J 7. surpluses   g. People's adjustments when price changes alter purchasing power.

B 8. equilibrium   h. Quantities supplied are positively related to price.

E 9. shortages   i. A movement along a demand curve.

C 10. diminishing marginal utility   j. Caused when prices are artificially held above equilibrium.

CHAPTER REVIEW (FILL-IN QUESTIONS)》

1. The relative prices that must be paid by purchasers are called ___market___ prices, but consumers won't buy unless these prices are in accord with their own ___subjective___ prices, which are their subjective estimates of the satisfaction gained or lost by consuming a bit more or less.

2-4. The law of demand states that consumers will purchase ___more___ of a good the lower its opportunity cost (relative price), and vice versa. The basic reason for this is the ___substitution___ effect, which reflects the adjustments people make solely because of changes in relative prices. A secondary reason for most goods is the ___income___ effect, which measures the adjustments people make because price changes alter consumers' ___purchasing p.___ Another way to explain the negative relationship between relative prices and quantities demanded is the principle of ___diminishing r.___, which suggests that a point is eventually reached where added consumption of any good yields ever ___smaller___ gains of satisfaction.

5-7. Factors other than the price of a good that can affect purchases include ___taste___ ___income___ ___# of buyers___, ___related goods___ ___taxes___, and ___gov. Reg.___.

8. The law of supply states that higher prices induce sellers to offer consumers ___more___ of their product, and vice versa. The supply curve depicts the ___max___ amounts of a good that firms are willing to place on the market at various prices.

9-10. Economists often call our market economy the ___price___ system. Markets permit buyers and sellers to communicate their desires and complete transactions. In so doing, markets reach ___equilibrium___. When quantity demanded exceeds quantity supplied, the current price is too low and a ___shortage___ exists. If the current is above the equilibrium price, there is a ___surplus___ of the good.

STANDARD MULTIPLE CHOICE

THERE IS ONE BEST ANSWER FOR EACH QUESTION.

_A_ 1. Demand prices and market prices are guides for rational choices when decisionmakers consider them as:
    a. relative prices.
    b. absolute prices.
    c. transaction costs.
    d. monetary prices.
    e. resources.

___ 2. Which term implies that people are able and willing to pay for something?
    a. Need.
    b. Demand.
    c. Requirement.
    d. Necessity.
    e. Desire.

___ 3. The market demand for a good is least affected by the:
    a. incomes of consumers.
    b. prices of related goods.
    c. costs of resources.
    d. number of buyers.
    e. expectations about price changes.

gov't reg
income
future price
tech
related goods
no. of buyers

___ 4. When demand decreases, the demand curve shifts:
    a. down and to the left.
    b. in a clockwise rotation.
    c. up and to the right.
    d. counter-clockwise.
    e. away from the origin.

___ 5. A demand curve would not shift if there were changes in the:
    a. tastes and preferences of consumers.
    b. size or distribution of national income.
    c. price of the good.
    d. number or age composition of buyers.
    e. expectations of consumers about availability.

___ 6. Demand is positively related to income for:
    a. inferior goods.
    b. normal goods.
    c. complementary goods.
    d. transitional goods.
    e. substitute goods.

_P↑_
income

___ 7. People's adjustments to relative price changes are termed:
    a. demonstration effects.
    b. substitution effects.
    c. wealth effects.
    d. adaptive effects.
    e. income effects.

___ 8. If price cuts in video recorders cause expanded cable TV hookups, these are:
    a. luxury goods.
    b. substitute goods.
    c. normal goods.
    d. inferior goods.
    e. complementary goods.

___ 9. In the short run, an increase in the relative price of a good increases the:
    a. state of technology.
    b. supply of the good.
    c. quantity of the good demanded.
    d. quantity of the good supplied.
    e. profits of capital owners.

_P↑_

10. Improvements in technology shift:
    a. demand up and to the right.
    b. production possibilities towards the origin.
    c. demand down and to the right.
    (d.) supply to the right, away from the vertical axis.
    ~~e. supply up and to the left.~~

11. Subsidies on a good tend to increase:
    a. supplies from buyers' perspectives.
    b. tax burdens on sellers.
    c. the time required for production.
    d. the rates at which returns diminish.
    e. consumer enjoyment from a unit of the good.

12. Decreases in the desire and willingness to pay for additional units of some good are best explained by the:
    a. substitution effect.
    (b.) principle of diminishing marginal utility.
    c. income effect.
    d. law of diminishing supply.
    e. law of demand.

13. Examples of joint goods (by-products in production) would include:
    a. shirts, ties, and socks.
    b. cameras and film.
    c. college tuitions and textbooks.
    d. vitamin pills and surgery.
    (e.) water skiing and electricity from a hydroelectric dam.

14. Expectations of price hikes for a durable good tend to:
    a. increase production, but only for later sale.
    b. cause firms to increase their inventories.
    c. decrease supply in the very short run.
    d. increase consumers' demands.
    (e.) All of the above.

15. Taxes on a good may cause which of the following:
    a. drive a "wedge" between demand prices and supply prices.
    b. tend to reduce supply from the perspectives of buyers.
    c. tend to reduce demand from the vantage points of sellers.
    d. reduce the amounts of the good produced and sold.
    e. all of the above.

16. The market for a good is in equilibrium if the:
    a. supply and demand are equal.
    b. price is equal to costs plus a fair profit.
    c. rate of technological change is steady.
    (d.) quantity supplied equals the quantity demanded.
    e. government properly regulates demands and supplies.

17. An increase in the quantity demanded of a good can be caused by an increase in:
    (a.) supply.
    b. inflationary expectations.
    c. consumer incomes.
    d. the price of a substitute good.
    e. federal income tax rates.

18. All transaction costs would be zero if:
    a. a law were passed requiring prices to be cut in half.
    (b.) information and transportation were costless.
    c. prices could not legally exceed production costs.
    d. inflation were eliminated.
    e. middleman operations were efficient.

19. Market prices that are below equilibrium tend to create:
    a. surpluses of the good.
    b. declines in resource costs.
    c. pressures for research and development.
    (d.) shortages of the good.
    e. buyers' markets.

below ceiling shortages
keep prices low in short run

above : surplus
below : shortage

41

___20. Among the influences of time on supply and demand is that:
- a. longer time intervals make these curves flatter because people can adjust more completely to price changes.
- b. production invariably absorbs more time than consumption.
- c. firms that are in business longer attract more customers.
- d. more experienced shoppers are less prone to buy on impulse.
- e. more goods become complements in both production and consumption as time elapses.

TRUE/FALSE QUESTIONS

T 1. Among the common denominators of markets are demands by people for goods or the resources that produce them and a willingness of sellers to supply these goods or resources.

F 2. The term demand can mean that people desire a good, but are still unable to afford it.

F 3. Most goods only cost money.

T 4. Transaction costs raise the opportunity costs of consumption above monetary prices.

F 5. For an entire demand curve to shift to the right, all determinants of demand except price must be stable.

T 6. Advertising may be beneficial and promote economic efficiency if it reduces transaction costs.

T 7. Purchases by individuals can be considered "dollar votes" which signal and direct business decisions.

T 8. Increases in income decrease supplies of inferior goods.

T 9. The demand curve for a good shows the relationship between its price and the quantity demanded, assuming that all other determinants are constant.

F 10. The longer the time interval considered, the more sensitive are quantities demanded and supplied to any price changes.

T 11. Most markets maintain stable equilibria for long periods.

T 12. Equilibrium supply prices exceed demand prices by the same ratio that quantity demanded exceeds quantity supplied.

T 13. If quantity demanded exceeds quantity supplied, then a shortage exists.

T 14. In equilibrium, a change in quantity demanded results if there is a change in supply.

T 15. In equilibrium, a change in quantity supplied implies that demand has shifted.

UNLIMITED MULTIPLE CHOICE

WARNING: EACH QUESTION HAS FROM ZERO TO FOUR CORRECT ANSWERS!

___ 1. According to the law of demand, relative prices:
  - a. and quantities demanded are negatively related.
  - b. decrease and cause demand to shift to the right.
  - c. are negatively related to consumers' desires for goods.
  - d. are determined by influences on consumer purchasing patterns, with supply effects being strictly secondary.

___ 2. In the short run, the market demand for ice cream should:
  - a. shift to the right upon the arrival of a heat wave.
  - b. slope upwards to depict the inverse relationship between its price and the quantity of ice cream demanded.
  - c. remain stationary when the price of ice cream falls.
  - d. grow to accommodate any increase in the supply of ice cream.

___ 3. In the market for gasoline, one would expect the:
  - a. supply curve to be stable in spite of OPEC's uneven history of trying to establish inordinately high oil prices.
  - b. demand curve to continually shift to the right, if more and more gas-guzzling automobiles are purchased.
  - c. demand for gasoline to decrease when acceptable and economical substitutes are developed and marketed.
  - d. supply curve to shift to the right if the government began taxing oil companies more heavily.

___ 4. The quantity demanded of a good adjusts to changes in: *Change in price only*
  - a. the price of a substitute good.
  - b. the price of a complementary good.
  - c. consumers' income.
  - d. tastes and preferences.

___ 5. Transaction costs are the costs associated with:
  - a. gathering information about commodities and services.
  - b. transporting goods or resources between markets.
  - c. working to secure income to buy goods and services.
  - d. driving 30 miles to buy goods at a clearance sale.

43

PROBLEMS

Problem 1.

Use the data in Table 1 to answer the following questions.

Table 1

CONSUMER X'S DEMAND SCHEDULE		CONSUMER Y'S DEMAND SCHEDULE		CONSUMER Z'S DEMAND SCHEDULE	
PRICE	QUANTITY DEMANDED	PRICE	QUANTITY DEMANDED	PRICE	QUANTITY DEMANDED
$10	0	$10	0	$10	0
9	0	9	3	9	1
8	0	8	5	8	5
7	1	7	7	7	8
6	2	6	9	6	11
5	4	5	12	5	12
4	6	4	15	4	15
3	10	3	18	3	18
2	15	2	21	2	20
1	21	1	24	1	23
0	25	0	25	0	25

a. Draw demand curves for consumers X, Y, and Z, respectively, in Panels A, B, and C of Figure 1.

b. Draw the resulting market demand curve in Panel D of Figure 1. Explain how you derived the demand curve for the entire market. _____

c. Assume that demands for this good by individuals X and Y double, but fall by half for individual Z. Revise their demand curves and then redraw the market demand curve.

Figure 1

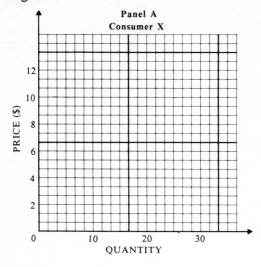

Panel A
Consumer X

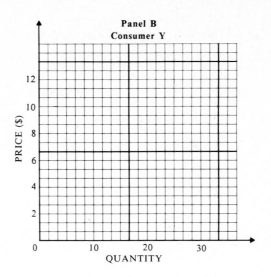

Panel B
Consumer Y

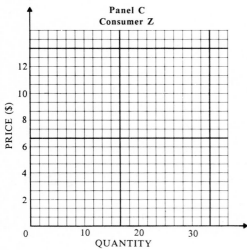

Panel C
Consumer Z

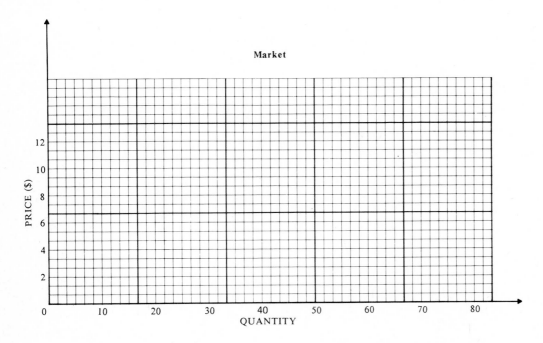

Market

45

Problem 2

Use the market demand curves D_0, D_1, and D_2, shown in Figure 2, to answer the following questions.

Figure 2

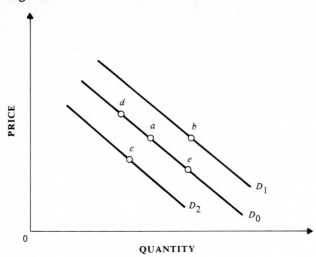

a. A movement from point *a* to point *b* represents what?_____ Why? _____ What might account for this movement? _____

b. A movement from point *a* to point *c* represents what? _____ Why? _____ What might account for this movement? _____

c. A movement from point *a* to point *d* represents what? _____ Why? _____ What might account for this movement? _____

d. A movement from point *a* to point *e* represents what? _____ . Why? _____ . What might account for this movement? _____

Problem 3

Use the market supply curves S_0, S_1, and S_2 in Figure 3 to answer the following questions about possible movements.

Figure 3

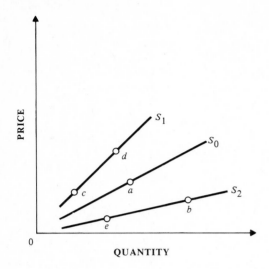

a. A movement from point *a* to point *b* represents what? _____. Why? _____ . What might account for this movement? _____ _____.

b. A movement from point *a* to point *c* represents what? _____. Why? _____ . What might account for this movement? _____.

c. A movement from point *c* to point *d* represents what? _____. Why? _____ . What might account for this movement? _____

d. A movement from point *b* to point *e* represents what? _____. Why? _____ . What might account for this movement? _____

Problem 4

Use the market supply and demand schedules for electric drills listed in Table 2 to answer the following questions.

Table 2

	PRICE	$10	$20	$30	$40	$50	$60	$70
THOUSANDS	Quantity Demanded	32	28	24	20	16	12	8
	Quantity Supplied	4	7	10	13	16	19	22

47

a. Draw the market supply and demand curves for electric drills in Figure 4.

Figure 4

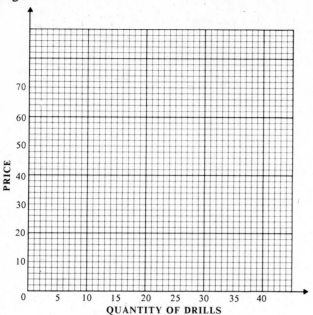

b. The equilibrium price in this market is _____.

c. The equilibrium quantity of drills is _____ thousand monthly.

d. If the price were $30, there would be a _____ of _____ thousand drills monthly.

e. If the price were $60, there would be a _____ of _____ thousand drills monthly.

Problem 5

The demand curve for Xebs is represented in Graph 1 by D_X. Graph 2 depicts the demand curve for Yoozs (D_Y), a substitute good for Xebs. Graph 3 represents the demand curve for Zorks (D_Z) a complement to product Xebs.

a. Suppose the price of Xebs increases. Indicate the effect(s) of this price change on the graphs in Figure 5.

Figure 5

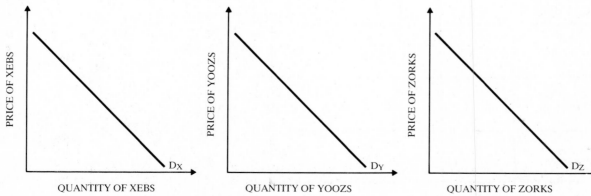

ANSWERS

Matching Key Terms and Concepts

SET I

Answer	Reference
1. f	p. 43
2. h	p. 53
3. j	p. 44
4. e	p. 60
5. i	p. 45
6. b	p. 49
7. d	p. 49
8. c	p. 49
9. a	p. 45
10. g	p. 44

SET II

Answer	Reference
1. d	p. 45
2. a	p. 45
3. i	p. 51
4. g	p. 45
5. f	p. 51
6. h	p. 52
7. j	p. 60
8. b	p. 59
9. e	p. 60
10. c	p. 45

Chapter Review (Fill-in Questions)

1. market, demand (subjective)
2. more, substitution
3. income, purchasing power
4. diminishing marginal utility, smaller
5-7. tastes and preferences; income; number of buyers; price of related goods; expectations; taxes, subsidies and government regulations
8. more, maximum
9. price, equilibrium
10. shortage, surplus

Standard Multiple Choice

Answer	Reference
1. a	p. 44-45
2. b	p. 44
3. c	p. 48-51
4. a	p. 51
5. c	p. 51
6. b	p. 49
7. b	p. 45
8. e	p. 49
9. d	p. 57
10. d	p. 55
11. a	p. 50, 56
12. b	p. 45
13. e	p. 56
14. e	p. 49
15. e	p. 50, 56
16. d	p. 59
17. a	p. 59-60
18. b	p. 60
19. d	p. 60
20. a	p. 57-58

True/False Questions

Answer	Reference
1. T	p. 43
2. F	p. 44
3. F	p. 44
4. T	p. 60
5. F	p. 51
6. T	p. 60
7. T	p. 44
8. F	p. 49
9. T	p. 45
10. T	p. 57
11. F	p. 60
12. F	p. 60
13. T	p. 60
14. T	p. 60
15. T	p. 60

Unlimited Multiple Choice

Answer	Reference
1. a	p. 45
2. ac	p. 48-50
3. bc	p. 51
4. None	p. 51
5. abd	p. 60

PROBLEM 1
Reference pp. 45-48

a. See Figure 6 (line with dots).

Figure 6

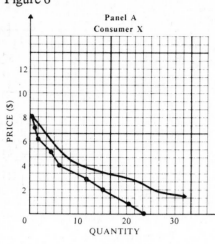

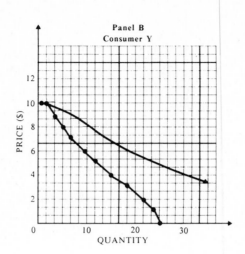

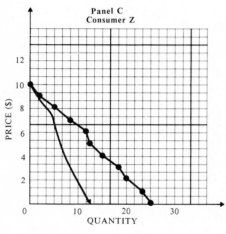

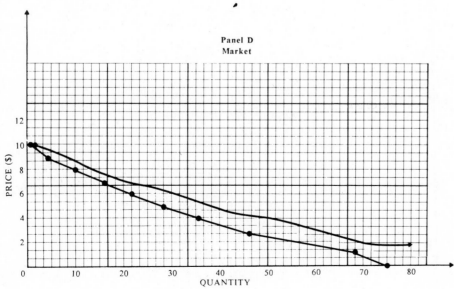

b. Horizontal summation of individual demand curves.   Figure 7

c. See Figure 6 (line without dots).

PROBLEM 2
Reference pp. 48-51

a. increase in demand; curve shifted rightwards; increase in income, more favorable consumer preferences, or some other parallel change in a determinant besides the good's own price.

b. decrease in demand; curve shifted leftward; decrease in income, increase in the price of a complement, or some other parallel change in a determinant besides the good's own price.

c. decrease in quantity demanded; movement along the curve; increase in the price of the good.

d. increase in quantity demanded; movement along the curve; decrease in the price of the good.

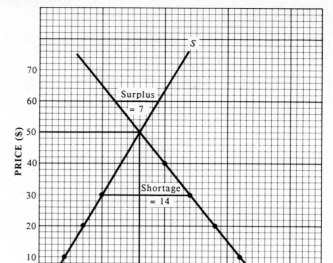

QUANTITY OF DRILLS MONTHLY

b. $50

c. 16

d. shortage, 14

e. surplus, 7

PROBLEM 3
Reference pp. 53-57

a. increase in supply; curve shifted to the right; decrease in resource price, technological advances, or some other change in determinant besides the good's price.

b. decrease in supply; curve shifted to the left; increasing resource prices, reduction in the number of sellers, or some other change in a determinant besides the good's price.

c. rise in quantity supplied; movement along a curve; increase in price.

d. decline in quantity supplied; movement along a supply curve; decrease in price.

PROBLEM 5
Reference pp. 49, 51

Figure 8

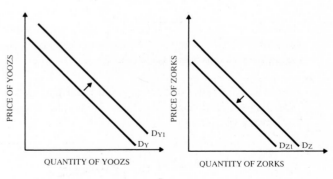

QUANTITY OF YOOZS   QUANTITY OF ZORKS

a. Demand for substitute good (Yoozs) increases, demand for complement (Zorks) decreases.

PROBLEM 4
Reference pp. 58-60

a. See Figure 7.

51

CHAPTER FOUR
MARKETS AND EQUILIBRIUM

CHAPTER OBJECTIVES

After you have read and studied this chapter you should be able to explain how prices and quantities change to reflect movements in supplies and demands; discuss the effects of taxes, subsidies, price floors, and price ceilings; describe the roles of speculators, arbitragers, and middlemen and predict how supply and demand interact to shape activities in markets you have not yet encountered.

CHAPTER REVIEW: KEY POINTS

1. Increases in supplies or decreases in demands tend to reduce prices. Decreases in supplies or increases in demands tend to raise prices. Increases in either supplies or demands tend to increase quantities. Decreases in either supplies or demands tend to shrink quantities. If both supply and demand shift, the effects on price and quantity may be either reinforcing or at least partially offsetting. (If these points make little sense to you, you need to review this important material.)

2. Prices may not move quickly to their equilibrium values, and can swing up and down as they slowly approach the intersections of demands and supplies.

 speculators later

3. *Middlemen* prosper only if they reduce the transaction costs associated with getting goods from the ultimate producers to the ultimate consumers. *Speculators* aid in movements towards equilibrium because they try to buy when prices are below equilibrium (increasing demand) and sell when prices are above equilibrium (increasing supply). This dampens price swings and reduces the costs and risks to others of doing business.

4. *Arbitrage* involves buying in a market where the price is low and selling in a market where the price is higher. If this price spread is greater than the transaction costs, arbitrage is risklessly profitable. **Competition** for opportunities to arbitrage dampens profit opportunities and facilitates efficiency by ensuring that price spreads between markets are minimal.

5. Government can set monetary prices at values other than equilibrium price, but *price ceilings* or *price floors* do not "freeze" opportunity costs; instead, these *price controls* create economic inefficiency and either shortages or surpluses, respectively.

6. Taxes and subsidies drive *wedges* into markets so that buyers and sellers have different perceptions about supplies and demands. The slopes of supplies and demands determine the proportions of tax burdens borne by buyers and sellers.

MATCHING KEY TERMS AND CONCEPTS

SET I

D 1. arbitrage

A 2. tax wedge

E 3. subsidy wedge

I 4. speculator

J 5. excess supply

F 6. price floor

H 7. price ceiling

C 8. middlemen

B 9. invisible hand

G 10. minimum wage laws

a. Reduces production so that demand prices exceed supply prices.

b. Adam Smith's name for automatic adjustments in a market system. *invisible hand*

c. Their incomes depend on cutting transaction costs for others. *middlemen*

d. Risklessly buying at a low price in one market and then selling at a higher price in another. *arbitrage*

e. Raises production so that supply prices exceed demand prices.

f. A legal limitation that causes a surplus. *price floor*

g. Price floors that may cause unskilled people to be unemployed. *minimum wage laws*

h. A legal limit that causes a shortage. *price ceiling*

i. Examples include ticket scalpers. *speculator*

j. A synonym for a surplus. *excess supply*

SET II

NOTE: More than one answer may correspond to adjustments a through h.

What happens to equilibrium price and quantity when:

A 1. both supply and demand increase? a. Equilibrium price and quantity will increase.

D 2. both supply and demand decrease? b. Equilibrium price and quantity will fall.

F 3. supply increases and demand decreases? c. Equilibrium price will fall and quantity will rise.

E 4. supply decreases and demand increases? d. Equilibrium price will rise and quantity will fall.

C 5. supply grows and demand is constant? e. Equilibrium price rises, but quantity changes are indeterminate.

A 6. demand grows; supply remains the same? f. Equilibrium price falls, but quantity changes are indeterminate.

D 7. supply falls and demand is constant? g. Equilibrium quantity rises, but price changes are indeterminate.

B 8. demand declines and supply is constant? h. Equilibrium quantity falls, but price changes are indeterminate.

___ 9. Corn prices rise; what happens to wheat?

___10. How will an oil strike affect gasoline?

CHAPTER REVIEW (FILL-IN QUESTIONS)

1. Market _equilibrium_ occurs at the price where quantity demanded equals quantity _supplied_.

2-3. A shortage occurs when the market price is _below_ the equilibrium price because a greater quantity of the good is _demanded_ than supplied. If the market price exceeds the equilibrium price, there is a _surplus_ because greater quantities of the good are _supplied_ than are demanded by consumers.

4-5. If demands increase while supplies decline, prices _raise_ (increase) but quantity changes are _intermediate_. When there are increases in both demands and supplies, _quantity_ will increase but the change in _price_ is indeterminate.

6-8. When a maximum legal price is set, it is termed a price _ceiling_, whereas if the government sets a minimum legal price, it is termed a price _floor_. Price ceilings do not hold economic prices down; opportunity costs rise because of increases in _transaction_ costs, and price ceilings typically cause _shortages_. Price floors on the other hand often cause _surpluses_; and the production costs of these surpluses are _above_ their values to consumers.

9-10. Successful speculators tend to reduce the volatility of ___prices___ and absorb the
___risks___ to others of doing business. Middlemen are successful only to the extent that
they are able to reduce the ___cost___ incurred in transmitting goods from producers to
consumers. The process of ___arbitrage___ entails buying at a low price in one market and selling
at a higher price elsewhere.

STANDARD MULTIPLE CHOICE

THERE IS ONE BEST ANSWER FOR EACH QUESTION.

_B_ 1. The first comprehensive work on economics
was written by Adam Smith in 1776 and
entitled *An Inquiry into the Nature and
Causes of the:*
  a. *Laws of Supply and Demand.*
  b. *Wealth of Nations.*
  c. *Sovereignty of the Marketplace.*
  d. *Distribution of Income Among the Social
     Classes.*
  e. *Efficiency Gained from Competition.*

_B_ 2. When the price of a good is below the
intersection of its supply and demand
curves, there will be:
  a. surpluses
  b. shortages
  c. "frozen" opportunity costs
  d. excessive unemployment
  e. none of the above

_B_ 3. If the supply and demand for a product both
increase, the:
  a. price will rise.
  b. quantity will increase.
  c. price will remain stable.
  d. profits of competitors will increase.
  e. welfare of society rises.

_D_ 4. The market price of video recorders will rise if:
  a. reading becomes more popular.
  b. supply increases.
  c. technology advances.
  d. imports are prohibited.
  e. consumers substitute towards cable TV.

_C_ 5. Buying low in one market and selling at a
higher price elsewhere is not:
  a. a riskfree way to make profits.
  b. called arbitrage.
  c. a cause of price spreads between markets.
  d. a mechanism that increases demand in the
     low-price market.
  e. a mechanism that increases supply in the
     high-price market.

_D_ 6. The transaction costs of conveying goods from
producers to consumers are reduced by
firms known as:
  a. arbitragers.
  b. efficiency consultants.
  c. commission houses.
  d. middlemen.
  e. consortiums.

_A_ 7. Speculators:
  a. increase the risks of legitimate businesses.
  b. tend to reduce the volatility of prices.
  c. are the causes of economic booms and
     busts.
  d. eliminate transaction costs.
  e. always make profits.

_B_ 8. Demand prices will be above supply prices in
equilibrium if:
  a. shortages cause consumers to form queues.
  b. inflationary pressures are anticipated by
     sellers.
  c. government subsidies cause more than
     optimal production.
  d. price floors create farm surpluses that
     must be stored.
  e. tax wedges cause prices paid to exceed
     those received.

55

9. Subsidies boost the incentives to produce and consume goods but tend to create inefficiency because the:
   a. other goods forgone may have been even more valuable.
   b. government agencies become extremely bureaucratic.
   c. shortages that result involve long queuing time.
   d. resulting high prices can be afforded only by the rich.
   e. incentives for research and development are destroyed.

10. Regulations create wedges that reduce the supply of a good to the extent that they:
    a. artificially stimulate demand.
    b. prevent pollution and industrial blight.
    c. raise the costs of production.
    d. are based on laissez faire government policies.
    e. generate cyclical shortages and then surpluses.

11. Laws used to keep market prices from rising are called:
    a. wage and/or price ceilings.
    b. rationing and subsidies.
    c. allocations and redemptions.
    d. arbitrage and arbitration.
    e. wedges and hedges.

E 12. Long term price ceilings are likely to cause:
    a. shortages.
    b. queues.
    c. black markets and corruption.
    d. economic inefficiency.
    e. all of the above.

 13. Minimum wage laws are examples of:
    a. government subsidies that aid people on welfare.
    b. direct benefits from union membership.
    c. price floors, and create surplus labor and unemployment.
    d. arbitrage exercised by government bureaucrats.
    e. price ceilings that create labor shortages.

14. Ignoring economic factors when designing social policies is:
    a. appropriate because morality does not depend on money.
    b. likely to cause results that are incompatible with intentions.
    c. recommended by advocates of laissez faire policies.
    d. a major reason why income is equitably distributed.
    e. mandated by the 27th amendment to the U.S. Constitution.

D 15. Harsher punishments for drug pushers than addicts cannot be blamed for higher:
    a. prices for illegal drugs than free market prices.
    b. rates of street crime by addicts.
    c. profits reaped by successful pushers who are uncaught.
    d. rates of addiction than would exist in a free market.
    e. police corruption because pushers can offer big bribes.

TRUE/FALSE QUESTIONS

F 1. Prices depend on demand alone, while quantities depend primarily on supply.

T 2. Long-term shortages or surpluses are almost without exception the results of government price controls.

F 3. Federal minimum wage laws are examples of price ceilings, and most utility rates are examples of price floors.

F 4. Increases in supplies put upward pressure on market prices and tend to increase the quantities of a good sold.

T 5. Price controls are legal restrictions that often prevent monetary prices from rising to equilibrium levels.

F 6. Speculation tends to hinder movements of prices and quantities towards market equilibrium.

T 7. Allocative efficiency is aided if decision makers consider all costs of their actions.

F 8. According to Adam Smith, the behavior of both business firms and individual consumers is governed by ~~altruism~~. *Invisible hand*

F 9. If the equilibrium price is below a price ceiling, a market tends to generate surpluses.

___10. The opportunity costs of consumption tend to increase if price ceilings below equilibrium price are imposed.

___11. Tax wedges are loopholes that enable people in high income brackets to avoid paying fair shares of government costs.

T 12. Arbitrage generates riskless profits from buying low in one market and then selling at a higher price in another.

T 13. Middlemen will fail unless they reduce the transaction costs of getting goods from ultimate producers to consumers.

T 14. Price supports for agricultural products generate surpluses that consumers value less than their costs to society.

T 15. Black markets and queues of consumers are signs that price ceilings restrict monetary prices <u>below</u> equilibrium.

UNLIMITED MULTIPLE CHOICE

The following questions have from zero to four correct answers.

___1. Market equilibrium is said to occur when the:
   a. government strictly controls price-gouging businesses.
   (b.) market experiences neither surpluses nor shortages.
   (c.) market price equates the quantities demanded and supplied.
   d. quantity demanded equals a governmentally imposed quota.

___2. Government policies drive wedges between demand and supply curves when:
   a. taxes cause demand prices to fall below supply prices.
   b. a price ceiling is below the market-clearing price.
   c. regulations raise the opportunity costs of production.
   d. subsidies divert production from more valuable goods to less valuable goods.

___3. Price ceilings that are below market-clearing prices keep: *shortage*
   (a.) monetary prices from rising except in black markets.
   b. a lid on opportunity costs.
   c. consumers from being "ripped off."
   d. incentives strong for the Invisible Hand to work its magic.

___4. Examples of "middlemen" operations include:
   (a.) speculators.
   (b.) retail outlets.
   (c.) arbitrating.
   (d.) ticket scalpers.

___ 5. Competitive markets:
  (a.) translate consumer wants into production
        by firms.
   b. are stationary by nature.
  (c.) aid buyers and sellers in communicating
        their wants, and facilitate beneficial
        exchanges of goods and resources.
   d. are all very similar.

PROBLEMS

Problem 1

Use the information in Table 1 to answer the following questions about the market for battery-powered thermal socks. (Quantities are in millions of pairs of socks annually.)

Table 1

QUANTITY DEMANDED	PRICE	QUANTITY SUPPLIED
0	$10.00	20
2	9.50	18
4	9.00	16
6	8.50	14
8	8.00	12
10	7.50	10
12	7.00	8
14	6.50	6
16	6.00	4
18	5.50	2
20	5.00	0

a. Plot the supply and demand curves in Figure 1, being sure to label both axes; label the curves S_0 and D_0 respectively.

Figure 1

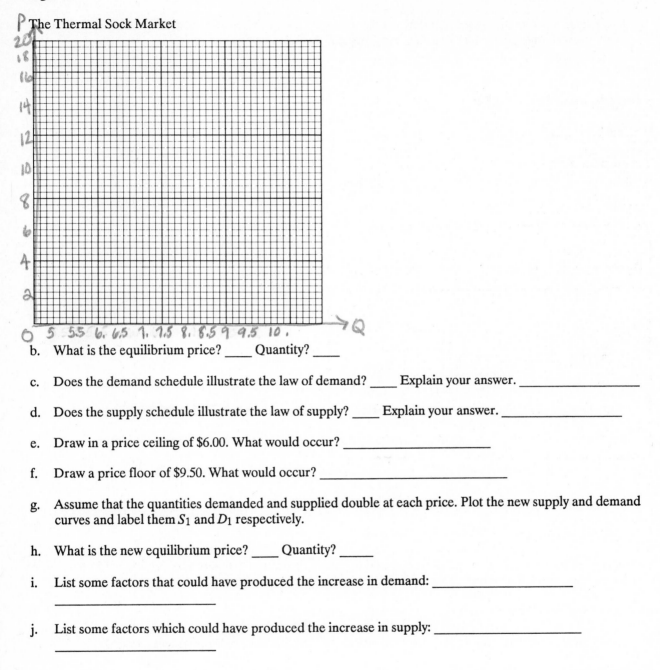

The Thermal Sock Market

b. What is the equilibrium price? _____ Quantity? _____

c. Does the demand schedule illustrate the law of demand? _____ Explain your answer. _____

d. Does the supply schedule illustrate the law of supply? _____ Explain your answer. _____

e. Draw in a price ceiling of $6.00. What would occur? _____

f. Draw a price floor of $9.50. What would occur? _____

g. Assume that the quantities demanded and supplied double at each price. Plot the new supply and demand curves and label them S_1 and D_1 respectively.

h. What is the new equilibrium price? _____ Quantity? _____

i. List some factors that could have produced the increase in demand: _____
_____

j. List some factors which could have produced the increase in supply: _____
_____

Problem 2

Use the original data from Table 1 to answer the following questions about the effects of government policies in the thermal sock market.

a. Use Figure 2 to replot the supply and demand curves for socks, and label them S_0 and D_0 respectively. Then slide (draw) a wedge between these curves representing a $2 tax on thermal socks.

Figure 2

Government and Thermal Socks

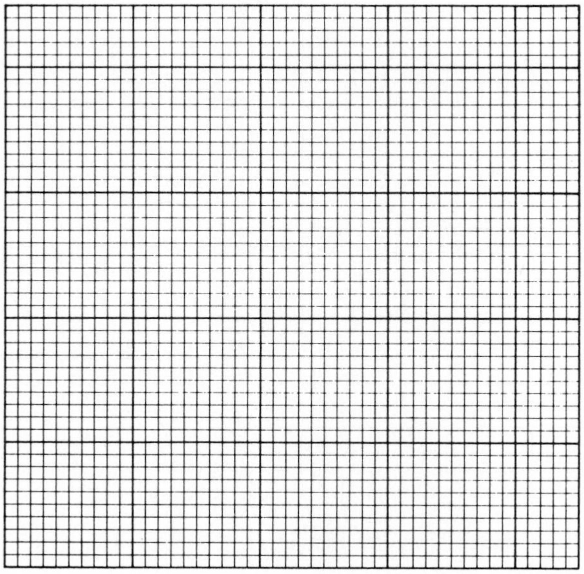

b. Now draw a dashed line representing the demand price of $____ for socks in this taxed equilibrium.

c. Draw a heavy solid line representing the supply price of $____ for socks in this taxed equilibrium.

d. The $2 tax reduces the quantity demanded and supplied to ____ million pairs annually.

e. The tax burden on thermal sock buyers is $____ per pair.

f. The tax burden on sock knitters is $____ per pair.

g. Draw a wedge in this figure to show what would happen if the tax were replaced by a subsidy of $1 per pair of socks. The buyers' demand price would be $____ in this new equilibrium.

h. The sellers' supply price would be $____ including the subsidy.

i. The $1 subsidy increases the equilibrium quantity to ____ million pairs of thermal socks annually.

j. Sock buyers realize a $____ gain from the subsidy for each pair of socks they buy.

k. Taxes cause equilibrium quantities demanded and supplied to ____; the opposite is true of subsidies.

l. On scratch paper, draw a demand curve twice as steep as D_0 and a supply curve half as steep as S_0. Drive a $2 tax wedge between these curves. Relative to the original curves, this market imposes more of the tax burden on _____ and less on _____. Naturally, the opposite is true in cases where demand curves are flatter and supply curves are steeper.

Problem 3

Supply and demand curves S_0 and D_0 in Figure 3 represent the original situation in the market for top quality Brahma bulls. Use the information in this figure to answer the following questions about this market.

Figure 3

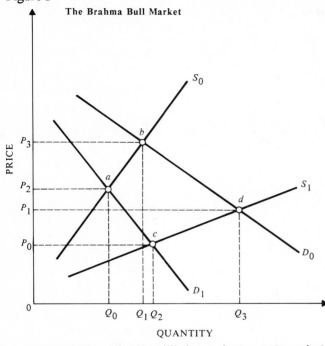

a. What is the original equilibrium price? ____ Quantity? ____

b. If demand moves to D_1 because dieticians recommend that all people over 40 become vegetarians, what is the new equilibrium price? _____ Quantity? _____

c. Beginning with the original curves, if supply shifts to S_1 with the introduction of beef-up antibotics, what is the new market-clearing price? ____ Quantity? _____

d. Assuming simultaneous shifts to D_1 and S_1, what is the new equilibrium price? _____ Quantity? _____

e. The movement from point a to point c represents what on the demand side? _____. What on the supply side? _____

f. The movement from point a to point b represents what on the demand side? _____ What on the supply side? _____

g. The movement from point b to point d represents what on the demand side? _____ What on the supply side? _____

h. The movement from point c to point d represents what on the demand side? _____ What on the supply side? _____

i. Looking only at the original set of demand and supply curves (D_0, S_0), what would occur if the price were set at $P2$? ____ Why? _____

j. Looking only at the new set of demand and supply curves (D_1, S_1) what would occur if the price were set at $P1$? ____ Why? _____

Problem 4

Demand curve D_L in Figure 4 represents the demand for unskilled labor services by business firms, and S_L represents the supply of unskilled labor services offered by households. Money wage rate W_e is the market-clearing wage rate, but W_m denotes the minimum money wage rate imposed on this labor market by federal law. Use this information to answer the following true/false questions.

Figure 4

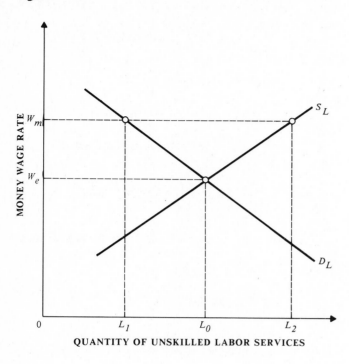

QUANTITY OF UNSKILLED LABOR SERVICES

___a.   The minimum money wage rate is an example of a price floor.

___b.   At wage rate W_e, the quantity of labor demanded equals the quantity supplied.

___c.   Employment is greater at W_m than at We.

___d.   The federal government has created a buyers' market in the labor market.

___e.   At wage rate W_m, unemployment equals L2 minus L1.

___f.   Unemployment would fall if the government discontinued its legal minimum for the money wage rate.

___g.   The minimum wage reduces employers' costs of discriminating.

ECONOMIC WORD SEARCH

SUPPLY AND DEMAND ANALYSIS

CLUES TO WORDS

1. The law of ____ is shown by a positively sloped curve.

2. What consumers do.

3. Gasoline and automobiles are _Comp_ goods.

4. The demand schedule is often represented as a ____.

5. Sets equilibrium price.

6. Often creates a surplus. _price floor_

7. Often creates a shortage. _price ceiling_

8. Advocated by some who view market results as inequitable.

9. Tea and coffee. _Subst. goods_

10. Occurs when price is artificially set too high.

11. The typical result from wage and price controls.

12. Fairly fickle component of consumer demand.

13. When demand and supply both rise, this also increases.

14. Market rationing device.

15. What people think will happen.

16. Results from the interactions of market transactors.

17. Affected by spending for research and development.

18. Typically, the more you have, the more you spend.

19. What your textbook is about.

20. Graphs depict this.

Figure 5

SUPPLY AND DEMAND ANALYSIS

```
A R F
O E Q
A C M B R                          Q E R
Y L P P U S                        N G P S
T X P R T X U                      A X G H
I E O U I P R R              Z T A N O
T A I   D C I M P          P R M I E
N M L   H E G Z L          R O F N B
A A S     A I N O U      O H N O E
U R U       B L T A S T E S C I G
Q E B         E I F R N S A T R
B M S           A N P Q R A B
J F T             R G P R E
S X I             W O S O C
E K T             D B N R O U R
R Q U           E Z O X M L R Z N
D E T         M P I Z P O F V L G R
M P E     A N T B L       E F I Q M
N A C     N E A G E       L H N E Z
R F R   D R T H M         U R C P N
P O N K M C A E           D L O A U
B E R N E M N             E N M O R
R A M P E T               H H E A
Q F X O A N E X A R O Z R S C I M O N O C E C A Z
L E P R C U V T E C H N O L O G Y E U N O S R V W
V W Y B L R A M E C J C K G M U I R B I L I U Q E
```

63

ANSWERS

Matching Key Terms and Concepts

SET I

Answer	Reference
1. d	p. 71
2. a	p. 73
3. e	p. 73
4. i	p. 71
5. j	p. 74
6. f	p. 73
7. h	p. 73
8. c	p. 69
9. b	p. 64
10. g	p. 75

SET II

Reference
pp. 66-68

Answer
1. g
2. h
3. f
4. e
5. c
6. a
7. d
8. b
9. a
10. c

Chapter Review (Fill-in Questions)

1. equilibrium, supplied
2. lower than, demanded
3. surplus, supplied
4. rise, indeterminate
5. quantity, price
6. ceiling, floor
7. transaction costs, shortages
8. surpluses, above
9. prices, risks
10. transaction costs, arbitrage

Standard Multiple Choice

Answer	Reference
1. b	p. 65
2. b	p. 73
3. b	p. 66-68
4. d	p. 66-68
5. c	p. 71
6. d	p. 69
7. b	p. 71
8. e	p. 73
9. a	p. 73
10. c	p. 73
11. a	p. 73
12. e	p. 73
13. c	p. 73
14. b	p. 79
15. d	p. 76

True/False Questions

Answer	Reference
1. F	p. 66-68
2. T	p. 73-75
3. F	p. 74-75
4. F	p. 66-68
5. T	p. 73
6. F	p. 71
7. T	p. 79
8. F	p. 65
9. F	p. 73
10. T	p. 73
11. F	p. 73
12. T	p. 71
13. T	p. 69
14. T	p. 75
15. T	p. 73

Unlimited Multiple Choice

Answer	Reference
1. bc	p. 66-68
2. bcd	p. 72-73
3. a	p. 73
4. abcd	p. 69-71
5. ac	p. 79

PROBLEM 1
Reference pp. 66-68

a. See Figure 6.

Figure 6

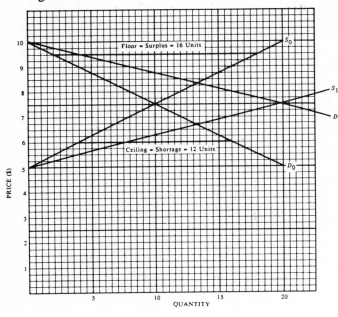

b. $7.50, 10 million

c. Yes, the relationship between price and quantity demanded is inverse (negative).

d. Yes, the relationship between price and quantity supplied is direct (positive).

e. See Figure 6; shortages since 16 units would be demanded but only 4 units would be supplied.

f. See Figure 6; surpluses since 18 units would be supplied but only 2 units would be demanded.

g. See Figure 6.

h. $7.50, 20 million pairs

i. favorable change in tastes and preferences, rise in income or the number of buyers, drop in price of a complementary good or rise in the price of a substitute good, increase in price expectations.

j. decline in resource costs, increase in technology, decreases in the prices of substitutes in production, cuts in the numbers of suppliers, expectations that durables' prices will fall.

PROBLEM 2
Reference pp. 72-73

a. See Figure 7.

Figure 7

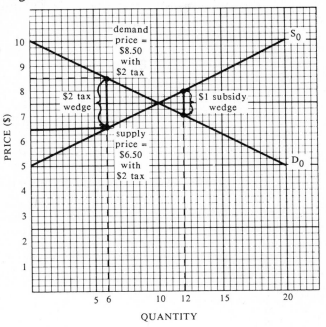

b. See Figure 7, $8.50

c. See Figure 7, $6.50

d. 6

e. 1

f. 1

g. See Figure 7; $7

h. $8

i. 12

j. $ 0.50

k. shrink

l. buyers; sellers

65

PROBLEM 3
Reference pp. 66-68, 73-74

   a. P_3, Q_1

   b. P_2, Q_0

   c. P_1, Q_3

   d. P_0, Q_2

   e. increase in quantity demanded, increase in supply

   f. increase in demand, increase in quantity supplied

   g. increase in quantity demanded, increase in supply

   h. increase in demand, increase in quantity supplied

   i. shortage, quantity demanded at P_2 exceeds quantity supplied

   j. surplus, quantity supplied at P_1 exceeds quantity demanded

PROBLEM 4
Reference pp. 73-75

   a. T
   b. T
   c. F
   d. T
   e. T
   f. T
   g. T

ECONOMIC WORD SEARCH

Figure 8

Economic Word Search--Supply and Demand Analysis

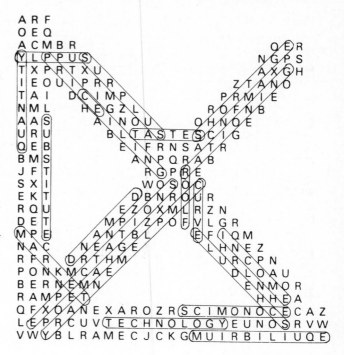

CHAPTER FIVE

ECONOMIC INSTITUTIONS:

HOUSEHOLDS, FIRMS, AND GOVERNMENT

CHAPTER OBJECTIVES

After you have read and studied this chapter you should be able to discuss the circular flow of resources, goods, and income; describe the economic roles of households and business firms; explain the economic functions of government; illustrate externalities and public goods; and differentiate regressive, proportional, and progressive taxes.

CHAPTER REVIEW: KEY POINTS

1. Households are both consumers of goods and providers of labor and other resources to business. Interactions between business and households are illustrated in *circular flow* models.

2. All household income is spent, saved, or taxed. Three major trends are discernible in U.S. household spending patterns during the past half century:
   a. consumption expenditures as a percentage of personal income have declined from 90 percent to 80 percent.
   b. taxes have increased from roughly 3 percent to nearly 14 percent.
   c. saving has been roughly stable as a percentage of income.

3. Wages and salaries make up approximately three quarters of the income of typical families. During the last two decades, women's rates of participation in the labor force have risen markedly while those of men have fallen slightly. The proportion of families in which both husband and wife are employed has also been climbing.

4. Six businesses out of seven are either *sole proprietorships* or *partnerships,* but *corporations* account for more than 80 percent of all goods and services sold and receive roughly two-thirds of all profits in the United States. Compared to corporations, however, sole proprietorships and partnerships are easily formed and less subject to government regulation. The major advantages of corporations are the limited liabilities of stockholders and better access to financial capital markets.

5. An erratic trend towards increased concentration of economic power in America has continued for more than a century--well over half of all manufacturing assets are held by the 200 largest corporations in the United States.

6. Corporate goals of making profits are under attack by people who believe "the new industrial state" is much too powerful, both politically and economically. These critics argue that big business should be "socially responsible."

7. Even though control of much of modern economic life is concentrated in the hands of those who control giant corporations, changing market shares and the growth of various imports are evidence that the processes of competition are still reasonably vigorous.

8. Where the price system is incapable of providing certain goods or fails to provide the socially optimal levels, *government* steps in to supplement the private sector in five major ways. It attempts to:
   a. provide a legal, social, and business environment for stable growth;
   b. promote and maintain competitive markets;
   c. redistribute income and wealth equitably;
   d. efficiently alter resource allocations where *public goods* or *externalities* are present; and
   e. stabilize income, employment, and prices.

9. If negative externalities (costs) exist, the private market will provide too much of the product and the market price will be too low because full production costs are not being charged to consumers. If positive externalities (benefits) exist, too little of the product will be produced by the private market and the market price will be too high, requiring a government subsidy or government production or provision of the commodity.

10. Once public goods are produced, it is extremely costly to exclude people from their use, and everybody can consume the goods simultaneously with everyone else. The free market will not adequately provide public goods because of the "free rider" problem.

11. Total spending on goods and services by all three levels of government exceeds 20 percent of GNP. State and local governments spend the bulk of their revenues on services that primarily benefit people in their local communities and rely heavily on the property and sales taxes as sources of revenue. Federal government spending is generally aimed at activities that are national in scope. Over 90 percent of federal revenue comes from individual and corporate income taxes plus social security and other employment taxes.

MATCHING KEY TERMS AND CONCEPTS

SET I

___ 1. conglomerate

a. supply-side entities that operate one or more plants.

___ 2. consumption + savings + taxes

b. consumers, resource owners, and ultimate holders of wealth.

___ 3. corporation

c. means that owners can lose only the amount they have paid for stock.

___ 4. partnerships and proprietorships

d. all firms competing in the same product market.

___ 5. horizontal integration

e. a combination that produces many diverse products.

___ 6. households

f. The ultimate uses of household income.

___ 7. limited liability

g. limited liability of owners is a major advantage.

___ 8. vertical integration

h. when a firm owns several plants that do the same things.

___ 9. firms

i. when a firm owns plants making intermediate goods that are inputs for other plants it owns.

___10. industry

j. firms owned by individuals who are personally liable for its debts.

___ 1. negative externality   a. national defense, public health service, space program.

___ 2. nonexclusion principle   b. the tax rate falls as income rises.

___ 3. progressive tax   c. competition produces too little of the good.

___ 4. positive externality   d. everyone can enjoy specific goods simultaneously.

___ 5. nonrival principle   e. no buyer or seller can noticeably influence market price.

___ 6. competitive market   f. litter

___ 7. public goods   g. when the marginal tax rate rises as income rises.

___ 8. proportional tax   h. when barring consumption is prohibitively expensive.

___ 9. transfer payments   i. the tax rate does not change as income changes.

___10. regressive tax   j. includes social security and welfare payments.

CHAPTER REVIEW (FILL-IN QUESTIONS)

1-2. The principal roles of households are as _____, as providers of labor and other _____, and as storehouses of _____. Household income is spent on consumer goods, is _____, or is paid to the government as taxes.

3-4. A _____ is a physical facility in a specific location involved in manufacturing, processing, or sales; _____ operate one or more. An _____ is comprised of all of the companies competing in the same product market. If one company provides a number of different products it is said to be _____.

5. A firm that operates at different production levels within an industry is _____. Firms that operate several plants making the same product are called _____.

6-7. The three basic forms of business organization are: _____, _____, and _____. In addition to superior access to markets for financial capital, a major advantage of the corporate form of business organization is _____.

8. If the market (price) signals from consumers to businesses are incorrect, too little or too much of a good will be provided. These problems usually exist when _____ are involved or when the commodity or service in question is a _____ good.

9. Public goods are subject to the _____ principle. It applies if, once a good is produced, everyone can consume it simultaneously. Public goods are also subject to the _____ principle, which means consumers cannot be barred from using the good.

10. A tax is said to be progressive if the percentage tax rate _____ as income rises. Regressive taxes are those where the tax rate _____ as income rises.

STANDARD MULTIPLE CHOICE

THERE IS ONE BEST ANSWER FOR EACH QUESTION.

___ 1. The movement of goods and income among firms, households, production, and resource markets is represented in the:
   a. national semiconductor chart.
   b. economic modulation graph.
   c. circular flow model.
   d. wage-price-labor-commodity diagram.
   e. production possibilities frontier model.

___ 2. Which of the following is not among the roles played by households in a market economy?
   a. storehouses of wealth.
   b. centers for consumption.
   c. ultimate ownership of all resources.
   d. centers for production.
   e. ultimate payers of all taxes.

___ 3. In market economies, the ultimate owners of productive resources are:
   a. major corporations.
   b partnerships and proprietorships.
   c. business firms, collectively.
   d. individual households.
   e. society as a whole.

___ 4. The labor force participation rate of which group has grown most markedly in the past three decades?
   a. senior citizens.
   b. nonwhite males.
   c. nonwhite females.
   d. white males.
   e. white females.

___ 5. Goods lasting more than a year are called:
   a. nonobsolescence goods.
   b. durable goods.
   c. expendables.
   d. nondurable goods.
   e. hard to find.

___ 6. The bulk of all income is in the form of:
   a. corporate profits.
   b. interest.
   c. wages and salaries.
   d. rental incomes.
   e. proprietor and partnership profits.

___ 7. Which of the following represent more than three-quarters of the total number of businesses in this country today?
   a. diversified firms.
   b. conglomerate firms.
   c. partnerships and proprietorships.
   d. corporations.
   e. financial institutions.

___ 8. Large, highly-diversified firms are also know as:
   a. conglomerate firms.
   b. financial intermediaries.
   c. vertically integrated firms.
   d. horizontally integrated firms.
   e. multiplant firms.

___ 9. Sole proprietorships are NOT characterized by:
   a. ease of organization.
   b simplicity of control.
   c. limited availability of capital.
   d. relatively free from regulation.
   e. limited liability.

___ 10. "Double taxation" refers to taxation of:
   a. last year's tax refund as this year's income.
   b. both corporate income and corporate dividends.
   c. interest accrued on a savings and loan account.
   d. dividends earned on shares in a credit union account.
   e. married people at rates that exceed those for "singles."

___11. Relative to other business organizations, corporations do not have the advantage of:
   a. little regulation of their activities.
   b. superior access to financial capital.
   c. permanence as long as the business is thriving.
   d. limited legal liabilities for their owners.
   e. better access to specialized professional managers.

___12. Providing a stable business environment, promoting growth, and maintain competitive markets are examples of the:
   a. social allocation of resources.
   b. economic functions of the governments.
   c. corrections for negative spillovers (costs).
   d. economic incidence on consumers.
   e. duties of trade unions.

___13. Government's macroeconomic role is most closely related to the goal of providing or promoting:
   a. the common defense.
   b. a stable legal system and business environment.
   c. purchasing power, employment, and economic growth.
   d. equity in the distribution of income.
   e. positive externalities in public goods.

___14. Negative (cost) spillovers:
   a. result in too much of a product at too low a price.
   b. are exemplified by air pollution and education.
   c. are exemplified by transportation and immunization.
   d. result in too little of a product at too high a price.
   e. are caused by wastes of taxpayers' dollars.

___15. Which of the following activities is least likely to generate negative externalities?
   a. Driving while intoxicated.
   b. Smoking a cigar in a restaurant.
   c. Parking on your front lawn for months while repairing your car.
   d. Failing to bathe during the hot summer months.
   e. Getting an inoculation against a contagious disease.

___16. Nonrivalness and nonexclusiveness characterize:
   a. pure private goods.
   b. goods embodying negative diseconomies.
   c. majority-rule voting systems.
   d. pure public goods.
   e. goods for which there is persistent excess capacity.

___17. Government provision of a pure public good does not necessarily require the good to be:
   a. scarce so that there are opportunity costs.
   b. nonrival.
   c. nonexclusive.
   d. produced by government.
   e. exclusive.

___18. Good examples of progressive taxes are:
   a. statutory taxes.
   b. sales taxes.
   c. social security taxes.
   d. tobacco and liquor taxes.
   e. income and inheritance taxes.

___19. If a good is nonexclusive, people will:
   a. all vote for maximum possible government provision.
   b. buy the good according to their tastes and preferences.
   c. not care if the good generates negative externalities.
   d. try to be "free riders".
   e. have a high benefit/cost ratio from its purchase.

___20. Transfer payments include payments:
   a. of sales taxes at the grocery store.
   b. of cash to someone who is not declaring the payment for purposes of income taxes.
   c. by the buyer of 100 shares of General Motors to the stock's seller.
   d. by a retail store of its telephone bill.
   e. of unemployment compensation to laid off autoworkers.

TRUE/FALSE QUESTIONS

___ 1.   Most of the personal saving in our economy is accomplished by those with incomes exceeding $60,000.

___ 2.   Saving is negatively related to income, all else equal.

___ 3.   Business firms are the ultimate holders of wealth.

___ 4.   Wages as percentages of national income have risen in part because many people who would have owned small farms or businesses in an earlier era now work for big companies.

___ 5.   Roughly 20,000 corporations each have assets exceeding $10 billion.

___ 6.   A plant is an entity which operates one or more firms.

___ 7.   Durable goods are economic goods whose expected life is less than one year.

___ 8.   Our economic system works most efficiently when it is not subjected to the interactions of consumers and firms.

___ 9.   Unhindered competition in a market system tends to yield an equilibrium combination of price and quantity that will maximize consumer satisfaction for a given distribution of income if goods are rival and exclusive and there are no externalities.

___10.   A tax is progressive if higher incomes are taxed proportionately less than lower incomes.

___11.   Most state and local governments rely on income taxes as their primary sources of revenue.

___12.   Pure public goods are rival but non-exclusive.

___13.   Externalities occur when parties other than those directly making decisions are affected by an activity.

___14.   In the market system, business firms seldom respond to signals from consumers.

___15.   Monopoly power tends to create economic inefficiency.

___16.   At present, well over half of all goods produced in our economy are directly controlled or allocated by government.

___17.   Since 1929, the United States has financed the bulk of its federal expenditures with a proportional income tax.

___18.   Corporate taxes are borne only by incorporated businesses.

___19.   Efficiency requires government to produce pure public goods.

___20.   National defense is the classic example of a negative externality.

UNLIMITED MULTIPLE CHOICE

WARNING: THERE ARE FROM ZERO TO FOUR ANSWERS FOR EACH QUESTION!

___ 1. Households:
   a. add directly to society's capital stock when they invest in bonds.
   b. are primarily producers of economic goods.
   c. provide labor services to business firms.
   d. are consumers.

___ 2. Corporations:
   a. are artificial beings sanctioned by state law.
   b. are not subject to extensive government regulations.
   c. are fruitful sources of tax revenue for government.
   d. enjoy unlimited liability.

___ 3. Public goods:
   a. are subject to the nonrival principle in consumption.
   b. are efficiently produced and sold in the market sector.
   c. are chosen by individual consumers who vote with money.
   d. are subject to the nonexclusion principle.

___ 4. A tax is:
   a. progressive if the percentage tax rate decreases as income increases.
   b. proportional if constant tax percentages apply to income.
   c. regressive when tax payments as a percentage of income decline as income declines.
   d. a source of financing to provide public goods.

___ 5. The economic functions of government include:
   a. to provide a reasonably certain legal, social, and business environment for stable growth.
   b. to promote and maintain competitive markets.
   c. to provide public goods and adjust for externalities.
   d. to stabilize income, employment, and the price level.

EXERCISE

Construct a simple, standard circular flow diagram showing flows of goods from firms to consumers through product markets, and resources from households to firms via resource markets. Be sure that you have shown the way payments are made with an opposite flow. Now add an additional (internal) loop showing how saving is channeled through financial institutions to provide investment funds to firms. (Hint: This is just a highly refined part of the market for resources.)

Problem 1

Use the tax and income information listed below to answer the following questions:

Income	Total Taxes
$10,000	$1,000
12,000	1,200
14,000	1,400
16,000	1,600
18,000	1,800
20,000	2,000

a. What kind of tax is depicted above? _____.

b. How much of total income is taxed at each income level? _____.

c. What is the marginal rate of taxation? (ΔTax/ΔIncome) _____.

d. Can you list examples of other taxes that are similarly related to income? _____
_____

Problem 2

Use the tax and income information listed below to answer the following questions:

Income	Total Taxes
$10,000	$ 5,000
15,000	6,750
20,000	8,000
25,000	8,750
35,000	9,000
50,000	10,000

a. Compute the average rate of taxation at each income level. _____.

b. What is the marginal rate of taxation when income increases from $10,000 to $15,000? _____.

c. What kind of tax is depicted above? _____ .

d. Can you think of any taxes that fit this pattern?_____.

Problem 3

Suppose that your salary is more than $100,000 per year and that you have $100,000 to invest. Your federal marginal tax rate is fifty percent on normal investment income.

a. How many extra after-tax dollars will you receive annually if you invest in tax free state and local bonds that yield an 8 percent return annually instead of the taxable 12 percent return you could realize if you bought corporate bonds? _____.

b. What return would make you indifferent between income from a tax free investment and the taxable 12 percent return on corporate bonds? _____

c. What will happen to rates of return generally for investments that generate income that receives preferential tax treatment? _____

d. Why?_____

e. What does this example suggest will happen to investment in sectors that have preferential tax treatments relative to possible investments not offering "loopholes"? _____ .

f. What does this example suggest about whether or not high income investors receive the full advantages of such loopholes? _____

ANSWERS

Matching Key Terms and Concepts

SET I

Answer	Reference
1. e	p. 85
2. f	p. 84
3. g	p. 86
4. j	p. 86
5. h	p. 86
6. b	p. 83
7. c	p. 87
8. i	p. 86
9. a	p. 85
10. d	p. 86

SET II

Answer	Reference
1. f	p. 91
2. h	p. 92
3. g	p. 94
4. c	p. 92
5. d	p. 92
6. e	p. 91
7. a	p. 92
8. i	p. 94
9. j	p. 90
10. b	p. 94

Chapter Review (Fill-in Questions)

1. consumers, resources
2. wealth, saved
3. plant, firms
4. industry, a conglomerate
5. vertically integrated, horizontally integrated
6. sole proprietorship, partnership
7. corporation, limited liability
8. externalities, public
9. nonrival, nonexclusion
10. rises, falls

Standard Multiple Choice

Answer	Reference
1. c	p. 83
2. d	p. 83
3. d	p. 84
4. e	p. 84
5. b	p. 84
6. c	p. 86
7. c	p. 85
8. a	p. 85
9. e	p. 86
10. b	p. 87
11. a	p. 86
12. b	p. 90
13. c	p. 90
14. a	p. 91
15. e	p. 91
16. d	p. 92
17. d	p. 92
18. e	p. 94
19. d	p. 92
20. e	p. 90

True/False Questions

Answer	Reference
1. T	p. 85
2. F	p. 85
3. F	p. 84
4. T	p. 85
5. F	p. 88
6. F	p. 85
7. F	p. 84
8. F	p. 83
9. T	p. 91
10. F	p. 94
11. F	p. 94
12. F	p. 92
13. T	p. 92
14. F	p. 87
15. T	p. 91
16. F	p. 89
17. F	p. 94
18. F	p. 87
19. F	p. 92
20. F	p. 92

Unlimited Multiple Choice

Answer	Reference
1. cd	p. 83
2. ac	p. 86
3. ad	p. 92
4. bd	p. 94
5. abcd	p. 90

EXERCISE

See Figure 1.

Figure 1

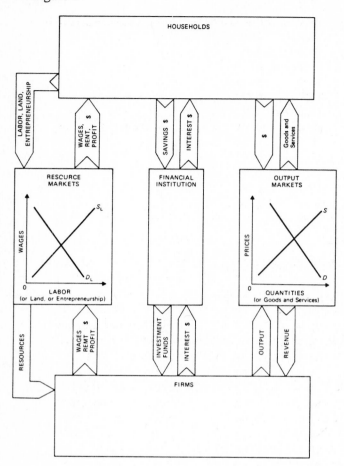

Problem 1
Reference p. 94

a. proportional tax

b. 10%

c. 10%

d. social security taxes (on wages only) below about $50,000; property taxes.

Problem 2
Reference p. 94

a. regressive

b. $10,000 - 50%
   15,000 - 45%
   18,000 - 40%
   25,000 - 35%
   35,000 - 25.7%
   50,000 - 20%

c. 35%

d. some sales taxes, tobacco and alcohol taxes.

PROBLEM 3
Reference p. 94

a. $8,000 - ($12,000/2) = $8,000 - 6,000 = $2,000 annually.

b. 6 percent return on the tax free investment.

c. They should fall until the after tax returns are roughly equal.

d. Competition among high income people for the advantages of loopholes will increase the supply of financial capital to sectors receiving preferential tax treatment, reducing its return. These sectors grow relative to sectors without loopholes.

e. The after-tax returns should be roughly equalized over time.

f. The loopholes yield only very small advantages to those who seek to exploit them.

CHAPTER SIX
UNEMPLOYMENT AND INFLATION

CHAPTER OBJECTIVES

After you have studied this chapter you should be able to examine various reasons for unemployment and enumerate the costs and benefits of each type; explain how inflation and unemployment are measured using index numbers and how indexes are constructed and used; and explore the various reasons for inflation and the benefits and costs of each type.

CHAPTER REVIEW: KEY POINTS

1. Major macroeconomic goals include full employment, price stability, and economic growth. Economic security is also an important goal.

    price stability, econ growth, full employment

2. People are involuntarily unemployed if they are able to work and are willing to accept prevailing wage rates for people with their skills, but cannot find work or have not yet secured suitable employment.

3. Unemployed people who are so discouraged about job prospects that they do not look for work are not counted in unemployment statistics. Some people who are not truly looking for work indicate that they are to receive unemployment compensation. Thus, unemployment statistics may either understate the true unemployment rate because of discouraged workers or overstate it because of dishonest nonworkers.

4. Unemployment arises in five major ways: (a) frictional, (b) structural, (c) seasonal, (d) cyclical, and (e) induced. Frictional unemployment arises because of transaction costs and is a by-product of normal entry and exit from the labor market, voluntary job changes, layoffs, or firings. Structural unemployment results from mismatches between workers and jobs because of changes in job requirements or individuals' lack of marketable skills. Seasonal unemployment arises from the annually recurring influences of weather, vacations, and the like on labor markets. Cyclical unemployment results from downturns in overall economic activity (recessions). Government policies that reduce work incentives cause induced unemployment.

5. Unemployment causes both economic and social costs. Society as a whole suffers because of lost output that unemployed individuals could have produced. Personal losses are cushioned by such programs as unemployment compensation. Individuals and their families suffer socially and psychologically when they are unemployed for long periods.

6. Unemployment is not distributed equally across all groups. Workers in manufacturing and construction are hit harder by cyclical unemployment during recessions than employees in most other lines of work.

7. Index numbers are used to compare particular variables over time. The Consumer Price Index (CPI) measures average price changes for a given bundle of consumer goods over time. The CPI is based on typical consumer patterns for approximately 80 percent of the urban population.

8. The CPI is used extensively as an escalator clause (cost-of-living adjustment) in many contracts. It is also an economic indicator and is used to convert nominal values to real values. Deflating nominal variables means dividing their monetary values by (1 percent of) a price index.

    real value = $\dfrac{\text{nominal value}}{\text{price index}/100}$

9. Among the major difficulties in computing the CPI are the problems inherent in adjusting the index for: (a) new products; (b) changes in the qualities of existing products; (c) changes in the composition of consumer expenditures; and, (d) already owned consumer durables such as housing.

10. The Producer Price Index (PPI) measures the changes in the prices of goods in other than retail markets. The GNP Implicit Deflator is used to adjust the GNP for changes in prices. It is composed of relevant portions of the CPI and the PPI, plus some additional prices covered by neither.

11. Inflation distorts relative prices and economic decision making and reduces incentives to save. Capital accumulation may be hampered by inflation, depending on business expectations and the availability of funds for investment. These are the distortions costs of inflation. Inflation causes resources that could be used productively elsewhere to be used for repricing. These are the repricing (menu) costs of inflation.

12. There are social costs of inflation because people feel greater uncertainty during inflationary periods. People living on fixed incomes are hurt by inflation, but many of today's transfer payments and wage contracts have escalator clauses that adjust payments for price level changes. Borrowers tend to gain from unexpected inflation, while the ultimate lender loses. When inflation boosts income, meeting a fixed mortgage payment becomes easier, so heavily mortgaged homeowners tend to gain.

13. The discomfort (misery) index is the sum of the inflation rate and the unemployment rate. It averaged 6-7 percent during the 1950s and 1960s. During the late 1970s and early 1980s, the index ranged from 13 to more than 20 percent. By the late 1980s, economic growth had pushed the index below 10 percent.

MATCHING KEY TERMS AND CONCEPTS

SET I

E   1. inflation

I   2. real values

B   3. structural unemployment

G   4. lost income costs of unemployment

D   5. menu costs of inflation

C   6. Consumer Price Index (CPI)

F   7. distortion costs of inflation

J   8. Producers Price Index (PPI)

A   9. frictional unemployment

H   10. nominal values

a. Caused by transactions costs in labor markets.

b. Typesetter replaced by computerized typesetters.

c. Measures average prices by comparing the costs of consumer market baskets over time.

d. Cost of upward revisions of price schedules.

e. An upward movement in the general price level.

f. Arise, in part, because inflated prices rise at different rates.

g. Include the opportunity costs of the output and income unemployed individuals could have produced.

h. The current dollar values of economic variables.

i. Variables measured by money but adjusted for price level changes.

j. Measures changes in prices in wholesale markets.

SET II

D   1.   "deflating" nominal values

I   2.   demand-pull inflation

G   3.   discomfort (misery) index

C   4.   cyclical unemployment.

H   5.   labor force

E   6.   cost-push inflation.

J   7.   hyperinflation

A   8.   seasonal unemployment.

B   9.   composition-shift inflation

F   10.   creeping inflation

a.   Regularly experienced by life guards and gold pros. *seasonal unemp.*

b.   Rising demand in one sector causes price hikes; falling demand in another causes layoffs. *composition shift*

c.   Caused by slumps in the overall economy. *cyclical unem*

d.   Adjusting for price level changes by dividing monetary variables by (1% of) a price index.

e.   Occurs, e.g., if union wage demands push prices up.

f.   Low levels of persistent price hikes.

g.   The sum of the rates of inflation and unemployment.

h.   Employed people plus unemployed people.

i.   Could be caused if the money supply grew too rapidly.

j.   Experienced by Germany after World War I.

CHAPTER REVIEW (FILL-IN QUESTIONS)

1-2. The idea that a lower price level encourages greater purchasing is shown in a(n) _ag demand_ curve, with a(n) _ag supply_ curve reflecting the idea that a higher average price level prompts greater production. Depressions and declining prices may emerge if the _demand_ curve shifts leftward, while a rightward shift of this curve will result in a(n) _rise_ in both the price level and aggregate output. A leftward shift of the _supply_ curve causes _stagflation_, a recently developed term that refers to periods when the price level climbs but output falls. *P↑ Output↓*

4.   Unemployment statistics as reported may understate true unemployment due to the failure to include _discouraged workers_, and may overstate the true level because of _cheaters_.

5.   When skill requirements for a given occupation change or people have no marketable skills, _structural_ unemployment results. _seasonal_ unemployment occurs because some types of work are dependent upon weather or the time of the year.

6.   Unemployment results in _lost income_ as well as _social_ costs such as foregone educations, increased family debt, and higher crime and suicide rates.

7-8. Inflation is defined as an increase in the _average_ level of money prices. The average level of prices is measured using a(n) _index_. The _____ (CPI) measures the changes in purchasing power by comparing the cost of a sample _market basket_ today with its cost at an earlier date.

9.   If inflation is at a relatively low rate, the economy is said to be suffering from _creeping_ inflation. However, when inflation exceeds roughly 50 percent annually, inflation is defined as _hyperinflation_.

10. The discomfort index is a combination of the rates of _unempl_ and _inflation_.

STANDARD MULTIPLE CHOICE

THERE IS ONE BEST ANSWER FOR EACH QUESTION.

___ 1. In the short run, rapid growth of Aggregate Demand relative to Aggregate Supply is LEAST likely to yield:
- a. deflationary growth.
- b. growth of aggregate output.
- c. inflation of the price level.
- d. declines in unemployment rates.
- e. widespread shortages if there are economy-wide price ceilings.

___ 2. If Aggregate Supply shrinks relative to Aggregate Demand, the likely result is:
- a. stagflation, with simultaneous inflation and rising unemployment.
- b. a deep depression, like that suffered during the 1930s.
- c. deflationary growth, with income rising and the price level falling.
- d. accelerating inflation of the sort suffered in post-World War I Germany.
- e. creeping inflation accompanied by moderate real growth, like the American experience of the 1950s and 1960s.

___ 3. Unemployed slide rule mechanics, typesetters displaced by automation, or ex-convicts whose only legal skills are making license plates, are all examples of what kind of unemployment?
- a. structural
- b. seasonal
- c. cyclical
- d. frictional
- e. institutional

___ 4. Which of the following statements would cause a respondent to be classified as unemployed?
- a. "I worked in my dad's store for 26 hours after school."
- b. "No I didn't work last week; we're on strike."
- c. "Are you kidding? I am in the Army."
- d. "No, I didn't work last week. I looked all over the city for a job. Didn't find anything though."
- e. "No, I didn't work last week, I'm on vacation."

___ 5. Macroeconomic policy makers are most concerned with unemployment that is:
- a. frictional
- b. cyclical
- c. structural
- d. voluntary
- e. out-on strike

___ 6. Unemployment statistics will be understated because of:
- a. unemployment compensation chiselers.
- b. unemployed college dropouts.
- c. discouraged workers.
- d. housewives.
- e. cyclical layoffs.

___ 7. Real income:
- a. always increases along with inflation.
- b. is the same as nominal income.
- c. is current monetary income divided by CPI/100.
- d. remains the same regardless of inflation.
- e. always rises when deflation occurs.

___ 8. The real costs of inflation do NOT include:
- a. lost income when a recession raises unemployment.
- b. the values of resources used in repricing goods.
- c. declines in capital accumulation caused by inflation.
- d. distortions due to uneven price increases.
- e. lost production because of mistakes emerging from inflation-caused confusion about what prices mean.

___ 9. The producer price index (PPI):
- a. currently includes over 50,000 retail products.
- b. is a general purpose index, measuring changes in prices in markets other than retail.
- c. does not distinguish list from transaction prices.
- d. will be less than 100 because markups are ignored.
- e. is synonymous with the GNP deflator.

80

10. Business firms may mark up their prices to compensate for increased risks they perceive from inflation. This is primarily an example of:
    a. menu costs.
    b. escalator costs.
    c. frictional costs.
    (d.) distortions costs.
    e. capitalist exploitation of misfortune.

11. The Consumer Price Index (CPI) is used:
    a. to convert real values to long-term nominal values.
    (b.) as an escalator in many contracts calling for future monetary payments.
    c. as an indicator of the strength of policies to dampen seasonal unemployment.
    d. as a direct measure of real economic growth.
    e. to ascertain the amounts consumers save by buying at discount stores and using coupons.

12. The most persistent period of rapid inflation in the United States occurred:
    a. during the Great Depression (1929-1939).
    b. following the Civil War (1865-1895).
    c. during World War II (1940-1946).
    d. during the Korean and Vietnam War eras (1950-1968).
    (e.) from the late 1960s into the early 1980s.

13. When the supply of money expands too rapidly relative to the growth of the supplies of goods, or when we are close to full employment and the government spends far more than its tax revenues, the likely result is:
    a. cost-push inflation.
    b. administered-price inflation. *P↑ more easily than ↓*
    c. composition-shift inflation.
    d. expectational inflation.
    (e.) demand pull inflation.

    demands ↑ in one sector P's ↑

14. Which of the following countries experienced the most rapid hyperinflation?
    a. China (1940-1950).
    b. Brazil (1950-1970).
    c. Germany (1919-1923).
    d. Russia (1922-1923).
    (e.) Hungary (1945-1946).

TRUE/FALSE

T 1. When using index numbers, the value of the index for the base period is normally 100.

F 2. Consumer buying patterns seldom if ever change.

F 3. Seasonal unemployment is that unemployment associated with the business cycle.

T 4. The United States Department of Labor surveys thousands of households monthly in determining the unemployment rate.

F 5. Altogether, incomes or other money payments received by more than 80 percent of our population are directly tied to the CPI.

F 6. Direct measurement of the value that consumers ascribe to quality changes in consumer goods is relatively easy.

F 7. The CPI undoubtedly understates hikes in the level of industrial prices.

T 8. Inflation roughly represents a zero sum game in terms of distribution.

___ 9. The income redistribution effects of inflation invariably reduce the real level of national production.

___10. In the short run, the Consumer Price Index (CPI) assumes fixed consumption patterns.

___11. When prices are rising consistently, but at relatively low rates, we must be suffering "demand-pull" inflation.

___12. The only country to suffer any significant hyperinflation in the twentieth century was Germany during World War II.

___13. Powerful unions that are able to increase the wages of their members are undoubtedly the principal reason for the inflation we face today.

___14. Widespread expectations of inflation generate inflationary pressures.

___15. When items on the shelf must be repriced due to inflation, the economy actually gains since workers are needed to accomplish these changes.

___16. Aggregate Supply and Demand curves operate quite differently from the demands and supplies for individual markets.

___17. Uncontrolled growth of Aggregate Supply is the major cause of stagflation.

UNLIMITED MULTIPLE CHOICE

WARNING: THERE ARE FROM ZERO TO FOUR CORRECT ANSWERS FOR EACH QUESTION!

___ 1. Frictional unemployment:
   a. could be eliminated by appropriate government programs.
   b. is a result of normal economic activity.
   c. usually results from serious structural change in the economy.
   d. arises due to transaction costs in labor markets.

___ 2. The presence of inflation:
   a. imposes no real costs on society.
   b. is of no concern to the government at present.
   c. means that relative prices may become distorted.
   d. means that the general price level has moved upward.

___ 3. Persons are classified as:
   a. unemployed if they are not employed but are available for work and made recent attempts to find jobs.
   b. unemployed if during the survey week they were waiting to report to a new job in three months.
   c. unemployed if during the survey week they were waiting to be recalled to a job from which they were laid off.
   d. part of the labor force if they were employed during the survey week.

___ 4. The major conceptual and statistical problems with the CPI occur because:
   a. the CPI is constructed primarily for adjusting Social Security payments and is of little use to younger families as a measure of the changes in the cost of living.
   b. such things as alcoholic beverage consumption and rock concerts are routinely excluded from all indexes.
   c. the value and prices for personal services cannot be estimated.
   d. criminal activity is missing from the market basket of goods and services.

_____ 5. The economy may gain from inflation if:
    (a.) business actually invests more today since it views rising prices as a signal that more profits can be made and that any future capital acquisitions will cost more.
    (b.) needed changes in relative prices occur more easily during inflationary periods.
    (c.) needed expansion of government is easier because tax revenues rise at a faster rate due to the progressivity of the personal income tax.
    d. the discomfort index for the economy grows as the inflation rate increases.

PROBLEMS

Problem 1

Given the numbers in Table 1 for nominal GNP and the GNP implicit price deflator, answer the following questions.

Table 1

$$\frac{103.4}{32.87/100}$$

YEAR	NOMINAL GNP (BILLIONS)	GNP IMPLICIT PRICE DEFLATOR (1972=100)	REAL GNP
1929	103.4	32.87	_____
1933	55.8	25.14	_____
1939	90.8	28.48	_____
1949	258.0	52.59	_____
1959	486.5	67.52	_____
1969	935.5	86.72	_____
1979	2,368.5	165.50	_____

GNP   .3787

a. Compute real GNP in 1972 prices and complete the table above.

b. What was the percentage increase in real GNP from 1929 to 1979? _____.

c. What has been the percentage increase in nominal GNP from 1929 to 1979? _____
_____.

d. What accounts for the difference between (b) and (c)? _____.

e. Compute the percentage increase in real GNP for the following decades:

1940s _____ 1950s _____

1960s _____ 1970s _____

Problem 2

Given in the next table are the dollar figures for the same bundle of consumer goods and services during a ten year period. Use these data to answer the following questions.

Table 2

YEAR	CURRENT DOLLAR VALUE OF BUNDLE	PRICE INDEX
1	$ 20	_____
2	22	_____
3	25	_____
4	30	_____
5	40	_____
6	50	_____
7	70	_____
8	80	_____
9	90	_____
10	110	_____

a. Compute the price index for each year, assuming that year 6 represents the base year.

b. Assume that during year 8 the industry producing one of the commodities in the market basket experienced a technological revolution, greatly enhancing product quality. If the price index was adjusted for this change in quality, what would happen to the values in the table?

Problem 3

Table 3 illustrates population and employment data for a hypothetical country. For simplicity's sake, assume that this country has no military personnel.

Table 3

	JULY 1985	DECEMBER 1985
Non-institutional Population	2,000,000	2,100,000
Labor Force	1,000,000	_____
Employed	920,000	900,000
Unemployed	_____	50,000
Employment Rate	_____	_____
Unemployment Rate	_____	_____
Labor Force Participation Rate	_____	_____

a. Complete the table.

b. What is the most likely cause of the population increase?

c. What has happened to the number employed? _____; and the employment rate? _____
   Does this result seem perverse? _____ Why or why not? _____

d. Why do you think the labor force declined over this period? _____ This type of
   "unemployment" is usually called _____

e. Are discouraged workers counted in any of the numbers above? _____ Which one(s)?
   _____

Problem 4

Listed in Table 4 is hypothetical data for a specific wage earner over the period 1944-1980. Using your knowledge of price indices and your ability to inflate or deflate variables, complete the table.

Table 4

Year	CPI (1967=100)	Nominal Income (Current dollars)	Real Income (1967 dollars)
1944	50	_____	12,000
1959	_____	10,000	15,000
1967	100	19,800	
1974	180	28,000	_____
1980	_____	40,000	16,000

Problem 5

Use Figure 1 that shows shifts of Aggregate Demand and Aggregate Supply curves for the entire economy to answer the following questions.

Figure 1

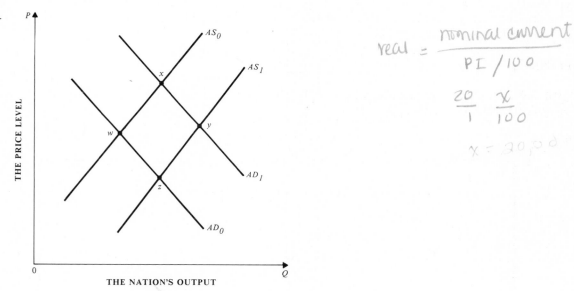

_____ a. Shifts of Aggregate Demand from AD_1 to AD_0 would cause recession and deflationary pressure on prices.

_____ b. President Reagan's "supply-side" policies were attempts to cause an upward shift like AS_1 to AS_0.

_____ c. Unemployment is likely to be more of a problem if Aggregate Demand moves from AD_0 to AD_1.

_____ d. Stagflation (simultaneous hikes in of both unemployment and inflation) can be described by a movement like AS_1 to AS_0.

_____ e. Deflationary growth is a likely consequence if the economy's equilibrium moves from w to z.

_____ f. Real output is likely to be comparatively unaffected, but prices will soar if Aggregate Supply moves from AS_0 to AS_1 while Aggregate Demand goes from AD_0 to AD_1.

_____ g. Employment and inflation will both be larger if the economy moves from equilibrium z to equilibrium x.

85

___ h. Substantial economic growth will occur with little inflation or deflation if Aggregate Demand moves from AD_0 to AD_1 while Aggregate Supply moves from AS_0 to AS_1.

___ i. A growing production possibilities frontier is paralleled by an upward movement of Aggregate Supply from AS_1 to AS_0.

___ j. The Great Depression followed a path like $y \rightarrow x \rightarrow w$.

Problem 6

On Figure 2 draw an Aggregate Demand curve and an Aggregate Supply curve. Label them AD_0 and AS_0, respectively. Now illustrate a situation where demand pull inflation will occur by labelling a new Aggregate Demand curve AD_1. Label the new intersection I. Finally, using the new Aggregate Demand curve AD_1, illustrate stagflation. Use the subscript AS_1 to label your new supply curve. Label the new intersection S.

Figure 2

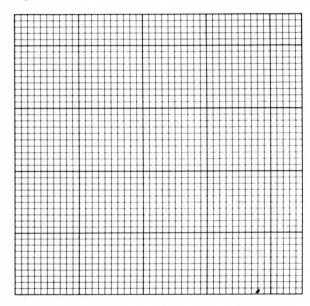

ANSWERS

Matching Key Terms and Concepts

SET I

Answer	Reference
1. e	p. 109
2. i	p. 111
3. b	p. 104
4. g	p. 107
5. d	p. 117
6. c	p. 110
7. f	p. 118
8. j	p. 112
9. a	p. 104
10. h	p. 110

SET II

Answer	Reference
1. d	p. 111
2. i	p. 114
3. g	p. 119
4. c	p. 105
5. h	p. 103
6. e	p. 115
7. j	p. 114
8. a	p. 104
9. b	p. 116
10. f	p. 114

Chapter Review (Fill-in Questions)

1. Aggregate Demand, Aggregate Supply
2. Aggregate Demand, rise
3. Aggregate Supply, stagflation
4. discouraged workers, dishonest nonworkers
5. structural, seasonal
6. lost income, social
7. average, index
8. Consumer Price Index, market basket
9. creeping, galloping or hyperinflation
10. unemployment, inflation

Standard Multiple Choice

Answer	Reference
1. a	p. 101
2. a	p. 101
3. a	p. 104
4. d	p. 105
5. b	p. 105
6. c	p. 103
7. c	p. 111
8. a	p. 117
9. b	p. 113
10. d	p. 117
11. b	p. 110
12. e	p. 114
13. e	p. 114
14. e	p. 114

True/False Questions

Answer	Reference
1. T	p. 109
2. F	p. 114
3. F	p. 104
4. T	p. 105
5. F	p. 110
6. F	p. 112
7. F	p. 112
8. T	p. 118
9. F	p. 118
10. T	p. 110
11. F	p. 114
12. F	p. 114
13. F	p. 115
14. T	p. 116
15. F	p. 117
16. F	p. 101
17. F	p. 101

Unlimited Multiple Choice

Answer	Reference
1. bd	p. 104
2. cd	p. 109
3. abcd	p. 105
4. none	p. 112
5. abc	p. 119

Problem 1
Reference p. 109-113

a. 1929 = 314.6
    1933 = 222.1
    1939 = 318.8
    1949 = 490.7
    1959 = 720.4
    1969 = 1,078.8
    1979 = 1,431.1

b. (1,431.1 - 314.6)/314.6 = 354.9%

c. (2,368.5 - 103.4)/103.4 = 2,190.6%

d. inflation

e. 1940s = (490.7 - 318.8)/318.8 = 53.9%
    1950s = (720.4 - 490.7)/490.7 = 46.8%
    1960s = (1,078.8 - 720.4)/720.4 = 49.8%
    1970s - (1,431.1 - 1,078.8)/1,078.8 = 32.7%

Problem 2
Reference pp. 109-113

a. 1.   40
    2.   44
    3.   50
    4.   60
    5.   80
    6.   100
    7.   140
    8.   160
    9.   180
    10. 220

b. The price index numbers should be lower after year
    8.

Problem 3
Reference pp. 102-107

a. See Table 5.

Table 5

	JULY 1985	DECEMBER 1985
Non-institutional Population	2,000,000	2,100,000
Labor Force	1,000,000	950,000
Employed	920,000	900,000
Unemployed	80,000	50,000
Employment Rate	92%	94.7%
Unemployment Rate	8%	5.3%
Labor Force Participation Rate	.50	.45

b. The birth rate over these six months greatly
    exceeded the mortality rate.

c. Employment has fallen. The employment rate has
    risen. No, because the labor force has declined
    substantially over this period.

d. The July figures include high school students who
    are no longer in the labor force in December.
    The December figures include many people
    temporarily employed for the holiday season.
    The term seasonal unemployment is usually used
    to describe such situations.

e. Discouraged workers are included in population
    and, therefore, labor force participation rate.

Problem 4
Reference pp. 108-111

See Table 6

Table 6

Year	CPI (1967=100)	Nominal Income (Current dollars)	Real Income (1967 dollars)
1944	50	6,000	12,000
1959	66.67	10,000	15,000
1967	100	19,800	19,800
1974	180	28,000	15,555
1980	250	40,000	16,000

Problem 5
Reference pp. 100-102

a. T
b. F
c. F
d. T
e. T
f. F
g. F
h. T
i. F
j. F

Problem 6
Reference p. 100-102

See Figure 3.

Figure 3

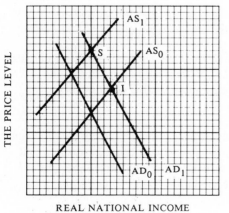

CHAPTER SEVEN
GROSS NATIONAL PRODUCT (GNP)

CHAPTER OBJECTIVES

After you have studied this chapter you should be able to, explain the concept and uses of Gross National Product (GNP); explain how income and expenditure approaches estimate GNP; explain the concept of value-added; explain how disposable personal income, personal income, national income and net national product are derived from GNP accounts; explain some limitations of GNP accounting, and evaluate GNP as a measure of social well-being.

CHAPTER REVIEW: KEY POINTS

1. GNP is the total market value of a nation's annual production. GNP measures estimate the economic performance of an economy and are important for government policy and business decisions.

2. The expenditures approach to GNP sums consumption spending (C), business investment spending (I), government purchases (G), and net exports (X-M): GNP = C + I + G + (X - M).

3. Gross Private Domestic Investment (GPDI) is the economic term for business spending. To arrive at net investment, we need to subtract depreciation from GPDI. $\left(NI = GPDI - Deprec.\right)$

4. Government purchases (G) do not include transfer (welfare) payments, which are treated as flows of income from some households to others.

5. The income approach to estimating GNP sums wages, interest, rent, and profits. We use the figures available, which are (a) wages and salaries, (b) proprietors' income, (c) corporate profits, (d) rental income, and (e) interest. The sum of these figures is National Income (NI). Addition of indirect business taxes, which is not anyone's income, yields Net National Product (NNP). The capital consumption allowance (depreciation) is the difference between GNP and NNP. $NI = Prop.\ income + corp.\ profits + interest + rent\ income$
$+ wages + salaries$

6. The value-added approach to GNP sums the sales of all firms and subtracts their purchases of intermediate products, which are goods bought by one firm from another for further processing. Failure to exclude purchases of intermediate goods from GNP figures would result in substantial double counting of production.

7. GNP figures should be used cautiously in any discussions of economic welfare. One problem is that they may be systematically biased and are often presented in an artificially precise fashion. Another problem is that they ignore most nonmarket production (for example, housewives' services and do-it-yourself projects). GNP accounts include as production many disproducts (for instance, pollution abatement equipment is added to GNP, while environmental decay is not subtracted).

8. A Measure of Economic Welfare (MEW), which attempts to correct for some of these flaws in GNP accounts, shows much less rapid growth than GNP.

MATCHING KEY TERMS AND CONCEPTS

SET I

G 1. exports

C 2. Gross National Product

A 3. Measure of Economic Welfare (MEW)

J 4. imports

I 5. indirect business taxes

D 6. Net National Product

B 7. Net Private Domestic Investment *GPDI-dep*

F 8. financial investment

H 9. transfer payments

E 10. per capita real income

a. GNP adjusted to better estimate economic welfare. *MEW*

b. Additions to society's stock of real capital. *NPDI*

c. National Income + Indirect business taxes + Depreciation. *GNP*

d. GNP minus depreciation of capital stock. *NNP*

e. Real national income divided by the population. *per capita*

f. Purchases of stocks and bonds. *financial inv.*

g. Goods produced in this country and purchased by foreigners. *exports*

h. Income taxed from one set of households and given to another set. *transfer payments*

i. Sales, excise, and property taxes. *indirect taxes*

j. Goods produced abroad and purchased by consumers in this country. *imports*

SET II

H 1. net private domestic investment

D 2. value-added

A 3. personal income

J 4. capital consumption allowance

C 5. retained earnings

F 6. government purchases

E 7. net exports

I 8. personal taxes

G 9. income approach

B 10. expenditure approach

a. NI + transfer payments - corporate taxes - retained earnings. *personal income*

b. C + I + G + (X - M) *expenditure approach*

c. Corporate income after taxes and dividends. *retained earnings*

d. A way to avoid the double-counting problem. *value added*

e. X - M *net exports*

f. Capital accumulation after adjusting for depreciation.

g. w + i + r + Π. *income approach*

h. Plus transfer payments equals government outlays. *gov't purch*

i. Subtracted from Personal Income to calculate Disposable PI. *NPDI personal taxes*

j. Known by accountants as depreciation. *capital consump. allowance*

© Scott, Foresman and Company

CHAPTER REVIEW (FILL-IN QUESTIONS)

1. Gross National Product (GNP) is the total *market value* of all production during one year. One of the major reasons for measuring GNP is to provide policymakers a regular, continuing and comparable *gauge* of total economic activity.

2. The two main conceptual approaches to measuring GNP are the *expenditure* approach and the *income* approach.

3-5. The expenditure approach looks at the expenditures of the *final* users of the product who include *govrn.* , *investors cons.* , and *foreign*. By adding these four expenditure categories *GNP* is obtained.

6-7. Alternatively, national income can be obtained by adding together all payments to the *owners of resources*. The biggest component of national income is *wages*. To reconcile national income and GNP, *depreciation* and *ind.* *bus. taxes* must be added to NI to obtain GNP.

8-9. While GNP does a pretty fair job of measuring economic performance, some notable limitations exist. Some national economic data is provided to the exact *dollar* where rounding would make more sense. Many forms of *household* production such as the value of housewive's services are excluded. Since many *gov't* services are not sold, valuing the output is difficult, so GNP statisticians use the next best estimate, the value of the *input*.

10. As a measure of well-being, GNP has many limitations. The value of *leisure* activities is ignored while expenditures for removing litter and pollution are included. To overcome these problems, two economists developed a(n) *Measure of Economic Welfare*.

STANDARD MULTIPLE CHOICE

THERE IS ONE BEST ANSWER FOR EACH QUESTION.

C 1. Gross National Product is the total market value of all:
   a. commodities sold in a year.
   b. services produced in a year.
   c. production during a year.
   d. consumer goods sold during a year.
   e. none of the above.

B 2. National Income is the sum of ALL of the following EXCEPT:
   a. wages.
   b. savings.
   c. interest.
   d. rent.
   e. profits.

A 3. Purchases of foreign-made goods should NOT be:
   a. included with other expenditures to compute our GNP.
   b. included in the GNP of the exporting country.
   c. included in the personal expenditures category of GNP, which is then adjusted by subtracting imports.
   d. value-added for the exporting country.
   e. none of the above.

C 4. GNP computations include only rough adjustments for:
   a. changes in the quantities of leisure time.
   b. changes in such 'disproducts' as pollution or crowding.
   c. increases or decreases in the quality of the goods we buy.
   d. how equitably wealth is distributed.
   e. the values of housewives' services.

5. The problem of "double counting" is partially cured by:
   a. summations of total sales by all firms.
   b. the expenditures approach.
   c. the income approach.
   (d.) summations of only the values added by each firm.
   e. capital consumption allowances.

6. The title "father of modern GNP accounting" belongs to:
   a. Oskar Morgenstern.
   b. Franscois Quesnay.
   c. John Stuart Mill.
   d. James Buchanan.
   (e.) Simon Kuznets.

7. Among the most vociferous critics of GNP accounting was:
   (a.) Oskar Morgenstern.
   b. John von Neumann.
   c. John Kenneth Galbraith.
   d. Paul Samuelson.
   e. Simon Kuznets.

8. Legalization of marijuana would cause the growth of GNP:
   (a.) to more accurately reflect wellbeing.
   b. to be overstated in the very short run.
   c. to be understated in the long run.
   d. to decline precipitously.
   e. to become stagnant.

9. Meased GNP would exclude the:
   a. market values of environmentally harmful goods.
   b. monetary costs incurred in cleaning up pollution.
   c. many items that never enter the marketplace such as military hardware.
   d. increases in inventories during business downturns.
   (e.) values of "do-it-yourself" projects.

10. Which of the following is Net National Product (NNP)?
    a. $C + GPDI + G + X - M$.
    b. $C + S + T + M$.
    c. GNP - IBT (indirect business taxes).
    (d.) GNP - depreciation.
    e. DPI + S.

11. The value-added approach estimates GNP as:
    a. the sum of the sales of all firms.
    b. the sum of all intermediate goods used by all firms.
    (c.) the sum of the sales of all firms less the purchases of all intermediate products.
    d. the sum of all final goods less costs of production.
    e. the sum of all sales minus labor costs.

12. Corporations use their profits to:
    a. pay salaries to employees.
    b. pay salaries and taxes or invest in capital goods.
    (c.) pay taxes to the government, dividends to their stockholders, and save to finance the firm's operations or expansion.
    d. buy insurance.
    e. contribute to charities, distribute foreign aid, and pay graft to politicians.

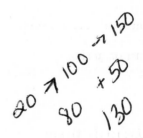

TRUE/FALSE QUESTIONS

F 1. For national income accounting purposes, stocks and bonds traded on the New York and American Stock Exchanges are considered real investments.

F 2. Changes in inventories are considered consumption. – Investment

T 3. Included in farm income is an estimate of the value of home-consumed food grown on farms but not marketed.

T 4. Indirect business taxes are treated as a part of NI since they are payments to the factors of production.

T 5. One way to avoid overstatement of GNP is to total the sales of all firms after subtracting the values of intermediate goods purchased by each firm.

F 6. National Income accounts only consider productive activity that takes place in the marketplace.

T 7. In computing the value of government services, government statisticians use the cost of the inputs used to produce the service.

F 8. GNP includes adjustments for the changing value of leisure time.

T 9. Individual income and spending are related positively to the level of economic activity.

F 10. Final economic goods are those goods used in the production of other economic goods.

UNLIMITED MULTIPLE CHOICE

WARNING: THERE ARE FROM ZERO TO FOUR CORRECT ANSWERS FOR EACH QUESTION!

___ 1. Economic investment includes:
   a. all final purchases of new capital equipment.
   b. changes in inventories.
   c. all construction.
   d. purchases of stocks, bonds, and old houses.

___ 2. National income:
   a. is the sum of incomes paid to owners of the various factors of production, plus retained earnings and corporate profit taxes.
   b. is normally broken down into wages, interest, rent, corporate income, and proprietor's income.
   c. equals Consumption + GPDI + Government purchases.
   d. equals GNP-(depreciation + indirect business taxes).

___ 3. Gross National Product (GNP) is:
   a. an important measure of total economic activity.
   b. a crude yardstick with which to measure national well-being.
   c. computed using a combination of several different accounting methods depending on the specific output or income measured.
   d. a valuable measure to policymakers trying to determine the needs of the economy.

___ 4. Profits are used by corporations:
   a. to pay corporate profit taxes.
   b. to finance investment projects.
   c. to pay dividends to households.
   d. as salary incentives to corporate officers who own stock.

___ 5. Interest income:
   a. includes payments made for the use of borrowed capital (usually financial capital).
   b. in recent years has been the most rapidly growing proportion of National Income.
   c. is usually associated with the renting of real property.
   d. represents profits received by entrepreneurs.

PROBLEMS

Problem 1

Listed below are various categories of expenditures and income used in GNP accounting. Using the numbers for these categories, specify formulas that will answer the following questions (e.g., 5 + 10 + 15).

1. Wages and salaries
2. Rental income
3. Interest
4. Indirect business taxes
5. Capital consumption allowance
6. Personal consumption expenditures
7. Gross Private Domestic Investment
8. Corporate profits
9. Proprietors' income
10. Government expenditures on goods
11. Personal income tax
12. Government transfer payments
13. Social security taxes
14. Corporate profits tax
15. Exports
16. Imports
17. Retained earnings
18. Personal savings
19. Consumer interest payments plus personal transfers to foreigners

a. Compute GNP using the expenditure approach.
b. Compute GNP using the income approach.
c. Compute National Income.
d. Compute Personal Income.
e. Compute Disposable Income.
f. Compute NNP in two different ways.

Scott, Foresman and Company

Problem 2

Information about a specific product is given in the table below. Stage #5 is the final stage of production.

Table 1

	DOLLAR VALUE OF INPUTS	DOLLAR VALUE OF GOOD IN MARKET	VALUE-ADDED
Stage 1	0	$ 100	100
Stage 2	$ 100	300	200
Stage 3	300	900	600
Stage 4	900	1,500	600
Stage 5	1,500	2,500	1000

a. Fill in the column for value added.

b. The value of this commodity to be counted in GNP is? ____ .

c. The sum of all values-added equals? _____ .

Problem 3

Use the data listed below from the first quarter of 1980 to compute the answers to questions a through f.

1. personal consumption expenditures: $1,634.1
2. compensation of employees: $1,552.4
3. personal taxes and consumer interest: $320.0
4. capital consumption allowance: $263.3
5. net interest: $147.2
6. federal purchases of goods and services: $187.3
7. rental income of persons: $27.0
8. Gross Private Domestic Investment: $388.8
9. corporate profits: $182.0
10. state and local purchases of goods and services: $331.0
11. exports: $299.4
12. proprietors' income: $131.3
13. imports: $320.4
14. personal income: $2,056.6
15. personal outlays: $1,677.6
16. Gross National Product in 1972 dollars: $1,444.2

a. Compute GNP _____ .
b. Compute Net National Product _____ .
c. Compute indirect business taxes _____ . sales, excise, property
d. Compute personal savings _____ .
e. Compute the GNP deflator (1972 = 100) _____ .
f. Compute National Income _____ .

Problem 4

Use (T) for true to indicate that the following items would be counted in GNP if known to government accountants, and (F) for false if they would not consider an item to be GNP.

_F_ a. You consume leisure that you value at $1,000 when you take a week long vacation in Hawaii.

_F_ b. Jocko grows marijuana in his backyard and sells it to Bonzo for $114,000.

_T_ c. I spend $40 for paint to repair an old house I just bought.

_T_ d. A Las Vegas casino wins $10,000 from a drunken tourist.

_T_ e. Tito runs his car into Franco's limousine and his insurance company pays $13,000 to repair both vehicles.

_T_ f. Marie Antoinette pays $7.00 for flour because she likes homemade cake best.

_F_ g. Mr. and Mrs. Richie Rich build a mansion worth a million dollars for their family's own occupancy, but have no out-of-pocket expenses because all materials were retrieved from the city dump and all work was done by family members during their summer vacation.

_T_ h. A carpenter repairs a neighbor's stairs for $200, but does not report it to the Internal Revenue Service.

_F_ i. Elvira now gets free swimming lessons, but before she married the lifeguard she paid $10 per lesson.

_T_ j. Engelbert pays $8.00 for a bottle of hairgrower that fails to cure his baldness. He later discovers that the local drugstore had the same brand on sale at two bottles for $6.99.

Problem 5

Calculate the value added for a wooden table given that the sum of all the value-added is $80.

Table 2

STAGE	COST OF INPUT	SALES RECEIPTS	VALUE-ADDED
Mill	-0-	_____	_____
Lumber distributor	15	_____	_____
Table maker	30	_____	_____
Delivered table	____	_____	25

Problem 6

Assume a simple economy with two people Robinson and Friday. Robinson is the boss because Friday possesses a meek personality. Robbie pays Friday $400 a year in wages to gather food and to make clothing, and a $100 a year to build new housing. Friday takes the $500 total wages and gives $100 to Robinson for rent and $400 to Robinson for clothes and food that Robbie has stored for Friday. Robbie reinvests the rental income into housing and assumes that $300 of Friday's money is for wages and $100 is entrepreneurial profit. Calculate GNP, NNP and NI from the expenditure and income approaches.

ANSWERS

Matching Key Terms And Concepts

SET I

Answer	Reference
1. g	p. 127
2. c	p. 123
3. a	p. 135
4. j	p. 127
5. i	p. 130
6. d	p. 130
7. b	p. 130
8. f	p. 126
9. h	p. 127
10. e	p. 124

SET II

Answer	Reference
1. f	p. 130
2. d	p. 130
3. a	p. 131
4. j	p. 130
5. c	p. 128
6. h	p. 126
7. e	p. 127
8. i	p. 132
9. g	p. 127
10. b	p. 125

Standard Multiple Choice

Answer	Reference
1. c	p. 123
2. b	p. 127
3. a	p. 127
4. c	p. 134
5. d	p. 130
6. e	p. 129
7. a	p. 133
8. b	p. 136
9. e	p. 134
10. d	p. 130
11. c	p. 130
12. c	p. 128

True/false Questions

Answer	Reference
1. F	p. 126
2. F	p. 126
3. T	p. 128
4. F	p. 128
5. T	p. 130
6. F	p. 127
7. T	p. 127
8. F	p. 135
9. T	p. 131
10. F	p. 130

Chapter Review (fill-in Questions)

1. market value, estimate
2. income, expenditure
3. final or ultimate, consumers
4. business investors, government
5. foreigners, Gross National Product
6. owners of resources, wages
7. capital consumption allowance, indirect business taxes
8. dollar, nonmarket
9. government, inputs
10. leisure, Measure of Economic Welfare (MEW)

Unlimited Multiple Choice

Answer	Reference
1. abc	p. 126
2. abd	p. 127
3. abcd	p. 124
4. abc	p. 128
5. ab	p. 129

Problem 1
Reference pp. 125-132

a. (6) + (7) + (10) + ((15) - (16)).
b. (1) + (2) + (3) + (8) + (9) + (4) + (5).
c. (1) + (2) + (3) + (8) + (9).
d. (18) + (6) + (19) + (11).
e. (18) + (6) + (19).
f. Answer (a) minus (5); or Answer (b) minus (5).

Problem 2
References p. 130

a. $100, $200, $600, $600, $1000
b. $2500
c. $2500

Problem 3
Reference p. 125-132

a. 2,520.2
b. 2,256. 9
c. 217.0
d. 59.0
e. 174. 5
f. 2,039. 9

Problem 4
Reference pp. 125-132

a. F
b. F
c. T
d. T
e. T
f. T
g. F
h. T
i. F
j. T

Problem 5
Reference p. 130

See table 3.

Table 3

STAGE	COST OF INPUT	SALES RECEIPTS	VALUE-ADDED
Mill	-0-	15	15
Lumber distributor	15	30	15
Table maker	30	55	25
Delivered table	55	80	25
	Sum of Value-Added		80

Problem 6
Reference pp. 125-132

GNP = C + I + G + (X-M) = 900 + 100 + 0 + (0) = 1000

GNP = NNP = NI since there is no depreciation and no government to collect indirect business taxes.

$$NI = w + i + r + \text{profit}$$
$$= 800 + 0 + 100 + 100$$
$$= 1000$$

99

CHAPTER EIGHT

MACROECONOMICS BEFORE KEYNES

CHAPTER OBJECTIVES

After you have read and studied this chapter you should be able to describe different phases of business cycles and explain early business cycle theories; explain the fundamentals of classical theory; describe the historical record of American business fluctuations; and use Aggregate Demand and Aggregate Supply curves to illustrate (crudely) movements of economy wide levels of prices, output, and employment.

CHAPTER REVIEW: KEY POINTS

1. Business cycles consist of alternating periods of economic expansion and contraction. From World War II into the early 1960s, many economists felt that the business cycle was obsolete because government could fine-tune the economy with monetary and fiscal policy. This optimistic point of view is no longer widely held.

2. The business cycle is typically broken down into four phases: (a) peak (boom), (b) contraction (recession or downturn), (c) trough (depression), and (d) expansion (recovery or upturn). Business cycles are measured from peak to peak and have averaged roughly 4 years although some have been as short as 18 months, while others have lasted a decade.

3. Business cycles are dated and analyzed by the National Bureau of Economic Research (NBER). Reference dates are established by a detailed examination of data from past cycles.

4. NBER has examined thousands of individual data series and classified those that seem systematically related to cycles into three groups: (a) leading indicators reach their respective highs and lows before the general cycle peak and trough; (b) coincident indicators tend to turn roughly with the general business cycle; and (c) lagging indicators reach their respective peaks and troughs after the general business cycle.

5. Business cycles leave their mark on people and families in many ways besides loss of income. Such things as mental and physical health problems, marital tensions, divorces, suicides, alcoholism, prostitution, illegitimacy, and both personal and property crime are closely related to changes in business conditions. Marriages and divorces alike tend to be positively related to the business cycle. Mental disorders and some physical diseases, suicides, crimes, and illegitimate births appear inversely related to business conditions. That is, they all rise when the economy turns down. Declines in income and the negative social effects of business slumps together have prompted policymakers to look for ways to keep the economy on a steady path.

6. Prosperity in the 1920s was caused primarily by the rapid growth of the automobile industry and the spread of such innovations as electricity, radio, and the telephone. A wave of optimism lasted through much of the period.

7. The Great Depression of the 1930s was the most severe in U. S. history. At its trough, a fourth of the labor force was unemployed and real disposable personal income had fallen by about 26 percent. Many were left homeless and hungry. The devastation of the Depression led to new economic theories and to numerous reforms in banking and social welfare programs.

8. World War II rapidly lifted the country out of the Depression. Massive government spending to fight the war brought unemployment down from 15 percent in 1940 to less than 3 percent during 1944-45. Inflation became a major problem after World War II as the federal government focused its policies on achieving full employment.

9. The 1960s were prosperous, consistent with the government's perceived ability to "fine-tune" the economy using the latest techniques of macroeconomic policy. President Johnson's decision to expand both domestic programs and the Vietnam conflict generally overheated the economy in the late 1960s and early 1970s.

10. In 1971, wage and price controls were used by President Nixon to slow the rate of inflation. In the middle 1970s, the economy was battered with large doses of both unemployment and inflation--a combination generally called stagflation. The economy remained sluggish, with substantial amounts of both unemployment and inflation lingering into the early 1980s. Attempts by the Reagan Administration to reduce both inflation and interest rates resulted in high unemployment in 1982, but a sustained recovery brought unemployment back down by the mid 1980s.

11. Many early business cycle theories were external force theories, focusing on events outside the economic system. The sunspot theory and other external force theories were based on changing weather conditions and wars as sources of instability.

12. Psychological theories of the business cycle use people's herd instincts to explain the effects of extended periods of optimism or pessimism. These theories may partially account for the cumulative nature of business cycle downturns or recoveries, but provide little insight into the reasons for turning points.

13. N. D. Kondratieff suggested that long waves of economic activity (40-60 years) underlie the minor reverberations that occur roughly every four to eight years. This long-wave theory has not been especially convincing to economists, being widely viewed as a statistical coincidence.

14. Joseph Schumpeter developed a business cycle theory around major innovations that may partially explain major long-term business fluctuations. He cited the developments of railroads, automobiles, and similar innovations as generating significant investment leading to tremendous economic growth for a period of time.

15. Classical theory is not a business cycle theory per se, but a systematic examination of how the economy operates. Classical theory is a conglomeration of the thoughts of many economic thinkers dating back to Adam Smith.

16. Classical economists based their theory on Say's Law: Supply creates its own demand. Coupled with assumptions that wages, prices, and interest rates are all perfectly flexible, Say's Law drives the economy towards full employment. All unemployment is considered voluntary--simply a refusal to work at the equilibrium wage. The protracted unemployment of the early 1930s diluted acceptance of classical theory and led to the development of the radically different Keynesian theory.

MATCHING KEY TERMS AND CONCEPTS

SET I

I 1. Aggregate Demand curve

H 2. business cycles

D 3. Say's Law

F 4. voluntary unemployment

A 5. flexible wages, prices, and interest

J 6. classical economics

G 7. Aggregate Supply curve

C 8. involuntary unemployment

E 9. Kondratieff long waves

B 10. spin-offs

a. Assure full employment in classical theory.

b. Mimicry of original innovations.

c. The result of excess supply in the labor market.

d. Supply creates its own demand.

e. Business cycle that oscillates every 40 to 60 years.

f. Unemployment that exists even at equilibrium.

g. A positive relationship between goods available economy-wide and the price level.

h. Alternating expansions and contractions in economic activity.

i. A negative relationship between economy-wide domestic production and the price level. prod ↓ price ↑

j. Predecessor of Keynesian Economics.

SET II

J 1. leading indicator

A 2. business cycles

F 3. recovery

C 4. recession

D 5. contraction

E 6. coincident indicator

I 7. peak-to-peak

H 8. trough

B 9. lagging indicator

G 10. the Great Depression

a. Alternating periods of expansion and contraction.

b. Typically hits its highs and lows after peaks or troughs.

c. The low point of a cyclical downturn.

d. Typically follows a peak.

e. Hits highs and lows simultaneously with a business cycle.

f. Typically follows a trough.

g. Lasted from 1929 until World War II.

h. Low point of a business cycle.

i. Averages four years, but with substantial variation.

j. Hits highs or lows ahead of a business cycle.

CHAPTER REVIEW (FILL-IN QUESTIONS)

1-2. Most early theories of business cycles focused on forces that were ___external___ to the economic system. Sunspot theories and other early theory stressed wars and shocks to the ___ag.___ industry. Psychological theories of the cycle concentrate on the herd instinct coupled with prolonged periods (or waves) of ___optimism___ and ___pessimism___.

3-4. The two long-wave theories of business cycles are associated with the names of ___K___ and ___S.___. Variations in the magnitudes and timing of ___innovation___ and then the process of adjusting to them were the driving forces behind long cycles according to Schumpeter. Karl Marx predicted the decline and eventual overthrow of capitalism as it moved through extended business expansions and contractions because of ever greater ___concentration___ of wealth in the hands of capitalists.

5. Classical economic theory was the result of numerous studies of how markets operate. Classical theory suggested that several automatic mechanisms operate to ensure _____. The first mechanism is Say's Law, which asserts that the very act of production creates an equivalent level of _____.

6. Classical economists suggested that full employment is assured by flexible _____ and _____ in labor and product markets.

7-9. The idea that a lower price level encourages greater purchasing is shown in a(n) ___demand___ curve, with a(n) ___supply___ curve reflecting the idea that a higher average price level prompts greater production. Depressions and declining prices may emerge if the ___demand___ curve shifts leftward, while a rightward shift of this curve will result in a(n) ___rise___ in both the price level and aggregate output. A leftward shift of the ___supply___ curve causes ___stag.___, a recently developed term that refers to periods when the price level climbs but output falls.

10. The business cycle exhibits a strong relationship with many ___social___ institutions and maladies. Suicides, crime, and illegitimate births tend to be ___neg.___ related to economic activity.

STANDARD MULTIPLE CHOICE

THERE IS ONE BEST ANSWER FOR EACH QUESTION

___ 1. Say's Law refers to:
  a. the concept that demand creates its own supply.
  b. an insignificant part of classical macroeconomic theory.
  c. the idea that the act of production creates an equivalent level of demand.
  d. an old law that held that workers could not sue business for on-the-job injuries because they (the workers) had assumed the risks of employment by accepting the job in the first place.
  e. a tendency towards unionization of the labor force.

___ 2. Classical economists thought that:
  a. flexible wages and prices were the principal causes of recessions.
  b. government policies and spending were needed to keep the economy at full employment.
  c. the Great Depression confirmed their view of the business cycle.
  d. price, wage, and interest rate flexibility can quickly cure any tendencies for a recession.
  e. communist relolutions would overthrow capitalism.

___ 3. Classical economists believe that people save primarily:
   a. to have cash for emergencies.
   b. to be able to consume more in the future.
   c. because investment was to risky.
   d. because insufficient consumer goods were available.
   e. All of the above.

___ 4. Classical macroeconomic theory assumes:
   a. Say's law.
   b. flexible prices.
   c. flexible wages.
   d. flexible interest rates.
   e. All of the above.

___ 5. Psychological theories of business cycles have not been given serious study by economists but:
   a. they can be used to predict turning points in the business cycle.
   b. they can explain the cumulative nature of economic recoveries or downturns.
   c. they illustrate why people do not behave as if they possessed a "herd instinct."
   d. it has been shown that waves of pessimism or optimism won't affect the economic cycles in any way.
   e. psychologists use them to explain suicides and other social problems.

___ 6. Joseph Schumpeter's theory of business cycles was:
   a. the sunspot theory: that sunspots affect the economy through changes in agricultural production.
   b. the psychological theory: herd instincts coupled with periods of optimism and pessimism.
   c. the innovation and long-wave theory: that the economy would expand with significant innovation, reach a saturation point, reevaluate, go into recession, and await another great innovation.
   d. the "long-waves" theory: the economy works on sine waves lasting 50-60 years.
   e. that population adjusts to the resources available, creating swings in supplies and demands.

___ 7. The "sunspot theory" of business cycles:
   a. says that booms commence when business becomes optimistic.
   b. correlates sunspot activity with creative innovations that spark growth.
   c. is an example of psychological theory.
   d. may be resurrected if our economic system becomes dependent on solar energy.
   e. is in accord with modern astrology.

___ 8. During periods prosperity, you might expect:
   a. fewer suicides.
   b. more marriages and divorces.
   c. less crime.
   d. fewer illegitimate births.
   e. All of the above.

___ 9. The development of the Keynesian theory was a response to:
   a. Kondratieff's Long Wave Theory.
   b. Schumpeter's Business Cycle Theory.
   c. Say's Law.
   d. the extensive unemployment of the 1930s.
   e. worldwide inflation after World War I.

___ 10. According to classical macroeconomic theory:
   a. all unemployment is involuntary.
   b. changing weather is a source of instability.
   c. minimum wages stabilize the economy.
   d. extended depressions cannot occur.
   e. high saving rates weaken an economy.

___ 11. The idea that human beings are ultimately destined to live at the minimal level for survival is associated with:
   a. new classical macroeconomics.
   b. Adam Smith and Thomas Malthus.
   c. Keynesian theory.
   d. Marxism.
   e. innovation theory.

___ 12. Classical economics suggests that increased desires to save cause:
   a. interest rates to fall.
   b. investment to shrink.
   c. cyclical unemployment.
   d. severe business cycles.
   e. government budgets to run deficits.

TRUE/FALSE QUESTIONS

T 1. During the Great Depression, unemployment rates approached 25 percent.

F 2. In the U.S., the unemployment rate plummeted from 25 percent in 1929 to nearly 3.2 percent in 1933.

T 3. Both the excesses of a boom and the repressive influence of a depression tend to leave indelible marks on social structures.

F 4. Classical economists strongly reject the idea that a capitalistic, laissez-faire economy automatically produces a full employment output.

F 5. The long wave theory of business cycles gained wide acceptance after several studies proved their existence.

F 6. Since information is costless in the real world, business firms know exactly what to do and what not to do.

F 7. Between 1830 and 1894, Karl Marx expounded a long-wave theory of business cycles by suggesting that economic growth and development in capitalistic systems are fueled by innovations.

T 8. During the Great Depression, the burden of economic assistance fell largely on private charities.

F 9. The decade of the 1950s in the US was a period of rapidly accelerating economic growth, with double-digit inflation becoming a slightly more serious problem as the years progressed.

T 10. In the U.S., the middle 1970s witnessed our first serious brush with supply induced double-digit inflation.

F 11. All saving is quickly invested according to classical theory.

F 12. Classical economists believe that flexible wages equate saving and investment to ensure full employment.

T 13. The Great Depression was responsible for many of the governmental institutions that exist today.

F 14. J. M. Keynes was the principal architect of classical economic analysis.

F 15. Growth of Aggregate Supply is the major cause of unemployment.

UNLIMITED MULTIPLE CHOICE

WARNING: EACH QUESTION HAS FROM ZERO TO FOUR CORRECT ANSWERS!

___ 1. According to Joseph Schumpeter, innovation included:
- (a.) the introduction of a new good.
- (b.) the introduction of a new technology.
- (c.) the opening of a new market.
- (d.) the major reorganization of an industry.

___ 2. Classical economic theory:
- a. easily explained the persistence of the Great Depression.
- b. viewed full employment in the economy as unattainable.
- c. was not a theory of the business cycle per se, but rather a systematic study of the functioning of the economy.
- d. relies heavily on unhindered supply and demand to WORK.

___ 3. Say's Law:
- a. was shown to be valid during the Great Depression.
- b. states that "supply creates its own demand."
- c. is an important proposition in classical economic theory.
- d. was named after J. B. Say, a nineteenth-century French economist.

___ 4. External force theories of the business cycle:
- a. were psychological in nature.
- (b.) include the "sunspot" theory.
- (c.) considered agriculture and war as major sources of instability.
- d. recognize that man is a herd animal.

___ 5. During the prosperous 1960s:
- (a.) tax cuts were effective in stimulating the U.S. economy.
- (b.) there appeared to be a trade-off between unemployment and inflation.
- c. the country suffered double-digit inflation rates.
- (d.) the expansionary effects of the Vietnam War helped push the U.S. economy to full employment.

PROBLEMS

Problem 1

The classical capital market is pictured below. Investment schedule I_0 depicts the investment demand curve. The original saving schedule is denoted S_0 while S_1 denotes the new supply of saving curve. Using this information to answer the following true/false questions.

Figure 1

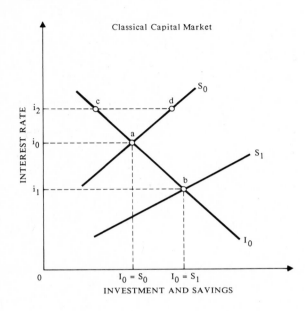

____ a. The economy is in equilibrium at point a after saving increases.

____ b. Say's Law holds at point b.

____ c. Say's Law does not hold at point a.

____ d. The new saving schedule S_1 indicates that people have decided to save less, and, therefore, to consume more, at each income level.

____ e. The movement from a to b represents an increase in investment demand.

____ f. The movement from a to b reflects an increase in the willingness to save.

____ g. In moving from a to b, the interest rate must fall to eliminate the excess supply of commodities created by the decrease in consumption.

____ h. Interest rate i_2 is an equilibrium rate of interest.

____ i. Say's Law holds true at point c.

____ j. The horizontal segment dc represents excess demand in the investment and savings market.

Problem 2

Pictured below is a classical labor market. The original labor supply and demand curves are denoted S_0 and D_0 respectively. The 'Ps' in parentheses indicate the price level. Use this information to answer the following true/false questions.

Figure 2

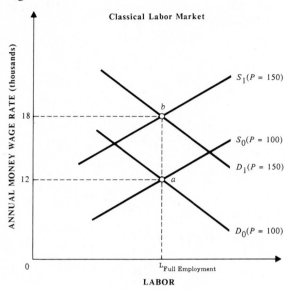

a. Labor decisions are based on the real wage rate.

b. The quantity of labor services demanded varies inversely with the money wage rate, assuming a constant price level.

c. When the demand for labor shifts from D_0 to D_1, this is an indication that the general price level has declined.

d. A 50 percent general increase in prices could cause the supply of labor curve to shift from S_0 to S_1.

e. A movement from point a to point b indicates an increase in the money wage rate.

f. A movement from point a to point b necessarily represents an increase in real wages.

g. At point b, voluntary unemployment is zero.

h. At point a, involuntary unemployment exists.

i. The movement from a to b shows that, as a result of an increase in the real wage rate, business firms decide to hire fewer workers and to produce less output.

j. In the graph, a movement from a to b would occur if the money wage rate and the general price level experience the same 50 percent increase.

k. The average level of prices has increased 50 percent in the graph as we move from a to b.

Problem 3

There are two graphs provided below. In graph A illustrate the classical view of the Aggregate Demand/Aggregate Supply relationship. Be sure to label the axes correctly and to indicate where full employment occurs. In graph B illustrate the Keynesian view of the Aggregate Demand/Aggregate Supply relationship. You have not seen this material presented yet so a description is in order. The Aggregate Demand curve does not change, but the Aggregate Supply curve allows for unemployment. As a matter of fact until there is full employment the Keynesian view is that output (and employment) can be expanded with NO change in the price level. P.S. If you find this too difficult, you can wait for a chapter or two and see the material presented.

Figure 3

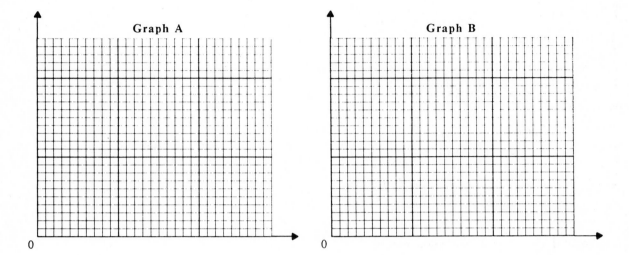

ANSWERS

Matching Key Terms And Concepts

SET I

Answer	Reference
1. i	p. 155
2. h	p. 142
3. d	p. 153
4. f	p. 154
5. a	p. 154
6. j	p. 152
7. g	p. 155
8. c	p. 154
9. e	p. 151
10. b	p. 149

SET II

Answer	Reference
1. j	p. 143
2. a	p. 142
3. f	p. 143
4. c	p. 143
5. d	p. 143
6. e	p. 143
7. i	p. 143
8. h	p. 143
9. b	p. 143
10. g	p. 146

Chapter Review (fill-in Questions)

1. external, agriculture
2. optimism, pessimism
3. Schumpeter, Kondratieff
4. innovations, concentration
5. full employment, demand
6. wages, prices
7. Aggregate Demand, Aggregate Supply
8. Aggregate Demand, rise
9. Aggregate Supply, stagflation
10. social, inversely or negatively

Standard Multiple Choice

Answer	Reference
1. c	p. 153
2. d	p. 154
3. b	p. 153
4. e	p. 153
5. b	p. 152
6. c	p. 150
7. d	p. 148
8. e	p. 143
9. d	p. 156
10. d	p. 155
11. b	p. 155
12. a	p. 155

True/false Questions

Answer	Reference
1. T	p. 146
2. F	p. 146
3. T	p. 143
4. F	p. 155
5. F	p. 151
6. F	p. 148
7. T	p. 151
8. T	p. 146
9. F	p. 147
10. T	p. 148
11. F	p. 155
12. F	p. 153
13. T	p. 145
14. F	p. 152
15. F	p. 155

Unlimited Multiple Choice

Answer	Reference
1. abcd	p. 149
2. cd	p. 153
3. bcd	p. 153
4. bc	p. 148
5. abd	p. 147

Problem 1
Reference pp. 152-155

a. T
b. T
c. F
d. F
e. F
f. T
g. T
h. F
i. F
j. F

Problem 2
Reference pp. 152-155

a. T
b. T
c. F
d. T
e. T
f. F
g. F
h. F
i. F
j. T
k. T

Problem 3

See Figure 4.

Figure 4

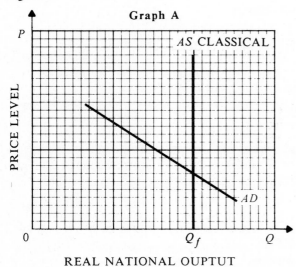

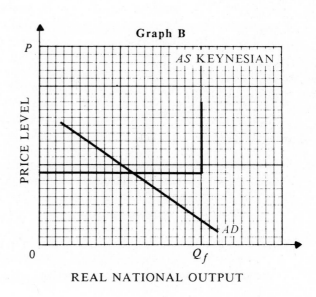

111

CHAPTER NINE

AGGREGATE EXPENDITURES: CONSUMPTION, INVESTMENT, AND GOVERNMENT SPENDING

CHAPTER OBJECTIVES

After you have read and studied this chapter you should be able to enumerate the components of Keynesian Aggregate Demand; discuss average and marginal propensities to consume and save; describe the major determinants of consumption and saving; explain the major determinants of investment; and describe how the major components add together to form Keynesian Aggregate Demand.

CHAPTER REVIEW: KEY POINTS

1. Keynesian analysis focuses on Aggregate Demand. During the Great Depression, the economy had considerable excess productive capacity. During a slow recovery from 1933 to 1940, real output expanded by more than 60 percent with only slight increases in the price level. Keynesian economics assumes that Aggregate Supply is flat in a depressed economy so that the price level is constant and can be ignored; it is primarily concerned with maintaining Aggregate Demand consistent with full employment.

2. Aggregate Expenditures (AE) is total spending on domestic output during a year. Aggregate Expenditures has four components: (a) personal consumption expenditures, (b) gross private domestic investment, (c) government purchases of goods and services, and (d) net exports of goods and services.

3. The single most important determinant of consumer spending is disposable income through its influence on induced consumption. Consumer spending is related directly to disposable income and is a stable component of Aggregate Expenditure. Other important determinants of consumption and saving include: (a) wealth and expectations of future income, (b) the average size and age composition of typical households, (c) the stocks of consumer goods on hand, (d) the level of household assets and debts, (e) consumer expectations regarding prices and availability of products. These determine the level of autonomous consumption (C_a). *household budget consumer expectations* *expectations of further income size + age composition stocks on hand*

4. The average propensity to consume (apc) is the share of total disposable income that is consumed (C/Y_d). The average propensity to save (aps) is the fraction of total disposable income that is saved (S/Y_d). In addition, apc + aps = 1. Until recently, the average propensities to consume and to save were relatively constant over time, at roughly 93 percent and 7 percent, respectively. The aps has only averaged 4-5 percent during the past decade. $APC = \dfrac{C}{Y_d}$ $APS = \dfrac{S}{Y_d}$

5. The marginal propensity to consume (mpc) is the change in planned consumption associated with a given small change in disposable income; it tells us how much of an additional dollar of income will be consumed. Similarly, the marginal propensity to save (mps) is how much of an additional dollar in income will be saved. Furthermore, mpc + mps = 1.

6. Capital investment refers to purchases of new output that can be used in the future to produce other goods and services. There are three major components of investment: (a) new business and residential structures, (b) machinery and equipment, and (c) inventory accumulation. *New business machinery + equipment inventory accum.*

7. The primary factors determining the quantity of investment are (a) expected returns from investment, (b) expectations about the business environment, (c) rates of technological change and innovation, (d) the level of existing stocks of business capital relative to total production, and (e) the costs of investment, including the interest rate. In simple Keynesian models, investment is treated as autonomous (I_a).

8. While government spending is probably influenced by changes in income, it is even more strongly affected by the state of international relations and domestic politics. Thus government spending as a component of Aggregate Expenditures is also treated as autonomous.

9. Exports and imports are reasonably balanced, so net exports (X - M) make a comparatively small contribution to Aggregate Expenditures. The foreign sector is, however, very important to the strength and vitality of our economy by providing markets for our production and imported goods that would be much more costly if produced only domestically. Simple Keynesian models treat net exports as autonomous.

[handwritten margin notes: expected returns, expected bus. env., tech change, exist. stock of bus. cap, cost of invest.]

MATCHING KEY TERMS AND CONCEPTS

[handwritten: $C_a + I_a + G_a + (X_a - m_a) + mpc(Y)$]
[handwritten: $AE = 175 + 100 + 150 + 25 + .5(y)$]
[handwritten: $1 - .5y = 450 + .5y$ $.5y = 450$]

B 1. interest rate

E 2. rate of return

H 3. autonomous expenditures

G 4. induced expenditures

I 5. marginal propensity to save

D 6. Keynesian Aggregate Demand

J 7. 45-degree Keynesian reference line

A 8. average propensity to save

F 9. marginal propensity to consume

K 10. breakeven level of income

C 11. dissaving

a. The proportion of income that is saved. *APS*

b. An important cost of investment. *interest rate*

c. Borrowing or drawing down savings. *dissaving*

d. C + I + G + (X-M). *Aggregate AD*

e. The annual percent of an income stream relative to the dollar outlay for a capital good. *rate of return*

f. The change in consumption divided by the change in income. *mpc* $\frac{\Delta C}{\Delta Y_d}$

g. Related to income. *induced expend*

h. Not a function of income.

i. 1-MPC. *MPS*   *MPC + MPS = 1*   *MPS = 1 - MPC*

j. Y = C + S.

k. The point where S is zero.

[handwritten: $MPS = \frac{S}{Y_d}$ $MPC + MPS = 1$ $MPC + MPS = 1$]

CHAPTER REVIEW (FILL-IN QUESTIONS)

1-3. Keynesian theory suggests that if Aggregate Supply exceeds Aggregate Demand, economic activity and employment will __decrease__ and there will be __decreasing__ pressures on prices. When Aggregate Demand exceeds Aggregate Supply, output will __increase__ and __increasing__ pressures on prices will result. Keynesian analysis focuses on situations of substantial _____ capacity and unemployment. Aggregate Supply is assumed to adjust to Aggregate Demand solely through quantity adjustments. Consequently, all prices are assumed __constant__. As a result, Keynesian analysis focuses on the __demand__ side of the economy.

113

4-6. The largest component of Keynesian Aggregate Demand is consumption and the most volatile is ~~investment~~. The most important determinant of consumer spending is __income__. Keynes's fundamental psychological law asserted that people will __increase__ their consumption as income increases, but by __less__ than the increase in income. When consumption exceeds income, __dissaving__ occurs. Autonomous consumption is __unrelated to__ income.

7-10. The level of investment is affected by business expectations about the business climate, new technologies and the stocks of _____ relative to total output. Production from capital, as with other factors of production, is subject to _____. One of the most important costs of investment is the _____, because it represents the opportunity cost of using funds. _____ investment refers to investment spending that is unrelated to income. Many _____ purchases are like investment in that the benefits are received over a long period of time. Government _____ are not considered a part of Keynesian Aggregate Demand because they do not directly affect demand until the recipient actually spends the money. Graphically, Keynesian Aggregate Demand is the _____ sum of all types of spending; consumption, investment, and government spending. _____ are normally ignored because they represent such a small part of overall economic activity.

STANDARD MULTIPLE CHOICE

THERE IS ONE BEST ANSWER FOR EACH QUESTION.

A 1. The marginal propensity to consume (MPC) is between zero and one according to:
   a. Keynesian consumption functions.
   b. the Law of Diminishing Returns.
   c. the Law of Demand.
   d. Say's Law.
   e. the Law of Entrophy.

D 2. Keynesian Aggregate Demand does not include:
   a. consumption (C).
   b. government purchases (G).
   c. investment (I).
   d. saving (S).
   e. net exports (X-M).

C 3. I spent $8,000 of my $10,000 income last year. My salary has increased to $12,000 and my MPC is .8. What will be the growth in my consumption?
   a. $2,000.
   b. $9,600.
   c. $1,600.
   d. $11,000.
   e. $400.

D 4. Investment is $100 billion at 6 percent interest. If the interest rate increases to 8 percent, investment will:
   a. climb to over $100 billion.
   b. remain at $100 billion.
   c. cause the rate of return from investment to fall.
   d. drop below $100 billion.
   e. decline until interest falls substantially below 6 percent, to compensate for the short term interest rate penalty.

B 5. The largest component of Aggregate Demand is:
   a. government spending.
   b. consumer spending.
   c. new office construction.
   d. inventory accumulation.
   e. investment.

C 6. Which one of the following is NOT an example of economic investment?
   a. inventory growth.
   b. business firms replacing worn out equipment.
   c. purchasing a government bond.
   d. newly constructed residential housing.
   e. newly installed telephone lines.

Annual Yd
10,000

Planned consump
8,000

MPC
.8

$Y = C + S$

$MPC = \dfrac{\Delta C}{\Delta Yd}$

$.8 = \dfrac{\Delta C}{2000}$

$mpc \quad \dfrac{\Delta C}{\Delta Yd}$

$\dfrac{.8}{1} = \dfrac{\Delta C}{2000}$

.8

B 7. If a wave of inflationary expectations newly arose and you were a new car dealer, you might expect your sales to:
  a. drop drastically.
  (b.) increase rapidly.
  c. remain constant.
  d. fluctuate up and down until the rumors subside.
  e. fall initially, but ultimately rise, stabilizing at a new high.

A 8. Keynesian theory suggests that when Aggregate Supply exceeds Aggregate Demand, the level of economic activity will:
  (a.) decline, with pressure on prices to fall.
  b. decline, with pressure on prices to rise.
  c. rise, with pressure on prices to fall.
  d. remain the same.
  e. rise, with pressure on prices to rise.

E 9. Which of the following is NOT an important determinant of consumption and saving:
  a. average size and age of the household.
  b. consumer expectation about prices and availability of products.
  c. stocks of consumer goods on hand.
  d. wealth.
  (e.) wages relative to rates of return on capital.

C 10. If income increases from $7,000 to $12,000 and saving increases by $500, the Marginal Propensity to Save is:
  a. .2.
  b. .3.
  (c.) .1.
  d. .05.
  e. .5.

$$MPS = \frac{\Delta S}{\Delta Y_d} \quad \frac{500}{5000}$$

$$mps = \frac{\Delta S}{\Delta Y_d} \quad \frac{500}{5000}$$

E 11. Investors will pursue investment opportunities as long as:
  a. the expected rate of return is greater than zero.
  b. saving is available for investment.
  c. they are more optimistic than pessimistic.
  d. the expected total profits over time exceeds current monetary outlays.
  (e.) the expected rate of return is at least as great as the interest rate.

A 12. Increases in which of the following will reduce Aggregate Demand?
  (a.) imports (M).
  b. investment (I).
  c. government spending (G).
  d. consumption (C).
  e. marginal propensity to consume (MPC).

TRUE/FALSE QUESTIONS

T 1. Consumption expenditures represent approximately two-thirds of GNP.

T 2. Whenever aggregate demand exceeds aggregate supply, the level of economic activity will tend to rise, and there will be pressures for output or prices, or both, to increase.

T 3. John Maynard Keynes was the first major economist to put forth the revolutionary notion of a positive relationship between consumption and the income level.

F 4. It is impossible for households to have negative savings.

F 5. The average propensity to consume tells us how much of an additional dollar of income will be consumed.

F 6. When the interest rate increases, the investor's opportunity cost of investment falls. rises

F 7. The marginal propensity to save indirectly indicates how much of an additional dollar of income will be consumed.

T 8. Consumption as a percentage of income increases as income increases.

F 9. Investment spending is unaffected by changes in business expectations about the economy.

T 10. Some economists attribute much of the volatility of investment to changes in the interest rate.

T 11. Keynesian Aggregate Demand is the vertical summation of consumption, investment, government spending, and net exports.

T 12. The average propensity to save refers to the proportion of total income saved.

T 13. The marginal propensity to save is equal to the slope of the consumption function.

F 14. The purchase of 100 shares of General Motors stock is not considered an investment for aggregate economic analysis.

T 15. The marginal propensity to consume and marginal propensity to save added together equal one in a simple Keynesian model.

UNLIMITED MULTIPLE CHOICE

WARNING: THE QUESTIONS MAY HAVE SEVERAL OR NO RIGHT ANSWERS!!!

1. Economic investment:
   a. is synonymous with financial investment.
   b. includes the purchase of stocks and bonds.
   c. is the most volatile component of Aggregate Expenditures.
   d. includes the purchase of an old house by a consumer.

2. The marginal propensity to save:
   a. is the change in income caused by a small change in saving.
   b. is the proportion of income that is saved.
   c. is computed by the ratio $\Delta S/\Delta Y$.
   d. plus the marginal propensity to consume balances to zero.

3. Major determinants of consumption and saving include:
   a. wealth and the average size and age of the household.
   b. the stocks of consumer goods on hand.
   c. the nature of the household's balance sheet.
   d. consumer expectations about product prices and availability.

4. Changes in inventories:
   a. are the most volatile component of investment spending.
   b. are signals to business firms of changing economic conditions.
   c. are only brought about by the actions of business firms.
   d. are uncontrollable by most business firms on a day-to-day basis.

5. The marginal propensity to consume (MPC):
   a. is the proportion of total income consumed.
   b. is the proportion of additional income consumed.
   c. is inconsistent with the fundamental psychological law of consumption as expressed by Keynes.
   d. is equal to (1-APS).

$mPC + mPS = 1$

PROBLEMS

Problem 1

Use responses a - g (representing line segments) to answer the following questions based on the diagram below:

a. $dY_2/0Y_2$

b. $ed/0Y_2$ or ed/eY_2

c. df/cf

d. $-ab$

e. $0Y_1$

f. ed

g. dY_2

Figure 1

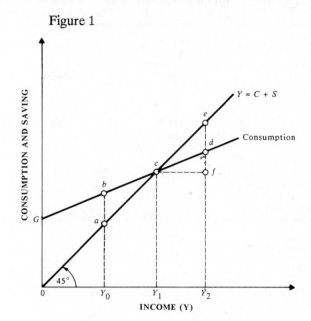

1. The breakeven level of income is ___E___ ?

2. Saving at income Y_0 is equal to ___D___ ?

3. The MPC is equal to _____ C ?

4. When income is Y_2, the APS is equal to ___B___ ?

5. When income is Y_2, the APC is equal to ___A___ ?

6. Consumption at income Y_2 is equal to ___G___ ?

7. Saving when income is Y_2 is equal to ___F___ ?

$$mpc = \frac{\Delta c}{\Delta y}$$

117

Problem 2

Answer the following questions based on the table below:

Table 1 $y = C + S$

Y (BILLION)	C	S	mpc	mps	apc	aps
$ 0	100	-100				
100	175	-75				
200	250	-50				
300	325	-25				
400	400	0				
500	475	25				
600	550					
700	625					
800	700					
900	775					
1,000	850					

a. Fill-in the table. Note that MPC + MPS = 1 = APC + APS.

b. How much is the autonomous component of consumption? _____

c. Using the diagrams below, plot the consumption and savings schedules.

d. Draw and label the Y = C + S (45-degree) line. What is the slope of this line? _____

Figure 2

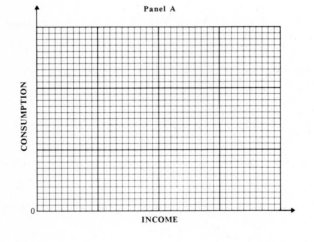

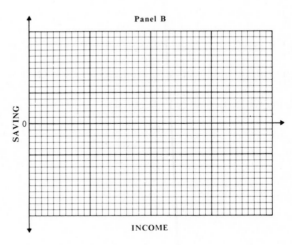

Problem 3

Use these consumption and investment functions to answer the following true/false questions.

Figure 3

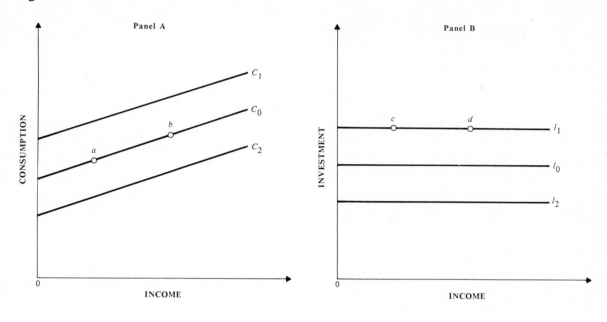

_____ a. The shift of the consumption function from C_0 to C_1 represents a decrease in consumption at all income levels.

_____ b. The shift of the investment function from I_0 to I_2 represents an increase in investment at all income levels.

_____ c. The movement from _a_ to _b_ along consumption function C_0 might be precipitated by a change in consumer expectations about future prices of goods.

_____ d. The movement from _b_ to _a_ along consumption function C_0 might be brought about by a decrease in autonomous saving.

_____ e. The movement from _c_ to _d_ along investment function I_1 represents an increase in investment at each income level.

_____ f. All other factors constant, an increase in autonomous consumption implies a concomitant decrease in autonomous saving.

_____ g. The movement from _a_ to _b_ along consumption function C_0 represents an increase in induced consumption brought about by an increase in income.

_____ h. The APC increases as the economy moves upward along consumption function C_2.

_____ i. All other factors constant, an upward shift in the saving function is always accompanied by a downward shift in the consumption function.

_____ j. A shift in the consumption schedule from C_1 to C_2 could be caused by a decreasing desire to save.

Problem 4

Use the information provided in the saving -income diagram below to answer the following questions.

Figure 4

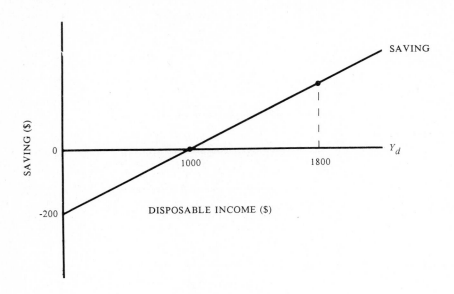

a. In this situation the level of autonomous saving equals _____; and the level of autonomous consumption equals _____.

b. The mpc equals _____; and the mps equals _____.

c. If the level of disposable income equals 1,000, then the apc equals _____; and the aps equals _____.

d. If the level of income is $1,800, then the level of induced consumption is _____; and the total level of consumption equals _____.

e. If the level of income were to rise to $2,200, then the amount of induced savings would equal _____; and the total level of savings would be _____; which naturally means that autonomous saving is still _____.

Problem 5

Refer to the Aggregate Expenditures diagram below to answer the following questions. Note that there is no government sector in this analysis.

Figure 5

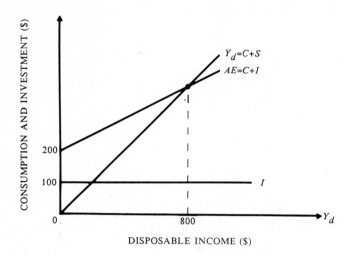

a. The equilibrium level of $800 is based on a marginal propensity to consume of _____.

b. The level of autonomous consumption equals_____; the amount of induced consumption is _____; and therefore total consumption equals _____.

c. The corresponding savings function that would go with this diagram would have autonomous saving equal to _____; a mps equal to _____; and induced savings of _____ at equilibrium.

d. If the level of autonomous consumption fell to $50, then the new level of equilibrium income would equal _____; the new equilibrium level of saving would be _____; and induced consumption would equal _____. At equilibrium, total consumption equals _____; and total saving equals _____.

$$mpc = \frac{\Delta c}{\Delta Y_d} \quad \frac{200}{800}$$

$$mpc = .25$$

ANSWERS

Matching Key Terms and Concepts

Answer		Reference
1.	b	p. 171
2.	e	p. 169
3.	h	p. 175
4.	g	p. 175
5.	i	p. 166
6.	d	p. 161
7.	j	p. 165
8.	a	p. 165
9.	f	p. 166
10.	k	p. 164
11.	c	p. 164

Chapter Review (Fill-in Questions)

1. decline, downward
2. grow, upward, excess
3. constant, demand
4. investment, disposable income
5. increase, less
6. dissaving, independent of, or unrelated to
7. capital, diminishing returns
8. interest rate, Autonomous
9. government, transfer payments
10. vertical, net exports

Standard Multiple Choice

Answer		Reference
1.	a	p. 166
2.	d	p. 175
3.	c	p. 166
4.	d	p. 171
5.	b	p. 168
6.	c	p. 168
7.	b	p. 170
8.	a	p. 161
9.	e	p. 168
10.	c	p. 166
11.	e	p. 169
12.	a	p. 174

True/False Questions

Answer		Reference
1.	T	p. 168
2.	T	p. 161
3.	T	p. 162
4.	F	p. 164
5.	F	p. 165
6.	F	p. 170
7.	T	p. 166
8.	F	p. 165
9.	F	p. 170
10.	T	p. 172
11.	T	p. 175
12.	T	p. 165
13.	F	p. 166
14.	T	p. 168
15.	T	p. 166

Unlimited Multiple Choice

Answer		Reference
1.	c	p. 168
2.	c	p. 166
3.	abcd	p. 167-168
4.	abd	p. 168
5.	b	p. 166

Problem 1
Reference p. 165, 167

1.	e
2.	d
3.	c
4.	b
5.	a
6.	g
7.	f

Problem 2
Reference pp. 164-167

a. See Table 2

Table 2

S	mpc	mps	apc	aps
-100				
- 75	.75	.25	1.75	-.75
- 50	.75	.25	1.25	-.25
- 25	.75	.25	1.08	-.08
0	.75	.25	1.00	0
+ 25	.75	.25	.95	.05
50	.75	.25	.92	.08
75	.75	.25	.89	.11
100	.75	.25	.88	.12
125	.75	.25	.86	.14
150	.75	.25	.85	.15

b. $100
c. See Figure 6

Figure 6

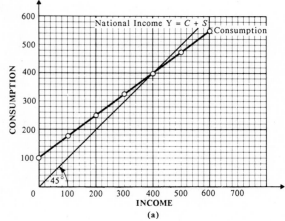

(a)

(b)

d. one

Problem 3
Reference pp. 164-173

a. F
b. F
c. F
d. F
e. F
f. T
g. T
h. F
i. T
j. F

Problem 4
Reference pp. 164-167

a. -$200; $200; autonomous saving and income are based on zero income.

b. .8; .2; as income rises from $0 to $1,000, savings increases by $200 (0-(-200)). Thus MPS = 200/1,000 = .2 and MPC = 1 - MPS = 1 - .2 = .8.

c. 1.0; 0; saving is zero, so C = Y and C/Y = 1.0 since 1 = APS + APC, APS = 0.

d. $1,440; $1,640; induced consumption is equal to MPC x Y = .8 x $1,800 = $1,440. The total level of consumption is induced plus autonomous ($1,440 + 200 = $1,640).

e. $440; $240; -$200; induced saving is equal to MPS x Y = .2 x $2,2400 = $440. The total level of savings is induced plus autonomous ($440 + (-200) = $240).

Problem 5
Reference pp. 165-167, 173

a. .75; since autonomous spending is $200 for an equilibrium income of $800, the multiplier must equal 4 and therefore the MPC is .75.

b. $100; $600; $700; since autonomous spending is $200 and autonomous investment is $100, autonomous consumption must equal $100. Induced consumption is MPC x Yd = .75 x $800 = $600. Total consumption is equal to autonomous plus induced or $100 + $600 = 700.

c. -$100; .25; $200; autonomous saving is the negative of autonomous consumption or -$100. The marginal propensity to save, MPS = 1 - MPC = 1 - .75 = 25. At equilibrium induced saving is equal to
MPS x Y = .25 x $800 = $200.

d. $600; $100; $450; equilibrium income is equal to autonomous spending ($150) times the multiplier (4) or $600. At equilibrium induced consumption is MPC x Y = .75 x $600 = $450 and total consumption is autonomous plus induced ($50 + $450 = $500). Therefore, since S = Y - C, savings is $100 ($600 - $500 = $100).

CHAPTER TEN

EQUILIBRIUM OUTPUT, EMPLOYMENT, AND INCOME

CHAPTER OBJECTIVES

After you have read and studied this chapter you should be able to explain equilibrium income and employment using the Aggregate Expenditures - National Income approach, and why Keynesians differ from classical economists by emphasizing demand over supply forces; explain macroequilibrium with the savings-investment approach; explain the differences between potential and actual GNP and the concepts of recessionary and inflationary gaps; and explain the relationships between Keynesian Aggregate Supply and Demand and the average level of prices in the economy.

CHAPTER REVIEW: KEY POINTS

1. Keynesian theory suggests that erratic changes in business investment spending (especially inventories) play a major role in causing fluctuations in aggregate income and employment.

2. Equilibrium income and employment occur at the output level at which Aggregate Spending equals National Output; firms desire to produce and sell exactly the amounts consumers and investors want to purchase. Any deviation from equilibrium income sets forces in motion to drive the economy towards a new equilibrium.

3. When planned saving equals planned investment (S = I), the economy will be in equilibrium. Actual saving and investment are equal at all times because inventory adjustments and similar mechanisms ensure this balance.

4. When autonomous spending in the economy increases by $1, income rises by an amount equal to the autonomous spending multiplier times the original $1. The multiplier exists because the original $1 in new spending becomes $1 in new income, parts of which are then spent by successive consumers and businesses. The simple autonomous spending multiplier equals: $\Delta Y / \Delta A = 1/mps = 1/(1 - mpc)$, where A represents some form of autonomous spending. More generally, the multiplier equals 1/(withdrawal fraction per spending round).

$$\frac{\Delta Y}{\Delta A} = \frac{1}{mps} = \frac{1}{1 - mpc}$$

5. Investment spending dropped precipitously during the 1929-33 period. The effect of this decline was to reduce equilibrium income sharply, and it may have been a principal cause of the Great Depression.

6. The paradox of thrift appears to be an important challenge to our conventional wisdom. If consumers decide to increase their saving, the result might be declining income, consumption, and saving.

7. Potential GNP is an estimate of the output the economy could produce at full employment. The GNP gap is the difference between potential and actual GNP.

8. The recessionary gap is the amount by which autonomous spending falls short of that necessary to achieve a full employment level of income; it is measured on the vertical axis. An inflationary gap is the amount that autonomous spending exceeds what is necessary for a full employment equilibrium and is a measure of upward pressure on the price level.

9. Keynes felt that in a depression, increases in output with no increase in the price level could be stimulated by raising demand. Simple Keynesian theory suggests that the Aggregate Supply curve is horizontal up to the point of full employment. Once full employment and the economy's capacity to produce are reached, the economy follows classical reasoning. The Aggregate Supply curve becomes vertical because higher prices cannot generate extra production. When the economy is at full employment, any increase in Aggregate Demand simply bids up prices and results in inflation.

MATCHING KEY TERMS AND CONCEPTS

D 1. equilibrium

H 2. National Output schedule

B 3. unintended inventory changes

F 4. recessionary gap

I 5. inflationary gap

G 6. paradox of thrift

J 7. potential GNP

C 8. actual investment

E 9. planned investment equals planned savings

A 10. autonomous spending multiplier

a. The reciprocal of the marginal propensity to save.

b. Ensures that actual investment equals actual saving. *autonomous spending muet*

c. Planned investment adjusted for unintended inventory changes.

d. Pressures for changes in a market system are balanced.

e. Condition for a private economy macroequilibrium. $S = I$

f. Deficiency in autonomous expenditure at full employment.

g. Attempts to save more actually yields less saving.

h. The amounts that producers are willing to offer, expecting to sell their outputs at prevailing prices.

i. Amount that autonomous spending exceeds that needed to achieve full-employment equilibrium with price level stability.

j. National output when resources are fully employed.

$$mps = \frac{\Delta S}{\Delta Y}$$

$$mps = \frac{\Delta S}{\Delta Yd}$$

$$\frac{\Delta Y}{\Delta I}$$

CHAPTER REVIEW (FILL-IN QUESTIONS)

1-3. Keynesian analysis focused on _____ [employ short run] problems and illustrated that the economy might be stuck in a short-run equilibrium in which substantial excess _____ [capacity] existed. In the simple Keynesian Aggregate Demand-National Income model, the National output schedule could be thought of as a Keynesian _____ schedule. All points along the National Income schedule represent potential equilibrium because aggregate output and income just equal aggregate spending. Whenever aggregate spending differs from aggregate income there is _____ . Equilibrium occurs when Keynesian Aggregate Demand is just equal to _____ . At this point, firms do not experience pressures to expand or contract output and they are able to maintain _____ at a level consistent with their desires.

4-6. Keynesian analysis assumes that only _____ adjustments will occur in situations of excess capacity. Whenever Keynesian Aggregate Demand exceeds national output, firms typically find their _____ shrinking. To correct for this problem, business will _____ output and as a result, _____ will increase. Consequently, national income and output expands. As income expands, aggregate spending expands until both _____ and _____ are equal.

7-9. When an autonomous injection of spending is introduced into the economy, its effect is _____ so that equilibrium income actually increases _____ than the autonomous injection. This effect is the result of a concept referred to as the _____ , and is defined by the ratio of the change in income to the change in _____ . The simple spending multiplier is also defined to be equal to _____ or _____ .

$$\frac{\Delta Y}{\Delta A} \quad \frac{1}{mps} \quad \frac{1}{1-mpc}$$

10. The paradox of thrift suggests that when people collectively desire to save more they actually end up saving _____ [less] . When the economy is slipping into a recession, people generally attempt to save more, _____ [increasing] the likelihood a recession will occur.

STANDARD MULTIPLE CHOICE

THERE IS ONE BEST ANSWER FOR EACH QUESTION.

___ 1. The Keynesian autonomous spending multiplier equals:
   a. government spending.
   b. 1 - MPC.
   c. 1/(1-MPS).
   d. 1/(1-MPC). (circled)
   e. unity.

$$1 - mpc$$
$$\frac{\Delta Y}{\Delta A} = \frac{1}{mps} = \frac{1}{1-mpc}$$

___ 2. As autonomous investment rises, Keynesians expect increases in:
   a. income.
   b. employment.
   c. consumption.
   d. Aggregate Demand.
   e. All of these. (circled)

$$\frac{1}{1-mpc} \quad \frac{1}{mps}$$

___ 3. Which of the following may NOT be true in equilibrium for a simple Keynesian model?
   a. the government budget balances. (circled)
   b. Y = A/(1-MPC).
   c. S + T = I + G.
   d. C + I + G = C + S + T.
   e. Y = A(1/mps).

___ 4. The Aggregate Supply curve during a Keynesian depression:
   a. is horizontal. (circled)
   b. is vertical.
   c. tilts downward to the right.
   d. tilts upward to the right.
   e. is the negative relation between unemployment and inflation.

price level is constant

5. A recessionary gap measures:
   a. the amount by which autonomous spending falls short of that needed to bring equilibrium income to full employment. *(circled)*
   b. The amount Aggregate Spending exceeds that needed to achieve full employment.
   c. the difference in real output between the Classical model and the Keynesian Depression model.
   d. the Paradox of Thrift.
   e. none of the above.

6. The Paradox of Thrift suggests that:
   a. "a penny saved is a penny earned."
   b. as consumption increases saving decreases.
   c. as saving increases investment declines. *(circled)*
   d. attempts to save more may actually reduce total saving.
   e. the less you pay, the lower your satisfaction.

7. Equilibrium is achieved in a private economy when desired: $S = I$
   a. consumption equals Aggregate Demand.
   b. consumption equals desired savings.
   c. investment equals desired saving. *(circled)*
   d. inventories equal desired saving.
   e. income equals net wealth.

8. Inventories play an important role in the economic equilibrium because:
   a. unintended inventory changes act as signals to producers to change their production plans. *(circled)*
   b. they are a major component of the multiplier effect.
   c. Aggregate Expenditures would be too hard to accurately measure without inventory changes.
   d. savings could not be converted to investment without inventories as the means of doing so.
   e. inventories are an extremely stable component of investment.

9. The Keynesian point of view suggests that:
   a. supply creates its own demand.
   b. demand creates its own supply. *(circled)*
   c. the market is always at equilibrium.
   d. full employment is achieved as the result of natural market forces.
   e. none of the above.

10. The major cause of the depression of the 1930s according to the Keynesian model was:
   a. increased government spending.
   b. reduced foreign exports.
   c. reductions in investment. *(circled)*
   d. declines in the money supply.
   e. none of the above.

11. How large will the change in income be from a change in investment of $25 if the marginal propensity to consume is .8?
   a. $5.
   b. $20.
   c. $25.
   d. $125. *(circled)*
   e. $200.

$$\frac{1}{mps} \quad \frac{1}{1-mpc} \quad \frac{\Delta Y}{\Delta I} = \frac{1}{1-.8}$$

12. An excess in autonomous spending relative to that needed for full employment is referred to as a(n):
   a. inflationary surplus.
   b. inflationary gap. *(circled)*
   c. recessionary gap.
   d. deflationary shortfall.
   e. demand shortage.

(handwritten notes in margins:)

$C = a + bY$

$\dfrac{1}{.2}\ \dfrac{\Delta Y}{25}$ $\dfrac{1}{1-.8}$

$\dfrac{\Delta Y}{} $

$\begin{array}{r} 4 \\ 25 \\ \underline{.8} \\ 120 \end{array}$

$\dfrac{\Delta Y}{25} = \dfrac{1}{.2}$

$.2y = 25$

$y =$

mpc
.8 mpc
.2 mps

$\dfrac{1}{.2}$

$\dfrac{1}{1-.8} \quad \dfrac{1.0}{.8} \quad \dfrac{1}{.2}$

TRUE/FALSE QUESTIONS

$mpc = \frac{\Delta c}{\Delta y}$ $mpc = \frac{\Delta c}{\Delta Y}$ $mpc \; \frac{\Delta c}{25}$ $\frac{.8}{1} = \frac{\Delta c}{25}$

F 1. An inflationary gap could be eliminated by increasing government expenditures.

T 2. Keynes viewed savers and investors as different groups who saved and invested for different reasons.

T 3. In Keynesian theory, planned investment is always equal to planned saving. $\frac{\Delta Y}{\Delta I}$

T 4. According to classical theory, consumption expenditure is a function of the level of income.

F 5. By definition, the recessionary gap is the amount by which Keynesian Aggregate Expenditures exceeds National Income at the full employment level of income.

F 6. Keynes upheld Say's Law in his *General Theory*.

T 7. Business firms increase production and employment in response to increasing sales and unplanned decreases in inventories.

F 8. The economy will stay in equilibrium whenever actual investment is equal to actual saving. $I =$

T 9. An inflationary gap occurs when Keynesian Aggregate Expenditures exceed National Income at full employment.

T 10. The Keynesian model suggests that autonomous injections into the economy are translated into much larger changes in incomes.

UNLIMITED MULTIPLE CHOICE

WARNING: THESE QUESTIONS MAY HAVE SEVERAL OR NO RIGHT ANSWERS!!!

___ 1. Macroeconomic equilibrium occurs in the simple Keynesian model whenever:
   a. actual investment is equal to actual saving.
   (b.) unplanned changes in inventories are zero.
   (c.) planned investment equals planned saving.
   (d.) the dollar value of desired expenditures equal the dollar value of goods produced.

___ 2. Unintended inventory changes:
   (a.) act as a balancing force for the economy.
   (b.) represent unplanned investment or disinvestment by business firms.
   (c.) resolve any differences between planned saving and planned investment.
   d. guarantee that planned investment and planned saving will be equal at all levels of income.

$\frac{\Delta Y}{\Delta A} = \frac{1}{mps} \; \frac{1}{1-mpc}$

___ 3. In a simple Keynesian model of the economy characterized by autonomous investment and no government, the autonomous spending multiplier is given by:
   (a.) 1/MPS.
   (b.) 1/(1-MPC).
   c. 1/MPC.
   d. 1/(MPC + MPS).

$\frac{1}{MPS} \quad \frac{1}{1-mpc}$

$\frac{\Delta Y}{\Delta A}$

___ 4. Keynesian theory suggests that Aggregate Supply curves:
   a. fail to embody the workings of the labor market and the state of technology.
   (b.) are vertical when the economy reaches full employment.
   (c.) show the relationship between real output and the price level.
   d. show the real output that producers are willing to purchase at various income levels.

5. In a simple Keynesian model, characterized by autonomous investment and no government, an autonomous spending multiplier of 5 implies that:
   a. the MPS equals .20.
   b. the MPC equals .50.
   c. new autonomous investment of $10 billion will cause income to grow by $20 billion.
   d. 1 - MPS = .80 = MPC.

mult = 5

$$\frac{1}{mps} \quad \frac{1}{1-mpe}$$

$$\frac{c}{Yd}$$

$$\frac{\Delta c}{\Delta Yd}$$

PROBLEMS

Problem 1

Use this table to answer the following questions:

Table 1

AGGREGATE EXPENDITURES	Y	C	I	S	apc	aps	mpc	mps
300	0	200	100	-200	0			
700	500	600	100	-100	1.2			
1100	1,000	1,000	100	0				
1500	1,500	1,400	100	100				
1900	2,000	1,800	100	200				
2300	2,500	2,200	100	300				
2700	3,000	2,600	100	400				

a. Complete the table and plot C, I, Y, and Aggregate Expenditures on the figure below.

Figure 1   C

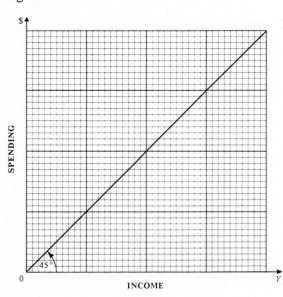

b. Equilibrium income is _____?

c. The multiplier is equal to _____?

d. If full employment income is equal to 2,500, the recessionary gap would be equal to _____ _____. Show the recessionary gap on the figure. The GNP gap is equal to _____? What causes these two to differ? _____.

Problem 2

Answer the following questions based on the table below:

Table 2

(1) INCOME (Y)	(2) SAVING (S)	(3) INVESTMENT (I)	(4) S₁	(5) I₁	(6) S₂
0	-60	40	_____	45	_____
100	-40	40	_____	45	_____
200	-20	40	_____	45	_____
300	0	40	_____	45	_____
400	20	40	_____	45	_____
500	40	40	_____	45	_____
600	60	40	_____	45	_____
700	80	40	_____	45	_____
800	100	40	_____	45	_____

a.   Graph the saving and investment schedules on the figure below.

Figure 2

$C = I + S$
$Y = C + S$

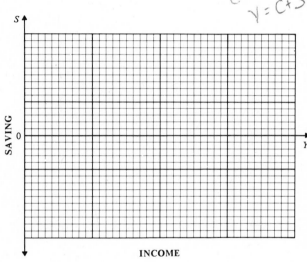

b.   Equilibrium income is _____ ?

c.   Equilibrium saving is _____ ?

d.   Equilibrium investment is _____?

e.   Equilibrium consumption is _____?

f.   The multiplier is _____ ?

g.   Now assume that savers decide to save 25 percent LESS at each income level and business invests $45 at each income level.

1.   Fill in column 4 of the table. Then graph the new saving and investment schedules and label them S_1 and I_1.

2.   The new equilibrium income level will be ___?

3.   Equilibrium saving will be _____?

4.   Equilibrium investment will be _____?

5.   The multiplier is _____?

h.   Beginning from the original table, assume that savers decide to save $20 more at each level of income. Label this saving function S_2 and fill in column 6 of the table.

1.   Equilibrium income will be? _____.

2.   Equilibrium consumption will be? _____.

3.   Equilibrium saving will be? _____.

4.   The marginal propensity to consume is? ____

5.   Have consumers really saved more ?_____.

6.   What has happened to their standards of living?_____. Why? _____.

Problem 3

Use letters in the figure below to answer the following questions:

a. If Keynesian Aggregate Spending is $C + I_1$, equilibrium income will be _____?

b. If $0Y_1$ represents full employment and Keynesian Aggregate Spending is $C + I_0$, the recessionary gap is equal to _____?

c. If $0Y_1$ represents full employment and Keynesian Aggregate Spending is $C + I_2$, the inflationary gap is equal to _____?

d. The multiplier is equal to _____?

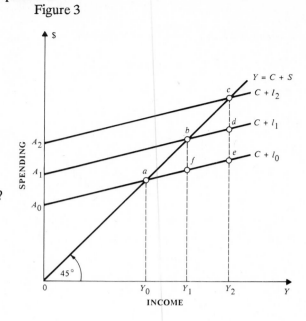

Figure 3

Problem 4

Use the figure below to answer the following questions:

a. Using saving and investment schedules S_2 and I, answer the following (use letters):

    1. Equilibrium income is _____?
    2. The MPC is equal to _____?
    3. Saving when income is Y_1 is _____?

b. Using S_1 as the original, which curve shows increased in desired saving by the public _____?

c. If consumers actually desire to save less, will they end up saving less _____?

d. The multiplier is equal to _____?

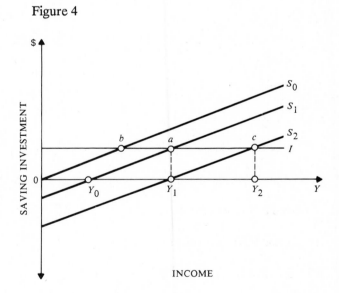

Figure 4

Problem 5

To answer this question you may want to review the optional material included at the end of Chapter Ten. Given below are equations for the components of Aggregate Expenditures (C + I). Use these equations to answer the following questions:

$$C = 250 + .75Y$$

$$I = 100$$

a. Graph C, I, and Aggregate Expenditures (AE) on the chart below.

Figure 5

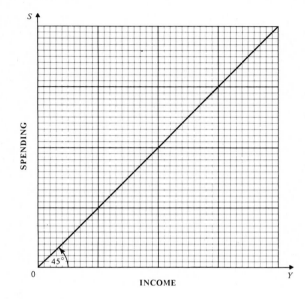

b. Equilibrium income is _____ ?

c. The autonomous spending multiplier equals _____ ?

d. Equilibrium consumption is _____ ?

e. Equilibrium saving is _____ ?

f. Write the equation for the saving function _____.

g. Assume that autonomous consumption expenditures increase from 250 to 400. What is the effect on equilibrium income _____ ? On equilibrium saving _____ ? Show these changes on the chart and label the new Keynesian Aggregate Expenditures curve AE_1 and the new consumption schedule C_1.

h. Assuming that full employment income is 1700, what is the recessionary gap to at the initial equilibrium level ____ ? The GNP gap is _____ ?

Problem 6

To answer this question, you should review the optional material included at the end of Chapter Ten. Given below are the equations for desired investment and saving. Use the equations to answer the following questions:

$$S = -300 + .20Y \qquad I = 200$$

a. Graph the saving and investment schedules on this figure.

b. Equilibrium income is _____?

c. The autonomous spending multiplier is _____?

d. Write the equation for the consumption function _____.

e. At an income level of 1500, planned saving is equal to ____? Planned investment is equal to ____? Is the economy in equilibrium? ____

Figure 6

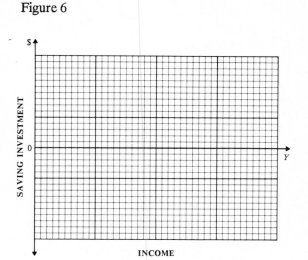

Problem 7

Refer to the figure 7 to answer the following questions.

a. The level of output Q_1 represents _____.

b. If Aggregate Demand were to fall from AD_1 to AD_0 what would be the impacts on price and quantity?_____

c. At Aggregate Demand level AD_0 the economy would most likely be in a _____.

d. Using Keynesian policy tools the move from AD_0 to AD_1 might be accomplished by _____.

e. If Aggregate Demand overshoots the AD_1 level and instead proceeds to AD_2, what would be the effect on price and quantity? _____

f. The range of the Aggregate Supply curve that corresponds to our simple Keynesian income-expenditure model is _____.

g. The classical school assumed that market forces always maintained full employment. Based on that logic, what would an Aggregate Supply curve look like for a classical macroeconomic model?_____

Figure 7

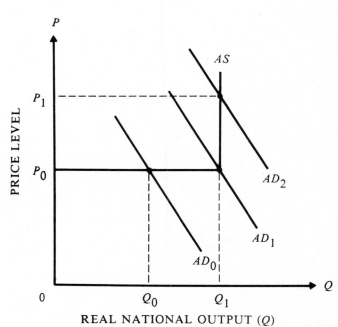

ANSWERS

Matching Key Terms and Concepts

Answer	Reference
1. d	p. 179
2. h	p. 179
3. b	p. 181
4. f	p. 190
5. i	p. 191
6. g	p. 186
7. j	p. 190
8. c	p. 183
9. e	p. 183
10. a	p. 185

True/False Questions

Answer	Reference
1. F	p. 191
2. T	p. 182
3. F	p. 183
4. T	p. 179
5. F	p. 190
6. F	p. 180
7. T	p. 181
8. F	p. 182
9. T	p. 191
10. T	p. 183

Chapter Review (Fill-in Questions)

1. short-run, capacity
2. Aggregate Supply, disequilibrium
3. National Income, inventories (or production)
4. quantity, inventories
5. increase, employment
6. National Income, Keynesian Aggregate Expenditures
7. multiplied, more
8. multiplier, autonomous spending or injections
9. $1/(1 - MPC)$, $1/MPS$
10. less, increasing

Unlimited Multiple Choice

Answer	Reference
1. bcd	p. 180-182
2. abc	p. 181
3. ab	p. 185
4. bc	p. 192
5. ad	p. 185

Standard Multiple Choice

Answer	Reference
1. d	p. 185
2. e	p. 183
3. a	p. 182
4. a	p. 192
5. a	p. 190
6. d	p. 186
7. c	p. 182
8. a	p. 182
9. b	p. 180
10. c	p. 186
11. d	p. 185
12. b	p. 190

Problem 1
Reference pp. 183-185, 190-191

a. See table 3 and Figure 8

Table 3

AGGREGATE EXPENDITURES	Y	C	I	S	apc	aps	mpc	mps
300	0	200	100	-200	- - - -	- - - -	- - - -	- - - -
700	500	600	100	-100	1.20	-.20	.80	.20
1,100	1,000	1,000	100	-0-	1.00	0	.80	.20
1,500	1,500	1,400	100	100	.93	.07	.80	.20
1,900	2,000	1,800	100	200	.90	.10	.80	.20
2,300	2,500	2,200	100	300	.88	.12	.80	.20
2,700	3,000	2,600	100	400	.86	.14	.80	.20

Figure 8

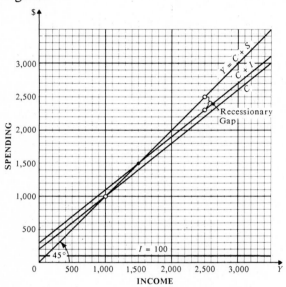

Problem 2
Reference pp. 183-185, 190-191

a. see Figure 9

Figure 9

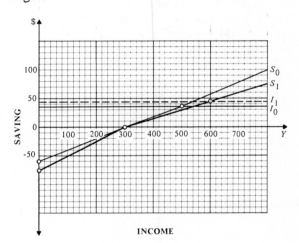

b. 1,500

c. 5

d. 200, see figure, 1000, the multiplier

b. 500

c. 40

d. 40

e. 460

f. 5

g. (1) see Figure 9
(2) 600
(3) 45
(4) 45
(5) 6.67 when S is positive

h. (1) 400
   (2) 360
   (3) 40
   (4) .8
   (5) no
   (6) it had declined. Increases in desired saving
       reduced both equilibrium income and
       consumption.

Problem 3
Reference pp. 183-185, 190-191
a. $0Y_1$

b. bf or de or A_0A_1

c. cd or A_1A_2

d. Y_0Y_1/bf or Y_2Y_1/cd or $0Y_1/0A_1$ or $0Y_0/0A_0$ or $0Y_2/0A_2$

PROBLEM 4
Reference pp. 182-185
a. (1) Y_2
   (2) cY_2/Y_1Y_2
   (3) zero

b. S_0

c. no

d. Y_2Y_1/cY_2 or $Y_1Y_0/aY_1 = 1/MPS$

PROBLEM 5
Reference pp. 195, 183-185,190-191
a. see Figure 10

Figure 10

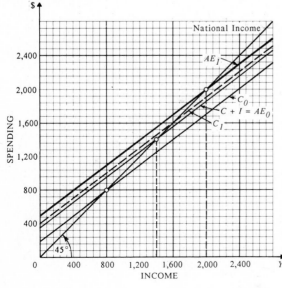

b. $Y = C + I$
   $Y = 250 + .75Y + 100$
   $Y = 350 + .75Y$
   $Y - .75Y = 350$
   $.25Y = 350$
   $Y = 350/.25 = 1400$

c. $k = 1/(1-MPC)$
   $= 1/(1-.75)$
   $= 1/.25$
   $= 4$

d. $C = 250 + .75(1400)$
   $= 250 + 1050$
   $= 1300$

e. 100

f. $S = Y - C$
   $= Y - (250 + .75Y)$
   $= Y - 250 - .75Y$
   $= -250 + .25Y$

g. increases by 600, stays the same, see graph

h. 75, 300

PROBLEM 6
Reference pp. 195, 183-185, 190-191

a. see Figure 11

Figure 11

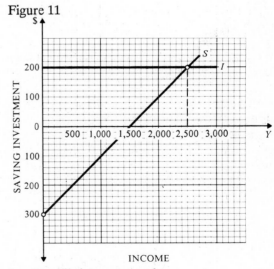

b. Equilibrium occurs when
   $S = I$
   $-300 + .20Y = 200$
   $.20Y = 500$
   $Y = 500/.2$
   $Y = 2500$

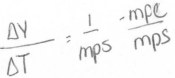

$$\frac{\Delta Y}{\Delta T} = \frac{1}{mps} \quad \frac{-mpc}{mps}$$

137

c. $k = 1/MPS = 1/.20 = 5$

d. $C = Y - S$
    $= Y - (-300 + .20Y)$
    $= Y + 300 - .20Y$
    $= 300 + .8Y$

e. zero, 200

PROBLEM 7
Reference p. 161

a. Output Q_1 represents full employment or full utilization of resources. It can also be viewed as a point on the production possibility frontier.

b. Under the assumptions of the Keynesian model as depicted here, price would not fall below P_0 but quantity would fall from Q_1 to Q_0.

c. recession or depression

d. new government expenditures. It could also be accomplished by increases in any of the other components of autonomous Aggregate Demand, such as consumption, investment or net exports.

e. Beyond AD_1 demand increases are converted into price level increases as there are no additional resources to put into the production process. Output stays at Q_1 but the price level rises from P_0 to P_1.

f. the horizontal portion where no price level changes occur.

g. Since Q_1 represents the fully employed level of economic activity, it would be reasonable to assume that a classical AS curve would be vertical at that level of output. Under these conditions all Aggregate Demand changes are translated into price level changes.

CHAPTER ELEVEN

FISCAL POLICY: GOVERNMENT TAXING AND SPENDING

CHAPTER OBJECTIVES

After you have read and studied this chapter you should be able to differentiate discretionary from automatic fiscal policy; and distinguish between Keynesian and Supply-sider fiscal policies.

CHAPTER REVIEW: KEY POINTS

1. Keynesian fiscal policy is the use of federal spending and tax policies to stimulate or contract Aggregate Spending and economic activity to offset cyclical fluctuations. Classical (supply-side) fiscal policies rely on low tax rates and minimal government spending to allow Aggregate Supply to grow.

2. Discretionary fiscal policy entails of deliberate changes in federal spending and taxation for stabilization purposes. Without congressional action automatic stabilizers such as corporate and personal income taxes and various transfer programs cause changes in spending and taxation as economic conditions change.

3. Increases in government spending increase Aggregate Expenditure and National Income through the multiplier process in the same way as changes in investment or autonomous consumer spending.

4. Changes in net tax revenues (tax revenues minus transfer payments) affect Aggregate Spending differently than changes in government spending. Changes in net taxes directly affect disposable income and, therefore, consumption and saving. These effects on income are transmitted into spending through the autonomous tax multiplier ($\Delta Y/\Delta T = 1 - 1/mps$, or $-mpc/mps$), which is weaker than the spending multiplier.

$$\frac{\Delta Y}{\Delta T} = 1 - \frac{1}{mps} \qquad -\frac{mpc}{mps}$$

5. In a Keynesian depression, the balanced-budget multiplier equals one, suggesting that equal increases (decreases) in government spending and taxes will increase (decrease) Aggregate Spending and equilibrium income by an equal amount. This result follows from the fact that the autonomous tax multiplier ($-mpc/mps$) is one minus the autonomous spending multiplier.

6. Automatic stabilizers tend to cushion the economy. When income falls, automatic stabilizers keep the level of disposable income from falling as rapidly as income. Our progressive income tax causes tax collections to fall proportionally faster when income is falling and to increase proportionally faster when income is rising.

7. These built-in stabilizers can become a problem. When potential income is rising, automatic stabilizers brake the economy and slow the rate of growth. This problem is referred to as fiscal drag.

8. The full employment budget is the amount of surplus or deficit that would be generated at full employment with the existing tax and expenditure structure. The full employment budget is a way of estimating the expansionary or contractionary influence of any tax and expenditure mix.

9. The Laffer curve indicates that high tax rates may impose such large disincentives to productive effort that Aggregate Supply and tax revenues are both restricted.

10. Structural deficits result directly from the mix of spending and tax policies enacted by Congress. The cyclical deficit is attributable to business conditions. As unemployment grows, the cyclical deficit grows, and vice versa.

MATCHING KEY TERMS AND CONCEPTS

E 1. fiscal policy

B 2. fiscal drag

C 3. automatic stabilizers

D 4. balanced budget multiplier

A 5. discretionary fiscal policy

J 6. simple autonomous spending multiplier

F 7. Laffer curve

G 8. high tax rates

I 9. government spending and transfers

M 10. full employment deficit

L 11. structural deficit

H 12. autonomous tax multiplier

K 13. cyclical deficit

a. Deliberate changes in spending and taxes for stabilization policy. *discretionary*

b. Retards growth in Aggregate Expenditures. *fiscal drag*

c. Examples of nondiscretionary fiscal policy. *automatic stabilizers*

d. Always equals one. *balanced budget mult.*

e. The use of government spending and tax policies to stimulate or contract economic activity to offset cyclical fluctuations. *fiscal policy*

f. Higher tax rates may either raise or lower government revenues. *Laffer Curve*

g. Keynesians see as dampening spending, while supply-siders emphasize the destructive effects on production incentives. *higher taxes*

h. -(MPC/MPS). *tax multiplier*

i. Keynesians perceive as bolstering spending, but supply-siders worry about disincentive effects on production. *gov't spending*

j. 1/MPS *auton. spending mult.*

k. Occurs if the economy has excessive idle capacity. *cyclical def.*

l. Also known as a full employment deficit. *struct def*

m. The difference between tax revenues and government outlays when the economy is producing at its capacity. *full emp def*

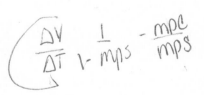

$$\frac{\Delta Y}{\Delta T} \quad \frac{1}{1-mps} \quad \frac{-mpc}{mps}$$

$$\frac{\Delta Y}{\Delta T} \quad \frac{1}{1-mpc} \quad \frac{1}{mps} \quad \frac{-mpc}{mps}$$

mps = .25

CHAPTER REVIEW (FILL-IN QUESTIONS)

1-4. Fiscal policy is the use of government spending and ____tax____ policies to stimulate or contract economic activity to offset _____ fluctuations. Discretionary fiscal policy is the intentional changes in government spending and taxation for the purpose of economic stabilization; whereas __auto. stab__ fiscal policies are changes in spending or taxing which take place ___auto___ (without congressional action) as economic conditions change. Because all changes in injections are subject to the multiplier principle, __changes__ in government spending will change Aggregate Expenditures by an amount equal to the changes in autonomous injections times the multiplier. At equilibrium, injections must equal withdrawals, so when both government spending and taxation are introduced, the new equilibrium condition becomes _____. The payment of taxes will come from both consumption and __saving__.

5-7. An old idea that hikes in very high tax rates may actually lower total tax _____ is depicted by a device called the _____ curve. Although Keynesians and supply-siders agree that cuts in _____ are stimulative, Keynesians view hikes in government _____ or _____ payments as stimulants for spending, while supply-siders view these outlays as retarding _____.

8-10. A law requiring annually balancing the budget would place policymakers in a dilemma. If declines in Aggregate Spending cause rising unemployment, balancing the budget requires that either tax revenues must be _____ or government outlays _____. Unfortunately, it is ambiguous as to whether higher tax _____ will yield more tax _____. Another problem is that recent estimates are that over three-fourths of all government outlays are uncontrollable. Moreover, raising taxes and cutting government outlays both cut into Aggregate _____ and would only aggravate a problem of deficient demand. To avoid the procyclical effects of annually balanced budgets, balancing spending and taxes over the _____ has been proposed.

STANDARD MULTIPLE CHOICE

THERE IS ONE BEST ANSWER FOR EACH QUESTION.

___ 1. Which of the following is NOT an automatic stabilizer?
   a. social security payments.
   b. unemployment compensation.
   c. an anti-inflationary tax increase.
   d. progressive personal income tax rates.
   e. the corporate income tax.

___ 2. Using a simple Keynesian model where the mpc = .75 and government outlays and taxes are equal to $250 billion, the multiplier is equal to:
   a. 4
   b. 1
   c. 3
   d. 2
   e. 5

___ 3. The autonomous tax multiplier equals:
   a. -MPC/MPS.
   b. 1/mpt.
   c. four.
   d. three.
   e. 1/mpc.

___ 4. When built-in (automatic) stabilizers retard growth in Aggregate Spending, the problem is known as:
   a. stagflation.
   b. fiscal drag.
   c. excessive retardation.
   d. frictional inflation and unemployment.
   e. crowding-out.

141

5. The balanced budget multiplier is:
   a. one.
   b. 1/mpc.
   c. 1/mps.
   d. 1/(1-mpc).
   e. -mpc/mps.

6. Equal increases in the amount of government expenditures and taxes:
   a. have no effect on equilibrium income.
   b. cause equilibrium income to fall.
   c. cause equilibrium expenditures to increase by the same amount.
   d. cause prices to fall.
   e. cause proportional increases in the price level and unemployment.

7. According to modern supply-siders, increases in which of the following would NOT pose disincentives for production?
   a. marginal tax rates on wage and salary incomes.
   b. corporate income tax rates.
   c. tax deductions and exemptions.
   d. government transfer programs.
   e. government purchases of goods and services.

8. The Laffer curve suggests a tradeoff between:
   a. unemployment and inflation.
   b. high tax rates and high tax revenues.
   c. consumption and investment.
   d. production and consumption.
   e. tax deductions or exemptions and a balanced budget.

9. Which of the following is smallest in absolute size?
   a. the autonomous spending multiplier.
   b. the marginal propensity to save.
   c. the balanced budget multiplier.
   d. the autonomous tax multiplier.

mps is smallest in absolute size

10. President Reagan's 1981-83 tax cuts were most compatible with the ideas of:
    a. modern supply-siders.
    b. Keynesians.
    c. advocates of laws requiring annually balanced budgets.
    d. functional finance.
    e. advocates of budget balance over the business cycle.

11. Keynesians and supply-siders would be most likely to agree on which of the following as a cure for a severe recession?
    a. substantial increases in government 'public works' projects.
    b. deep cuts in government transfer programs.
    c. slashes in government purchases but hikes in transfer programs.
    d. the need to balance the federal budget.
    e. cuts in tax rates.

12. Huge government budgets cause problems, according to supply siders, for ALL of the following reasons EXCEPT:
    a. fiscal drag causing disincentives for spending.
    b. high taxes causing disincentives for work and investment.
    c. big transfer programs discouraging work effort.
    d. massive government provisions of goods causing people who don't work to excessively enjoy life without labor.
    e. All of these cause problems, according to supply-siders.

TRUE/FALSE QUESTIONS

F 1. If tax rates are increased to pay increased interest on public debt, incentives to work and invest might be diminished.

T 2. The biggest sources of federal tax revenues are social security, personal, and corporate income taxes.

F 3. Fiscal drag refers to the retarding effect that ~~decreased~~ *increased* government expenditures have on the economy.

F 4. Discretionary variations in spending and taxes are the only governmental mechanisms to control unemployment and inflation.

T 5. Automatic stabilizers are the mechanisms inherent in the economy to automatically dampen swings in economic activity.

T 6. Given the unpredictable nature of economic activity, an inflexible commitment to annually balancing the budget could prove disastrous, especially during recessionary periods.

___ 7. In the classical model, an increase in desired Aggregate Expenditures will always induce greater production.

___ 8. In the classical macroeconomic model, a decrease in desired Aggregate Expenditures is followed by a decrease in equilibrium real production and real income.

T 9. Changes in government spending change Keynesian Aggregate Expenditures and National Income through the multiplier process in the same manner as changes in investment or autonomous consumer spending.

F 10. Because government outlays involve both spending for goods and services and transfer payments, the balanced budget multiplier is only slightly bigger than one.

F 11. Automatic stabilizers are also know as discretionary fiscal policy.

T 12. The tax increase of 1932 probably contributed to the severity of the Great Depression.

T 13. Supply siders and Keynesians agree that big government spending programs will boost the economy out of a slump.

T 14. Massive supply-side tax cuts quickly eliminated huge federal deficits in the early 1980s.

T 15. Cutting tax rates will tend to cure both fiscal drag and disincentives for production.

UNLIMITED MULTIPLE CHOICE

WARNING: THERE ARE FROM ZERO TO FOUR ANSWERS FOR EACH QUESTION!

___ 1. Supply-siders and Keynesians would probably agree that :
   a. tax rate hikes reduce equilibrium income.
   b. cuts in government spending reduce national income.
   c. cuts in government transfer payments increase real income.
   d. expanding taxes and spending equally results in equivalent growth of our national income.

___ 2. Macroeconomic equilibrium occurs:
   a. when planned injections are greater than planned withdrawals.
   b. at the point where autonomous taxes equal autonomous government expenditures, assuming a balanced budget fiscal policy, and no induced government expenditure or induced taxation.
   c. when autonomous consumption equals autonomous saving.
   d. only at full employment income in the Keynesian model.

___ 3. Incorporating autonomous taxes (T_a) into simple Keynesian models:
   a. shifts the withdrawal schedule upward by MPC x T_a.
   b. shifts the investment schedule downward by the same amount as tax revenue.
   c. shifts the government expenditure function upward.
   d. shifts the Aggregate Expenditures schedule downward by an amount exceeding tax revenues.

___ 4. An autonomous spending multiplier of 4 implies:
   a. that an increase in autonomous consumption of $10 billion will cause income to increase by $40 billion.
   b. that a decrease in autonomous investment of $40 billion will cause income to fall by $160 billion.
   c. that a simultaneous increase in both autonomous government expenditures and autonomous taxes of $20 billion will cause income to increase by $20 billion, all else equal.
   d. an MPC of .80, assuming consumption to be the only induced demand expenditure.

___ 5. A Constitutional amendment requiring annual balance of the federal budget:
   a. may be self-defeating if tax hikes and spending cuts are used in attempts to cure deficits occurring during a deep recession.
   b. would have been an excellent cure for the Great Depression.
   c. might result in inflationary policies if the economy was at full employment and the full employment budget yields a large surplus.
   d. would result in much lower tax burdens throughout the remainder of this century.

144

PROBLEMS

Problem 1

Use the table below to answer the following questions:

Table 1

(1) INCOME (Y)	(2) SAVING (S)	(3) INVESTMENT (I)	(4) GOVERNMENT (G)
0	-60	40	40
100	-40	40	40
200	-20	40	40
300	0	40	40
400	20	40	40
500	40	40	40
600	60	40	40
700	80	40	40
800	100	40	40
900	120	40	40
1000	140	40	40
1100	160	40	40
1200	180	40	40

Figure 1

Graph A

Graph B

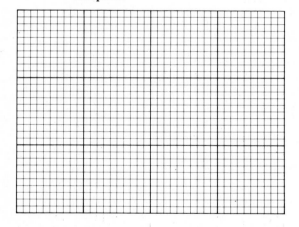 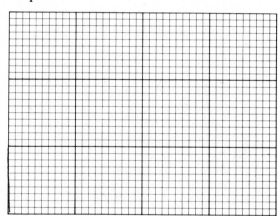

a. On graph A plot the schedules for consumption and Keynesian Aggregate Expenditures (C + I + G + (X - M)). On graph B plot the saving, investment, and investment with government spending schedules.

b. Equilibrium income without government spending is _____

c. Equilibrium saving without government spending is _____

d. With government spending of $40, equilibrium income is _____

e. With government spending, equilibrium saving rises by _____

145

Problem 2

Three different desired expenditure schedules are drawn below.

Figure 2

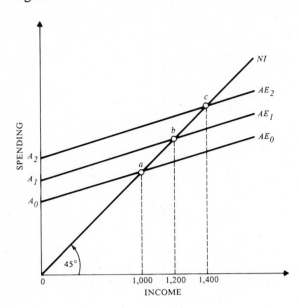

Use this information to answer the following T/F questions. Assume that $1,200 billion represents full employment national income and that the autonomous spending multiplier is 4.

___ a. A recessionary gap exists when the economy produces an income of $1,400 billion.

___ b. Desired autonomous expenditures corresponding to Keynesian Aggregate Expenditure schedule AE_0 is $300 billion.

___ c. An inflationary gap exists when the economy produces an income of $1,200 billion.

___ d. As the economy moves along the nominal income line from a to b, real output increases.

___ e. As the economy moves from b to c, real output increases, and the absolute price level remains unchanged.

___ f. A recessionary gap of $50 billion exists when the economy produces an income of $1,000 billion.

___ g. An inflationary gap of $50 billion exists when the economy produces an income of $1,400 billion.

___ h. The movement from b to c ultimately yields only pure price inflation.

___ i. If the economy was in equilibrium at point a, the government could exactly eliminate the recessionary gap by increasing its spending by $200 billion.

___ j. If the economy was in equilibrium at point c, full employment (without inflation) could be restored by decreasing both government spending and taxes by 200.

Problem 3

Use the table below to answer the following questions:

Table 2

BEFORE GOVERNMENT				AFTER GOVERNMENT						
Y	C	S	I	G	T	Y-T	C_1	S_1	$S_1 + T$	$I + G$
0	400	___	100	200	200	___	___	___	___	___
200	500	___	100	200	200	___	___	___	___	___
400	600	___	100	200	200	___	___	___	___	___
600	700	___	100	200	200	___	___	___	___	___
800	800	___	100	200	200	___	___	___	___	___
1000	900	___	100	200	200	___	___	___	___	___
1200	1000	___	100	200	200	___	___	___	___	___
1400	1100	___	100	200	200	___	___	___	___	___
1600	1200	___	100	200	200	___	___	___	___	___
1800	1300	___	100	200	200	___	___	___	___	___
2000	1400	___	100	200	200	___	___	___	___	___

a. Complete the column labeled "S."

b. Equilibrium income without government is _____

c. Now assume that government enters the picture and spends 200 without taxing. Equilibrium income would be _____ Equilibrium saving would become _____

d. Now assume that government continues to spend 200, but now levies taxes equal to 200 as well.

   (1) Complete the "Y-T" column.
   (2) Complete the adjusted consumption schedule (C_1). Remember that only a portion (the MPC) of taxes comes from consumption.
   (3) Remember that only a portion (the MPS) of taxes come from savings. Complete the "S_1 + T" and "I + G" columns.

e. With the balanced budget (G = T = 200), equilibrium income is _____?

f. The increase in income accompanying the balanced budget hike was _____?

g. In the graph below, plot the S, S_1, I, G, T, I+G, and S_1+T schedules. Label the original equilibrium (without government) as "a" and the new equilibrium (budget balanced at 200) as "b."

Figure 3

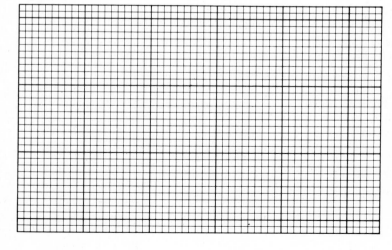

$$\frac{\Delta Y}{\Delta A} = \frac{1}{1-mpc} = \frac{1}{mps}$$

$$\frac{\Delta Y}{\Delta T} = \frac{-mpc}{mps} = \frac{1}{1-mps}$$

Problem 4

Answering Problems 4, 5, and 6 may require reviewing the Optional Material at the end of Chapters Ten and Eleven. Use the table below to answer the following questions:

Table 3

Y	C	I	G	T
0	300	100	50	50
100	375	100	50	50
200	450	100	50	50
300	525	100	50	50
400	600	100	50	50
500	675	100	50	50
600	750	100	50	50
700	825	100	50	50
800	900	100	50	50
900	975	100	50	50
1000	1050	100	50	50

a. Write an equation for the consumption function without taxes. _____

b. Write an equation for the saving function without taxes. _____

c. Write an equation for investment expenditure. _____

d. Write an equation for government expenditure. _____

e. Write an equation for the tax function. _____

f. Write an equation for the consumption function with taxes. _____

g. Write an equation for the saving function with taxes. _____

h. Solve for equilibrium output, including the government's budget. _____

i. What are the equilibrium values for C?_____ I?_____ G?_____ S?_____ T?_____

j. What kind of fiscal policy is the government pursuing in this example? _____

k. Write the condition for macroeconomic equilibrium when government both spends and taxes._____

l. Assume that $\Delta Ga = \Delta Ta = \$40$ billion, all other things held constant. Solve for equilibrium output or income. _____

m. Write an equation for the new consumption function with taxes. _____

n. Write an equation for the new saving function with taxes. _____

o. What are the equilibrium values for C?_____ I?_____ G?_____ S?_____ T?_____

p. Show that the balanced-budget multiplier is one. _____

Problem 5

If $G_a = 40$, $I_a = 30$, and $S = -100 + .20\,Y$;

a. What are equilibrium values for C?_____ I?_____ G?_____ Y?_____

b. If full employment national income is 700, is there an inflationary or recessionary gap?_____

c. What is the value of the inflationary or recessionary gap?_____

d. How could a tax change be used to close this gap? _____

e. What are the equilibrium values of C, I, G, and Y after solving question d for:
   C?_____ I?_____ G?_____ Y?_____

Problem 6

Given that $I_a = 100$, $G_a = 250$, and $C = 400 + .9Y$;

a. What are the equilibrium values of C?_____ I?_____ G?_____ Y?_____

b. If the GNP gap equals 200, is the situation inflationary or recessionary? _____

c. Solve for the fully employed equilibrium using a balanced budget approach. What are the full employment equilibrium values of C?_____ I?_____ G?_____ Y?_____ T?_____ S?_____

ANSWERS

Matching Key Terms and Concepts

Answer	Reference
1. e	p. 196
2. b	p. 204
3. c	p. 202
4. d	p. 202
5. a	p. 197
6. j	p. 198
7. f	p. 207
8. g	p. 207
9. i	p. 203
10. m	p. 206
11. l	p. 206
12. h	p. 201
13. k	p. 206

True/false Questions

Answer	Reference
1. T	p. 208
2. T	p. 203
3. F	p. 204
4. F	p. 202
5. T	p. 202
6. T	p. 202
7. F	p. 196
8. F	p. 196
9. T	p. 197
10. F	p. 202
11. F	p. 202
12. T	p. 210
13. F	p. 209
14. F	p. 212
15. T	p. 208

Chapter Review (Fill-in Questions)

1. tax, cyclical
2. nondiscretionary, automatically
3. changes, $I + G = S + T$
4. saving
5. revenues, Laffer
6. tax rates, purchases
7. transfer, production or Aggregate Supply
8. increased, reduced
9. rates, revenues
10. Expenditures, business cycle

Unlimited Multiple Choice

Answer	Reference
1. a	p. 207
2. none	p. 198
3. a	p. 200
4. abc	p. 202
5. ac	p. 206

Standard Multiple Choice

Answer	Reference
1. c	p. 202
2. a	p. 202
3. a	p. 201
4. b	p. 204
5. a	p. 202
6. c	p. 202
7. c	p. 207-209
8. b	p. 207
9. b	p. 202
10. a	p. 212
11. e	p. 208
12. a	p. 207-209

Problem 1
Reference pp. 197-199

a. See Figure 4

Figure 4

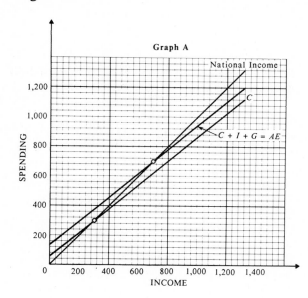

Graph A

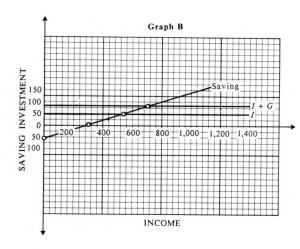

Graph B

b. 500
c. 40
d. 700
e. 40

Problem 2
Reference pp. 197-199

a. F
b. F
c. F
d. T
e. F
f. T
g. T
h. T
i. F
j. T

Problem 3
Reference pp. 197-202

a. See Table 4.

Table 4

BEFORE GOVERNMENT				AFTER GOVERNMENT						
Y	C	S	I	G	T	$Y-T$	C_i*	S_i*	S_i*$+T$	$I+G$
0	400	-400	100	200	200	-200	300	-500	-300	300
200	500	-300	100	200	200	0	400	-400	-200	300
400	600	-200	100	200	200	200	500	-300	-100	300
600	700	-100	100	200	200	400	600	-200	0	300
800	800	0	100	200	200	600	700	-100	100	300
1000	900	100	100	200	200	800	800	0	200	300
1200	1000	200	100	200	200	1000	900	100	300	300
1400	1100	300	100	200	200	1200	1000	200	400	300
1600	1200	400	100	200	200	1400	1100	300	500	300
1800	1300	500	100	200	200	1600	1200	400	600	300
2000	1400	600	100	200	200	1800	1300	500	700	300

* Altered consumption and saving schedule with introduction of taxes,
keeping in mind that, mpc = .5 and mps = .5.

b. 1000; saving and investment are equal at Y = 100 without government
c. 1400, 300; I + G = S when Y = 1,400.
d. See Table 4
e. 1200
f. 200
g. See Figure 5.

Figure 5

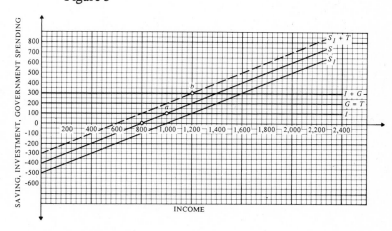

Problem 4
Reference pp. 197-202

a. $C = 300 + .75Y$

b. $S = -300 + .25Y$

c. $I = 100$

d. $G = 50$

e. $T = 50$

f. $C = 262.50 + .75Y$; the consumption function is shifted down by the MPC x taxes or $.75 \times 50 = 37.50$. Thus, autonomous consumption becomes $262.50 \ (300 - 37.50)$.

g. $S = -312.50 + .25Y$

h. $Y = 1,650$
$Y = C + I + G$
$Y = 262.50 + .75Y + 100 + 50$
$Y = 412.50 + .75Y$
$Y .75Y = 412.50$
$Y = 412.50 /.25$
$Y = 1,650.$

i. $C = 1,500 \ I = 100 \ G = 50 \ S = 100 \ T = 50$

j. Balanced budget, since $G = T$

k. $I + G = S + T$

l. $1,690$

m. $C = 232.50 + .75Y$

n. $S = -322.50 + .25Y$

o. $C = 1,500 \ I = 100 \ G = 90 \ S = 100 \ T = 90$

p. Balanced budget multiplier $= \Delta Y/(\Delta Ga = \Delta Ta)$
$= 40/(40 = 40) = 1$

Problem 5
Reference pp. 197-202

a. (1) $S = I + G$
$-100 + .2Y = 40 + 30$
$-100 + .2Y = 70$
$.2Y = 170$
$Y = 170/.2 = 850$

(2) $C = Y - S$
$C = 850 - (-100 + .2(850))$
$C = 850 + 100 - .2(850)$
$C = 850 + 100 - 170$
$C = 780$

(3) $I = 30$

(4) $G = 40$

b. Since we have more than sufficient spending to fully employ the economy we have an inflationary gap.

c. GNP gap $= 700 - 850 = 150$;
inflationary gap $= -150/5 = -30$, where the multiplier $= 5$

d. Our objective is to decrease autonomous aggregate expenditures by 30 units so we must increase taxes. Since only 80% of our tax change is translated into autonomous aggregate demand, we must increase taxes by an amount greater than 30 units. This number can be obtained by dividing 30 by .8 which equals 37.5. In other words raising taxes by 37.5 units decreases consumption by 30 units.

e. $C = 630, I = 30, G = 40, Y = 700.$

Problem 6
Reference pp. 197-202

a. $C = 7,150, I = 100, G = 250, Y = 7,500.$

b. Since the GNP gap is positive we know that there is deficient aggregate demand; therefore the situation is recessionary.

c. Fully employed equilibrium equals 7,700. Since the balanced budget multiplier always equals 1 the solution is to increase government expenditures by 200 units and increase taxes by 200 units. After solving $C = 7,150, I = 100, G = 50$, and $Y = 7,700$. Note that even though total consumption is equal in the before and after situations the breakdown of autonomous and induced consumption is, in fact, different.

CHAPTER TWELVE
MONEY AND ITS CREATION

CHAPTER OBJECTIVES

After you have read and studied this chapter you should be able to describe the functions money performs in a market system; differentiate between alternative forms of money and definitions of the money supply; differentiate between potential money multipliers, actual money multipliers, and the monetary base; and explain how the interactions between banks and their customers determine the amount of money in circulation.

CHAPTER REVIEW: KEY POINTS

1. Barter requires a double coincidence of wants--trade can only occur if each party has what the other wants and if divisibility poses no problems.

2. Money ensures this double coincidence of wants--the seller will accept money because of what it will buy, while the buyer is willing to exchange money (and, thus, all else it will buy) for the good or service in question.

3. Money facilitates specialization and exchange by decreasing transaction costs. The more sophisticated the financial system, the greater the level of production and consumption and the higher the standard of living.

4. Money is a medium of exchange. It is used for most transactions in monetary economies.

5. Money is a measure of value. Used as a standard unit of account, it is the common denominator for pricing goods and services.

6. Money is a store of value. It is among the most nominally secure of all assets people can use to hold their wealth.

7. Money is a standard of deferred payment. Serving as a link between the past, present, and future, it is used as a measure of credit to execute contracts calling for future payments.

8. Liquidity is negatively related to the transaction costs incurred in exchanges of assets. Time, certainty regarding price, and the quality of information in a market are all dimensions of liquidity. Assets are liquid if transaction costs are low, illiquid if transaction costs are high.

9. Commodity monies (precious metals, stones, or arrowheads) have values that are independent of what they will buy. Fiat money (paper currency) is valuable only because it is money; its use is based on faith.

10. The profit governments make from printing money or stamping coins is called seignorage.

11. According to Gresham's Law, "Bad money drives out good."

12. The very narrowly defined money supply (M1) is the total of: (a) currency (coins and bills) in the hands of the nonbanking public, plus (b) demand deposits (checking accounts of private individuals, firms, and nonfederal government units in financial institutions).

13. Some highly liquid assets are viewed as near-monies and are included in broader definitions of the money supply (M2 and M3) by monetary analysts who believe the spending of the public can be predicted better if these assets are included. Examples of such highly liquid assets include short-term time deposits (savings accounts) or certificates of deposit (CDs). The assets included in "money supplies" defined more broadly than M1 are judgmental because these assets are not mediums of exchange.

14. Banks and some thrift institutions "create" money through loan-based expansions of demand deposits (checking account money). They make loans based on reserves they hold and these loans take the form of new demand deposit money.

15. Banks hold reserves that are far less than their deposit liabilities. The larger the proportion of deposits held as either excess or required reserves, the smaller are the money multiplier and resulting money supply, given some fixed total amount of reserves.

16. The potential money multiplier (m_p) equals $1/rr$, where rr is the banking system's planned or legally required reserves as a percentage of deposits. The actual money multiplier is much smaller because: (a) households and firms hold currency that could be used as a base for the money creation process were this currency held in bank vaults as reserves against deposits; and (b) banks hold excess reserves to meet withdrawals of deposits. The actual money multiplier equals MS/MB, where MS is the money supply and MB is the monetary base, or high-powered money.

MATCHING KEY TERMS AND CONCEPTS

SET I

B 1. credit

C 2. money multiplier

E 3. M1

H 4. currency

A 5. Federal Reserve System

G 6. barter

I 7. seignorage

F 8. value of money

D 9. M2, M3 and L

J 10. liquidity

a. Created in 1913 to mitigate the impact of financial crises.

b. Extension of money; uses money as a standard of deferred payment.

c. Always equals one in a 100 percent reserve banking system.

d. Broader definitions of the money supply.

e. Currency plus "checkable" deposits.

f. Purchasing power of money.

g. Requires double coincidence of wants.

h. Coins and paper money.

i. Profits made by government when it prints or coins money.

j. Inversely related to the transactions costs incurred when an asset is bought or sold.

SET II

F 1. measure of value

I 2. potential money multiplier

A 3. store of value

J 4. reserves

H 5. fiat money

G 6. Gresham's Law

B 7. medium of exchange

E 8. actual money multiplier

D 9. standard of deferred payment

C 10. commodity money

a. Money as an asset.

b. Goods trade for money, and money trades for goods.

c. Money that is valuable in itself.

d. Money as a standard of credit.

e. $m_a = MS/MB$.

f. Standard unit of account.

g. "Bad money drives out good."

h. Money valued only for what it buys.

i. 1/(reserve requirement ratio).

j. Cash in bank vaults.

CHAPTER REVIEW (FILL-IN QUESTIONS)

1. In a(n) __Barter__ economy, exchange occurs only when each trader has precisely what the other desires; that is, there must be a(n) __coincidence__ of wants.

2-4. As a _____, money provides a common denominator through which the relative prices of goods may be compared. As a _____, money is exchanged for goods, and goods are exchanged for money. As a _____, money is a relatively riskless way to hold your wealth. As a _____, money binds the past, the present, and the future so that contracts are possible calling for future payments for goods delivered now. _____ money has intrinsic value because it is made of something valuable, while _____ money is only valuable because of its purchasing power.

5-8. In a fractional reserve banking system, the ready cash in bank vaults, called _____, is far less than bank liabilities, or _____. The money creation process occurs when banks issue _____ when they make _____ to their customers. The factor by which banks can expand a given amount of reserves into new demand deposits is called the _____. Its potential value is _____, where rr stands for the reserve requirement ratio. It reaches this potential value only when banks are _____ loaned-up, and when consumers and businesses hold _____.

9-10. When only a few banks have outflows of deposits so great that they may not be able to cover all of their liabilities instantly, they can sell _____ to other banks or borrow funds from banks having _____. The banking network facilitating these interbank borrowings is the _____ market. As a last resort, banks can borrow from the federal "bankers' bank," which is known as the _____.

STANDARD MULTIPLE CHOICE

THERE IS ONE BEST ANSWER FOR EACH QUESTION.

___ 1. An asset's "liquidity" refers to:
   a. how low are transaction costs incurred in dealing in the asset.
   b. the time it takes to convert it to cash.
   c. the "backing" behind a financial instrument.
   d. whether it may be bought or sold.
   e. whether the asset is water soluble.

___ 2. Money is NOT a:
   a. medium of exchange.
   b. measure of value or standard unit of account.
   c. means of interpersonal utility comparison.
   d. store of value.
   e. standard of deferred payment.

___ 3. "Bad money drives out good" according to:
   a. Gresham's Law.
   b. Say's Law.
   c. Fisher's Law.
   d. Keynes' Law.
   e. Friedman's Corollary.

___ 4. An appropriate commodity money would NOT be:
   a. durable.
   b. divisible.
   c. optimally scarce.
   d. heterogeneous.
   e. portable.

___ 5. Fiat money has value because:
   a. it is backed by gold or silver.
   b. it is made of a precious metal.
   c. the government that issues it says it has a given value.
   d. it has no value at all as a commodity.
   e. none of the above.

___ 6. The number of relative prices in an n-good, barter economy is:
   a. n.
   b. n^2.
   c. $(n(n-1))/2$.
   d. 2^n.
   e. np.

___ 7. Relative to barter, money:
   a. facilitates specialization and exchange.
   b. increases the frequency of transactions.
   c. reduces transaction costs.
   d. finesses the "double coincidence of wants" requirement.
   e. all of these.

___ 8. A fractional reserve banking system relies most on:
   a. extensive government regulation.
   b. people keeping most of their money in banks.
   c. a stable money multiplier.
   d. a commodity base for money.
   e. none of these.

___ 9. The profits made by government when it prints/mints money are known as:
   a. exorbitant.
   b. fiat returns.
   c. legal tender.
   d. seignorage.
   e. budgetary revenue.

___10. If no currency exists outside bank vaults, and banks loan exactly 80 percent of total reserves, then there will be:
   a. "runs" on banks.
   b. five times as much money as reserves.
   c. excess liquidity.
   d. inflation.
   e. financial collapse.

___11. The potential value of the money multiplier equals:
  a. 1/mpc.
  b. 1/mps.
  c. 1/rr.
  d. 1/(rr + xr).
  e. 10rr.

___12. The actual money multiplier, m_a, is calculated as:
  a. -MPC/MPS.
  b. 1/rr.
  c. 1/(1-mpc).
  d. $\Delta M/\Delta rr$.
  e. MS/MB.

TRUE/FALSE QUESTIONS

T 1. Currency held in bank vaults is not included in the money supply.

T 2. The value of money and the cost of credit are both determined by supply and demand in much the same manner as the prices of other economic goods are determined.

F 3. Commodity money is valuable only because of its purchasing power, while fiat money has substantial value independently of what it will buy.

F 4. The most important service that money provides is that it is used to express the relative prices of goods.

T 5. Wealth is the monetary value of all of your assets.

F 6. Financial assets are liquid if transaction costs incurred in trading them are high, while financial assets are illiquid if the transaction costs incurred in trading them are low.

T 7. The amount of funds held in the vault to meet withdrawals of deposits are called the bank's reserves.

T 8. The major function performed by money to eliminate the necessity of a double coincidence of wants in a barter system is that of a medium of exchange.

F 9. Standards of living tend to be very high in money-less economies.

F 10. By definition, credit cards are counted as money.

UNLIMITED MULTIPLE CHOICE

WARNING: THERE MAY BE FROM ZERO TO FOUR CORRECT ANSWERS TO EACH QUESTION!

___1. In an economy characterized by barter:
  a. the costs of securing information about potentially profitable transactions are negligible.
  b. goods are exchanged for goods.
  c. transactions can only be carried out when there exists a double coincidence of wants.
  d. few of the advantages of specialization are ever realized.

___2. Money serves as a:
  a. medium of exchange.
  b. measure of value.
  c. store of value.
  d. common denominator by which relative prices are expressed.

157

___ 3. The potential money multiplier:
   a. is always equal to one in a fractional reserve banking system.
   (b) is given by the reciprocal of the reserve requirement ratio.
   (c) indicates the extent to which demand deposits can be expanded as the result of an initial deposit.
   d. is equal to zero in a 100 percent reserve banking system.

___ 4. The total amount of deposits in any single bank is not likely to be highly volatile because:
   (a) flows of deposits between banks do not affect the total amounts of reserves in the banking system.
   b. the average daily amount in a given account is fairly stable on a month to month basis.
   (c) most people have reasonably stable patterns of income and spending, and seldom allow their accounts to drop below some minimum value.
   d. most people seldom use their checking accounts in purchasing goods.

___ 5. Which measures (estimates) of money are correct?
   (a) M1 = currency in the hands of the nonbanking public plus funds in "checkable" accounts.
   b. L = the total market value of all assets in an economy.
   (c) M2 = M1 plus small time deposits.
   d. M3 = M2 plus gold, silver, and long-term negotiable bonds.

PROBLEMS

PROBLEM 1

Table 1 shows the initial T-account for our monopoly bank. Assume that the reserve requirement ratio is 20 percent. Also, assume that all money in the community is held in the bank, and that our monopoly bank is a profit maximizer, which means that it will always expand loans (IOUs) by the maximum amount permitted by law. (Thus, the bank's excess reserves are always zero; by definition, excess reserves = total (legal) reserves minus required reserves.) Use this information to answer the following questions:

Table 1

ASSETS	LIABILITIES		
Cash reserves	$1,000	Demand deposits	$5,000
Loans	$4,000		
	$5,000		$5,000

a. What is the size of the money multiplier?_____

b. Write the formula for the money multiplier._____

c. Is this a fractional reserve banking system? _____ Why?_____.

d. Assume that $2,000 is deposited in the monopoly bank. Please balance the bank's T-account.

e. By how much will demand deposits increase? _____

f. By how much have loans increased?_____

g. Explain why the monopoly bank is able to expand its loans by the maximum amount permitted by law._____

h. Why won't this be true for each bank in a multi-bank example? _____.

PROBLEM 2

Table 2 shows the initial T-account for another monopoly bank. Assume that the reserve requirement ratio is 10 percent. Also, assume that unless otherwise indicated, all money is held in this bank, which is always fully loaned up as soon as possible. That is, desired excess reserves will always be zero.

Table 2

ASSETS		LIABILITIES	
Cash reserves	$ 1,000	Demand deposits	$10,000
Loans	$ 9,000		
	$10,000		$10,000

a. How big is the size of the money multiplier? _____

b. Write the formula for the money multiplier. _____

c. Assume that an additional $2,000 is deposited in our monopoly bank. Please balance the bank's T-account. By how much will demand deposits increase? _____

d. By how much will loans increase? _____

e. Notice that ΔLoans = Money Multiplier x Excess reserves. Establish this for yourself. Also, ΔDemand deposits = Initial deposit + Loans. Establish this for yourself.

f. Assume that $1,000 is now withdrawn from our monopoly bank. Please balance the bank's T-account.

g. By how much will demand deposits decrease? _____

h. By how much will loans decrease? _____

i. Assume that $500 more is withdrawn. Please balance the bank's T-account.

j. By how much will demand deposits decrease? _____

k. Why?_____

l. By how much will loans decrease? _____

m. What are total demand deposits? _____

n. Total cash reserves? _____

o. Total loans?_____

PROBLEM 3

Assume that there are roughly 1,000 banks in our fractional reserve banking system. Assume also that the reserve requirement ratio is 20 percent, that each bank holds an extra 5 percent as excess reserves, but that the public holds no cash. Using this information, assume that $2,000 is deposited in the first bank.

a. Show, using the first ten banks in the system, how the money supply will increase as each bank expands its loans by the full amount of any reserves greater than 25 percent of deposits.

b. What is the size of the money multiplier?_____

c. By how much will demand deposits increase for the system as a whole?

_____

d. By how much will loans increase for the system as a whole? _____

e. Explain why the creation of money in a multi-bank world is a cumulative process.

_____

f. Why should each bank only increase its loans by reserves in excess of 25 percent of deposits?

_____

PROBLEM 4

This problem combines elements of the first three problems. Assume that the required reserve ratio is 20% and that each bank in the system is fully loaned up. In this example there is no difference between the potential money multiplier and the actual money multiplier. (i.e. the banks hold no excess reserves and the non-banking public places all its cash in the banking system) Assume that there is an initial $2,000 cash deposit into the system by a patron of bank "A" into his or her checking account. The bank retains the required reserve and loans out the excess reserve. Complete the table below for banks "B" through "H" and then sum the columns indicated as if this transaction had passed through 1,000 or more banks in the system.

Table 3

BANK	TOTAL RESERVES	REQUIRED RESERVES	EXCESS RESERVES	LOAN/MONEY EXPANSION
"A"	$2,000.00	$400.00	$1,600.00	$1,600.00
"B"	$1,600.00	320		
"C"	1280.00	256		
"D"	1024.00	204.8		
"E"	819.20	163.84		
"F"	655.36	131.10		
"G"	524.29			
"H"	419.43			
·	·	·	·	·
·	·	·	·	·
·	·	·	·	·
Banking System				

PROBLEM 5

This problem is designed to help you practice the various values that a money multiplier might take. In order to complete the table below assume that there is a large banking system (1,000 or more banks). Additionally assume that the banks always hold enough reserves to exceed the required reserve ratio by 5%. For example, if the required reserve ration were 25% the banks would in reality hold 30%. Assume that the non-banking public holds no cash reserves.

Table 4

CASH DEPOSIT	REQUIRED RESERVE RATIO	ACTUAL MONEY MULTIPLIER	SINGLE BANK EXPANSION	BANKING SYSTEM EXPANSION
$2,000	.20	___	___	___
$1,000	.15	___	___	___
$5,000	.1166	___	___	___
$3,500	.05	___	___	___
$500	.075	___	___	___

$rr = .05 \ (5\%)$

$\frac{1}{rr}$ potential mm

$\frac{ms}{mb}$ 400

$\frac{1}{rr}$

← initial 2,000 cash dep.
.20 rr

$\frac{1}{.2}$

$2\overline{)1.0}$ $\frac{5.}{}$

$15\overline{)1.00}$ $\frac{6.}{}$ $\frac{90}{10}$

$\frac{.15}{3}$

2000

1600

ANSWERS

Matching Key Terms and Concepts

SET I

Answer	Reference
1. b	p. 219
2. c	p. 230
3. e	p. 225
4. h	p. 224
5. a	p. 226
6. g	p. 218
7. i	p. 223
8. f	p. 220
9. d	p. 225
10. j	p. 222

SET II

Answer	Reference
1. f	p. 220
2. i	p. 230
3. a	p. 220
4. j	p. 227
5. h	p. 222
6. g	p. 224
7. b	p. 219
8. e	p. 230
9. d	p. 221
10. c	p. 222

Standard Multiple Choice

Answer	Reference
1. a	p. 222
2. c	p. 220
3. a	p. 224
4. d	p. 222
5. c	p. 222
6. c	p. 221
7. e	p. 219
8. b	p. 227
9. d	p. 223
10. b	p. 230
11. c	p. 230
12. e	p. 230

True/False Questions

Answer	Reference
1. T	p. 225
2. T	p. 219
3. F	p. 222
4. F	p. 220
5. F	p. 219
6. F	p. 222
7. T	p. 227
8. T	p. 219
9. F	p. 218
10. F	p. 225

Chapter Review (Fill-in Questions)

1. barter, double coincidence
2. standard unit of account, medium of exchange
3. store of value, standard of deferred payment
4. Commodity, fiat
5. reserves, deposits
6. new demand deposits, loans
7. money multiplier, 1/rr
8. fully, zero cash balances
9. loans, excess reserves
10. federal funds , Federal Reserve System

Unlimited Multiple Choice

Answer	Reference
1. bcd	p. 219
2. abcd	p. 219-221
3. bc	p. 230
4. bc	p. 227
5. ac	p. 225-226

Problem 1
Reference pp. 227-232

a. 5

b. $m_p = 1/rr = 1/.20 = 5$.

c. Yes; bank holds less than 100% against deposit liabilities.

d. See Table 5

Table 5

ASSETS		LIABILITIES	
Cash reserves	$ 3,000	Demand deposits	$15,000
Loans	$12,000		
	$15,000		$15,000

e. $10,000

f. $8,000

g. Monopolist doesn't have to worry about withdrawn money not returning.

h. Flows between banks in multi-bank systems prevent each from making maximum loans.

Problem 2
Reference pp. 227-232

a. 10

b. $m_p = 1/rr = 1/.10 = 10$
c. $20,000 (See Table 6)

Table 6

ASSETS		LIABILITIES	
Cash reserves	$ 3,000	Demand deposits	$30,000
Loans	$27,000		
	$30,000		$30,000

d. $18,000

e. On new demand deposits of $2,000, excess reserves will be $1,800 times the money multiplier (10) equals $18,000. The change in demand deposits will equal the initial new deposits plus the new loans because the new loans all become new deposits.

f. See Table 7

Table 7

ASSETS		LIABILITIES	
Cash reserves	$ 2,000	Demand deposits $20,000	
Loans	$18,000		
	$20,000		$20,000

g. $10,000

h. $9,000

i. See Table 8

Table 8

ASSETS		LIABILITIES	
Cash reserves	$ 1,500	Demand deposits $15,000	
Loans	$13,500		
	$15,000		$15,000

j. $5,000

k. Bank will rebuild its reserve position by not renewing old loans or offering new ones a sold ones are paid off.

l. $4,500

m. $15,000

n. $1,500

o. $13,500

Problem 3
Reference pp. 227-232

a. See Table 9

Table 9

```
┌─────────────────────────────────────────────┐
│                  BANK 1                       │
├──────────────────────────┬────────────────────┤
│ Reserves = 500           │ Deposits = 2,000   │
│    Req/Res = 400         │                    │
│    Exc/Res = 100         │                    │
│ Loans = 1,500            │                    │
├──────────────────────────┴────────────────────┤
│                  BANK 2                        │
├──────────────────────────┬────────────────────┤
│ Reserves = 375           │ Deposits = 1,500   │
│    Req/Res = 300         │                    │
│    Exc/Res = 75          │                    │
│ Loans = 1,125            │                    │
├──────────────────────────┴────────────────────┤
│                  BANK 3                        │
├──────────────────────────┬────────────────────┤
│ Reserves = 281.25        │ Deposits = 1,125   │
│    Req/Res = 225         │                    │
│    Exc/Res = 56.25       │                    │
│ Loans = 843.75           │                    │
│                  etc.                          │
└────────────────────────────────────────────────┘
```

b. 4.

c. Demand deposits = $8,000

d. Loans = $6,000

e. Each bank is limited to loans equalling
    .75 (New deposit).

f. The danger of outflows making it impossible to
    meet withdrawals.

Problem 4
Reference pp. 227-232

Table 10

BANK	TOTAL RESERVES	REQUIRED RESERVES	EXCESS RESERVES	LOAN/MONEY EXPANSION
"A"	$2,000.00	$400.00	$1,600.00	$1,600.00
"B"	$1,600.00	$320.00	$1,280.00	$1,280.00
"C"	$1,280.00	$256.00	$1,024.00	$1,024.00
"D"	$1,024.00	$204.00	$ 819.20	$ 819.20
"E"	$ 819.20	$163.84	$ 655.36	$ 655.36
"F"	$ 655.36	$131.07	$ 524.30	$ 524.30
"G"	$ 524.30	$104.86	$ 419.44	$ 419.44
"H"	$ 419.44			
.		.		.
.		.		.
.		.		.
.		.		.
Banking System		$2,000.00		$10,000.00

Problem 5
Reference pp. 227-232

Table 11

CASH DEPOSIT	REQUIRED RESERVE RATIO	ACTUAL MONEY MULTIPLIER	SINGLE BANK EXPANSION	BANKING SYSTEM EXPANSION
$2,000	.20	4	$1,500.00	$ 6,000
$1,000	.15	5	$ 800.00	$ 4,000
$5,000	.1166	6	$4,166.66	$25,000
$3,500	.05	10	$3,150.00	$31,500
$500	.075	8	$ 437.50	$ 3,500

166

CHAPTER THIRTEEN

THE FEDERAL RESERVE SYSTEM AND FINANCIAL INSTITUTIONS

CHAPTER OBJECTIVES

After you have read and studied this chapter you should be able to describe the purposes of a central bank such as the Federal Reserve System (FED); explain the nature of the FED's primary and secondary tools, and how these tools may be used; discuss and evaluate the effects of various rules and regulations on the efficiency of the financial sector, and discuss the differences between the various types of financial intermediaries.

CHAPTER REVIEW: KEY POINTS

1. Since fractional reserve banking makes it impossible for all banks to pay all demand deposits simultaneously, resolutions of monetary crises may require intervention by a central bank, or "bankers' bank."

2. The value of the potential money multiplier (m_p) is the reciprocal of the reserve-requirement ratio ($1/rr$). Excess reserves in the financial system and cash holdings by the public are drains on the potential multiplier. The actual multiplier (m_a) is the amount of currency and bank reserves (MB) issued by the Federal Reserve System (FED) divided into the money supply (MS): $m_a = MS/MB$.

3. The Federal Reserve System's most powerful but least used primary tool is its power to change reserve requirements (rr). Increases in rr reduce the money multiplier and money supply, and vice versa.

4. The most useful tool of the FED is open-market operations (OMO). After all adjustments, open-market operations affect the monetary base, not the money multiplier. When the FED sells government bonds, bank reserves are reduced and the money supply declines. FED purchases of bonds increase bank reserves and the money supply.

5. The discount rate (d) is the interest rate the FED charges member banks. When the discount rate is low relative to market interest rates, banks hold few excess reserves and will borrow funds from the FED. Consequently, the money supply increases. High discount rates relative to market interest rates cause banks to borrow less from the FED and provide incentives for larger holdings of excess reserves. The actual money multiplier and total bank reserves fall, and the money supply falls. Changes in the discount rate alter both the monetary base and the money multiplier..

6. The FED's other tools include margin requirements to limit stock-market credit and jawboning.

7. Financial institutions facilitate flows and payments of funds and provide secure places for savers' deposits. Their most important economic function is to channel funds from savers to investors and other borrowers through a process called financial intermediation. Commercial banks, savings and loan associations, credit unions, insurance companies, and stock exchanges are all financial intermediaries.

8. Usury laws reduce the availability of credit to the poor. Interest ceilings on deposits hold down interest rates paid depositors, and may cause higher interest rates to be charged to borrowers.

MATCHING KEY TERMS AND CONCEPTS

SET I

H 1. jawboning

A 2. reserve requirements

D 3. discount rate

J 4. financial intermediation

C 5. usury laws

E 6. increases in currency held by the public

B 7. excess reserves

F 8. open market operations

I 9. commercial banks

G 10. margin requirements

a. The FED's most powerful tool.

b. Legal reserves minus required reserves.

c. Legal ceilings on interest rates chargeable on loans.

d. Now 'pegged' slightly above the federal funds rate.

e. Decreases the total reserves in the banking system.

f. The FED's most useful tool.

g. Sets 'down payments' on purchases of stock.

h. Exercising persuasive powers to induce changed behavior.

i. "Full service" banks

j. The process by which saving is made available to people desiring to spend more than their incomes.

SET II

G 1. financial efficiency

D 2. credit rationing

E 3. Federal Open Market Committee   x

A 4. federal funds market   x

F 5. monetary base (MB)

C 6. thrift institutions

H 7. Comptroller of the Currency

B 8. F.D.I.C.   x

J 9. central bank   x

I 10. program trading   x

a. Interbank lending of excess reserves.

b. Insures deposits in commercial banks.

c. Savings and loans, credit unions.

d. Limiting loans to affluent, low-risk customers.

e. Sets policies for trading in U.S. bonds to vary the money supply.

f. Bank reserves plus currency held by the nonbanking public.

g. Minimum differences between interest rates charged and received.

h. Charters national banks.

i. Has been blamed in part for the 1987 Stock Market Crash

j. Government's bank and 'lender of last resort.'

CHAPTER REVIEW (FILL-IN QUESTIONS)

1-4. In addition to the FED, national banks are regulated by the _____, which charters national banks and the _____, which insures deposits in commercial banks. Although most deposits are in national banks, most banks are _____ banks, and are regulated by _____. Of these regulatory bodies, the _____ has the most influence on macroeconomic activity, and its most powerful decisionmaker is the _____. Although nominally owned by member banks, the FED's governors are appointed by the _____. The United States is divided into _____ regions served by FED district banks.

5-7. Although it is not especially useful, the FED's most powerful tool is its ability to set _____. By lowering this tool, the FED initially causes banks to have _____. As banks extend new loans, the _____ grows, causing the _____ to expand. In the long run, however, this tool does not affect total legal reserves, nor is the division between excess reserves and required reserves affected. Thus, changes in reserve requirements operate primarily by causing changes in the _____. Hikes in the reserve requirements ratio would cause _____ in the money supply.

8. The FED may also change its policies about extending loans to banks, a tool known as _____. The interest rate the FED charges banks is called the _____ rate.

9-10. The FED's most useful tool is its conduct of _____. _____ operations occur when the FED, through the "open market" trading desk in New York, sells some of the U.S. Treasury bonds in its portfolio. Banks expand their holdings of bonds, but _____ in the banking system decline. Consequently, the money supply falls when banks _____.

STANDARD MULTIPLE CHOICE

THERE IS ONE BEST ANSWER FOR EACH QUESTION.

___ 1. If the FED sells bonds to commercial banks:
   a. total bank reserves increase.
   b. the money supply decreases.
   c. the money supply increases.
   d. it offsets such policies by cutting reserve requirements.
   e. All of the above.

___ 2. The most powerful tool at the FED's disposal is:
   a. the ability to set reserve requirements.
   b. the discount rate.
   c. open market operations.
   d. Regulation Q.
   e. margin requirements.

___ 3. If bankers want to retain reserves of 25 percent against all deposits, if the FED issues $100 billion in currency, and if private individuals keep all money in banks, then, once banks are "fully loaned-up" the money supply will be comprised of:
   a. $400 billion in demand deposits.
   b. $100 billion in currency + $300 billion in DDs.
   c. no additional loans could be made if the FED printed more currency.
   d. $2,500 billion total in cash and DDs.
   e. none of the above.

   $.25x = 100$

___ 4. The most effective and efficient tool of the FED is:
   a. the reserve requirement.
   b. discount operations.
   c. Regulation Q.
   d. open market operations.
   e. jawboning.

___ 5. The FED attempts to control stock speculation through:
   a. reserve requirements.
   b. margin requirements.
   c. Regulation Q.
   d. jawboning.
   e. open market operations.

___ 6. Usury laws and other limits on interest do NOT:
   a. keep interest rates down for rich people.
   b. make more credit available to the poor.
   c. cause inefficient flows of loanable funds.
   d. create "credit crunches" that shock the housing market.
   e. none of the above.

___ 7. The FED's reserve requirement ratio:
   a. is its most powerful monetary tool.
   b. aids in stabilizing the money multiplier.
   c. reduces the value of the money multiplier.
   d. reduces the money supply relative to the monetary base.
   e. All of these.

___ 8. The FED's "margin requirements" refer to:
   a. down payments on stock.
   b. bank capitalization requirements.
   c. interest rate ceilings.
   d. credit controls.
   e. buying U.S. government bonds.

___ 9. Usury laws:
   a. limit credit to the poor.
   b. cause economic inefficiency.
   c. ignore inflation's effects on real interest rates.
   d. limit interest payments to lenders.
   e. all of these.

___ 10. A major purpose of the FED is to:
   a. print money to cover all government spending not covered by tax revenues.
   b. set interest rate ceilings as low as possible.
   c. act as a "lender of last resort. "
   d. ensure the profitability of commercial banks.
   e. ensure the liquidity of social assets.

___ 11. The most powerful entity in the Federal Reserve system is the:
   a. Director of Open Market Operations.
   b. President of the New York Federal Reserve Bank.
   c. Chairman of the FED.
   d. Unified District Bank Presidents.
   e. Reserve Requirements Regulator.

___ 12. The Federal Reserve System is:
   a. privately owned and operated.
   b. extremely profitable for its investors.
   c. the tax collector for all government agencies.
   d. the central bank of the United States.
   e. the core of the International Monetary Fund (IMF).

TRUE/FALSE QUESTIONS

___ 1. Independently of FED policies, banks may influence the money supply through variations in the percentage of total demand deposits held as excess reserves.

___ 2. Banks will generally want to hold the same percent of excess reserves against demand deposits regardless of the reserve requirement ratio, since the percentage fluctuations of bank deposits depend on people's behavior rather than on the Federal Reserve System's reserve requirements.

___ 3. If the FED buys more bonds than it sells, total bank reserves are increased and the money supply grows.

___ 4. The Federal Reserve System's Open Market Committee has no influence over the total amount of currency in circulation.

___ 5. Banks and other financial intermediaries are less closely supervised than automakers.

___ 6. The reserve requirement ratio is the FED's most powerful tool.

___ 7. If the FED decided to reduce the money supply, it could buy bonds from commercial banks.

___ 8. In the 1920's, you could purchase stock "on margin" with a down payment of as little as 10 percent.

___ 9. The Chairman of the Board of Governors is the real power in the FED.

___10. Governmental constraints on interest paid generates both inefficiency and inequality.

___11. Ceilings on the interest rates payable to depositors help keep general interest rates down.

___12. Regulatory ceilings on interest rates depress the returns to low-income savers and limit credit availability to low income households.

UNLIMITED MULTIPLE CHOICE

WARNING: THERE ARE FROM ZERO TO FOUR RIGHT ANSWERS FOR EACH QUESTION!

___ 1. When commercial banks:
   a. are faced with higher discount rates, they lend more money to the FED, shrinking their excess reserves and expanding the money supply.
   b. receive higher margin requirements, they increase lending.
   c. confront lower reserve requirements ratios, they create more money from a given monetary base.
   d. buy bonds from the FED, bank reserves are decreased, and the banking system will decrease loan-based demand deposits.

___ 2. Regulation of the financial system:
   a. is undertaken in the hope that savers will be protected.
   b. results in a more equitable distribution of income than that which would exist without regulation.
   c. results in a more efficient allocation of financial resources.
   d. has caused widespread, artificial differentiation between financial intermediaries.

___ 3. Central banks commonly:
   a. act as 'lenders of last resort.'
   b. control monetary policies where they operate.
   c. collect taxes like the Internal Revenue Service under their direct control.
   d. determine tax rates and collect revenues for governments.

___ 4. The discount rate:
   a. represents the most powerful tool wielded by the FED to control the money supply.
   b. is seldom changed.
   c. is generally changed to reflect changes in market interest rates and the federal funds rate.
   d. is now pegged slightly above federal funds rates to discourage banks from borrowing reserves from the FED.

___ 5. When constraints exist on interest rates:
   a. market rates of interest are always in equilibrium.
   b. the rate of inflation can easily be incorporated into the interest rates charged by financial institutions.
   c. funds are allocated to borrowers according to their credit-worthiness rather than their willingness to pay.
   d. relative interest rates in financial markets are distorted.

171

PROBLEMS

Problem 1

BOXING DIRECTIONAL CHANGES: Put an upward pointing arrow in the box for increases, downward pointing arrows for decreases, zeros for no change situations, and dashes if the answer cannot be determined.

Table 1

	TOTAL BANK RESERVES	MONETARY BASE	POTENTIAL MONEY MULTIPLIER	ACTUAL MONEY MULTIPLIER	MONEY SUPPLY
a					
b					
c					
d					

a.   The long-run effect if the FED sells bonds.

b.   The long-run effect if the FED raises the discount rate.

c.   The long-run effect if the FED raises reserve requirements.

d.   The long-run effect if the public wants more currency relative to deposits.

Problem 2

Without looking at your responses to Problem 1, what happens if the changes in questions a-d are reversed?

Table 2

	TOTAL BANK RESERVES	MONETARY BASE	POTENTIAL MONEY MULTIPLIER	ACTUAL MONEY MULTIPLIER	MONEY SUPPLY
a					
b					
c					
d					

Problem 3

In the T-account provided, illustrate the balance sheet of the Federal Reserve Bank and a Member Bank when the Federal Reserve Bank sells $2,000 in securities to the Member Bank.

Table 3

FEDERAL RESERVE BANK	
ASSETS	LIABILITIES
____ Treasury Bonds	____ Reserves held for Member Bank

MEMBER BANK	
ASSETS	LIABILITIES
____ Loanable Reserves	
____ Treasury Bonds	

Problem 4

Use the graph provided below to graph the supply and demand for loanable funds when a ceiling exists on the rate of interest payable to savings accounts. (Assume the ceiling is below the equilibrium interest rate.)

Graph 4

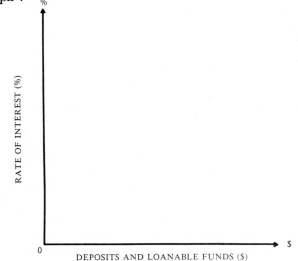

b. What would be the graphical result of such a policy?

c. Given the graphical result of b, what would happen in the real world?

ANSWERS

Matching Key Terms and Concepts

SET I

Answer	Reference
1. h	p. 244
2. a	p. 240
3. d	p. 243
4. j	p. 245
5. c	p. 250
6. e	p. 244
7. b	p. 239
8. f	p. 240
9. i	p. 246
10. g	p. 243

SET II

Answer	Reference
1. g	p. 250
2. d	p. 250
3. e	p. 238
4. a	p. 239
5. f	p. 244
6. c	p. 246
7. h	p. 236
8. b	p. 236
9. j	p. 236
10. i	p. 244

Chapter Review: Key Points

1. Comptroller of the Currency, FDIC
2. state, state banking authorities
3. FED, Chairman
4. President, 12
5. reserve requirements, excess reserves
6. money multiplier, money supply
7. money multiplier, a reduction
8. discounting operations, discount
9. open market operations, contractionary
10. reserves, reduce loans

Standard Multiple Choice

Answer	Reference
1. b	p. 240
2. a	p. 240
3. a	p. 240
4. d	p. 240
5. b	p. 243
6. b	p. 250
7. e	p. 240
8. a	p. 243
9. e	p. 236
10. c	p. 236
11. c	p. 236
12. d	p. 244

True/False Questions

Answer	Reference
1. T	p. 240
2. T	p. 240
3. T	p. 241
4. F	p. 241
5. F	p. 235
6. T	p. 240
7. F	p. 241
8. T	p. 243
9. T	p. 239
10. T	p. 250
11. F	p. 250
12. T	p. 250

Unlimited Multiple Choice

Answer	Reference
1. cd	p. 240-241
2. ad	p. 246, 250
3. ab	p. 236, 243
4. cd	p. 243
5. cd	p. 250

PROBLEMS

Problem 1
Reference pp. 240-243

See table below.

Table 4

	TOTAL BANK RESERVES	MONETARY BASE	POTENTIAL MONEY MULTIPLIER	ACTUAL MONEY MULTIPLIER	MONEY SUPPLY
a	▼	▼	0	0	▼
b	▼	▼	0	▼	▼
c	0	0	▼	▼	▼
d	▼	0	0	▼	▼

Problem 2
Reference pp. 240-243

All arrows are the opposite of those in Problem 1.

Problem 3
Reference pp. 240-243

See T-account below.

Table 5

FEDERAL RESERVE BANK	
ASSETS	LIABILITIES
-$2,000 Treasury Bonds	-$2,000 Reserves held for Member Bank

MEMBER BANK	
ASSETS	LIABILITIES
-$2,000 Loanable Reserves +$2,000 Treasury Bonds	

Problem 4
Reference p. 250

See graph below.

Figure 2

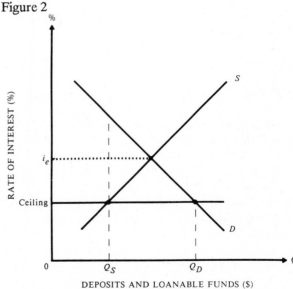

DEPOSITS AND LOANABLE FUNDS ($)

b. The expected result would be a shortage of loanable funds due to the interest rate ceiling.

c. Without sufficient funds for all people seeking loans at the current lending rate, the financial intermediary would most likely ration the funds based on credit worthiness.

CHAPTER FOURTEEN
MONETARY THEORY AND POLICY

CHAPTER OBJECTIVES

After you have read and studied this chapter, you should be able to differentiate between the classical, Keynesian, and modern monetarist approaches to the demand for money; explain how variations in the quantity of money might influence macroeconomic activity, given various states of the economy; and explain why interest rates and bond prices are inversely related.

CHAPTER REVIEW: KEY POINTS

1. You increase your spending when you have "too much" money; your rate of saving increases when you have "too little" money.

2. People hold money for predictable spending (transaction demands) with a cushion for uncertain outlays or income receipts (precautionary demands). People also have asset demands for money because: (a) money is relatively riskless, (b) transaction costs associated with less liquid assets may exceed expected returns, or (c) people speculate by holding money when they expect the prices of alternative assets (e.g., stocks, bonds, or real estate) to fall.

3. According to classical monetary theory, the sole rational motive for holding money is to consummate transactions.

4. Interest rates and bond prices are inversely related. Bond prices fall if interest rates rise, and vice versa.

5. The costs of holding nominal amounts of money are: (a) the reciprocal of the price level (1/P) if the choice is between saving money or buying consumer goods; or (b) the interest rate, if money is viewed as an asset substitutable for some highly liquid income-generating asset, say a bond. Inflation also imposes costs on holdings of money.

6. The income velocity (V) of money equals nominal GNP (PQ) divided by the money supply (M).

7. The equation of exchange, a truism, is written MV = PQ. Therefore, the percentage change in the money supply plus the percentage change in velocity roughly equals the percentage change in the price level plus the percentage change in real output:

$$\frac{\Delta M}{M} \quad + \quad \frac{\Delta V}{V} \quad = \quad \frac{\Delta P}{P} \quad + \quad \frac{\Delta Q}{Q}.$$

8. Classical economics assumes that velocity (V) and output (Q) are reasonably constant and independent of the money supply (M) and the price level (P). Classical economists believe that changes in the money supply result in proportional changes in the price level and expressed this belief in early versions of the quantity theory of money. The quantity theory of money is more accurately a monetary theory of the price level.

9. Keynes's attack on the quantity theory disputes the assumptions that: (a) the natural state of the economy is full employment, (b) the velocity of money is inherently stable, and (c) the only rational motive for holding money is for transactions purposes.

10. Modern monetarists perceive a direct link between the money supply and national income. Since the demand for money is relatively stable, growth of the money supply puts excess money balances in the hands of consumers and investors who, in turn, spend this surplus money on goods and services. Monetary growth may expand output in the short run, but modern monetarists conclude that in the long run, higher prices will result.

11. The difficulties confronting monetary and fiscal policymakers have caused many economists to favor putting the economy on "automatic pilot." The advocates of replacing discretionary policy with monetary growth rules would replace the Federal Open-Market Committee with a couple of reliable but unimaginative clerks. Their job would be to increase the money supply by a fixed small (3 percent?) increase annually, and the federal budget would be set to balance at full employment.

MATCHING KEY TERMS AND CONCEPTS

___ 1. hoarding

___ 2. crude quantity theory of money

___ 3. transaction demand

___ 4. precautionary demand

___ 5. asset demand

___ 6. real money balances

___ 7. liquidity trap

___ 8. income velocity of money

___ 9. opportunity cost of money

___10. Equation of Exchange

a. Causes income velocity of money to decrease.

b. Arises because of transaction costs, risk aversion, and speculation that interest rates might rise soon.

c. Horizontal money demand curve; might occur if people expected currently low interest rates to rise sharply and very soon.

d. Varies directly with the level of income and inversely with the frequency with which households receive income payments.

e. Positively related both to income and to uncertainty about future purchases.

f. Assumes $\Delta Q/Q = \Delta V/V = 0$, so that the price level is proportional to the nominal money supply.

g. The interest rate if the alternative to holding money is buying bonds; 1/CPI if the next best alternative is consumption.

h. GNP/M

i. $MV = PQ$

j. M/P

CHAPTER REVIEW (FILL-IN QUESTIONS)

1-5. Why do people want to hold money? Perhaps the most important motive is the _____ demand for money, which arises because people expect that they will make certain outlays of money in the near future. In addition, uncertainty about future expenditures creates a _____ demand for money. Finally, uncertainty about the future values of potential investments generates the _____ demand for money. Part of this last source of the demand for money is fear that _____ will rise. _____ fall when interest rates rise, so bondholders lose. Keynes identified this part of the asset demand for money as the _____ demand for money. Aversion to _____ and _____ costs are other foundations of the asset demand for money. Classical economists had focused on the _____ demand for money, which is directly related to _____ and negatively related to the frequencies of receipts and payments.

6. Irving Fisher helped formalize classical monetary theory by developing the Equation of _____, which is written _____.

7-9. Keynes introduced the _____ motive for holding money, which is reasonably compatible with classical theory, and the _____ demand for money, which raised the possibility that even huge increases in the money supply might be _____ rather than spent if the economy were caught in a _____. In addition, Keynes argued that _____ is much influenced by the "animal spirits of investors" and relatively insensitive to variations in _____.

10. According to the Keynesian _____, expansion of the money supply only influences autonomous spending by reducing interest slightly, which stimulates _____ slightly, which then, through the multiplier principle, increases Aggregate Expenditures somewhat.

STANDARD MULTIPLE CHOICE

THERE IS ONE BEST ANSWER TO EACH QUESTION.

___ 1. The total demand for money does not include:
   a. transactions demands.
   b. stocks and bonds.
   c. asset demands.
   d. precautionary demands.
   e. any of these.

___ 2. The crude "Quantity Theory of Money" did NOT:
   a. assume full employment.
   b. assume velocity was erratic.
   c. predict money and the price level to be proportional.
   d. blame inflation on too much monetary growth.
   e. rely heavily on the transactions demand for money.

___ 3. Precautionary demands originate in:
   a. people's desire for "mad money."
   b. fear that interest rates will rise.
   c. fear that prices will rise.
   d. expectations of economic booms.
   e. expectations of stock market crashes.

___ 4. People will hold more money if they:
   a. think prices will rise.
   b. expect interest rates on bonds to fall.
   c. expect interest rates on bonds to rise.
   d. expect tremendous economic growth.
   e. are paid more frequently.

___ 5. The person most responsible for the reemergence of monetarism during the past quarter century is:
   a. Paul Samuelson.
   b. John Maynard Keynes.
   c. John Kenneth Galbraith.
   d. Milton Friedman.
   e. Irving Fisher.

6. We can infer that you have too little money if you:
   a. are a typical college student.
   b. must spend money as quickly as you receive it.
   c. wear ragged clothes and eat cheap food.
   d. increase the amount of cash you save from each paycheck.
   e. use credit cards extensively.

7. People's money-holdings tend to grow with:
   a. higher expected inflation.
   b. greater interest rates paid on money.
   c. higher interest rates on bonds.
   d. higher purchasing power of each dollar (1/CPI).
   e. easier access to credit.

8. The asset demand for money will increase if:
   a. for a given expected return, the risk of holding other assets rises.
   b. people want greater liquidity than previously.
   c. the interest rate is expected to rise.
   d. the prices of bonds is expected to fall.
   e. all of the above.

9. The transaction demand for money is most closely related to its use as a:
   a. medium of exchange.
   b. standard unit of account.
   c. measure of value.
   d. store of value.
   e. standard of deferred payment.

10. Keynesian monetary theory assumes that the cost of holding money is best measured by:
    a. 1/CPI.
    b. CPI.
    c. the interest rates on bonds.
    d. the interest banks pay to owners of demand deposits.
    e. the realized rate of inflation.

11. The Equation of Exchange is written:
    a. $MQ = PV$.
    b. $M = QVP$.
    c. $MV = PQ$.
    d. $V = PQ/M$.
    e. $\Delta M/M + \Delta V/V = \Delta P/P + \Delta Q/Q$.

12. In a "liquidity trap," expansionary monetary policies:
    a. rapidly cure inflationary pressures.
    b. have no effect except on people's money holdings.
    c. reduce interest rates, increase investment and, hence, Aggregate Demand.
    d. quickly pull a sluggish economy out of the doldrums.
    e. create new inflationary pressures.

TRUE/FALSE QUESTIONS

1. According to classical theory, any changes in the nominal money supply will be reflected in proportional changes in the absolute price level.

2. In classical theory, the interest rate determines the level of saving while, in the Keynesian theory, the interest rate determines the composition of an income-determined level of saving.

3. Variations in the money supply affect investment similarly in the classical and Keynesian theoretical models.

4. Keynesian and classical economists agree that equilibrium investment occurs when the rates of return on investment projects are equal to the prevailing market rate of interest.

5. According to J. M. Keynes, expansionary monetary policy propels an economy out of a depression.

___ 6. Keynesian economists believe investors' expectations about rates of return to be quite stable, and explain wide swings in investment as responses to small changes in interest rates.

___ 7. Classical economic models allow the possibility that a market economy could be in equilibrium at less than full employment.

___ 8. Milton Friedman argues that the demand for money varies inversely with the interest rate on bonds, the rate of return on physical capital, and the expected rate of inflation.

___ 9. Most Keynesian models ignore the institutional mechanisms used to create money.

___10. The Monetarist prescription for a healthy economy is active federal management of Aggregate Demand.

UNLIMITED MULTIPLE CHOICE

WARNING: THERE ARE FROM ZERO TO FOUR ANSWERS FOR EACH QUESTION!

___ 1. Classical economists contend that the:
   a. income velocity of money is reasonably constant.
   b. quantity of money demanded varies inversely with the interest rate.
   c. investment demand is highly sensitive to changes in the expectations of firms.
   d. market system is inherently unstable.

___ 2. Modern Monetarists believe that the:
   a. demand for money is a positive function of income.
   b. demand for money varies inversely with the amount of human capital as a percentage of total wealth.
   c. expected rate of inflation does not influence the demand for money.
   d. basic cause of instability in a market economy is erratic governmental policy.

___ 3. According to the Keynesian monetary transmission mechanism:
   a. an increase in the nominal money supply makes people feel wealthier, and they eliminate their excess holdings of money by spending more on goods immediately.
   b. an increase in the money supply causes the interest rate to decrease, resulting in an increase in investment and then income.
   c. changes in the money supply will affect consumer spending directly.
   d. money's affect on interest rates induce changes in aggregate spending.

___ 4. Both Keynesian and classical writers:

   a. agree that very high rates of investment lead to somewhat lower rates of return, but disagree about how fast this occurs.
   b. believe that investment will occur as long as the expected rate of return to investment at least equals the interest rate.
   c. believe that interest rates are determined in the money market.
   d. view economic transactors as confronted by much uncertainty.

___ 5. The crude quantity theory of money:
   a. posits that market economies never deviate much from full- employment levels of output.
   b. assumes that velocity is reasonably constant.
   c. treats velocity as unaffected by the price level, by the level of real output, and by the nominal money supply.
   d. posits that people hold money only to consummate transactions.

PROBLEM 1

Fill in the blanks for interest rates, annual payments, bond prices, etc., so that the following statements are true.

a. An interest rate equaling _____ percent would make assured perpetual annual payments of $5,000 worth $100,000 today.

b. A perpetual bond would be worth _____ if the interest rate were 12.5 percent annually and the bond paid $2,000 each year.

c. A perpetual bond would need to yield annual payments of roughly ___ to be worth $10,000 if the interest rate were 16.67 percent.

d. If a perpetual bond is priced at $70,000 and pays $10,500 annually, the interest rate yielded is _____ percent.

e. An annual after-tax rental value of a parcel of property equalling $30,000 combined with a current interest rate of 10 percent would make its present value _____ .

f. A National Football League franchise costing $12 million is worth buying if the current interest rate is 12 percent and it is forecast to generate ____ million annually after all other expenses.

PROBLEM 2

On the graphs provided below illustrate the Keynesian transmission mechanism. Note the steep slope of the investment demand function. Use primes (') to illustrate an expansionary monetary policy.

Figure 1

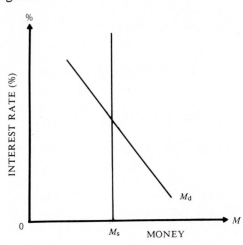

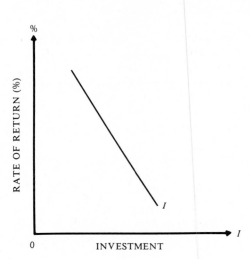

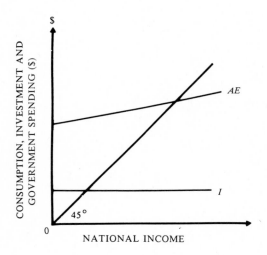

PROBLEM 3

Now that you have developed this Keynesian linkage perhaps a numerical example would be helpful. Suppose that the FED buys $5 million in treasury bonds from the banking system. If the required reserve ratio is 10%, all the banks are fully loaned up, and the non-banking public holds no cash;

a. What is the actual money supply expansion? _____

b. Assume that the money demand curve is linear over the relevant range. If an increase of $20 million in the money supply decreases the interest by 1%, who much will the interest rate decrease? _____

c. Suppose the investment demand curve is linear and that a 1% decrease in the interest rate increases investment by $1 million. How much will investment increase? _____

d. If the MPC = .8, who much will equilibrium income increase? _____

ANSWERS

Matching Key Terms and Concepts

Answer	Reference
1. a	p. 264
2. f	p. 261
3. d	p. 254
4. e	p. 255
5. b	p. 255
6. j	p. 267
7. c	p. 264
8. h	p. 258
9. g	p. 256
10. i	p. 258

Chapter Review (fill-in Questions)

1. transactions, precautionary
2. asset, interest rates
3. bond prices, speculative
4. risk, transactions
5. transactions demand, income
6. Exchange, $MV = PQ$
7. precautionary, asset or speculative
8. hoarded, liquidity trap
9. investment, interest rates
10. monetary transmission mechanism, investment

Standard Multiple Choice

Answer	Reference
1. b	p. 253-256
2. b	p. 261
3. a	p. 255
4. c	p. 256
5. d	p. 268
6. d	p. 254
7. b	p. 256
8. e	p. 255
9. a	p. 254
10. c	p. 256
11. c	p. 258
12. b	p. 263

True/False Questions

Answer	Reference
1. T	p. 261
2. T	p. 262
3. F	p. 262
4. T	p. 264
5. F	p. 267
6. F	p. 265
7. F	p. 262
8. T	p. 267
9. F	p. 271
10. F	p. 274

Unlimited Multiple Choice

Answer	Reference
1. a	p. 256
2. ad	p. 262
3. bd	p. 267
4. ab	p. 271
5. abcd	p. 274

Problem 1
Reference pp. 255-256

a. 5
b. $16,000
c. $1,667
d. 15
e. $300,000
f. $1.44

Problem 2
Reference pp. 265-266

See graph below.

Figure 2

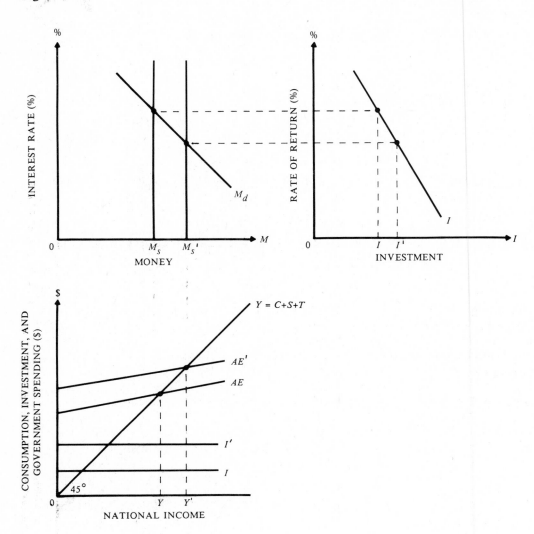

Problem 3
Reference pp. 265-266

a. $50 million
b. 2.5%
c. $2.5 million
d. $12.5 million

CHAPTER FIFTEEN

FINANCING GOVERNMENT:

DEFICITS AND THE PUBLIC DEBT

CHAPTER OBJECTIVES

After you have read and studied this chapter you should be able to describe various problems encountered in balancing the budget; discuss the 'crowding out' hypothesis; differentiate between government and private budget constraints; and evaluate the impact of national debt on future generations.

CHAPTER REVIEW: KEY POINTS

1. The budget deficit equals annual government outlays minus receipts. The public debt is total federal indebtedness resulting from current and past deficits.

2. Balancing the budget annually might result in incorrect fiscal actions to combat either inflation or recession. Some have suggested balancing the budget over the business cycle. This would entail running deficits during recessions and surpluses over the boom. Unfortunately, business cycles are not symmetric, and the budget may not be easy to balance over the cycle without hampering prosperity. Advocates of functional finance believe that the size of the public debt is unimportant. They suggest that we ignore the problem of balancing the budget and focus on balancing the economy instead.

3. The federal government can finance public spending by collecting taxes, printing money, selling government securities, or through confiscation. All of these techniques are drains on gross private saving (production minus private consumption) that can crowd out private economic activities. The notion called Ricardian equivalence suggests that whether government spending is financed by taxes or borrowing is irrelevant.

4. The crowding-out hypothesis states that increases in government purchases inevitably reduces private consumption, investment, or leisure.

5. Federal deficits can be financed by increasing domestic saving, securing the savings of foreigners, or by reducing domestic investment or exports. A growing budget deficit may cause growth of a trade deficit.

6. Some government spending is uncontrollable (roughly three quarters today). These programs are long-range or are committed by law each and every year. Reducing these outlays is virtually impossible.

7. A major difference between private and public debt is that private debt is entirely owned by persons external to the issuing institution, while the bulk of public debt is internal, being owed to ourselves. Private debt has grown faster than public debt since the early 1950s and is currently over twice as large.

8. The real burden of the national debt stems from the federal government "crowding out" private investment as it drives interest rates up when competing with the private sector for loanable funds. As a result, future generations may inherit a smaller capital stock and a smaller production-possibilities frontier.

9. Among the major benefits of the public debt are its use as a stabilization instrument and as a risk-free asset for savers.

MATCHING KEY TERMS AND CONCEPTS

___ 1. confiscation

___ 2. Ricardian Equivalence

___ 3. uncontrollable spending

___ 4. crowding-out hypothesis

___ 5. government budget constraint

___ 6. external debt

___ 7. roll over

___ 8. internal debt

___ 9. functional finance

___10. national debt

a. IOUs the repayment of which entail no loss of purchasing power.

b. The best way to finance government outlays depends on the least costly policies available.

c. Long term programs like Social Security.

d. Repaying old debts by taking out new loans.

e. The cumulation of all budget deficits through history.

f. Eminent domain and the military draft are examples.

g. The idea that governmental growth entails opportunity costs.

h. $G = T + \Delta B + \Delta MB$.

i. How government debt is financed is irrelevant.

j. Purchasing power is lost when this is repaid.

CHAPTER REVIEW (FILL-IN QUESTIONS)

1-7. Government can obtain resources through sales of existing _____ or current _____, by _____ from citizens, corporations, foreigners or commercial banks, through _____, _____, or by _____. Recognizing that confiscation is a relatively minor source of government revenues, the governmental budget can be summarized by the equation _____. The idea that increases in outlays by government inevitably cause reductions in private consumption or investment is known as the _____ hypothesis. When increased governmental purchases crowds out private individuals, they lose leisure or purchasing power through _____ or higher _____. Issuance of bonds increases the demand for loanable funds which typically drives up _____ imposing an added burden on potential borrowers and investors. If there is efficient and full employment of all resources and government purchases are increased either _____, _____ or _____ must decline.

8-10. The major difference between private and public debt is that the latter is primarily _____ held. Because private debt is owned by _____ persons their claim on the real assets of the firm or individual can deplete the net worth of private parties. When the government issues new bonds, the purchasing power sacrificed by American bond-buyers just _____ the government's gain in purchasing power. However, increased debt may impose several burdens on the society. If taxes must be raised to pay the interest on the debt, _____ to work and invest may be reduced. Further, if interest rates rise as more public debt is floated, private borrowing may be _____. This could squelch _____ so that the national debt did impose a burden on future generations by reducing growth in the stock of capital.

MULTIPLE CHOICE

THERE IS A SINGLE BEST ANSWER FOR EACH OF THESE QUESTIONS.

___ 1. The public debt:
   a. results from cumulative budgetary deficits.
   b. is a stabilization instrument.
   c. provides a relatively riskless investment.
   d. is held primarily by U.S. citizens and institutions.
   e. all of the above.

___ 2. Which has grown fastest since World War II?
   a. national debt.
   b. state and local debt.
   c. private debt.
   d. gross national product.
   e. unemployment.

___ 3. "Crowding-out" is most significant:
   a. at full employment.
   b. during inflation.
   c. during recession.
   d. during war time.
   e. during stagflation.

___ 4. "Crowding-out" refers to:
   a. cuts in private activities caused when government grows.
   b. TANSTAAFL.
   c. the public burdens of increased private purchases.
   d. the decline in unemployment forced by more rapid inflation.
   e. all of the above.

___ 5. Major differences between private and public debt are:
   a. the private debt is used as a risk free asset.
   b. the private debt is almost entirely owned by external persons.
   c. the public debt is entirely owned by external persons.
   d. all of the public debt is owed to Americans.
   e. none of the above.

___ 6. Government cannot secure extra resources by:
   a. collecting taxes.
   b. backing the dollar with gold.
   c. printing money.
   d. selling government securities.
   e. issuing bonds.

___ 7. If private owners are compelled to sell when the government buys land for public use, it is applying:
   a. the right of eminent domain.
   b. the law of economic efficiency.
   c. political rights of taxpayer preference.
   d. the rights of economic expansion.
   e. an unconstitutional power that the Supreme Court will overturn.

___ 8. A fairly recent legislated attempt to control deficits is the:
   a. Ricardian Equivalence Act.
   b. Structural Deficit Act.
   c. Stop-Gap Act.
   d. Gramm-Rudman Act.
   e. Functional Finance Act.

___ 9. "The mix that works best should be used" best describes:
   a. the growth of public of debt.
   b. Ricardian Equivalence.
   c. the government's use of eminent domain.
   d. the functional finance approach.
   e. a chocolate chip cookie recipe.

___ 10. An example of uncontrollable spending would be:
   a. increasing annual budget deficits.
   b. increased imports of crude oil.
   c. local outlays for construction of a new park.
   d. a $50,000 spending binge at Bloomingdales.
   e. federal outlays for postal service.

___11. Robert Barro's argument that loans and taxes are equivalent is based upon:
   a. the notion of Functional Finance.
   b. the relationship specified in the government constraint.
   c. Richardian Equivalence.
   d. international trade theory.
   e. Keynesian analysis.

___12. The amount of money 'printed' by the FED when it buys Treasury bonds issued to cover a federal budget deficit:
   a. is new monetary base, and consequently causes the money supply to grow even more through the bank 'money creation' process.
   b. somewhat replaces crowding-out that would have been accomplished by higher interest rates with crowding-out through inflation.
   c. reduces the amount of national debt in the public's hands.
   d. results in greater growth of Aggregate Spending than would have occurred without such expansionary open market operations.
   e. All of the above.

TRUE/FALSE QUESTIONS

___ 1. Selling assets or borrowing to secure resources are methods used by both private and governmental decisionmakers.

___ 2. Consumption by households is financed by sales of current assets, by current income, and by borrowing against current assets or expected income.

___ 3. The distribution of the opportunity costs associated with government among the public is not a crucial consideration in determining who really pays for government.

___ 4. Private debt is primarily internally held while public debt is primarily externally held.

___ 5. The Gramm-Rudman Act calls for a balanced budget every fiscal year.

___ 6. The military draft fully covers the opportunity costs of resources through taxing, borrowing, and printing new money.

___ 7. Crowding-out does not need to be considered if there are many idle resources during a deep recession.

___ 8. When the government issues bonds to cover a budget deficit, interest rates tend to rise and crowd-out investment.

___ 9. Taxes have been used almost exclusively to finance most of the wars in which the United States has been involved.

___10. Government outlays for medicare are an example of uncontrollable spending.

___11. Budget deficits were dramatically reduced during the Reagan Administration.

___12. Our government is forbidden by the Constitution from acquiring resources from their owners unless the owners voluntarily agree by contract to surrender their assets.

UNLIMITED MULTIPLE CHOICE

NOTE: EACH QUESTION HAS FROM ZERO TO FOUR CORRECT RESPONSES.

___ 1. The federal government can:
   a. finance a deficit by printing money.
   b. finance a deficit by buying bonds from the public.
   c. retire some public debt when tax revenue exceeds expenditure.
   d. finance a deficit by selling bonds to the public.

___ 2. According to the crowding-out hypothesis:
   a. an increase in government spending has no adverse impact on the private sector.
   b. increased government outlays necessarily decrease private consumption or investment if the economy is at full employment.
   c. profitable private investment opportunities decrease if government borrowing pushes the interest rate upward.
   d. increases in taxes drive up the interest rate.

___ 3. It is unavoidably true that government budgetary:
   a. deficits cause increases in the national debt.
   b. surpluses permit either a reduction in the monetary base or retirement of part of the public debt.
   c. deficits require retirement of part of the public debt or reduction of the money supply.
   d. surpluses cause increases in national debt or in the money supply.

___ 4. Which of the following represent possible example of crowding-out by the government:
   a. losses of leisure by previously idle workers.
   b. reduced purchasing power of households caused by inflation.
   c. reduced investments caused by higher interest rates.
   d. reduced borrowing by consumers because of higher interest rates.

___ 5. Which of the following is a form of taxation if it is defined as the loss in purchasing power that occurs when government outlays increase?
   a. Extra consumption induced via the Keynesian multiplier process when government spending grows to combat a serious depression.
   b. Confiscation, as when a military draft is used to acquire labor resources for the Department of Defense.
   c. Inflation following an increase in the monetary base caused when the FED 'monetizes' a huge deficit.
   d. Jumps in the interest rate caused by an enormous budget deficit.

PROBLEMS

PROBLEM 1

On the axes provided illustrate the concept of "crowding out" caused by the government issuing bonds to cover expenditures.

Figure 1

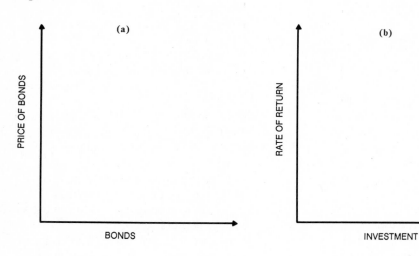

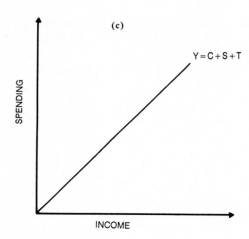

PROBLEM 2

Use Figure 2 to answer the following True/False questions.

Figure 2

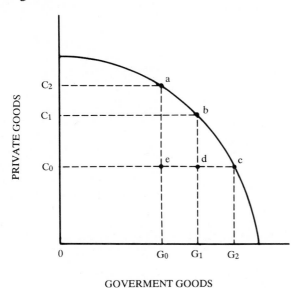

GOVERMENT GOODS

___ a. An increase in government spending from G_0 to G_1 will result in crowding out of the private sector equal to $C_2 - C_1$ in an economy with idle resources.

___ b. In an economy with idle resources an increase in government spending from G_0 to G_1 might result in induced consumption equal to $b - d$.

___ c. In a fully employed economy an increase in government spending from G_1 to G_2 will result in a reduction in private spending equal to $C_1 - C_0$.

___ d. If an increase in government spending from G_0 to G_1 results in movement from point e to point b, the distance between b and d is equal to the multiplier times the change in government spending.

___ e. An increase in government spending from G_1 to G_2 will result in crowding out equal to $d - c$ in an economy with idle resources.

___ f. If the economy is at point e, an increase in government spending can enable the economy to move to point a through induced consumption.

___ g. If the economy is at point a an increase in government spending from G_0 to G_1 will result in a decrease in private spending equal to $C_2 - C_1$.

___ h. A movement from point b to point a illustrates crowding out of the private sector by government spending.

___ i. In order to move from point d to point b, the government will have to increase its outlays and, in the process, crowd out the private sector.

___ j. A decrease in government spending from G_2 to G_1 must result in a movement from point c to point d.

PROBLEM 3

Use your knowledge about the government budget constraint to answer the following True/False questions, given the following information:

$$G = 700 \text{ billion} \qquad\qquad T = 500 \text{ billion}$$

___ a. The government budget is balanced.

___ b. If there is no change in the monetary base, the change in national debt is equal to $200 billion.

___ c. If the change in national debt is equal to $75 billion, the change in the monetary base is equal to $125 billion.

___ d. If taxes are increased to a total of $800 billion, the government can retire $100 billion of the national debt and contract the monetary base.

___ e. If taxes are increased to a total of $750 billion, the government can contract the monetary base by $50 billion if there is no change in the national debt.

___ f. In an open economy (international trade takes place) a $100 billion domestic savings surplus will necessitate a $100 billion trade deficit.

___ g. In an open economy a $300 billion domestic savings surplus will necessitate a $100 billion trade deficit.

___ h. In an open economy a $100 billion trade surplus will necessitate a $300 billion domestic savings surplus.

___ i. In an open economy a $200 billion trade surplus will necessitate a domestic savings surplus equal to zero.

___ j. In an open economy a $200 billion trade deficit will necessitate a domestic savings surplus equal to zero.

ANSWERS

Matching Key Terms and Concepts

Answer	Reference
1. f	p. 283
2. i	p. 282
3. c	p. 289
4. g	p. 285
5. h	p. 284
6. j	p. 292
7. d	p. 294
8. a	p. 292
9. b	p. 281
10. e	p. 292

Chapter Review (Fill-in Questions)

1. assets, production
2. borrowing, taxation
3. confiscation, printing money
4. $G = T + \Delta B + \Delta MB$, crowding out
5. inflation, taxes
6. interest rates, consumption
7. investment, exports
8. internally, external
9. equals, incentives
10. crowded out, investment

Multiple Choice Questions

Answer	Reference
1. e	p. 279
2. c	p. 296
3. a	p. 287
4. a	p. 285
5. b	p. 292
6. b	p. 284
7. a	p. 283
8. d	p. 291
9. d	p. 281
10. e	p. 290
11. c	p. 282
12. e	p. 284

True/False Questions

Answer	Reference
1. T	p. 283
2. T	p. 283
3. T	p. 285
4. F	p. 292
5. F	p. 291
6. F	p. 283
7. F	p. 285
8. T	p. 287
9. F	p. 288
10. T	p. 288
11. F	p. 279
12. F	p. 283

Unlimited Multiple Choice

Answer	Reference
1. abcd	p. 284
2. bc	p. 285-287
3. b	p. 284
4. abcd	p. 285-287
5. bcd	p. 283, 287

Problem 1
Reference p. 286

See Figure 3

Figure 3

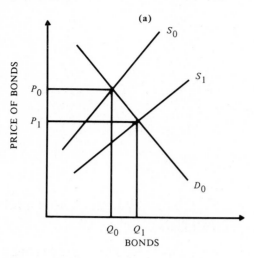

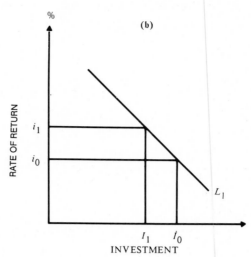

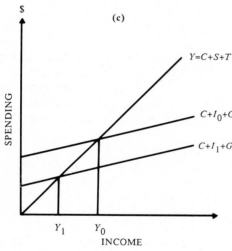

Problem 2
Reference p. 285

a. F
b. T
c. T
d. T
e. F
f. F
g. T
h. F
i. F
j. F

Problem 3
Reference p. 284-289

a. F
b. T
c. T
d. F
e. T
f. T
g. F
h. T
i. F
j. T

CHAPTER SIXTEEN
AGGREGATE DEMAND AND SUPPLY

CHAPTER OBJECTIVES

After you have read and studied this chapter you should be able to explain the basics of Aggregate Supply and Demand curves and their major determinants; explain what causes shifts in Aggregate Supply and Demand Curves; and describe the processes of supply-side and demand-side inflation.

CHAPTER REVIEW: KEY POINTS

1. Stagflation, a contraction of the terms stagnation and inflation, is the simultaneous occurrence of high rates of both unemployment and inflation.

2. Decreases in the Aggregate Supply curve cause supply-side inflation and declines in real incomes and output. Excessive increases in the Aggregate Demand curve cause demand-side inflation, which initially is accompanied by increased incomes and output.

3. If Aggregate Demand grows excessively in a fully employed economy, the first phase of the demand-side cycle entails rising prices, outputs, employment, and incomes. In the second phase, supply-side adjustments to the demand-originated disturbances cause prices to continue to rise, but total employment, production, and income fall. Demand-side inflation induces a counterclockwise adjustment path of inflation versus real output. If the economy starts at less than full employment, only the first phase necessarily occurs when Aggregate Demand is increased.

4. Supply-side inflation generates a clockwise adjustment pattern. During the first phase of a supply-side (cost-push) cycle, prices rise while real output and incomes fall. If the government attempts to correct for the resulting inflationary recession by increasing Aggregate Demand, the second phase occurs--prices continue to rise, but real output and income rise as well.

5. Mild but increasing demand-side inflation accompanied the prosperity of the 1960s. From the mid-1970s into the early 1980s, stagflation took over with a vengeance. Whether this stagflation was the supply-adjustment phase of the earlier demand-pull cycle or originated solely from supply-related shocks cannot be established conclusively. It seems likely, however, that even if the economy had been stable when the supply shocks listed previously emerged, considerable supply-side inflation would have plagued the American economy from 1973 to 1980.

6. Disinflation is a significant reduction in the rate of inflation. Most people adjust their behavior if they expect inflation. Their expectations cause disinflation to entail losses in real income before it restores the economy to a relatively stable growth path. Thus, the 1981-83 recession was especially severe.

MATCHING KEY TERMS AND CONCEPTS

___ 1. wealth effect

___ 2. stagflation

___ 3. demand-side inflationary cycle

___ 4. money (inflation) illusion

___ 5. incomes policies

___ 6. supply-side inflationary cycle

___ 7. rightward shift of economy's supply curve

___ 8. leftward shift of economy's demand curve

___ 9. rightward shift of economy's demand curve

___10. leftward shift of economy's supply curve

a. Caused by increased preference for leisure by labor.

b. Can exist in the short run, but not in the long run.

c. Employment rises in the initial stage of this process.

d. May occur if the reserve requirement ratio is cut.

e. One reason why the Aggregate Demand curve is negatively sloped.

f. Generates a clockwise adjustment path of the price level versus real output.

g. May be caused by a decline in monopoly power.

h. Attempts to curb inflation without cutting Aggregate Demand.

i. Induced by, e.g., reduced government spending.

j. Inflationary recession.

CHAPTER REVIEW (FILL-IN QUESTIONS)

1. The short run Aggregate Demand curve is negative sloped in part because the stock of money is assumed constant. This means that _____ will rise when the price level increases, shrinking consumer spending on durable goods, spending by state and local governments, and _____ spending by business firms.

2-3. In sum, the main determinants of Aggregate Supply are the quantities and costs of _____, production _____, _____ about inflation or deflation, and governmental _____.

4-6. Price hikes may initially 'fool' workers through a process called _____, so that firms' _____ do not rise as fast as prices. During such a period, the _____ rate tends to fall and output grows. Eventually, however, workers adjust their inflationary expectations. Real wages will tend to _____ and output fall because, even though prices continue to rise, _____ will grow even faster. A complete demand-side inflationary cycle follows a _____ path.

7-8. A supply-side inflationary cycle originates from an initial shift of the Aggregate Supply curve to the left. This drives up both the rates of _____ and _____. Policymakers commonly try to combat the recessionary trend with _____ demand management policies. As a result, the longer-term equilibration path for a supply-side inflationary cycle is _____.

9-10. The empirical evidence of actual equilibration paths suggests that the inflation of the 1960s was primarily _____, while the inflation of the 1970s was essentially _____. The very high rates of unemployment and inflation that plagued the early 1980s might be interpreted as the latter phases of a _____ cycle, or as the beginnings of a _____ cycle.

STANDARD MULTIPLE CHOICE

THERE IS ONE BEST ANSWER FOR EACH QUESTION.

___ 1. Rightward shifts of the Aggregate Supply curve cause:
   a. stagflation.
   b. high unemployment.
   c. cost-push inflation.
   d. high interest rates.
   e. deflationary pressure.

___ 2. Aggregate Supply might grow because of:
   a. reductions in the bargaining strength of organized labor.
   b. enhanced unemployment compensation programs.
   c. increased inflationary expectations by labor.
   d. increased preference for leisure by labor.
   e. All of the above.

___ 3. Which of the following actions would cause a shift to the right in the Aggregate Demand curve?
   a. Congress decides to terminate all highway and water projects.
   b. The President's call for a permanent tax decrease is approved.
   c. The FED changes the reserve requirement from 17% to 20%.
   d. Sales of U.S. bonds to commercial banks by the FED are increased.
   e. Welfare spending is slashed.

___ 4. A shift in the Aggregate Supply curve to the left will initiate _____ while a shift in the Aggregate Demand curve to the right will initiate _____:
   a. cost-pull inflation; demand; push inflation.
   b. demand-push inflation; cost-pull inflation.
   c. demand-pull inflation; cost-push inflation.
   d. cost-push inflation; demand-pull inflation.
   e. deflation; recession.

___ 5. Rapid technological advances tend to shift the:
   a. economy's supply of capital leftward.
   b. economy's labor supply curve leftward.
   c. Aggregate Expenditures curve rightward.
   d. Aggregate Supply curve rightward.
   e. price level upward.

___ 6. Stagflation is a contraction of _____ and _____:
   a. stagnant; deflation.
   b. stable; defoliation.
   c. stagnation; inflation.
   d. stabilization; repugnant.
   e. staggered; contraction.

___ 7. Stagflation involves simultaneous high levels of:
   a. unemployment and interest rates.
   b. interest rates and inflation.
   c. unemployment and inflation.
   d. economic growth and inflation.
   e. stagnation and degeneracy.

___ 8. Which of the following is NOT a reason why Aggregate Supply curves are positively sloped?
   a. Costs adjust less quickly than prices do to changes in demand.
   b. Price changes trigger wealth effects.
   c. Diminishing returns causes it to become ever more difficult to expand output as the economy approaches its capacity.
   d. Higher prices are needed to cover rising production costs as larger amounts of output are demanded.
   e. Expanding production causes more intense competition for resources when the economy nears full employment.

___ 9. Which of the following would be the LEAST likely to cause demand-pull inflation?
   a. a tax cut.
   b. an increase in government spending.
   c. a hike in the discount rate.
   d. a cut in reserve requirements.
   e. the FED buys bonds from banks.

___ 10. Stagflation occurs when Aggregate:
   a. Demand and Aggregate Supply shift right.
   b. Demand shifts right.
   c. Demand shifts left.
   d. Supply shifts right.
   e. Supply shifts left.

___11. Cost-push inflation is a likely result if the:
   a. money supply grows faster than our productive capacity.
   b. Aggregate Demand shifts right.
   c. Aggregate Supply curve shifts left.
   d. federal government runs a huge deficit.
   e. Congress repeals all inefficient regulations.

___12. A supply-side inflationary cycle follows a _____ path.
   a. clockwise.
   b. counterclockwise.
   c. cyclical.
   d. countercyclical.
   e. sinusoidal.

TRUE/FALSE QUESTIONS

___ 1. If no one suffers from money illusion, demand-pull inflation still initially yields both higher employment and higher prices.

___ 2. Monetary and fiscal policies can both increase the Aggregate Demand curve but require varying amounts of time before they become effective.

___ 3. Increasing Aggregate Supply can be done quite quickly.

___ 4. Aggregate Supply curves shift because of changes in monetary or fiscal policies or changes in consumption or investment expenditures.

___ 5. External shocks to the economy that increase resource costs or other production costs will cause the economy's demand curve to shift leftward.

___ 6. New regulations that facilitate efficiency cause the Aggregate Supply curve to shift to the right.

___ 7. The supply of labor is partially determined by individual preferences for work versus leisure.

___ 8. Hikes in the money wage rates imposed by powerful labor unions tend to cause the Aggregate Supply curve to shift leftward.

___ 9. Labor contracts are easily renegotiated when there are major increases in the rate of inflation.

___10. Money wage rates can be increased at a rate equivalent to the rate of labor productivity gain without causing price inflation.

UNLIMITED MULTIPLE CHOICE

WARNING: EACH QUESTION HAS FROM ZERO TO FOUR CORRECT ANSWERS.

___ 1. Workers are said to suffer from money illusion when:
   a. they make their work decisions after adjusting prevailing money wage rates for expected inflation or deflation.
   b. they anticipate real wage rates that are not realized.
   c. they work more but realize only decreased real wages because of inflation.
   d. their expected rate of inflation equals realized inflation.

___ 2. Incomes policies:
   a. include a variety of measures intended to reduce inflationary pressures without decreasing Aggregate Demand.
   b. may reduce labor's inflationary expectations.
   c. include such measures as wage and price controls.
   d. may worsen inflationary pressures if their inefficiencies cause the Aggregate Supply curve to shift inward and to the left.

___ 3. The Aggregate Supply curve:
   a. would be nearly vertical if workers quickly secured increases in money wage rates offsetting any increases in the price level.
   b. would be nearly vertical if workers' expected rates of inflation were much less than the actual rates of inflation.
   c. shifts rightward as workers revise their inflationary expectations upward.
   d. shifts leftward as business firms lower the prices they charge for goods.

___ 4. During the initial stage of a demand-side inflation:
   a. business firms offer higher money wages for more labor to produce more output at higher prices.
   b. the demand for labor schedule shifts to the left.
   c. the supply schedule of labor will shift leftward, assuming that labor suffers from money illusion.
   d. workers suffering from money illusion actually offer more labor services at a reduced real wage rate.

___ 5. Inflationary recession occurs during the:
   a. initial stage of a demand-side inflation.
   b. initial stage of a supply-side inflation.
   c. latter stage of a demand-side inflation as workers adjust their inflationary expectations to agree with actual inflation.
   d. latter stage of a supply-side inflation as government resorts to demand-management policies to restore full-employment.

PROBLEMS

Problem 1

Use information drawn from the Aggregate Supply and Demand curves depicted to answer the following True/False questions.

Figure 1

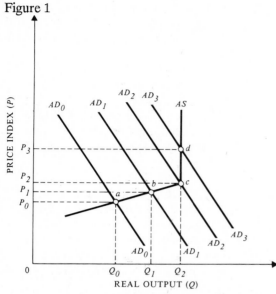

_____ a. Full employment occurs at output level Q_2.

_____ b. The shift of the Aggregate Demand curve from AD_0 to AD_1 could be accomplished by increased government expenditures.

_____ c. The price level is stable as the economy moves from a to b.

_____ d. As the economy moves from c to d, the percentage increase in the money wage rate equals the percentage increase in the absolute price level.

_____ e. Assuming a constant money wage rate, as the economy moves from b to c, the real wage rate increases, causing firms to hire less labor.

_____ f. A technological advance could shift the Aggregate Supply curve outward and to the right.

_____ g. The Aggregate Supply curve depicted is composed of both a Keynesian segment and a Classical segment.

_____ h. As the economy moves up along the Keynesian segment of its supply curve, the real wage rate remains unchanged.

_____ i. The movement from c to d represents pure price inflation.

_____ j. An increase in the money wage rate would shift the Keynesian portion of the supply curve upward and to the left.

_____ k. An increase in autonomous saving might shift the Aggregate Demand curve from AD_1 to AD_2.

_____ l. The demand curve for labor services corresponding to the Keynesian portion of the supply curve is a horizontal line.

200

Problem 2

Depicted below are the original Aggregate Supply (AS₀) and Demand (AD₀) curves for an economy, with output Q_e representing full employment. Use this information to answer the following True/False questions.

Figure 2

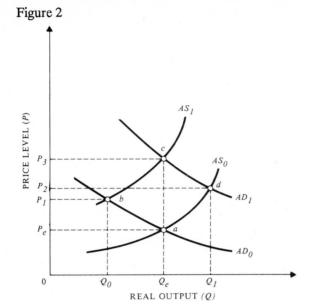

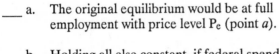

___ a. The original equilibrium would be at full employment with price level P_e (point *a*).

___ b. Holding all else constant, if federal spending increased or if the FED decided to increase the money supply, Aggregate Demand could increase from AD₀ to AD₁.

___ c. As the economy moves from point *a* to point *d*, the real wages of workers increase.

___ d. Realizing that wages have not kept pace with inflation at point *d*, workers will compensate by reducing their supplies of labor, so that Aggregate Supply shifts from AS₀ to AS₁.

___ e. This sequence of events (the economy moving from point *a* to point *d* to point *c*) is often referred to as Supply-side inflation.

___ f. Stagflation occurs when the economy moves from *a* to *b*.

___ g. Real wages fall as the economy moves from *a* to *b*.

___ h. Real wages rise during a move from *b* to *c*.

___ i. All things equal, the real wage at *c* is equal to the real wage at *a*.

___ j. The sequence of events described by the economy moving from *a* to *b* to *c* is referred to as Demand-side inflation.

___ k. The rightward shift of the Aggregate Demand curve from AD₀ to AD₁ could have been induced by a decrease in the discount rate.

___ l. Unemployment rates are higher at *a* than at *b*.

___ m. A movement from *b* to *c* could be generated if policymakers tried to combat a recession originally caused by supply shocks.

___ n. In the short-run, labor probably suffers from inflationary (money) illusion.

___ o. In the long run, labor adjusts to unexpectead inflation by shrinking the labor supply curve.

___ p. A shift in Aggregate Supply from AS₁ to AS₀ could be caused by an increase in the capital gains tax.

___ q. Policies to reduce monopolistic practices could shift Aggregate Demand from AD₀ to AD₁.

___ r. A movement from *a* to *b* could represent a situation where external supply shocks induce an inflationary recession.

Problem 3

On the graph provided, using Aggregate Supply and Aggregate Demand analysis, illustrate an economy at full employment with the normal amount of frictional unemployment. Label the demand curve AD_0, the supply curve AS_0, and the output level Q_f. Label the equilibrium point a.

Figure 3

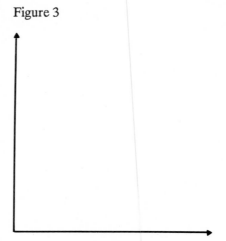

a.   Illustrate the resulting shift caused by a reduction in the discount rate. Label the new curve with a subscript 1. Label the new equilibrium point b.

b.   In the long run workers will react to the illusion created by the situation in "a" above. Illustrate by a shift of the appropriate curve to a new equilibrium point c. Label the curve you have shifted with a subscript 1. What is the level of real output after the adjustment?

c.   What kind of cycle have you illustrated?

Problem 4

Using the graph provided, illustrate an economy with Aggregate Demand and Aggregate Supply analysis. The economy is operating at full employment with the normal amount of frictional unemployment.

Label the original demand curve AD_0, the original supply curve AS_0, the initial equilibrium point a, and the initial level of output Q_f.

Figure 4

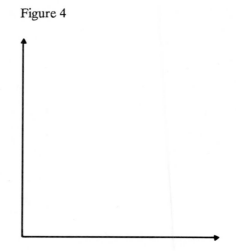

a.   Due to lax enforcement of antitrust laws and intense merger activity there is a major macroeconomic activity. Illustrate this shift on your graph by labeling the new curve with a subscript 1. Label the new equilibrium point b, and the new level of output Q_1.

b.   The leader of the country is fearful of the situation described above. She decides to pressure the central bank into lowering the reserve requirement. Illustrate the likely result of this policy on your graph. Label your new curve with a subscript 1. Label the new equilibrium point c. What is the level of real output?

c.   The situation described above is what kind inflation?

202

ANSWERS

Matching Key Terms and Concepts

Answer	Reference
1. e	p. 307
2. j	p. 306
3. c	p. 317
4. b	p. 312
5. h	p. 315
6. f	p. 319
7. g	p. 314
8. i	p. 310
9. d	p. 310
10. a	p. 314

Chapter Review (fill-in Questions)

1. interest rates, investment
2. resources, technology
3. expectations, regulations
4. money (inflation) illusion, wage costs
5. unemployment, rise
6. nominal wages, counterclockwise
7. inflation, unemployment
8. expansionary, clockwise
9. demand-side, supply-side
10. demand-side inflationary, supply-side inflationary

Standard Multiple Choice

Answer	Reference
1. e	p. 314
2. a	p. 314
3. b	p. 310
4. d	p. 316-318
5. d	p. 314
6. c	p. 306
7. c	p. 306
8. b	p. 309
9. c	p. 317
10. e	p. 314
11. c	p. 320
12. a	p. 320

True/False Questions

Answer	Reference
1. F	p. 316
2. T	p. 310
3. F	p. 314
4. F	p. 314
5. F	p. 310
6. T	p. 314
7. T	p. 312
8. T	p. 314
9. F	p. 312
10. T	p. 313

Unlimited Multiple Choice

Answer	Reference
1. bc	p. 312
2. abcd	p. 315
3. a	p. 314
4. ad	p. 317
5. bc	p. 319

Problem 1
Reference pp. 307-316

a. T
b. T
c. F
d. T
e. F
f. T
g. T
h. F
i. T
j. T
k. F
l. F

Problem 2
Reference pp. 307-316

a. T
b. T
c. F
d. T
e. F
f. T
g. F
h. F
i. T
j. F
k. T
l. T
m. T
n. T
o. T
p. F
q. F
r. T

Problem 3
Reference pp. 316-317

a.   See Figure 5

Figure 5

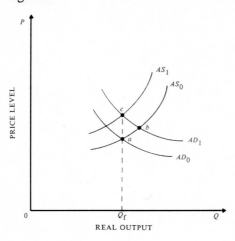

b.   See Figure 5, Q_f

c.   Demand-side inflation

Problem 4
Reference pp. 318-320

a.   See Figure 6

Figure 6

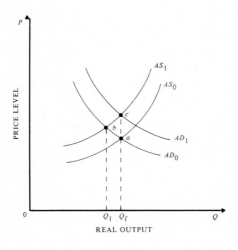

b.   See Figure 6, Q_f

c.   Supply-side inflation

204

CHAPTER SEVENTEEN
THE POLICYMAKER'S DILEMMA

CHAPTER OBJECTIVES

After you have read and studied this chapter you should be able to describe alternative interpretations of the Phillips curve hypothesis that inflation and unemployment are inversely related; discuss possible reasons for the stagflation of the 1970s; evaluate various policies to fight inflation and stagflation, including 'supply-side' policies, discuss the natural real rate of interest, hypothesis, and the Keynes and Fisher effects; and discuss New Classical Macroeconomic theories such as competitive markets, efficient markets, and rational expectations.

CHAPTER REVIEW: KEY POINTS

1. The Phillips curve depicts a trade-off for policymakers between unemployment and inflation. Lower unemployment rates presumably might be purchased through higher inflation, or vice versa; it is up to policymakers to choose the least harmful mix of evils. The Phillips curve appeared to be relatively stable through the 1960s, but it shifted sharply in the 1970s and early 1980s so that much higher rates of unemployment appeared necessary to dampen inflationary pressures. The reasons for the instability of the Phillips curve are the subject of a continuing debate within the economics profession.

2. The natural rate theory of the instability in the Phillips trade-off focuses on worker expectations of inflation. As labor begins to anticipate inflation, greater increases in wages are required for a given level of real output. Thus, accelerating inflation is required if policymakers desire to hold unemployment below its "natural rate," but even this policy will not work forever. Natural rate theory suggests that there is no long run tradeoff between unemployment and inflation; the long run Phillips curve is vertical at the natural rate of unemployment.

3. Modern Keynesian analysis suggests that several factors in addition to inflationary expectations can cause stagflation and instability in the Phillips curve. A critical assumption is that wages and prices are "sticky", especially in a downward direction. Unexpected shocks to the supply side, rapid compositional changes in demand or output, changes in labor institutions that generate disincentives for work, and changes in public regulatory policies all are capable of shifting the Phillips curve. The Keynesian structuralist approach emphasizes production "bottlenecks" as foundations for the Phillips curve.

4. If interest rate targets or unemployment rate objectives are set below their "natural rates," expansionary policies may actually cause nominal interest rates to rise, not fall. Natural-rate theorists believe that only temporary reductions in interest rates or unemployment can be obtained through expansionary policies, and even in the short run, only by "fooling" lenders or workers.

5. The Keynes effect predicts that monetary growth will decrease interest rates, and vice versa. The Fisher effect is the adjustment of nominal interest rates when transactors' inflationary expectations change.

6. The new classical macroeconomics is based on the model of perfect competition, or efficient markets, which suggests that even in the short run, macropolicy only works only if either (a) policy changes are so erratic that the public cannot predict them, or (b) when the economy is operating inefficiently--a situation that never occurs.

7. The theory of rational expectations suggests that people eventually figure out how a given change in policy affects the economy and learn to predict how policymakers react to swings in economic activity. Thereafter, people will focus on what policymakers are doing and make adjustments that prevent the policies from accomplishing their objectives.

MATCHING KEY TERMS AND CONCEPTS

___ 1. rational expectations theory

a. The percentage annual monetary premium paid for borrowing.

___ 2. Keynes effect

b. Trade-offs between inflation and unemployment.

___ 3. demand-side stagflation

c. People learn to anticipate the results of policies

___ 4. Keynesian 'shock' and 'structuralist' hypotheses

d. Deviations from normal frictional unemployment are caused by macropolicy.

___ 5. nominal interest rate

e. Monetary interest adjusted for inflation.

___ 6. Fisher effect

f. Expanding the money supply unexpectedly initially causes nominal interest rates to fall.

___ 7. real interest rate

g. Contracting the money supply unexpectedly ultimately causes the nominal interest rate to fall.

___ 8. natural rate theory

h. Workers adjust to anticipated inflation by reducing labor supplies.

___ 9. Phillips curves

i. Falling Aggregate Supply boosts prices and unemployment.

___ 10. supply-side stagflation

j. Explains Phillips curves by labor market "bottlenecks" and changing intensities of shocks to our economy.

CHAPTER REVIEW (FILL-IN QUESTIONS)

1-2. Between the 1960s and 1970s many economists believed that a reasonably _____ inverse relationship existed between unemployment and inflation. This idea is known as the _____ curve tradeoff. Phillips curves are inverse relationships between unemployment and inflation and the _____ curve indicates a positive relation between the level of output (and thus employment) and the price level; thus, the two curves _____ each other.

3-6. One Keynesian explanation for the Phillips curve suggests that as _____ is approached, it becomes increasingly costly to produce added output because labor market _____ become increasingly severe. The monetarist explanation for shifts of the Phillips relation focuses on rising _____ expectations of workers and their adjustments that shift Aggregate Supply to the _____. Modern Keynesian explanations emphasize the _____, especially downwards, of wages and prices. Shocks are continually bombarding the economy causing changes in demand for various products. In sectors where demands increase, _____ tend to rise. Where demand declines, workers are reluctant to accept wage _____, so firms commonly cut their production costs through layoffs and _____ in production.

7-8. Natural rate theory assumes that lenders and borrowers focus on the _____, which is the _____ after adjusting for inflation. In equation form, loan contracts will be struck so that _____, in anticipation of realizing "purchasing power paid" for the use of borrowed money can be approximated with the formula _____.

9-10._____ suggests that economic profits are almost purely the result of luck. A related theory, _____, suggests that people will learn to anticipate any predictable consequence of policy, so that overly expansionary policies will result in high rates of _____ and _____, but nothing else. Instantaneous adjustments eliminate all other effects.

STANDARD MULTIPLE CHOICE

THERE IS ONE BEST ANSWER FOR EACH QUESTION.

___ 1. The Phillips curve posits a tradeoff between:
   a. economic stability and growth.
   b. consumption today vs. tomorrow.
   c. unemployment and inflation.
   d. low interest rates and low taxes.
   e. gasoline service stations and screwdrivers.

___ 2. Second phases of demand-pull inflationary cycles entail:
   a. cost-push inflation.
   b. substantial layoffs of workers.
   c. rising unemployment.
   d. accelerating inflation.
   e. All of the above.

___ 3. The Phillips Curve:
   a. shifted inward during the 1970s.
   b. has been very stable.
   c. shows the tradeoff between balanced budgets and inflation.
   d. demonstrates stable economic growth.
   e. None of these.

___ 4. According to "natural rate" theory, macropolicy can't influence long-run rates of:
   a. inflation and unemployment.
   b. real interest and unemployment.
   c. nominal economic growth.
   d. financial capital accumulation.
   e. All of the above.

___ 5. Hikes in nominal interest rates when people expect higher inflation are examples of the:
   a. Keynes effect.
   b. Fisher effect.
   c. real wealth effect.
   d. Friedman effect.
   e. Kuznets effect.

___ 6. In broad terms, natural rate theory assumes:
   a. balanced budgets at full employment.
   b. stable unemployment/inflation tradeoffs.
   c. inflationary biases in healthy economies.
   d. prices rise more easily than they decline.
   e. independence between monetary and "real" variables.

___ 7. The idea of combatting inflation by shrinking Aggregate Demand does NOT involve which of the following theories:
   a. recessions moderate labor's inflationary expectations.
   b. recessions foster inflation that improves political incumbents' reelection prospects.
   c. periods of slack demand aid firms in eliminating 'deadwood'.
   d. fear of stimulates labor productivity.
   e. recessions dampen the inflationary expectations of workers, investors, business firms, and consumers.

___ 8. The "natural rate" theory of the Phillips curve suggests that expansionary macroeconomic policy may temporarily reduce unemployment with only minor inflation because:
   a. workers are temporarily fooled by higher money wage offers.
   b. workers find long-term employment easier during business booms.
   c. policymakers are fooled by businessmen into expanding Aggregate Demand.
   d. business decisionmakers are fooled by workers who are lazier than they represent themselves to be.
   e. everyone is happier to work when recessions end.

___ 9. Many modern Keynesians suggest that, for the most part, the stagflation of the 1970s was caused by:
   a. workers ceasing to be fooled by inflation.
   b. policymakers seeing past the inflation illusion of the 1960s.
   c. business expectations being confronted by reality.
   d. such shocks to the economy as OPEC price hikes and the souring of the Russian Wheat Deal.
   e. All of the above.

___10. Overly expansionary monetary and fiscal policies tend to cause:
   a. unemployment to fall temporarily.
   b. rising expectations of inflation.
   c. nominal interest to rise in the long run.
   d. no long-term effect on employment.
   e. All of the above.

___11. The "supply-side" policies adopted in the early 1980s to counter inflation and stimulate economic growth did not include selective:
   a. accelerated depreciation allowances.
   b. investment tax credits.
   c. cuts in corporate income taxes.
   d. tax deductions for savers.
   e. hikes in the tax rate of wage earners.

___12. The explanation of Phillips curves as consequences of labor and product market "bottlenecks" is at the core of the:
   a. modern monetarist approach.
   b. "natural rate" approach.
   c. Keynesian "composition-shift" approach.
   d. Keynesian 'structuralist' approach.
   e. classical approach.

TRUE/FALSE QUESTIONS

___ 1. Some firms use cost-plus pricing strategies so that rising costs are quickly reflected in higher prices.

___ 2. High unemployment generates political pressures for full employment policies that raise Aggregate Supply.

___ 3. The stagflation phase of demand-side inflation resembles the initial phase of supply-side inflation.

___ 4. In the early 1960s, Keynesian policy prescriptions seemed to steer the economy along a prosperous path.

___ 5. External economic shocks may cause the Aggregate Supply to shift to the right, worsening the tradeoff between unemployment and inflation.

___ 6. Natural rate theorists believe that long run Phillips curves are vertical at the natural rate of unemployment.

___ 7. Classical theory suggests that policymakers are faced with a relatively stable Phillips curve tradeoff.

___ 8. Expansionary fiscal policy reduces frictional unemployment because workers are afraid to change jobs.

___ 9. The Phillips curve for the United States shifted to the left during the 1970s.

___10. When Aggregate Demand shifts to the left, the Phillips curve shifts to the left.

___11. Aggregate Supply shifts cause Phillips curve shifts.

___12. As workers anticipate higher inflation the short- run Phillips relation shifts outward (up and to the right).

___13. The particular interest rate paid by a borrower to a lender reflects default risk, length of time to maturity of the note or bond, the anticipated rate of inflation, and legal constraints.

___14. The Fisher effect refers to the change in nominal interest rates as borrowers and lenders compensate for expected inflation.

___15. Advocates of natural rate theory tend to favor the replacement of rules with discretionary policy making.

UNLIMITED MULTIPLE CHOICE

WARNING: EACH QUESTION HAS FROM ZERO TO FOUR RIGHT ANSWERS.

___1. According to the natural rate hypothesis:
   a. attempts to drive unemployment and real interest rates permanently below their natural rates are futile.
   b. the government can induce a permanent increase in the employment rate by pursuing demand-management policies.
   c. frictional unemployment can only be reduced temporarily.
   d. each Phillips curve exists only for a particular expected rate of inflation.

___2. Real interest rates are the annual percentage:
   a. monetary premiums paid to use money.
   b. of real purchasing power paid to a lender by a borrower for the use of money.
   c. of extra goods that can be enjoyed if consumption is deferred.
   d. premiums necessary to induce savers to defer gratification.

___3. According to the rational expectations branch of monetarism:
   a. government can fool the public continually.
   b. policy goals can be predictably achieved in neither the short run nor the long run.
   c. nominal interest rates adjust immediately to expected inflation, if the public knows about past countercyclical policies.
   d. some policy goals might be achievable in the short run only if macroeconomic policies are disguised from the public.

___4. Markets will operate efficiently if there is:
   a. substantial information about profit making opportunities.
   b. vigorous competition among sellers for profit making opportunities.
   c. federal control of wages and prices.
   d. business collusion to fix prices.

___5. According to natural rate theory, if the FED pursues an expansionary monetary policy by buying bonds:
   a. the nominal rate of interest will be reduced permanently.
   b. the initial decline in the interest rate is called the Fisher effect.
   c. the supply of loanable funds initially decreases, causing the nominal interest rate to increase.
   d. despite an initial increase in the real rate of interest, it will return to its natural rate.

PROBLEMS

PROBLEM 1

Interpret information from the figure below to answer the following True/False questions as a "Natural Rate" theorist would.

Figure 1

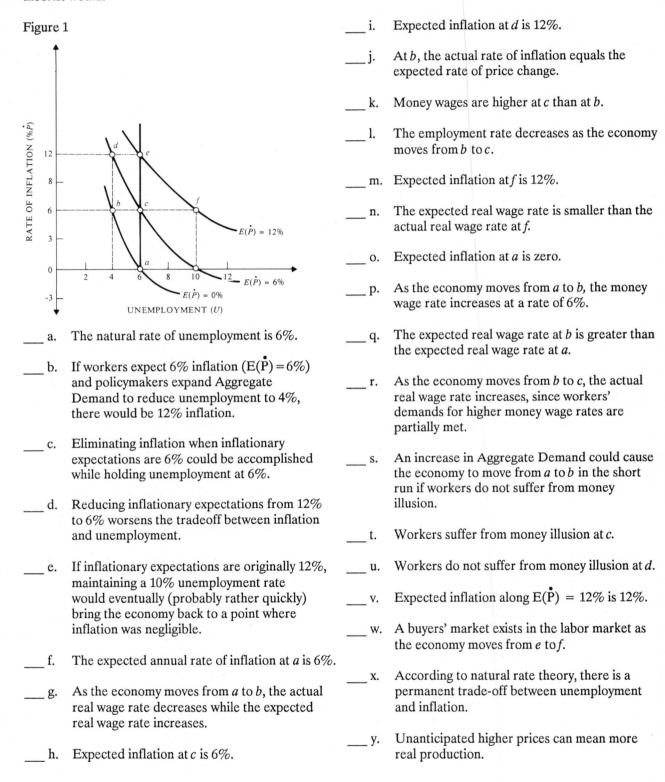

___ a. The natural rate of unemployment is 6%.

___ b. If workers expect 6% inflation $(E(\dot{P}) = 6\%)$ and policymakers expand Aggregate Demand to reduce unemployment to 4%, there would be 12% inflation.

___ c. Eliminating inflation when inflationary expectations are 6% could be accomplished while holding unemployment at 6%.

___ d. Reducing inflationary expectations from 12% to 6% worsens the tradeoff between inflation and unemployment.

___ e. If inflationary expectations are originally 12%, maintaining a 10% unemployment rate would eventually (probably rather quickly) bring the economy back to a point where inflation was negligible.

___ f. The expected annual rate of inflation at a is 6%.

___ g. As the economy moves from a to b, the actual real wage rate decreases while the expected real wage rate increases.

___ h. Expected inflation at c is 6%.

___ i. Expected inflation at d is 12%.

___ j. At b, the actual rate of inflation equals the expected rate of price change.

___ k. Money wages are higher at c than at b.

___ l. The employment rate decreases as the economy moves from b to c.

___ m. Expected inflation at f is 12%.

___ n. The expected real wage rate is smaller than the actual real wage rate at f.

___ o. Expected inflation at a is zero.

___ p. As the economy moves from a to b, the money wage rate increases at a rate of 6%.

___ q. The expected real wage rate at b is greater than the expected real wage rate at a.

___ r. As the economy moves from b to c, the actual real wage rate increases, since workers' demands for higher money wage rates are partially met.

___ s. An increase in Aggregate Demand could cause the economy to move from a to b in the short run if workers do not suffer from money illusion.

___ t. Workers suffer from money illusion at c.

___ u. Workers do not suffer from money illusion at d.

___ v. Expected inflation along $E(\dot{P}) = 12\%$ is 12%.

___ w. A buyers' market exists in the labor market as the economy moves from e to f.

___ x. According to natural rate theory, there is a permanent trade-off between unemployment and inflation.

___ y. Unanticipated higher prices can mean more real production.

PROBLEM 2

You are the chief economic advisor to the president. She asks you for your policy prescription for the current economic climate which features high unemployment and high price inflation (stagflation). You believe in the Keynesian structuralist approach.

a. Illustrate this using Aggregate Demand and Aggregate Supply analysis in panel A of Figure 2. Label your initial curves with a subscript 1.

b. Illustrate, by movements of the curves in panel A and corresponding shifts of the Phillips curves in panel B, what the impact of your program would be. Label your original Phillips curve that corresponds to your initial Aggregate Demand-Aggregate Supply equilibrium PC_1. Label each succeeding curve AS_2, AS_3, PC_2, PC_3.

c. What are some of your proposals to attain this goal? _____
_____
_____

Figure 2

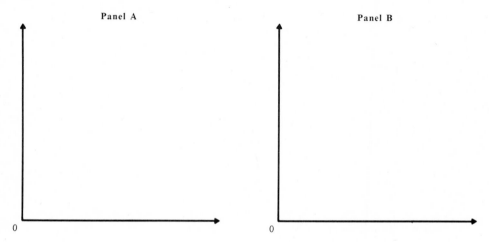

ANSWERS

Matching Key Terms and Concepts

Answer	Reference
1. c	p. 346
2. f	p. 342
3. h	p. 338
4. j	p. 336
5. a	p. 342
6. g	p. 343
7. e	p. 342
8. d	p. 334
9. b	p. 329
10. i	p. 339

Chapter Review (fill-in Questions)

1. stable, Phillips
2. Aggregate Supply, mirror
3. full employment, bottlenecks
4. inflationary, left
5. stickiness, prices and wages
6. cuts, cutbacks
7. real rate of interest, nominal rate of interest
8. $i = r_d + E(\dot{P})$, $r = i - \dot{P}$
9. efficient, rational expectations
10. interest, inflation

Standard Multiple Choice

Answer	Reference
1. c	p. 329
2. e	p. 333
3. e	p. 329
4. b	p. 334, 341
5. b	p. 342
6. e	p. 334
7. b	p. 336
8. a	p. 333
9. d	p. 338
10. e	p. 334, 341
11. e	p. 339
12. d	p. 336

True/false Questions

Answer	Reference
1. T	p. 347
2. F	p. 332
3. T	p. 333
4. T	p. 331
5. F	p. 336
6. T	p. 334
7. F	p. 331
8. F	p. 333
9. F	p. 331
10. F	p. 331
11. T	p. 331
12. T	p. 334
13. T	p. 342
14. T	p. 343
15. F	p. 336

Unlimited Multiple Choice

Answer	Reference
1. acd	p. 334
2. bcd	p. 342
3. bcd	p. 346
4. ab	p. 346
5. none	p. 343

Problem 1
Reference p. 332-343

a. T
b. T
c. F
d. F
e. T
f. F
g. T
h. T
i. F
j. F
k. T
l. T
m. T
n. T
o. T
p. F
q. T
r. T
s. F
t. F
u. F
v. T
w. T
x. F
y. T

Problem 2
Reference p. 337-339

a. See Figure 3.

Figure 3

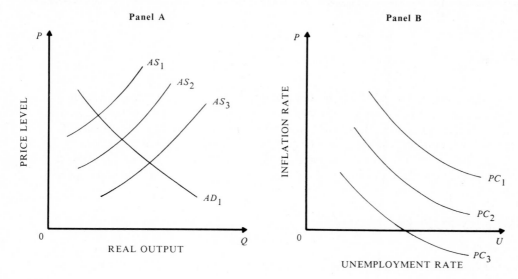

b. See Figure 3 panel A and B.

c. Any proposals that reduce rigidity and bottlenecks
in the economy, will help solve stagflation
problems by shifting the Phillips curve to the left
and the Aggregate Supply curve to the right.
Most of the policies described in the textbook
are mentioned under Supply- side economics,
but some programs of the 1970s, particularly job
training, were designed to increase Aggregate
Supply.

CHAPTER EIGHTEEN
LIMITATIONS OF STABILIZATION POLICY

CHAPTER OBJECTIVES

After you have read and studied this chapter you should be able to explain the difficulties for macroeconomic policymaking posed by such factors as missed timing, improper dosages of stimulation or contraction, and how private adjustments may frustrate even well intended discretionary policymaking; discuss the ways that policymaking may be misused to introduce "political" business cycles and a long-term trend for growth in government relative to the private sector; discuss incomes policies and their possible effects on the economy; and discuss nation economic planning and national industrial policy, and how they apply to the United States.

CHAPTER REVIEW: KEY POINTS

1. Macroeconomic policymaking is at least as much art as it is a science. A multitude of problems preclude perfect analysis and policy.

2. A recognition lag occurs because it takes time to get even a modestly accurate picture of changes in the state of the economy. An administrative (implementation) lag exists because it takes a while to get the tax and monetary machinery in gear even when policymakers' plans are made. An impact lag confounds the proper timing of policy; the economy budges only stubbornly to the prods of the policymakers' tools. These lags, which may be long and variable, may cause discretionary policy to be more destabilizing than stabilizing.

3. Lack of precise knowledge about recessionary gaps, inflationary gaps, and GNP gaps, as well as uncertainty about multipliers and velocity, mean that estimating the correct doses of monetary and fiscal medicine is extremely difficult.

4. Some modern Keynesians challenge the long-term effectiveness of monetary policy, arguing that adjustments in financial technologies will ultimately insulate financial institutions and make monetary tools inoperative.

5. Incumbents' prospects for return to office improve as per capita disposable income grows immediately prior to elections. There is some evidence that policymakers try to manipulate Aggregate Demand to enhance their positions in the eyes of voters, which induces political business cycles.

6. Some critics of Keynesian fiscal policies also suggest that the government grows relative to the private sector when policymakers increase spending and cut taxes during downturns. Policymakers neither cut spending nor restore taxes, however, during periods of prosperity or inflation.

7. Intentional recessions can decompress accumulated inflationary pressures and inflationary expectations. However, recessions tend to be very hard on political incumbents, so many politicians favor incomes policies of various sorts.

8. Incomes policies (mandatory wage-price freezes or controls, voluntary guidelines, or "jawboning") muzzle the effectiveness of the price system, creating shortages and widespread misallocations of resources.

9. The Humphrey-Hawkins Full Employment and Balanced Growth Act of 1978 makes government the "employer of last resort" and requires that the administration submit continuous five-year plans for achieving various macroeconomic objectives. It also encourages coordination of government macroeconomic policies.

10. National industrial policy involves government policies designed to support targeted industries. Proponents argue that a coherent industrial policy is needed to increase economic growth, enhance U.S. industrial competitiveness and counteract industrial policies of foreign governments. Opponents maintain that free markets will provide the appropriate investment in various industries and that an industrial policy will misallocate resources to politically powerful, heavily unionized industries.

MATCHING KEY TERMS AND CONCEPTS

___ 1. Incomes Policies

    a. Caused by underestimation of multipliers or overestimation of the economy's capacity.

___ 2. National Industrial Policy

    b. Financial institutions learn to counteract monetary policies.

___ 3. Political business cycles

    c. The period between adoption and effect of a change in policy.

___ 4. Wage and price freezes

    d. Most stringent form of incomes policy.

___ 5. Overdose of expansionary policy

    e. Range from moral suasion to freezes.

___ 6. Underdoses of contrationary policy

    f. The period between an event and the availability of information about it.

___ 7. Recognition lag

    g. The money supply grows rapidly in years divisible by 4.

___ 8. Administration lag

    h. Caused by overestimating multipliers or the economy's capacity.

___ 9. Impact lag

    i. The time required to alter the course of policy.

___ 10. Financial insulation effect

    j. Government intervention applied to target industries.

CHAPTER REVIEW (FILL-IN QUESTIONS)

1-5. Even well-intentioned policymakers suffer from a _____ lag because it takes time and resources to acquire sufficient _____ about the state of the economy to make judgments about the proper course of policy. Once such judgments are made, there is a(n) _____ lag because it takes time for _____ policymakers to tilt open market directions properly, and even more time for _____ policymakers to change _____ laws or alter appropriations for government outlays. Then, from the time policy is changed, the time it takes for policy to affect economic activity results in a(n) _____ lag. The _____ lag is usually longer for fiscal policy than monetary policy, while the _____ lag is longer for monetary policy if changes in _____ policies are the tools used by fiscal policymakers.

6. "Tight money policies may teach financial institutions new ways to conserve on their holdings of reserves. Such changes in financial technology are known as _____, and make repeatedly used monetary policies _____ or useless in their effects on macroeconomic activity.

7-8. Reluctance in using recessions to combat inflation has channeled many political decisionmakers into experiments with _____ policies. Wage-price curbs have ranged from _____, which typically involves _____ by the president, to mandatory _____.

9. Opponents point to the wage-price controls of _____ to show that incomes policies do not work. They argue that controls can create expectations that prices will _____ when controls are lifted.

10. Many policymakers interpreted the stagflation of the 1970s as evidence of structural change in the U.S. economy. This belief has led to the recommendation that a _____ _____ _____ should be adopted. This policy would _____ specific industries where government intervention should be used.

STANDARD MULTIPLE CHOICE

THERE IS ONE BEST ANSWER FOR EACH QUESTION.

___ 1. Which of the following laws deals with full-employment?
a. Robinson-Patman Act.
b. Wheeler-Lea Act.
c. Clayton Act.
d. Sherman Antitrust Act.
e. Humphrey-Hawkins Act.

___ 2. Which lag is longer for fiscal policy than for monetary policy?
a. discretionary lag.
b. recognition lag.
c. administration lag.
d. dosage lag.
e. impact lag.

___ 3. In the 1960s and 1970s:
a. monetary growth was the greatest just before presidential elections.
b. budgetary surpluses emerged after election years.
c. total government spending fell relative to GNP.
d. the U.S. experienced consistent and extraordinary growth.
e. none of these.

___ 4. Incomes policies disturb the price system and cause:
a. efficient usage of resources.
b. surpluses.
c. politicians' jawbones to swell.
d. inflation upon their implementation.
e. shortages and misallocation of resources.

5. Mandatory price controls are an example of:
a. monetary policy.
b. fiscal policy.
c. automatic stabilizers.
d. tax policy.
e. incomes policies.

___ 6. Some neo-Keynesians believe that financial technologies change in response to changes in:
a. the size of the workforce.
b. monetary policy.
c. the capital stock.
d. fiscal policy.
e. All of these.

___ 7. Assume OPEC hikes the price of oil, and policymakers attempt to offset the resulting tendency for the economy to slide into a recession. Which of the following is NOT a likely consequence of these events?
   a. The "real" price OPEC gets for oil will be less than it expects.
   b. The "real" wages of labor will fall.
   c. "Real" national income will fall because of the OPEC hike.
   d. Our "real" national income will fall solely because of overly expansionary policies.
   e. The price level will rise.

___ 8. Wage and price controls are intended to:
   a. dampen inflationary expectations.
   b. shift the economy's supply curve to the left.
   c. shift the economy's demand curve to the right.
   d. reduce corporate profits.
   e. increase corporate profits.

___ 9. Price ceilings are likely to result in:
   a. shortages.
   b. black markets.
   c. queuing.
   d. rationing by favoritism.
   e. all of the above.

___ 10. Incumbent policymakers that manipulate macroeconomic policies to obtain reelection may cause:
   a. political business cycles.
   b. stagflation.
   c. excessive unemployment.
   d. countercyclical cycles.
   e. tax rates to rise just before election.

___ 11. Government support of targeted industries is known as:
   a. macro planning.
   b. financial insulation.
   c. national industrial policy.
   c. national industrial policy.
   d. micro planning.
   e. government organization.

___ 12. Critics of discretionary monetary and fiscal policy point to:
   a. political manipulation of the business cycle.
   b. failures to raise taxes and cut spending during inflation.
   c. problems with lags and incorrect doses.
   d. these policies reliance on "fooling" people.
   e. all of these.

TRUE/FALSE QUESTIONS

___ 1. The recognition lag occurs because it is generally difficult for monetary and fiscal policymakers to determine quickly how much of which policies to use in steering our sluggish economy along a proper course.

___ 2. Since changes in monetary policy can be implemented quickly through the FED's Open Market Committee, administration lags are not much of a problem for monetary policymaking.

___ 3. Wage and price controls have a long history of considerable success at reducing inflation.

___ 4. The impact lag of monetary policy is comparatively regular and short.

___ 5. Critics contend that wage and price controls may actually increase inflationary expectations.

___ 6. The longer that wage and price controls are in force the more difficult it is for economic transactors to discern real from artificial price signals .

___ 7. Japan's Industrial Policy is responsible for the decline of the U.S. Steel industry.

___ 8. The Federal Funds Market provides banks with the opportunity to lend or to borrow millions of dollars for one or two days at comparatively low interest rates.

___ 9. Various studies indicate that voters tend to re-elect incumbents more often the faster disposable income grows during the year immediately preceding elections.

___ 10. Macroeconomic policy which is effective in sustaining high employment and low inflation rates may mitigate the need for a national industrial policy.

UNLIMITED MULTIPLE CHOICE

THERE ARE FOUR TO ZERO ANSWERS FOR EACH QUESTION.

___ 1. It may be difficult to design and to implement appropriate countercyclical policies:
   a. because of the timing problems inherent in both monetary and fiscal policies.
   b. because adjustments made by private individuals and firms to certain monetary and fiscal policies can eliminate the desired effects of the countercyclical measures.
   c. because policymakers do not possess current or perfect information about the condition of the economy.
   d. because politicians sometimes base policy on the effects that specific countercyclical measures might have on their prospects for re-election.

___ 2. Mandatory wage and price controls:
   a. have typically been associated with wartime efforts.
   b. were imposed by President Nixon in August of 1971.
   c. are imposed to mitigate recessionary pressures which develop automatically in the economy.
   d. seldom distort relative prices.

___ 3. Wage and price guideposts and guidelines:
   a. assume that rates of price increases can parallel increases in labor productivity without causing upward pressure on wage rates.
   b. have traditionally been mandatory.
   c. are typically tied to a socially accepted level of unemployment.
   d. are very effective in relieving inflationary pressures.

___ 4. Proponents of incomes policies argue that controls:
   a. effectively reduce deflationary expectations.
   b. make the public more aware of the problems of inflation.
   c. distort relative price signals and misallocate resources.
   d. can reconcile the goals of monopolistic industries with the goals of society.

___ 5. The Humphrey-Hawkins Act of 1978:
   a. explicitly identifies several economic priorities and objectives.
   b. directs the President to numerically specify certain goals.
   c. does nothing to improve the coordination and development of economic policy between the President, the Congress, and the Federal Reserve System.
   d. requires the Federal Reserve Board to report its activities to the Congress daily.

PROBLEM 1

Answer the True/False questions below based on the following scenario:

After moderate sales during the Christmas season of 1990, business pessimism leads to a decline in production in the first part of 1991. Consumers' expectations mirror business' hesitation, and outlays on durable goods are delayed or forgotten. First quarter statistics compiled in mid April indicate that a contraction is taking place. Upon receiving the news, the FED undertakes actions to boost the money supply. In Congress rumors begin to circulate about a possible tax cut to deal with the downturn in business activity.

___ a.   The time between January 1991 and mid April 1991 is known as a recognition lag.

___ b.   If the FED implements an expansion of the money supply by mid May, the administrative lag (of monetary policy) is approximately one month.

___ c.   The impact lag will most likely be longer for a tax cut than for open market operations which expand the money supply.

___ d.   The administrative lag will most likely be longer for monetary policy as compared to fiscal policy.

___ e.   The recognition lag is longer for fiscal policy than for monetary policy.

___ f.   Government purchases to combat declining Aggregate Demand will have a shorter administrative lag than lowering the discount rate.

___ g.   The impact lag of open market purchases will be of short duration because money expansion is almost instantaneous.

___ h.   If a tax cut is finally passed in November of 1991 and implemented in 1992, there is a chance that the tax cut will help to overheat the economy (cause inflation).

___ i.   The impact lag of expansionary monetary policy will increase if banks are reluctant to loan out additionally funds acquired through the sale of government securities to the FED.

___ j.   The recognition lag could be decreased by compiling business statistics at intervals of 1 month as opposed to each quarter.

ANSWERS

Matching Key Terms and Concepts

Answer	Reference
1. e	p. 364
2. j	p. 367
3. g	p. 361
4. d	p. 365
5. a	p. 358
6. h	p. 358
7. f	p. 355
8. i	p. 355
9. c	p. 355
10. b	p. 358

True/false Questions

Answer	Reference
1. T	p. 355
2. T	p. 356
3. F	p. 365
4. F	p. 357
5. T	p. 366
6. T	p. 365
7. F	p. 368
8. T	p. 358
9. T	p. 361
10. T	p. 370

Chapter Review (fill-in Questions)

1. recognition, information
2. administration, monetary
3. fiscal, tax
4. impact, administration
5. impact, tax
6. finaicial insulation, unpredictable
7. incomes, moral suasion
8. jawboning, wage/price freezes
9. 1971-73, rise more rapidly
10. national industrial policy, target

Unlimited Multiple Choice

Answer	Reference
1. abcd	p. 355
2. ab	p. 365
3. none	p. 365
4. bd	p. 365
5. ab	p. 367

Problem
Reference pp. 355-358

a. T
b. T
c. F
d. F
e. F
f. F
g. F
h. T
i. T
j. T

Standard Multiple Choice

Answer	Reference
1. e	p. 367
2. c	p. 357
3. a	p. 362
4. e	p. 365
5. e	p. 364
6. b	p. 358
7. d	p. 357
8. a	p. 364
9. e	p. 365
10. a	p. 361
11. c	p. 367
12. e	p. 357

CHAPTER NINETEEN
ECONOMIC GROWTH AND DEVELOPMENT

CHAPTER OBJECTIVES

After you have read and studied this chapter, you should be able to describe the processes of economic growth and development; discuss the special hurdles to development faced in poor countries; and discuss the pros and cons of the "trap of underdevelopment" argument.

CHAPTER REVIEW: KEY POINTS

1. Economic growth refers to quantitative changes in the capacity to produce goods and services in a country. It occurs through expanding capital or labor resources, discoveries of new sources of raw materials, or development of more productive technologies. Economic development refers to improving the qualitative aspects of economic growth, including changes in the quality of life.

2. The Rule of 72 is a rule of thumb for estimating how long it takes for a variable to double in value given some percentage growth rate. Simply divide 72 by the growth rate. For example, if growth in GNP is occurring at 6 percent per year, GNP will double in approximately 12 years (72/6 = 12).

3. Diminishing returns because of the fixity of land cause output to grow more slowly, even if labor and capital increase in fixed proportions.

4. Population S curves are theories of the growth paths of populations as they approach their biological limits. Reverend Thomas Malthus and other nineteenth-century economists theorized that equilibrium is attained only when bare subsistence is common to all.

5. Population growth tends to slow as a country develops. The least developed countries of the world tend to have the highest rates of population growth.

6. Capital formation requires high saving rates. If voluntary saving is used to finance development, greater incomes, higher interest rates paid to savers, and (perhaps) less equal income distributions will lead to higher rates of investment. Involuntary saving may be used to free investment resources through confiscation, taxation, or inflation.

7. Capital widening occurs when the capital stock and labor force grow at the same rates. Capital deepening requires the capital stock to grow faster than the labor force.

8. Technological advances occur when the same amounts of resources acquire greater productive capacity.

9. Rapid development requires a strong social infrastructure--education, communications, transportation, and other networks that facilitate production.

MATCHING KEY TERMS AND CONCEPTS

SET I

___ 1.	"*S*" curve	a.	According to Karl Marx, follows the 'dictatorship of the proletariat' and the 'withering away of the state'.
___ 2.	involuntary saving	b.	A population growth path.
___ 3.	Rule of "72"	c.	Expansion of productive capacity.
___ 4.	economic development	d.	Individual choice between present and future consumption.
___ 5.	economic growth	e.	Investment is proportionally greater than population growth.
___ 6.	communism	f.	A quick way of estimating "doubling" times.
___ 7.	capital deepening	g.	Qualitative expansion.
___ 8.	capital to labor ratio (K/L)	h.	Associated with underdevelopment.
___ 9.	high birth rates	i.	Accomplished by taxes or inflation.
___10.	voluntary saving	j.	A crucial determinant of labor productivity.

SET II

___ 1.	technological advance	a.	Percentage of a population in the work force.
___ 2.	infrastructure	b.	A stage in Rostow's growth theory.
___ 3.	"Trap of underdevelopment"	c.	Net investment and population growth are proportional.
___ 4.	high voluntary saving rate	d.	A factor temporarily expanding LFPRs.
___ 5.	Malthusian equilibrium	e.	High tax rates hinder Aggregate Supply and economic growth.
___ 6.	"takeoff"	f.	Inhibits Keynesian Aggregate Spending but facilitates economic growth.
___ 7.	Labor Force Participation Rate (LFPR)	g.	The edge of starvation.
___ 8.	Laffer curve	h.	Producing more from given resources.
___ 9.	capital widening	i.	Low income prevents rapid capital accumulation.
___10.	low birth rates	j.	An integral part of economic development.

CHAPTER REVIEW (FILL-IN QUESTIONS)

1-5. Economic _____ occurs when an economy's capacity expands; economic _____ entails qualitative improvements in economic conditions. The time required for doubling any variable is approximated through calculations using the _____. Dividing the percentage annual change in a variable into _____ yields the number of years required for the variable to double its value. Economic growth is the long-run process of expanding the limits to _____. Increasing the amounts of _____ available for production is one source of growth. Per capita income tends to rise when the workforce increases through rising _____ rates, although less than proportionally because of declining _____ ratios, assuming investment does not also rise. Productive capacity may also rise if the _____ grows, but _____ is likely to fall because of the growing number of mouths to feed.

6-7. Many early economists, accepting the analyses of the Rev. _____, argued that population would always tend towards the maximum sustainable with given resources, so that people would, on the average, live only at _____ levels. This led critics of the day to term economics "the dismal science." Malthus believed population has a natural tendency to grow, in his terms, _____, while food supplies grow only _____.

8-10. High levels of investment and research and development expenditures create improvements in _____ and/or physical capital resources in a society. Economy-wide technological changes occur with the development of social overhead capital, also known as the _____. This road to economic development entails sophisticated and efficient _____, _____, and _____ networks, and an educated and disciplined _____.

STANDARD MULTIPLE CHOICE

THERE IS ONE BEST ANSWER FOR EACH QUESTION.

___ 1. The number of years that it takes some variable to double is approximately its annual percentage growth rate divided into:
   a. its current value.
   b. 72.
   c. 76.
   d. 82.
   e. none of the above.

___ 2. Economic development in a primitive society would NOT be fostered by:
   a. an increase in the population growth rate.
   b. expanded investment in capital embodying new technology.
   c. improvements in the education of the work force.
   d. better transportation, communications, and banking networks.
   e. adoption of advanced agricultural technology.

___ 3. Output per capita would probably rise, but output per worker would probably fall if:
   a. capital deepening occurred rapidly.
   b. the labor force participation rate of a given population rose.
   c. technical education of the work force increased.
   d. involuntary saving was increased.
   e. income were distributed equally.

___ 4. In Karl Marx's theory of economic development:
   a. a 'takeoff stage' precedes the dictatorship of the proletariat.
   b. feudalism comes just before a 'withering away of the state'.
   c. communism immediately follows the overthrow of capitalism.
   d. capitalism is succeeded by a dictatorship of the proletariat.
   e. high savings rates launch a takeoff into high mass consumption.

5. Voluntary saving is enhanced by higher:
   a. tax rates and inflation.
   b. surplus values and more central planning.
   c. interest rates and income.
   d. confiscation and inflation.
   e. degrees of equality in the distribution of income.

6. According to Karl Marx, which event immediately precedes pure communism?
   a. the "withering away of the state."
   b. feudalism.
   c. a "dictatorship of the proletariat."
   d. distribution "from each according to need, to each according to ability."
   e. a non-sexist, non-racist, non-exploitative Utopia.

7. A problem NOT part of "Trap of Underdevelopment" is:
   a. a high birth rate.
   b. low per capita income.
   c. a low capital to labor ratio.
   d. low productivity.
   e. high pollution from dirty technology.

8. The growth paths to subsistence are described as:
   a. Phillips curves.
   b. Malthusian curves.
   c. population "S" curves.
   d. rectangular parabolas.
   e. Laffer curves.

9. An economist who argued that population adjusts to a biological subsistence level given available resources was:
   a. David Ricardo.
   b. Karl Marx.
   c. W. W. Rostow.
   d. Thomas Carlyle.
   e. Rev. Thomas Malthus.

10. Which of the following is called into question by the Laffer curve as an effective method to force the rate of saving up to secure resources for capital formation?
    a. policies to increase interest rates.
    b. policies to increase national income.
    c. direct governmental confiscation of surplus values.
    d. high tax rates intended to raise high tax revenues.
    e. extensive social investment in human capital.

TRUE/FALSE QUESTIONS

1. The labor force as a percentage of the population is known as the capital to labor ratio.

2. An important determinant of the size of the labor force relative to the size of the population is the rate of population growth.

3. Increases in the labor force generally result in an increase in potential real output.

4. Net investment represents net new capital formation during a given time period.

5. Capital widening increases real per capita income.

6. A government can rapidly increase potential Aggregate Supply by pursuing appropriate demand-management policies.

7. An increase in the interest rate received by savers increases the price of present consumption relative to future consumption.

8. Widespread poverty inhibits saving and capital accumulation.

9. Higher interest rates charged investors and lower payments to savers will lead to larger capital stocks over time.

10. Any smoothly functioning economy needs a sophisticated and efficient financial system.

UNLIMITED MULTIPLE CHOICE

CAUTION: EACH QUESTION HAS FROM ZERO TO FOUR CORRECT RESPONSES!

___ 1. Economic growth:
  a. is synonymous with economic development.
  b. refers to qualitative change experienced by an economic system.
  c. occurs when an economic system acquires greater productive capacity.
  d. always results in increased real per capita output or income.

___ 2. An increase in the capital to labor ratio:
  a. increases the productive capacity of an economy.
  b. tends to increase real per capita income.
  c. increases labor productivity more in a less developed country than in a developed country.
  d. generally results in economic growth and development.

___ 3. Saving:
  a. occurs when output is devoted to the production of capital goods.
  b. is necessary for the accumulation of capital.
  c. is voluntary when individuals decide on their own to defer consumption to some future date.
  d. is most positively related to the level of income, according to the classical model.

___ 4. Potential Aggregate Supply:
  a. is determined partially by the state of technology.
  b. might be increased by a government which employs highly inflationary policies and secures large tax revenues.
  c. is determined strictly by Aggregate Demand.
  d. is determined by both the quality and the quantity of productive inputs available.

___ 5. Capital deepening:
  a. is an increase in the ratio of labor to capital.
  b. necessarily increases real per capita output or income.
  c. is less likely to be effective in fostering growth in rich countries than in poor countries.
  d. can occur when saving rates are zero.

PROBLEMS

Problem 1

Given in Figure 1 are production possibility frontiers confronting two different economic systems. A_0 denotes the original production possibility frontiers for both economies and A_1 denotes the new ones. Each economy begins at point a. Use this information to answer the following True/False questions.

Figure 1

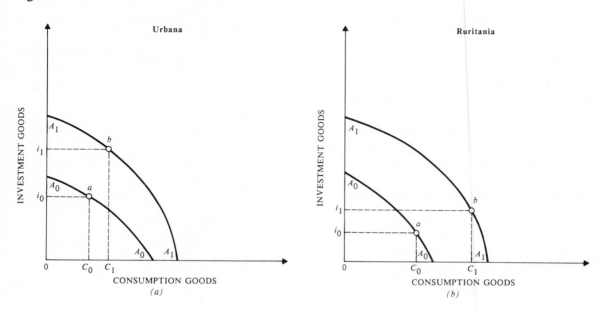

a. the rate of capital accumulation in Urbana exceeds the rate of capital accumulation in Ruritania.

b. Ruritania has experienced economic growth.

c. Urbana must be experiencing economic development.

d. The production possibility frontier for Ruritania has shifted outward the most because of the relatively large amount of net investment that was made at point a.

e. The net addition of real capital in Urbana is probably better suited to the production of investment goods than to the production of consumption goods.

f. Urbana has experienced economic growth.

g. Consumers in Ruritania more strongly prefer present consumption over future consumption relative to those in Urbana.

h. Consumers in Urbana relatively prefer to defer present consumption to some future date.

i. Technological advancement may best explain the relative economic growth that Ruritania has experienced.

j. Consumers in Urbana save more of their incomes than do the consumers in Ruritania.

Problem 2

Use the "Rule of 72" to answer the following T/F questions.

___ a. A country's population will double in 72 years if annual population growth is 1 percent.

___ b. Financial investments will double in value in 18 years if the compounded annual interest rate is 4 percent.

___ c. Financial investments will double in 7.2 years if the annual interest rate is 15 percent.

___ d. A population that grows at an annual rate of 7.2 percent will double in 10 years.

___ e. If the annual rate of inflation in consumer prices is 2 percent, it will take 36 years for the CPI to double.

___ f. If an economy experiences an annual increase of 3.6 percent in real output, it will take 20 years for the economy to double its production of output.

___ g. Financial investments will double in 30 years if the annual interest rate is 2.4 percent.

___ h. Financial investments will double in 7 years if the annual interest rate is 10.28 percent.

___ i. A country's population will double in 60 years if population growth is 1.2 percent annually.

___ j. A country's population will double in 40 years if population growth is 1.8 percent annually.

Problem 3

Figure 2 contains the supply and demand curves for the market for financial capital. Assume that the nominal interest rate is pegged below the equilibrium level by the FED at i_0, that it is then raised to i_1; and that i_e is the unattainable equilibrium interest rate. Assume that the rate of price inflation is 10 percent per annum. Use this information to answer the following True/False questions.

Figure 2

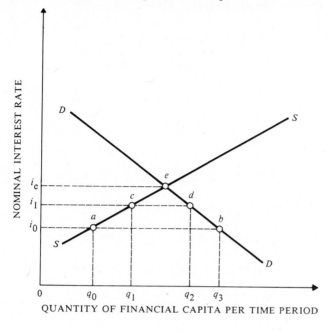

___ a. The supply of saving is a positive function of the money rate of interest.

___ b. There is a shortage of financial capital at interest rate i_0 this market.

___ c. The capital stock increases as the nominal interest rate increases from i_0 to i_1.

___ d. The real interest rate remains constant as the nominal interest rate increases from i_0 to i_1.

___ e. The quantity demanded of financial capital increases as the real interest rate rises as the economy moves from a to c.

___ f. In this market, the rate of capital accumulation is positively related to the nominal interest rate but negatively related to the real interest rate.

___ g. The relative price of present consumption would rise if the nominal interest rate declined from i_1 to i_0.

___ h. The relative price of future consumption decreases as the nominal interest rate increases from i_0 to i_1.

___ i. The rate of saving is greater at i_1 than it is at i_0.

___ j. The rate of present consumption is greater at i_0 than it is at i_1.

Problem 4

You have retained your job as chief economic advisor based on your fine performance in chapter 17. The president, once again, does not seem convinced that you are competent. You have just told him that fixed land and other resource constraints make it impossible to have continual radial expansions of the PPF without diminishing returns. The initial situation involves 2,000 units of labor and 2,000 units of capital and allows the economy to produce up to 100 tons of wheat or 100 military airplanes.

a. Graph this situation. Label the curve PPF1.

Figure 3

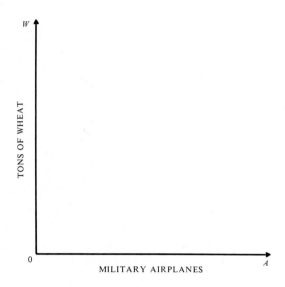

b. Illustrate an increase of 2,000 units of labor and 2,000 units of capital if there is no diminishing returns. Label this curve PPF2.

c. Illustrate a scenario where an additional 2,000 units of labor and capital are added to the production process. This time, however, the additional inputs are constrained by the amount of land in the production process. This constraint is particulary severe in the production of grain where you are only able to get half as much grain output per additional unit of input as before. On the defense side you encounter no resource constraint. Label this curve PPF3.

ANSWERS

Matching Key Terms and Concepts

SET I

Answer	Reference
1. b	p. 384
2. i	p. 388
3. f	p. 382
4. g	p. 381
5. c	p. 381
6. a	p. 392
7. e	p. 389
8. j	p. 389
9. h	p. 385
10. d	p. 387

SET II

Answer	Reference
1. h	p. 390
2. j	p. 391
3. i	p. 392
4. f	p. 387
5. g	p. 385
6. b	p. 392
7. a	p. 383
8. e	p. 389
9. c	p. 389
10. d	p. 383

Chapter Review (fill-in Questions)

1. growth, development
2. Rule of 72, 72
3. production, resources
4. labor force participation, capital to labor
5. population, per capita income
6. Thomas Malthus, subsistence
7. geometrically, arithmetically
8. human, infrastructure
9. financial, communications
10. transportation, labor force

Standard Multiple Choice

Answer	Reference
1. b	p. 382
2. a	p. 383
3. b	p. 383
4. d	p. 392
5. c	p. 387
6. c	p. 392
7. e	p. 392
8. c	p. 384
9. e	p. 384
10. d	p. 389

True/False Questions

Answer	Reference
1. F	p. 383
2. T	p. 383
3. T	p. 383
4. T	p. 386
5. F	p. 389
6. F	p. 393
7. T	p. 387
8. T	p. 388
9. F	p. 387
10. T	p. 391

Unlimited Multiple Choice

Answer	Reference
1. c	p. 381
2. abcd	p. 389
3. abc	p. 387
4. abd	p. 389-390
5. c	p. 389

Problem 1
Reference pp. 385-388

a. T
b. T
c. F
d. F
e. T
f. T
g. T
h. T
i. T
j. T

Problem 2
Reference p. 382

a. T
b. T
c. F
d. T
e. T
f. T
g. T
h. T
i. T
j. T

Problem 3
Reference pp. 385-388

a. T
b. T
c. T
d. F
e. F
f. F
g. F
h. T
i. T
j. T

Problem 4
Reference p. 383

a-c. See Figure 4.

Figure 4

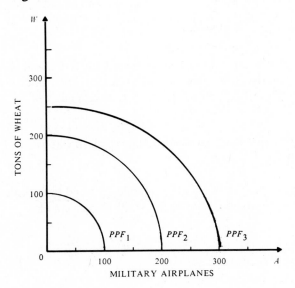

CHAPTER TWENTY
ELASTICITY AND MARGINALISM

CHAPTER OBJECTIVES

After you have read and studied this chapter, you should be able to describe the concept of elasticity and some specific elasticities; indicate the relationships between the incidence of various tax burdens and the price elasticities of supply and demand; compute elasticities from numerical observations; understand why marginal units are important for decisionmaking; and explain the law of equal marginal advantage and its relevance for economic efficiency.

CHAPTER REVIEW: KEY POINTS

1. The price-elasticity of demand is a measure of the responsiveness of the amount demanded to small price changes and is defined as:

$$e_p = \frac{\text{relative change in quantity demanded}}{\text{relative change in price}}$$

$$\approx \frac{\%\,\Delta Q}{\%\,\Delta P}.$$

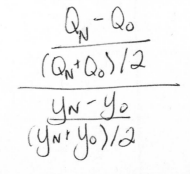

2. Problems result when calculating elasticity if initial prices and quantities are used as bases. As a result, economists typically use *midpoint bases*. The price-elasticity of demand is negative but, for convenience, we use absolute values to avoid the negative sign.

3. If price elasticity is less than one, then demand is relatively unresponsive to changes in price and is said to be *inelastic*. If elasticity is greater than one, the demand is very responsive to price changes and is *elastic*. Demand is *unitarily elastic* if the elasticity coefficient equals one.

4. Elasticity, price changes, and total revenues (expenditures) are related in the following manner: If demand is inelastic (elastic) and price increases (falls), total revenue will rise. If demand is elastic (inelastic) and price rises (falls), total revenue (expenditures) will fall. If demand is unitarily elastic ($e_p = 1$), total revenue will be unaffected by price changes.

5. Along any negatively sloped linear demand curve, parts of the curve will be elastic, unitarily elastic, and inelastic. The price-elasticity of demand rises as the price rises.

6. Income-elasticity of demand is the proportional change in the amount of a good demanded divided by a given proportionate change in income. Normal goods have income-elasticities above zero, while inferior goods have negative income-elasticities.

$$\frac{\dfrac{Q_N - Q_0}{(Q_N + Q_0)/2}}{\dfrac{y_N - y_0}{(y_N + y_0)/2}}$$

7. Cross-elasticity of demand measures the responsiveness of the quantity demanded of one good to price changes in a related good. That is, price cross-elasticity is the proportional change in the quantity of good X (Chevrolets) divided by a given proportional change in the price of good Y (Fords). If the cross-elasticity of demand is positive (negative), the goods are *substitutes (complements)*.

$$\frac{Q_{NX} - Q_{0X}}{(Q_{NX} + Q_{0X})/2}$$

8. The *price-elasticity of supply* measures the responsiveness of suppliers to changes in prices, and is defined to parallel that for the price-elasticity of demand: the proportional change in the amount supplied divided by a given proportional change in price. The price-elasticity of supply is typically positive, reflecting the positive slope of the supply curve.

$$\frac{P_{INX} - P_{0X}}{(Q_{NX} + P_{0X})/2}$$

9. The individual who actually loses purchasing power because of a tax is said to bear the tax's *economic incidence (tax burden)*. This may be quite different from the individual who is legally responsible for the tax, who bears its *legal incidence*. When these individuals differ, the tax has been shifted. A tax can be *forward-shifted* (to consumers) or *backward-shifted* (to labor or other resource owners).

10. If demand is perfectly inelastic or supply is perfectly elastic, a tax will be completely forward-shifted. If supply is perfectly inelastic or demand is perfectly elastic, the tax will be completely backward-shifted.

11. *Incremental* or *marginal* changes direct rational decision making. If a marginal unit of something is positive (negative), its total will rise (fall). If the marginal unit is zero, the total is unaffected. If the marginal exceeds (is less than) an average, the average rises (falls). The average is unchanged if marginal equals average.

12. The *law of equal marginal advantage* dictates that similar resources be used in equally valuable ways to achieve efficiency.

MATCHING KEY TERMS AND CONCEPTS

SET I

E 1. incremental

D 2. normal goods

J 3. complementary goods

F 4. luxury goods

I 5. unitary price elasticity of demand

C 6. substitute goods

H 7. law of equal marginal advantage

A 8. inferior goods

B 9. marginalism

G 10. elasticity

a. Income elasticity < 0.

b. The view that rational decisions weigh the costs and benefits of the last extra bit of an activity.

c. Positive cross-elasticity of demand.

d. income elasticity > 0.

e. A near synonym for marginal.

f. Income elasticity > 1.

g. The ratio of proportionate changes between two related variables.

h. Equivalent resources must be used in equally valuable ways.

i. Total revenue is immune to price changes.

j. Negative price cross-elasticity of demand.

G 1. perfectly inelastic demand   a. A straight line through the origin when graphed.

H 2. relatively inelastic demand   b. A tangent to this curve intersects the horizontal axis.

E 3. unitary demand elasticity √   c. A horizontal curve when perfect substitutes are available.

F 4. relatively elastic demand √   d. Land is the best single example.

C 5. perfectly elastic demand √   e. When graphed, this is a rectangular hyperbola.

D 6. perfectly inelastic supply   f. Price cuts yield increases in revenue and spending.

B 7. relatively inelastic supply √   g. No one has ever been able to give a satisfactory example.

A 8. unitarily elastic supply √   h. A firm faced by this will profit by raising its prices.

I 9. relatively elastic supply √   i. When sellers respond vigorously if the price rises slightly.

J 10. perfectly elastic supply √   j. Makes vast amounts of a good available at a constant price.

CHAPTER REVIEW (FILL-IN QUESTIONS)

1. _Elasticity_ is a general concept measuring the _relative_ changes between two related variables.

2-4. If large changes are involved, we use _midpoint_ as bases for computing the relative changes in the variables. Because of problems of scale, etc., _slope_ is often a misleading indicator of elasticity. If the price elasticity of demand exceeds one, demand is _relatively_ and price hikes will cause total revenues (spending) for a good to _fall_. Total revenue is unaffected by price when demand curves are _rectang._ hyperbolas; such demand curves are _unitary_ elastic.

5. Elasticity changes along a negatively-sloped, linear demand curve; as the price falls and quantity _increases_, the price elasticity of demand _falls_.

6. The _income_ elasticity of demand indicates how the consumption of a good varies as a family's purchasing power changes, and is computed as the relative change in the amount of the good demanded divided by the relative change in _income_.

7. Cross elasticities of demand measure the relative changes in the amount demanded of one good divided by the relative change in price of some related good. Positive coefficients indicate that the goods are _substitutes_, while negative coefficients indicate that the goods are _complements_ in consumption.

8-9. The price elasticity of supply is the relative change in quantity supplied divided by the relative change in the price of a good. Unlike its demand counterpart, it is normally a _positive_ number without adjustments. Both demand and supply elasticities tend to _increase_ as the time for adjustment is increased, as the closeness of _substitute_ goods increase, or as the ability to shift into other forms of _production_ is enhanced.

10. The _margin_ of a thing is the last bit of that thing; _marginalism_ is the idea that rational decisions are based on assessments of the costs and benefits of the final increments of an activity.

STANDARD MULTIPLE CHOICE

THERE IS A UNIQUELY "BEST" ANSWER TO EACH OF THESE QUESTIONS!

1. Price elasticities of demand tend to be larger:
   a. for necessities than for luxuries.
   b. when producers have good alternatives available.
   c. the higher are the opportunity costs of production.
   d. the larger are the number of uses for a good.
   e. None of these.

2. Cuts in a good's supply tend to cause increases in the:
   a. demand for a complementary good.
   b. industry revenues if its demand is price elastic.
   c. industry revenues if its demand is income inelastic.
   d. demand for the good itself.
   e. demand for a substitute good.

3. As price falls and quantity rises along a negatively-sloped linear demand curve:
   a. total revenue falls up to the point where elasticity equals zero; thereafter, it rises.
   b. the price elasticity of demand decreases.
   c. there is a contradiction to the law of supply.
   d. the incentive for substituting away from the good rises.
   e. a constant negative slope ensures a fixed elasticity.

4. Which of the following lists of taxes or taxed goods is in correct order from most backward-shifted to most forward-shifted?
   a. tobacco, property, payroll, general sales.
   b. land, payroll, property, tobacco.
   c. tobacco, payroll, corporate income, property.
   d. income, inheritance, gift, sales.
   e. gambling, amusement, inheritance, land.

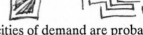

5. Cross-price elasticities of demand are probably most positive for:
   a. shoe repairs and new shoes.
   b. syrup and waffles.
   c. gasoline and limousines.
   d. college tuitions and textbooks.
   e. coal and iron.

6. From which of the following data might you estimate a price elasticity of supply?
   a. A price hike from $7 to $13 causes shirt sales to fall from 16,000 to 8,000 monthly.
   b. Farmers increase soybean plantings 15 percent when the price increases 5 percent.
   c. Ford's production increases because GM raises Chevette prices.
   d. The output of tennis balls slumps 8 percent when the prices of racquets go up 12 percent.
   e. Steel production and sales rise 18 percent when national income grows 13 percent.

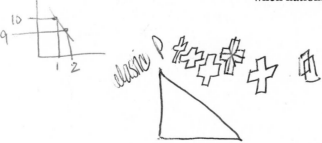

235

_____ 7. Which of the following suggest that supply is most price elastic?
   a. A pay hike from $400 to $800 monthly for new recruits raises new army enlistments from 12,000 to 28,000 monthly.
   b. A 20 percent increase in goat milk production follows a 40 percent rise in the price of cow milk.
   c. When wheat prices fall from $8 to $5 per bushel, world output drops from 460 million tons down to 340 million tons.
   d. Per capita income rises from $2,500 to $3,500 and auto sales rise from 6 million to 18 million units annually.
   e. New record releases climb from 1,800 annually to 2,400 annually when album prices rise from $6 to $9 each.

_____ 8. Pairs of substitute goods include:
   a. organic vegetables and french fries.
   b. polyester fabrics and cotton cloth.
   c. transistor radios and televisions.
   d. jogging shoes and bicycles.
   e. All of these.

_____ 9. Sets of complementary goods include:
   a. auto repairs and new cars.
   b. gasoline and gasohol.
   c. diving boards and swimming pools.
   d. saunas and steam baths.
   e. pipes, chewing tobacco, and snuff.

_____ 10. Demand for which of the following products is probably the least income elastic for most people?
   a. Rolls Royces.
   b. Big Macs.
   c. pinto beans.
   d. housing.
   e. health care.

_____ 11. If each 1-percent price hike causes the amounts sold to fall 2 percent, the price elasticity of demand for bacon is roughly:
   a. 0.5.
   b. 2.0.
   c. .02.
   d. unitary.
   e. .01.

$$\frac{\%\Delta Q}{\%\Delta P}$$

_____ 12. If attendance at basketball games falls from 10,000 per game to 8,000 when ticket prices are raised from $6 to $8, the price elasticity of demand is roughly:
   a. 2.00.
   b. 0.78.
   c. 3.33.
   d. 1.29.
   e. 0.50.

$$\frac{Q_n - Q_o}{(Q_n + Q_o)/2} \qquad \frac{P_n - P_o}{(P_n + P_o)/2}$$

$$\frac{8-10}{(8+10)/2} \qquad \frac{8-6}{(8+6)/2} \qquad \frac{2}{7}$$

_____ 13. National income booms from $3.75 trillion to $4.25 trillion and new car sales flourish, rising from 3 million to 5 million annually. The income elasticity of demand for new cars is:
   a. 0.5.
   b. 1.0.
   c. 2.0.
   d. 3.0.
   e. 4.0.

$$\frac{5-3}{(5+3)/2} \qquad \frac{4.25-3.75}{(3.75+4.25)/2}$$

$$\frac{2}{4} \qquad \frac{.5}{4}$$

_____ 14. Electric heater prices fall from $50 to $30 and the sales of Alaskan igloos melt from 750 to 450 per month. These goods are _____ and the price cross-elasticity of demand equals _____.
   a. inferior; 1.5
   b. necessities; 3.0
   c. substitutes; 1.0
   d. luxuries; -2.0
   e. complementary; -1.0

$$\frac{450-750}{(450+750)/2} \qquad \frac{30-50}{(30+50)/2}$$

$$\frac{300}{600} \qquad \frac{20}{40}$$

_____ 15. The average jail term for being convicted of driving while intoxicated rises from 1 month to 3 months, and traffic fatalities decline from 70,000 to 50,00 per year. The imprisonment elasticity of traffic fatalities is roughly:
   a. - 0.333.
   b. 0.667.
   c. 0.333.
   d. 1.000.
   e. - 3.000.

$$\frac{5000-70,000}{(5000+70,000)/2} \qquad \frac{3-1}{(3+1)/2}$$

$$\frac{-65000}{37500} \qquad \frac{2}{2} = 1$$

16. New competition causes exercise machines to be slashed from $650 to a rock bottom $350 and sales rise from 70,000 to 210,000 annually. The price elasticity of demand is roughly:
    - a. 1.667.
    - b. 0.600.
    - c. 3.333.
    - d. 0.333.
    - e. 1.000.

$$\frac{210,000 - 70,000}{(210,000 + 70,000)/2} \qquad \frac{350 - 650}{(350 + 650)/2}$$

$$\frac{140000}{14,0000} \qquad \frac{-300}{500}$$

$$\frac{1}{1} \quad \frac{5}{3} \qquad \frac{3}{5}$$

17. Soaring demand causes the price of sole-sucker beach sandals to rise from $10 to $14 a pair. An influx of new producers raises the total amount available from 3 million to 13 million annually. The price elasticity of supply is:
    - a. 0.375.
    - b. 0.750.
    - c. 3.750.
    - d. 1.000.
    - e. 7.500.

$$\frac{13000000 - 3000000}{("" + "")/2} \qquad \frac{14 - 10}{(14 + 10)/2}$$

$$\frac{5,000,000}{10,000,000} \qquad \frac{3}{1}$$

$$\frac{8,000,000}{4,000,000}$$

18. An economist who used the phrase "marginal returns" would probably be referring to:
    - a. such a poor investment that it should be abandoned.
    - b. an appropriate markup over production costs.
    - c. the gains or losses from slightly altering a situation.
    - d. the close outcome of a major election.
    - e. tendencies for students to skimp while studying economics.

19. The idea that rational decisionmaking entails carefully weighing the costs and benefits from slightly expanding or contracting an activity is known as:
    - a. instrumentalism.
    - b. pragmatism.
    - c. scholasticism.
    - d. marginalism.
    - e. realism.

$$-\frac{300}{600}$$

$$\frac{Q_n - Q_0}{P_n - P_0} \quad \frac{450 - 750}{(450 + 750)/2}$$

$$\frac{30 - 50}{(30 + 50)/2} \quad \frac{-20}{40}$$

$$+\frac{1}{2} \quad \frac{2}{1}$$

20. Which of the following statements is most compatible with the law of equal marginal advantage?
    - a. A shopper disregards transaction costs while trying to push the family grocery bill towards zero by using coupons.
    - b. Investors who have been receiving a 7 percent rate of return all shift their funds when they discover a similarly risky investment yielding 9 percent.
    - c. A professor requires that all term papers be typed, double-spaced, with 2 inch margins, and at least 20 pages long.
    - d. The manager of a hardware store decides to mark up every item sold using a uniform $2.00 margin.
    - e. Everyone gets big advantages from 8 hours of sleep nightly.

$$\frac{\Delta Q}{Q} \qquad \frac{2000}{8000} \qquad \frac{2}{8}$$

$$\frac{\Delta P}{P} \qquad \frac{1}{4} \quad \frac{8}{2} 2$$

$$\frac{8.5}{1} \frac{5}{2} \quad \frac{.5}{4.25} \quad \frac{2}{5}$$

TRUE/FALSE QUESTIONS

T 1. A point of unitary price elasticity is found at the midpoint of every negatively-sloped linear demand curve.

F 2. All demand curves possess an elastic range, an inelastic range, and a unitarily elastic range.

T 3. Total revenue varies directly with price in the inelastic range of a demand curve.

T 4. Total revenue varies inversely with price in the elastic range of a demand curve.

T 5. Negative price elasticities of demand are conventionally treated as absolute (positive) coefficients.

F 6. The price elasticity of supply is a measure of the slope of a supply curve.

T 7. Substitutes have positive price cross-elasticities of demand.

Midpoint Changes

$$\frac{Q_n - Q_0}{(Q_n + Q_0)/2} \Bigg/ \frac{P_n - P_0}{(P_n + P_0)/2}$$

237

$$\frac{-2000}{9000} \qquad \frac{8000 - 10,000}{8000 + 10,000/2}$$

$$\frac{2}{7} \qquad \frac{8 - 6}{8 + 6/2}$$

$$1000$$

$$\frac{2000}{9000} \quad \frac{7}{2}$$

_F_ 8. The law of equal marginal advantage suggests that people consistently gain if they work instead of enjoy their leisure.

_F_ 9. Any tax burden is synonymous with its legal incidence.

_T_ 10. Normal goods have positive income elasticities of demand; inferior goods have negative income elasticity coefficients.

_F_ 11. Using the metric scale, incremental units are 10 times larger than marginal units.

_F_ 12. Marginal utility refers to a baseball player who plays each position with equal lack of competence.

UNLIMITED MULTIPLE CHOICE

CAUTION: EACH QUESTION HAS FROM ZERO TO FOUR CORRECT ANSWERS!

___ 1. The price elasticity of demand is:
a. generally negative, so we normally consider its absolute value.
b. a measure of the absolute change in the quantity demanded of a good evoked by an absolute change in its price.
c. directly related to the time period allowed for consumers to adjust to changes in relative prices.
d. a measure of the slope of the demand curve.

___ 2. The income elasticity of demand is:
a. the relative change in the amount of a good demanded divided by the relative change in real income.
b. positively related to price cross elasticities of demand.
c. greater than one for superior goods.
d. negative for inferior goods.

___ 3. Total revenue is:
a. positively related to the price of an inelastically demanded good.
b. negatively related to the price of an elastically demanded good.
c. decreased if the price increases in the elastic range of the demand curve.
d. decreased if the price decreases in the inelastic range of the demand curve.

___ 4. The price elasticity of supply is:
a. normally positive.
b. the relative change in the price of a good caused by a change in the quantity of the good supplied.
c. positively related to the responsiveness of the quantity of a good demanded to changes in its price.
d. positive for upward-sloping supply curves.

___ 5. The price-cross elasticity of demand is:
a. positive for substitute goods.
b. negative for complementary goods.
c. the absolute change in the amount of a good demanded caused by an absolute change in the price of another good.
d. roughly zero for totally unrelated goods.

inelastic $P\uparrow$ $P\downarrow$
$0 < e < 1$ $TR\uparrow$ $TR\downarrow$
$\infty > e > 1$ $TR\downarrow$ $TR\uparrow$
elastic

PROBLEMS

Problem 1

Compute the elasticities for the following problems.

a. The Hobbit family buys 72 vegetarian specials annually at a price of $3.00 each but would consume 192 per year if the price dropped to $2.40. Their price elasticity of demand is _____.

b. The Sea Slug Glee Club bought 170 motor scooters when the price was $875 each, but ordered only 30 when the price soared to $2,125. The group's price elasticity of demand for scooters is _____.

c. If weight watchers gulp 205 million milkshakes at $1.15 apiece, but cut back to 155 million weekly when the price rises to $1.85 each, the price elasticity of their demand for shakes equals _____.

d. If a $9.98 sale on regular $19.95 watch fobs raises a store's sales from 30 to 300 per week, the price elasticity of the demand faced by the store is roughly _____.

e. If a strong recovery raises national income from $4.0 trillion to $4.4 trillion and diamond sales jump from 3 to 13 million carats annually, the income elasticity of demand for diamonds is _____.

f. If each 1-percent hike in the price of pencils causes a 2-percent decline in the quantity of erasers sold, the price cross-elasticity of demand for these complementary goods is roughly _____.

g. When J. R. Ewing can sell totem poles for $1,800 each, he markets 60 annually, but when the price falls to $600 apiece, he is willing to sell only 24 each year. His price elasticity of supply is _____.

h. When the temperature drops from $102°$ F to $54°$ F, sales of surf boards slip from 56,000 monthly down to 14,000 for diehard surfers. The temperature elasticity of the demand for surf boards is _____.

i. When 200,000 gallons of water are applied per acre, 4 tons are harvested from each acre of linguini trees annually, but cutting back to 160,000 gallons causes the crop per acre to fall to 2 tons annually. The water elasticity of linguini production is _____.

j. If doubling your viewing of soap operas to 16 hours per week causes your IQ score to fall from a genius level of 140 to a sluggish 70, your TV elasticity of brainpower is _____.

Problem 2

Table 1 shows data for four different markets.

	MARKET A	MARKET B	MARKET C	MARKET D
P_0	$10	$400		$.25 for X
Q_0	16 million	600,000	16	160 tons of Z
P_1	$16	$800		$.35 for X
Q_1	10 million	1,800,000	40	240 tons of Z
Y_0			$20,000	
Y_1			$40,000	

Complete the blanks in statements a through d, which correspond to markets A through D, respectively.

a. The _____ elasticity of _____ is _____ .

b. The _____ elasticity of _____ is _____ .

c. The _____ elasticity of _____ is _____ and this is a(n) _____ good.

d. The ____ elasticity of ____ is ____ and goods X and Z are ____ goods.

Problem 3

Table 2 shows the demand schedule for books per year for the Scholar family.

Table 2

PRICE ELASTICITY OF DEMAND	NUMBER OF BOOKS DEMANDED	PRICE PER BOOK	TOTAL SPENDING (OR REVENUE)
—	0	$20	
	10	18	
	20	16	
	30	14	
	40	12	
	50	10	
	60	8	
	70	6	
	80	4	
	90	2	
	100	0	

a. Compute the coefficient of price elasticity for the price ranges given in the schedule and complete the first column of the table.

b. Why is it conventional to use the absolute values of such numbers when discussing price elasticities of demand? _____

c. Identify the three ranges of price elasticity of demand in this schedule. (You can only approximate the three ranges.) _____

d. Fill in the total revenue (spending) column.

e. How does total spending vary with book prices in the elastic range? _____
   Why? _____

f. How does total spending vary with book prices in the inelastic range? _____
   Why? _____

g. Total spending attains a maximum value approximately in which range of price elasticity? _____
   _____ Why? _____

h. Graph the demand curve for books in Figure 1.

Figure 1

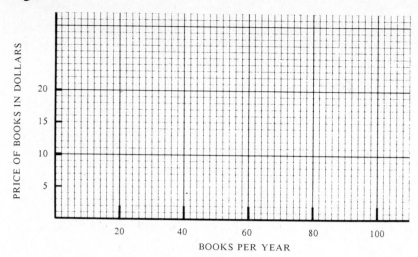

PRICE OF BOOKS IN DOLLARS

BOOKS PER YEAR

i. Why is the price elasticity of demand different from the slope of a demand curve? _____ .

j. Interpret the coefficient of price elasticity that you computed for the seventh price range: $8 to $6.
    _____ Do the same for the coefficient corresponding to the second price range.
    ($18 - $16) _____

Problem 4

Table 3 contains a supply schedule for bouquets of roses. Use these data to answer the following questions.

Table 3

PRICE ELASTICITY OF SUPPLY	BOUQUETS OF ROSES SUPPLIED	PRICE $
————	0	2
_____	2	4
_____	4	6
_____	6	8
_____	8	10
_____	10	12
_____	12	14
_____	14	16

a. Compute the coefficient of price elasticity of supply for the seven price ranges shown and complete the table.

b. What do you notice about the algebraic signs of the values you just computed? Explain why this is so.

    _____

c. Express the price elasticity of supply as the ratio of a marginal concept and an average concept. _____
    _____ Explain why all linear supply curves emanating from the origin manifest unitary price
    elasticity.

    _____

241

Problem 5

Figure 2 shows the supply and demand curves for three different markets. Use this information to answer the following true/false questions, assuming that the legal incidence of taxes is on firms.

Figure 2

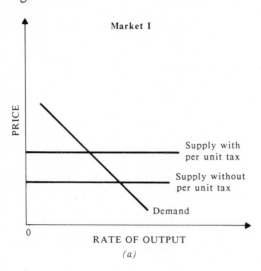

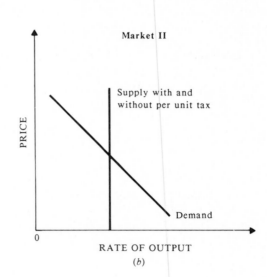

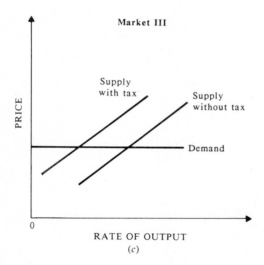

___ a. The tax is shifted forward completely in Market I.

___ b. The economic incidence of the tax is identical with its legal incidence in Market II.

___ c. The demand curve in Market III is perfectly price elastic.

___ d. The supply curve in Market II is perfectly price inelastic.

___ e. The economic incidence of the tax is identical with its legal incidence of the tax in Market I.

___ f. The supply curves in Market I have zero price elasticity.

___ g. The tax is completely shifted backward in Market III.

___ h. The economic incidence of the tax is different from its legal incidence in Market III.

___ i. The equilibrium price of the good sold in Market II is a demand determined price.

___ j. The tax is shifted backward completely in Market II.

Problem 6

Figure 3 shows the markets for four different goods. The numerical subscripts denote the analytic sequence of the demand curves: "0" denotes the original curve, "1" denotes the new curve. Assume that real income has increased by 10 percent. Use income elasticity to determine the kind of good represented in each market.

Figure 3

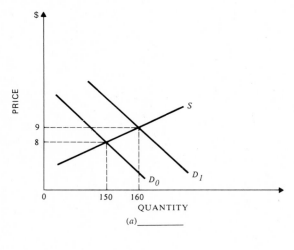

(a)_____

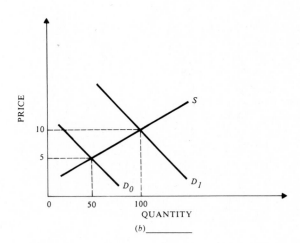

(b)_____

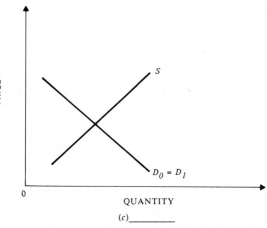

(c)_____

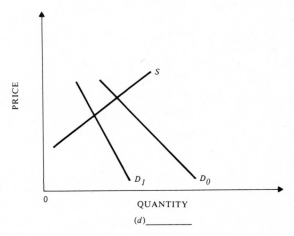

(d)_____

Problem 7

Suppose that if you work 40 hours a week at a straight-time wage, your income is $240; but if you put in 42 hours, your income rises to $258.

a. Assuming that your hourly overtime wage is constant once you exceed 40 hours of work weekly, draw the relationship between hours worked and income in Figure 4.

Figure 4

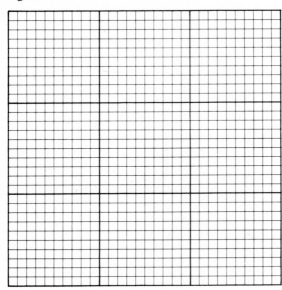

b. What is the overtime wage rate? _____

c. What is your average wage if you work 42 hours? _____

d. What is your average wage if you work 43 hours? _____

e. Once you have worked 42 hours, will whether you are willing to work the 43rd hour or not depend on your average wage or on the marginal (overtime) wage? _____

Problem 8

What happens to:

a. your average score over the course of this class if you fail the first exam, do a bit better on the second (marginal) test, and then ace (100 percent) the final? _____

b. the average income in this class if a late registering (marginal) student happens to be a prominent medical doctor who enjoys taking classes part time and hopes studying economics will make him richer? _____

c. the average height of people in Denver, Colorado when the Seattle Supersonics come to town to play a game of basketball with the Denver Nuggets? _____

d. the total and average revenue from TV sales if Reliable Ralph takes an unusual price mark-down in order to sell one more set this month? _____ Why? _____

244

ANSWERS

Matching Key Terms and Concepts

SET I

Answer	MIC	ECO
1. e	p. 113	417
2. d	p. 107	411
3. j	p. 108	412
4. f	p. 107	411
5. i	p. 104	408
6. c	p. 108	412
7. h	p. 114	418
8. a	p. 107	411
9. b	p. 113	417
10. g	p. 101	405

SET II

MIC pp. 102-104, 108-109; ECO pp. 406-408, 412-413

Answer
1. g
2. h
3. e
4. f
5. c
6. d
7. b
8. a
9. i
10. j

Chapter Review (Fill-in Questions)

1. Elasticity, proportionate or relative
2. mid-points, slope
3. relatively elastic, fall
4. rectangular, unitarily
5. increase, falls
6. income, income
7. substitutes, complements
8. positive, rise
9. substitute, production
10. margin or increment, marginalism

Standard Multiple Choice

Answer	MIC	ECO
1. d	p. 102	406
2. e	p. 108	412
3. b	p. 106	410
4. b	p. 110	414
5. a	p. 108	412
6. b	p. 108	412
7. a	p. 108	412
8. e	p. 108	412
9. c	p. 108	412
10. c	p. 107	411
11. b	p. 101	405
12. b	p. 101	405
13. e	p. 107	411
14. c	p. 108	412
15. a	p. 101	405
16. a	p. 101	405
17. c	p. 101	405
18. c	p. 113	417
19. d	p. 113	417
20. b	p. 114	418

True/False Questions

Answer	MIC	ECO
1. T	p. 104	408
2. F	p. 104	408
3. T	p. 102	406
4. T	p. 102	406
5. T	p. 101	405
6. F	p. 108	412
7. T	p. 108	412
8. F	p. 114	418
9. F	p. 112	416
10. T	p. 107	411
11. F	p. 113	417
12. F	p. 113	417

Unlimited Multiple Choice

Answer	MIC	ECO
1. ac	p. 101, 105	405, 409
2. acd	p. 107	411
3. abcd	p. 102	406
4. ad	p. 108	412
5. abd	p. 108	412

Problem 1
MIC pp. 101-102; *ECO pp. 405-406*

    a. 45/11 or 4.09
    b. 42/25 or 1.68
    c. 25/42 or .595
    d. 27/11 or 2.456
    e. 105/8 or 13.125
    f. -2.0
    g. 6/7 or .857
    h. 39/20 or 1.95
    i. 3.0
    j. -1.0

Problem 2
MIC pp. 101-102, 107-108; *ECO 405-406, 411-412*

    a. price; demand; 1.0 (unitary)
    b. price; supply; 1.5
    c. income; demand; 1.286 or 9/7; luxury
    d. price cross; demand; 1.2 or 6/5; substitutes

Problem 3
MIC pp. 102-106; *ECO 406-410*

a. See Table -4.

Table 4

PRICE ELASTICITY OF DEMAND	NUMBER OF BOOKS DEMANDED	PRICE PER BOOK	TOTAL REVENUE
--	0	$20	0
19.0	10	18	180
5.67	20	16	320
3.0	30	14	420
1.86	40	12	480
1.22	50	10	500
.82	60	8	480
.54	70	6	420
.33	80	4	320
.18	90	2	180
.05	100	0	0

b. Before adjustments the price elasticity of demand is negative because demand curves are negatively sloped.

c. elastic range: $20 to $10
    unitary range: roughly $10
    inelastic range: $10 to $0

d. See Table 4.

e. As price is lowered total revenue rises; the percentage change in quantity demanded exceeds the percentage change in price.

f. As price is lowered total revenue falls; the percentage change in quantity demanded is less than the percentage change in price.

g. The unitary range, because on each side of this range, if price is increased, demand is elastic and TR falls, and if price is lowered, demand is inelastic and TR falls.

h. See Figure 5.

Figure 5

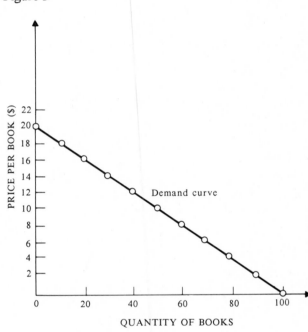

i. As can be seen in Table 4 and Figure 2, elasticity varies all along the curve, but the slope is constant.

j. The price elasticity computed for the seventh range is 0.54 and indicates that at a price between $8 and $6 the demand for books is inelastic. The coefficient for the second price change ($18-$16) is 5.67, indicating an elastic demand.

Problem 4
MIC pp. 108-109; *ECO 412-413*

a.   See Table 5

Table 5

PRICE ELASTICITY OF SUPPLY	UNITS SUPPLIED	PRICE
--	0	2
3.00	2	4
1.4	4	6
1.285	6	8
1.222	8	10
1.182	10	12
1.153	12	14
2	14	16

b.   The values are positive because the supply is positively sloped.

c. $e_s = (\Delta Q/Q)/(\Delta P/P) = (\Delta Q/\Delta P)/(Q/P) = (\Delta Q/\Delta P) \times (P/Q)$. All linear supply curves emanating from the origin have a unitary elasticity since the ratio of change in Q and P is always equal to the ratio of ΔP to ΔQ.

Problem 5
MIC pp. 110-112; *ECO 414-416*

a.   T
b.   T
c.   T
d.   T
e.   F
f.   F
g.   T
h.   F
i.   T
j.   T

Problem 6
MIC p. 108; *ECO 412*

a.   normal
b.   superior
c.   neutral
d.   inferior

Problem 7
MIC p. 106; *ECO 410*

1.   (a) See Figure 6.

Figure 6

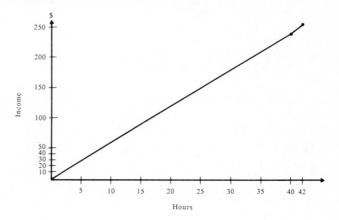

(b) $9.00 hourly

(c) $6.14 + hourly

(d) $6.16 + hourly

(e) It will depend on the $9 hourly overtime (marginal) wage.

Problem 8
MIC p. 106; *ECO 410*

(a) Your class average rises with both the second and final exams.

(b) The average income in the class rises.

(c) The average height in Denver rises.

(d) Total revenue rises, but average revenue declines. Marginal revenue is positive or Ralphie would raise prices substantially. Thus, total revenue rises when the price is cut. But average revenue (the price) falls when goods are sold at special low prices.

CHAPTER TWENTY-ONE
THE FOUNDATIONS OF CONSUMER CHOICE

CHAPTER OBJECTIVES

After you have read and studied this chapter, you should be able to distinguish the substitution and income effects of price changes; use utility analysis to explain negatively-sloped demand curves; and describe consumer equilibrium, the relevance of the law of diminishing marginal utility, and the principle of equal marginal utilities per dollar.

CHAPTER REVIEW: KEY POINTS

1. *Substitution effects* are the changes in consumer purchasing patterns that emerge if relative prices change, artificially assuming that the purchasing power of income is constant.

2. *Income effects* are changes in buying patterns that occur solely because the purchasing power of one's income changes when the prices of individual goods rise or fall.

3. *Utilitarianism* proposes that the best society is the one that provides the greatest happiness for the greatest number of people.

4. Marginal utility is the extra satisfaction gained from consuming a bit more of a good. The *law of diminishing marginal utility* states: The marginal utility of any good eventually declines as the amount consumed increases.

5. Measured in dollars, the declining portion of a marginal utility curve translates into a demand curve.

6. Maximum consumer satisfaction (*consumer equilibrium*) requires that the last cent spent on any good yield the same gain in satisfaction as the last cent spent on any other good: $MU_a/P_a = MU_b/P_b = \ldots = MU_z/P_z$. This is known as the *principle of equal marginal utilities per dollar.*

7. *Consumer surplus* is the area above the price line and below the demand curve. It is a consumer's gain from buying at a uniform price instead of paying prices equal to the marginal utility of each unit.

8. We are seldom certain about the *attributes* of any unit of a good. Information is costly and its marginal benefits may be trivial. Thus, our decisions are based on less than full information; we are *rationally ignorant* because we pursue information only as long as its expected benefit exceeds its expected cost.

9. Moral hazard occurs when a contract creates an incentive for opportunistic behavior that raises the costs or lowers the benefits to the other party. *Adverse selection* occurs when a party to a contract has been deceived about the qualities it expects to receive from a transaction. Rational ignorance, moral hazard, and adverse selection are all reasons why our effective consumer demands may not maximize our satisfaction.

10. There is an increasing tendency towards government edict as a means of overcoming transaction costs or solving the problems of rational ignorance and uncertainty. Do government experts know better than you do what things are good for you and what things will harm you?

MATCHING KEY TERMS AND CONCEPTS

SET I

I 1. consumer surplus ?

F 2. marginal utility

E 3. income effect ?

C 4. subjective demand price ?

H 5. *caveat emptor*

D 6. utilitarianism

J 7. services

B 8. equal marginal utilities per dollar

A 9. *caveat venditor*

G 10. law of diminishing marginal utility

a. "Let the seller beware." *caveat vendor*

b. Each final bit of money spent must yield equal satisfaction. *equal marginal utilities per dollar*

c. The marginal utility of one good relative to another (MU_x/MU_y).

d. "The greatest happiness for the greatest number." *utilitarianism*

? e. The change in buying patterns when purchasing power changes because of price changes. *income effect*

f. Satisfaction gained from additional consumption of a good. *marginal utility*

g. As more and more is consumed, after some point less and less extra satisfaction is derived from additional consumption. *law of dim. marg utility*

h. "Let the buyer beware." *caveat emptor*

i. Any difference between what you would willingly pay and what you do pay. *consumer surplus*

j. All goods must be rendered into these to generate utility. *services*

249

(NOTE: * = optional material from the end of the chapter.)

D 1. normal goods   *a.* Maximized satisfaction given income constraints. *consumer eq.*

I 2. substitution effect *I*   b. Constraints determined by income and market prices.

E 3. inferior goods   *c.* Explained by the difference between total and marginal utility. *diamond-water paradox*

H 4. attributes   *d.* Associated with positive income effects. *normal good*

G 5. commodity   *e.* Associated with negative income effects. *Inferior g. income ↑ 0 inf G ↑*

C 6. diamond-water paradox   f. All bundles yielding identical satisfaction to a consumer.

A 7. consumer equilibrium   *g.* A produced tangible good that can be owned. *commodity*

8. budget lines *   *h.* Qualities of goods that add or detract from satisfaction. *attributes*

9. indifference curve *   *i.* Always negative. *subst. effect*

10. tangency between #8 and #9 *   j. Graphically portrays consumer equilibrium.

CHAPTER REVIEW (FILL-IN QUESTIONS)

1-4. If satisfaction could be recorded in ___*utils*___ , a mythical measurement, then social lpolicies could be assessed straightforwardly. Unfortunately, it cannot. However, the law of diminishing *marginal utility* suggests that ever greater consumption of any good ultimately yields declining gains in satisfaction and leads to the law of demand. In equilibrium, a consumer must gain the same satisfaction from the last *dollar* ___*cent*___ on each good; an idea known as the principle of *equal marginal utility per dollar*. For example, if *applies* $MU_x/P_x > MU_y/P_y$, the consumer can gain by buying less of ___X___ and more of ___*Y*___ *can.* As this occurs, the marginal utility of X (MU_x) will ___*decrease*___ and the marginal utility of Y (MU_y) will ___*increase*___ , until $MU_x/Y_x = MU_y/P_y$.

5. Price changes alter consumer equilibria. For example, if initially $MU_x/P_x = MU_y/P_y$, increases in P_x cause $MU_x/P_x < MU_y/P_y$; your resultant decrease in purchases of ___X___ and increased purchases of ___*y*___ will, by the law of diminishing marginal utility increase MU_x and decrease MU_y until equilibrium is restored.

6. For ___*inferior*___ goods, the income effect is ___*negative*___ because price cuts increase real income ($\Delta I > 0$) and induce greater consumption ($\Delta Q > 0$); thus, $\Delta Q/\Delta I > 0$.

7-9. *consumer surplus* the difference between the amounts people would willingly pay for various amounts of specific goods and the amounts they do pay at ___*market*___ prices. It is roughly the area ___*below*___ the ___*demand*___ curve and above the ___*price*___ line. The *diamond-water* paradox was a knotty problem for economists because some "necessities" yield huge consumer surpluses but sell at low prices, while some frivolous luxuries are quite expensive. The key to resolving this puzzle is to realize that the subjective demand prices that are brought into equilibrium with market prices reflect marginal, not total, utilities.

10. Much of our consumer theory assumes that we have good information about the products we buy. The legal doctrine of *Caveat emptor* or "Let the buyer beware," assumes that consumers are the best judges of their individual well-being. Where complex goods that are infrequently purchased by most consumers cause sellers' information to be superior to that possessed by buyers, imposing risks on sellers under the doctrine of *caveat vendor* may make sense. However, government regulation increasingly restricts the choices available to us when some of the attributes of goods are viewed as so individually or socially harmful that certain goods are forbidden.

STANDARD MULTIPLE CHOICE

EACH QUESTION HAS A SINGLE "BEST"ANSWER!

1. The founder of "utilitarianism" was:
   a. Stanley Jevons.
   b. John Stuart Mill.
   c. Jeremy Bentham.
   d. Thorstein Veblen.
   e. Adam Smith.

2. The principle of equal marginal utilities per dollar suggests that:
   a. the additional satisfaction from consuming a good eventually declines.
   b. every good for which you spend identical total amounts are equally useful.
   c. $1,000 worth of water and a $1,000 diamond are identically satisfying to consumers.
   d. the last cent spent on any item yields the same satisfaction as the last cent spent on any other item.
   e. All of these.

3. If your marginal utility from a 25 cent candy bar is 50 utils and the marginal utility of a 30 cent cola is 60 utils, you can:
   a. not add to your satisfaction by changing this mix.
   b. gain by buying less candy and more cola.
   c. gain by devoting less money to both candy and cola.
   d. gain by buying less cola and more candy.
   e. None of these.

4. A corollary of the law of equal marginal advantage is the principle of:
   a. diminishing marginal utility.
   b. equal marginal utilities per dollar.
   c. diminishing returns.
   d. substitution.
   e. demand and supply.

5. Even if your income is adjusted for price changes, your buying patterns respond to changes in relative prices because of the:
   a. substitution effect.
   b. wealth effect.
   c. income effect.
   d. utility-maximizing effect.
   e. marginal utility equality effect.

6. *Caveat emptor* means:
   a. Let the seller beware!
   b. Everything else held constant.
   c. Let things change if they must.
   d. Charge whatever the market will bear.
   e. Let the buyer beware!

7. Substitution away from a good is greater when its price rises:
   a. the more close substitutes there are for the good.
   b. the more different uses to which the good has been put at the previous price.
   c. the longer is the time period allowed for adjustment.
   d. the fewer are the complements for the good.
   e. All of the above.

8. Thorstein Veblen was:
   a. a major early advocate of the view that people are rational.
   b. a savage critic of economics as a scientific discipline.
   c. a famous mathematical economist.
   d. a pioneer in developing modern consumer theory.
   e. the first to apply the concept of elasticity to demand curves.

251

C 9. If your income is closely tied to the price of a given product, an increase in its price may cause:
a. an income effect that, in extreme cases, yields a positively sloped demand curve.
b. you to go bankrupt.
c. a powerful positive substitution effect.
d. elimination of any meaningful budget constraint.
e. an early heart attack.

C 10. From which of the following goods do typical Americans derive the greatest consumer surpluses?
a. soap.
b. whole wheat bread.
c. water.
d. gold jewelry.
e. alarm clocks.

B 11. The intrinsic characteristics that create or detract from the satisfaction derived from consuming a good are known as:
a. factors.
b. attributes.
c. utilities.
d. anomalies.
e. pedigrees.

E 12. The idea that, in equilibrium, the more you pay for a good the more it is worth (at the margin) to you is most closely related to the:
a. law of diminishing returns.
b. equal satisfaction corollary.
c. increasing cost hypothesis.
d. Veblen effect.
e. principle of equal marginal utilities per dollar.

C 13. Wise use of coupons at grocery stores is likely to increase the amount of:
a. consumer surplus.
b. deadweight loss.
c. measured social utility.
d. entrepreneurial profit.
e. capitalistic exploitation.

A 14. When goods are nonstandardized and infrequently purchased by an individual, a presumption that sellers will have superior knowledge of product characteristics is an argument for applying the legal doctrine of:
a. caveat emptor.
b. nolo contendere.
c. no-fault insurance.
d. ceteris paribus.
e. caveat venditor.

B 15. NOT a part of the utilitarian philosophy was the assumption that:
a. "the greatest good for the greatest number" is an appropriate social goal.
b. individual utilities are summable to a measure of social welfare.
c. pleasure adds to utility, while pain detracts from utility.
d. people differ significantly in the ability to enjoy certain goods.
e. people seek pleasure and try to avoid pain.

A 16. Purchasing a defective pair of skis because the seller "tricked" you is an example of:
a. adverse selection.
b. a moral hazard.
c. rational ignorance.
d. the substitution effect.
e. stupidity.

D 17. When consumers reduce their purchases of a good because of a rise in price, the:
a. total utility enjoyed from other goods declines.
b. income effect reduces purchases of inferior goods.
c. marginal utility derived from the good rises.
d. substitution effect is positive.
e. law of diminishing returns is violated.

the amount you would willingly pay

free

you do pay at mkt prices

E 18. Which of the following might contradict the law of diminishing marginal utility?
  a. Dagmar bursts with pride when her pie wins first prize at the fair.
  b. Jethro is jealous because Elmer becomes an Eagle Scout.
  c. Ninotchka is disgusted because she must work overtime at the steel mill to meet her production quota.
  d. Engelbert would rather be promoted than get a big raise.
  (e.) Melba enjoys her tenth vodka of the night more than her second.

C 19. A consumer will buy goods until their relative market prices are proportional to the individual's:
  a. cost/benefit ratio.
  b. opportunity costs of production.
  (c.) subjective demand prices.
  d. comparative advantages.
  e. substitution effect.

20. If, in equilibrium, the marginal utility of a $10 haircut is 25 utils, then the willing purchase of an extra $2 hamburger must generate:
  a. the production of one-fifth of a haircut.
  (b.) 5 utils.
  c. an extra 20 minutes of work for a short order cook.
  d. 250 utils.
  e. 2 utils.

$$\frac{10}{25} \quad \frac{2}{5}$$

$10 \quad 25
$2 \quad 5

$$\frac{25}{10} \quad \frac{5}{2} \qquad \$10 \quad 25 \qquad \frac{10}{25} \quad \frac{2}{5}$$

$2 \quad X \qquad \frac{1}{5}$

TRUE/FALSE QUESTIONS

F 1. According to the central normative utilitarian principle, superior social organizations are those that fulfill the wishes of an elite group of leaders.

F 2. Marginal utility equals the satisfaction generated by a given rate of consumption of a particular good.

F 3. Recent scientific advances now allow interpersonal comparisons of utility to be made.

F 4. The law of diminishing marginal utility states that as one consumes equal successive units of a good, a point is inevitably reached where total utility begins to increase at an increasing rate when consumption is extended.

F 5. Even though marginal utility cannot be measured directly, total satisfaction can be approximated quantitatively by scientific market research.

T 6. Total utility is maximized when the marginal utilities of all goods consumed are exactly proportional to their prices.

T 7. For consumers in equilibrium, the ratios of the subjective demand prices of the goods purchased are the same as the relative market prices of the goods.

F 8. It has been shown empirically that total utility and income are inversely related.

F 9. Utilitarianism is now advocated by most moral philosophers.

F 10. The substitution effect shows the impact that a change in real income has on the consumption pattern of the consumer.

253

T 11. Many goods embody both positive and negative attributes.

E 12. The substitution effect is positive for luxury goods, roughly zero for most normal goods, and negative for inferior goods.

E 13. Similar attributes tend to make goods substitutes; complementarily tends to require goods to have dissimilar attributes.

T 14. Resources and commodities are only valuable to the extent that they embody streams of useful services.

T 15. Goods may become bads if they are excessively available.

F 16. Adverse selection occurs when all the "good" toppings at the salad bar have been consumed, leaving only the "icky" ones behind.

F 17. *Caveat emptor* has increasingly been replaced by government edict and the doctrine of *caveat venditor*.

T 18. Low-priced, standardized goods that are frequently purchased by most consumers are especially appropriate for the doctrine of *caveat emptor*.

T 19. Complicated goods that are infrequently purchased and have high prices are good candidates for imposition of the doctrine of *caveat venditor*.

F 20. Jeremy Bentham especially admired Adam Smith's idea that an "invisible hand" leads to a natural harmony in human behavior.

UNLIMITED MULTIPLE CHOICE

CAUTION: EACH QUESTION HAS FROM ZERO TO FOUR CORRECT ANSWERS.

___ 1. Marginal utility:
   a. is the gain in satisfaction generated by consuming an additional unit of a good.
   b. is computed by dividing the level of consumption of a particular good into the change in total utility.
   c. declines constantly as additional units of a good are consumed.
   d. is given by: Δ Total utility/ Δ Quantity of good.

___ 2. The substitution effect:
   a. is always positive.
   b. refers to changes in a consumer's buying patterns caused by changes in relative prices, assuming constant real income.
   c. is generally so powerful that it underpins the law of demand.
   d. shows that rational consumers always substitute relatively cheaper goods for relatively more expensive goods.

___ 3. In a world with only two commodities (X and Y) and money (M), total utility is maximized by a consumer when:
   a. $MU_x/P_y = MU_y/P_x = MU_m/P_m$.
   b. $MU_x = MU_y = MU_m$.
   c. $MU_x/MU_y = P_y/P_x$.
   d. $MU_x/P_x = MU_y/P_y = MU_m/P_m$.

___ 4. The income effect:
   a. is negative for inferior goods.
   b. shows the impact on the consumption pattern of the consumer of a change in real income caused by price changes.
   c. makes the demand curve for normal goods more negatively sloped.
   d. is positive for most economic goods.

5. According to the principle of equal marginal utilities per dollar, the consumer maximizes total utility when:
   a. the last cents spent on each good yield equal satisfaction.
   b. there is no reallocation of given money income that could increase total utility.
   c. at the margin, each dollar of money income is allocated in ways that are equally advantageous to the consumer.
   d. the last dollar one spends on any good yields the same satisfaction as the last dollar expended on any other good.

PROBLEMS

Problem 1

A consumer's total utilities from consuming various quantities of hats (H) and jelly (J) are provided in Table 1, along with three sets of price and income data.

Table 1

HATS (H)	TOTAL UTILITY	MARGINAL UTILITY	JELLY (J)	TOTAL UTILITY	MARGINAL UTILITY
0	0	—	0	0	—
1	100		1	50	
2	190		2	95	
3	270		3	135	
4	340		4	170	
5	400		5	200	
6	450		6	225	
7	490		7	245	
8	520		8	260	
9	540		9	270	
10	550		10	275	

DATA SET 1	DATA SET 2	DATA SET 3
Price of hats = $2	Price of hats = $1	Price of hats = $2
Price of jelly = 1	Price of jelly = $1	Price of jelly = $1
Income = $12	Income = $10	Income = $30

a. Complete the marginal utility columns for both goods.

b. What observed tendency or law do the marginal utility columns illustrate? Define this law.

   _____.

c. Graph total utility and marginal utility for each good in Figure 1. What do you notice about the rate at which total utility increases as consumption of each good is increased? _____.

d. Using the first data set for money prices and income, state real income in terms of hats _____ and in terms of jelly _____. At equilibrium, the consumer purchases _____ hats and _____ jars of jelly, and the MU_h is _____, while the MU_j is _____; total utility equals _____. State the marginal condition for utility maximization _____. The relative price of hats in terms of jelly is _____, while the relative price of jelly in terms of hats is _____.

e. Based on the second data set for money prices and income, real income in terms of hats is _____; in terms of jelly, it is _____. At equilibrium, the consumer purchases _____ hats and _____ jars of jelly, and the MU_h is _____, while that of jelly is _____; total utility equals _____, and the marginal utility of money is _____. The relative price of hats in terms of jelly is _____, while the relative price of jelly in terms of hats is _____.

f. Using the third data set for money prices and income, real income in terms of hats is _____; in terms of jelly it is _____. At equilibrium, the consumer purchases _____ hats and _____ jars of jelly, and the MU_h is _____, while the MU_j is _____; total utility equals _____. In equilibrium, the marginal utility of money is _____. The relative price of hats in terms of jelly is _____; while the relative price of jelly in terms of hats is _____.

g. Your answers to questions d through f suggest that total utility varies _____ with _____; and the marginal utility of money varies _____ with _____.

Figure 1

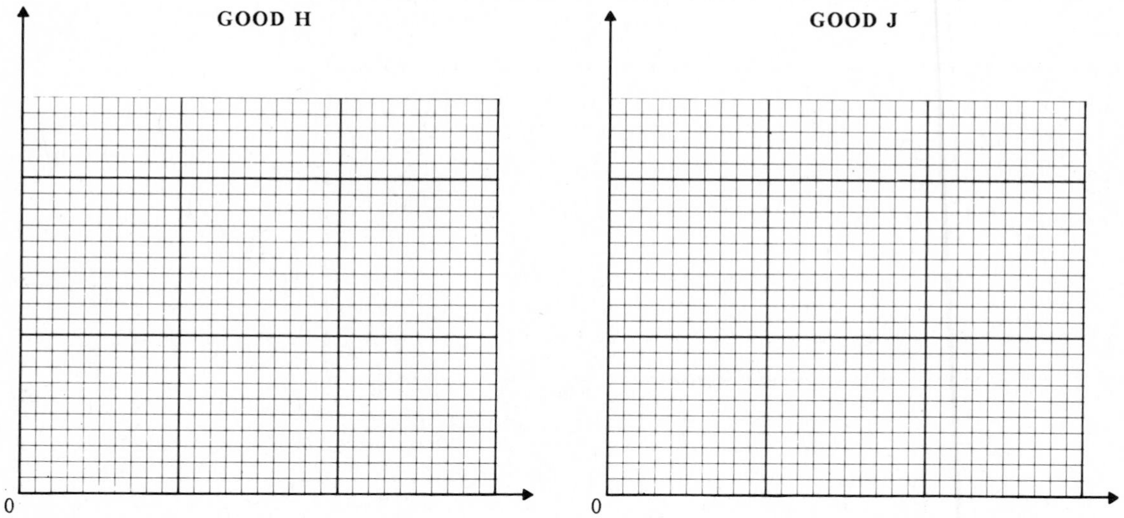

GOOD H

(a)

GOOD J

(b)

Problem 2

Ruby and Jeter Hapsburg want their daughter, Magda, to become a concert violinist. Figure 2 shows their demand for violin lessons and the supply facing them.

Figure 2

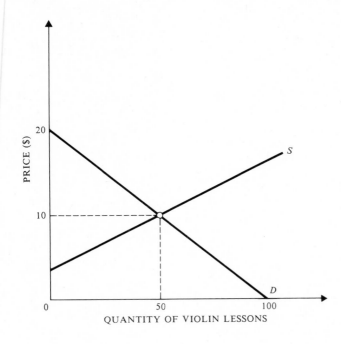

a. What is the dollar value of the total utility they would derive from the first 100 lessons? _____.

b. What is the dollar value of the total utility the Hapsburgs would derive from the first 50 lessons? _____.

c. In equilibrium, what is the dollar value of the Hapsburg's consumer surplus? _____ .

d. Approximately what is the dollar value of the marginal utility from the 100th lesson? _____. How much would the Hapsburgs willingly spend on the 100th lesson? _____. Why? _____.

e. How much extra consumer surplus do the Hapsburgs derive from the 50th lesson when lessons cost $10? _____.

Problem 3

*Optional material. Four of Caleb's indifference curves for avocados and balloons are mapped in Figure 3, along with budget constraint lines *UV* (original) and *UW* (new). Points *a* and *b* denote the two points of consumer equilibrium and Caleb's money income is $20. Answer the following true/false questions.

Figure 3

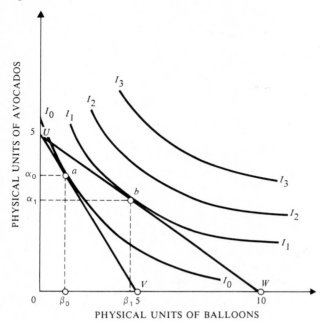

___ a.   Budget constraint *UV* has a slope of -2.

___ b.   Caleb originally maximizes total utility at point *a* because no spending reallocation can raise total utility.

___ c.   Balloons are originally $2 each.

___ d.   Avocados are originally $4 each.

___ e.   Caleb can move to a higher indifference curve because his real income rises when the budget line shifts from *UV* to *UW*.

___ f.   Growth of money income allows Caleb to move from *UV* to *UW*.

___ g.   These indifference curves show that the more balloons Caleb has, the fewer avocados he will trade for an additional balloon.

___ h.   Indifference curve I_1 has a slope of -1/2 at point *b*.

___ i.   At point *a*, $MU_a/P_a > MU_b/P_b$.

___ j.   Along budget constraint *UW*, the price of balloons is $2.

___ k.   At point *a*, $MU_b = 2MU_a$.

___ l.   At point *b*, $MU_a = 2MU_b$.

___ m.   The slope of budget constraint UV shows the original market rate of substitution between avocados and balloons.

___ n.   At point *b*, the price of balloons is $8 each.

___ o.   At point *a*, the price of avocados is $8 each.

___ p.   The substitution effect solely explains why Caleb moves from point *a* to point *b*.

___ q.   The shift from *UV* to *UW* is caused by a decrease in the price of balloons.

258

ANSWERS

Matching Key Terms and Concepts

SET I

Answer	MIC	ECO
1. i	p. 127	431
2. f	p. 123	427
3. e	p. 121	425
4. c	p. 127	431
5. h	p. 132	436
6. d	p. 121	425
7. j	p. 120	424
8. b	p. 126	430
9. a	p. 132	436
10. g	p. 123	427

SET II

Answer	MIC	ECO
1. d	p. 121	425
2. i	p. 120	424
3. e	p. 121	425
4. h	p. 129	433
5. g	p. 120	424
6. c	p. 128	432
7. a	p. 126	430
8. b	p, 136	440
9. f	p. 137	441
10. j	p. 138	442

Chapter Review (Fill-in Questions)

1. utils, marginal utility
2. bits of money, equal marginal utilities per dollar
3. *Y, X*
4. fall, rise
5. *X, Y*
6. normal, positive
7. Consumer surplus, market
8. below, demand
9. price, diamond-water
10. *caveat emptor, caveat venditor*

Standard Multiple Choice

Answer	MIC	ECO
1. c	p. 121	425
2. d	p. 126	430
3. a	p. 126	430
4. b	p. 126	430
5. a	p. 120	424
6. e	p. 132	436
7. e	p. 120	424
8. b	p. 130	434
9. a	p. 121	425
10. c	p. 127	431
11. b	p. 129	433
12. e	p. 126	430
13. a	p. 127	431
14. e	p. 132	436
15. d	p. 121	425
16. a	p. 132	436
17. c	p. 125	429
18. e	p. 123	427
19. c	p. 127	431
20. b	p. 126	430

True/False Questions

Answer	MIC	ECO
1. F	p. 121	425
2. F	p. 123	427
3. F	p. 123	428
4. F	p. 123	428
5. F	p. 123	428
6. T	p. 126	430
7. T	p. 127	431
8. F	p. 126	430
9. F	p. 121	425
10. F	p. 120	424
11. T	p. 129	433
12. F	p. 129	433
13. T	p. 129	433
14. T	p. 120	424
15. T	p. 119	423
16. F	p. 132	436
17. T	p. 132	436
18. T	p. 132	436
19. T	p. 132	436
20. F	p. 122	436

Unlimited Multiple Choice

Answer	MIC	ECO
1. ad	p. 123	427
2. bc	p. 120	424
3. d	p. 126	430
4. abcd	p. 121	435
5. abcd	p. 126	430

PROBLEM 1
MIC pp. 123-127; *ECO 427-431*

a. See Table 2.

Table 2

UNITS OF Q	TOTAL UTILITY	MARGINAL UTILITY	UNITS OF Z	TOTAL UTILITY	MARGINAL UTILITY
0	0	--	0	0	--
1	100	100	1	50	50
2	190	90	2	95	45
3	270	80	3	135	40
4	340	70	4	170	35
5	400	60	5	200	30
6	450	50	6	225	25
7	490	40	7	245	20
8	520	30	8	260	15
9	540	20	9	270	10
10	550	10	10	275	5

b. Law of diminishing marginal utility; as you consume equal successive units of a commodity, a point is eventually reached where the consumption of an additional unit yields less satisfaction (utility) than that of the preceding unit.

c. It increases at a diminishing rate.

d. 6; 12; 4; 4; 70 utils; 35 utils; 510 utils; $MU_h/P_h = MU_j/P_j$; 35 utils; 2; 1/2.

e. 10; 10; 7; 3; 40 utils; 40 utils; 625 utils; 40 utils; 1; 1.

f. 15; 30; 10; 10; 10 utils; 5 utils; 825 utils; 5 utils; 2; 1/2.

g. directly, real income; inversely, real income.

PROBLEM 2
MIC pp. 127-128; *ECO 431-432*

a. $1,000 (the area under the demand curve from $P = 20$ to $P = 0$).

b. $750 (the area under the demand curve from $P = 20$ to $P = 10$).

c. $250 (the area of the triangle above $10 and below the demand curve).

d. 0; 0; because the consumer receives only infinitesimal satisfaction (or utility) from consuming the 100th unit.

e. Infinitesimal (arbitrarily close to 0).

PROBLEM 3
MIC pp. 135-139; *ECO 439-443*

a. F
b. T
c. F
d. T
e. T
f. F
g. T
h. T
i. F
j. T
k. F
l. T
m. T
n. F
o. F
p. F
q. T

CHAPTER TWENTY-TWO
FOUNDATIONS OF PRODUCER DECISIONMAKING

CHAPTER OBJECTIVES

After you have read and studied this chapter, you should be able to discuss production relationships between inputs and outputs; describe the linkages between production and costs as a firm's output rises or falls; and distinguish accounting and economic concepts of profits and costs.

Note: This relatively technical chapter requires concentrated effort.

CHAPTER REVIEW: KEY POINTS

1. A *production function* expresses a relationship between inputs and output. Production transforms goods to make them more valuable in form, place, time, or possession. A *total physical product curve* shows how output is affected as the amount of only one input changes.

2. The *short run* is a period in which at least one resource and one cost are fixed. In the long run all resources can be varied, but technology is assumed constant. These periods, therefore, are not defined by time, but rather by the nature of the adjustment process.

3. Economic costs include both explicit and implicit costs. *Explicit costs* involve outlays of money for goods or resources. *Implicit costs* are the opportunity costs of resources provided by a firm's owner. Payments for rent, electricity, and wages are explicit costs, whereas the values of the owner's labor and capital are implicit costs.

4. Bookkeeping rarely considers implicit costs, while both implicit and explicit costs are included in economic costs. Consequently, *accounting profits* often overstate the economic profitability of an enterprise because the opportunity costs of owner-provided resources are ignored.

5. The *average physical product of labor (APP$_L$)* equals q/L. The *marginal physical product of labor (MPP$_L$)* equals $\Delta q/\Delta L$, and is the output generated by an additional unit of labor.

6. When increasing amounts of a variable resource are applied to a fixed resource, although the marginal physical product of the variable factor may initially rise, beyond some point its marginal product inevitably falls according to the *law of diminishing marginal returns*.

7. A firm's total costs can be separated into *fixed costs* (or *overhead*) and *variable* (or *operating*) *costs*. Fixed costs do not vary with output and do not alter rational decisions. Leases, utility hookup charges, opportunity costs of an owner's resources, and other overhead expenses are fixed costs in the short run. Wages paid employees, bills for raw materials, and other costs that change when output is changed are variable costs.

8. When total fixed costs and total variable costs are each divided by output, *average fixed costs (AFC)* and *average variable costs (AVC)* are obtained, respectively. Summing the two yields average total cost *(ATC)*. *Marginal cost (MC)* is defined as the additional cost of producing one more unit of a good and equals $\Delta TC/\Delta q$.

© 1989 Scott, Foresman and Company

9. Firms can enter or leave an industry in the long run because all resources are variable. The *long-run average cost curve (LRAC)* is an **envelope curve** under all short-run average cost curves (different-sized plants). It shows the minimum long-run average costs for each output level. Long-run average cost curves typically have *economies of scale* (*LRAC* falling) over some portion of the curve, but eventually exhibit *diseconomies of scale* (*LRAC* rising).

10. Measuring long-run costs is a complex and difficult problem. One method is to examine the size (and cost structure) of firms that have been successful and have "survived" in an industry over a long period of time, but reasons other than efficiency may explain why one firm survives while another fails.

11. *Technological progress* increases output from given resources. New technology resides in new knowledge or improved nonhuman resources, and results in new products or lower costs. Technological improvements account for much of our long-term economic growth and rising productivity.

MATCHING KEY TERMS AND CONCEPTS

SET I

F 1. survival principle F
A 2. sunk costs ✓ A
B 3. psychic income B
G 4. production function G
J 5. accounting profits J
E 6. explicit costs ✓ E
H 7. short run H
I 8. implicit costs I
C 9. economic profits C
D 10. long run D

a. A type of fixed cost.

b. Non-monetary satisfaction derived from an activity.

c. Total revenue minus both explicit and implicit costs.

d. All resources and costs are variable.

e. Out-of-pocket payments by a firm.

f. Only efficiently-sized firms pass the market test.

g. Relationship between inputs and outputs.

h. At least one factor or cost cannot be altered.

i. The use value of the entrepreneur's resources.

j. Total revenue minus explicit costs.

TR -

SET II

H 1. average fixed cost (AFC)

D 2. marginal cost (MC)

J 3. average physical product (APP$_L$)

F 4. fixed cost (TFC)

C 5. total variable cost (TVC)

I 6. average variable cost (AVC)

E 7. marginal physical product (MPP$_L$)

G 8. average total cost (ATC)

B 9. total product curve

A 10. total cost (TC)

a. TFC + TVC. *TC*

b. Increases at an increasing rate, then at a decreasing rate, and may finally decline. *Total prod. curve*

c. Costs incurred only when production occurs. *TVC*

d. The extra cost of an added unit of output. *MC*

e. Output per additional worker. *MPP$_L$*

f. Costs incurred regardless of the level of output. *TFC*

g. Per unit costs of production. *ATC*

h. Declines continuously as output rises. *AFC*
Output ↑

i. Per unit costs excluding "overhead." *AVC*

j. Output per worker.
APP$_L$

SET III

I 1. law of diminishing marginal returns

J 2. normal profits

H 3. equal marginal productivities per dollar

B 4. overhead costs

C 5. long run average cost (LRAC) curve

G 6. operating costs

D 7. diseconomies of scale

E 8. least cost production

F 9. technological change

A 10. economies of scale

a. LRAC falls as output grows. *cost ↓ output ↑*

b. A synonym for fixed cost.

c. An "envelope" curve under the minimal SRAC for each output level.

d. LRAC rises as output grows. *cost ↑ output ↑*

e. Occurs when the principle of equal marginal productivities per dollar is met. *least cost production*

f. Increases output with a given set of resources.

g. Also known as variable cost or direct cost.

h. MPP$_L$/w = MPP$_K$/i = ...

i. Additions of variable inputs to some fixed influence on production ultimately yield less and less additional output.

j. An economic cost, but not an accounting cost. *Normal profit*

CHAPTER REVIEW (FILL-IN QUESTIONS)

1-2. In the _SR_ , at least one _resource_ and the firm's cost of acquiring it are fixed, but in the _LR_ all inputs and costs are _variable_ .

3. _economic_ costs include out-of-pocket expenses plus such _implicit_ costs as the values of the entrepreneur's resources--labor and owned capital, etc.

4. Total costs (TC) include both _TFC_ costs that do not change with output, and _TVC_ costs, which do.

5. Because fixed cost does not change with output, marginal cost can be written as $\Delta TC/\Delta Q$ or as $\Delta TVC/\Delta Q$.

6. The vertical distance between the ATC and AVC curves equals _AFC_ which, when graphed alone, is a _rectangular_ _hyperbola_ because AFC = TFC/Q, so Q x AFC = TFC, which is a constant.

7-8. When the law of _dim. marg returns_ sets in, total product continues to _grow_ but at a _decreasing_ rate; total cost and total variable cost will also rise, but now at _increasing_ rates.

9. By enveloping from below the short run average cost curves associated with various possible levels of the fixed resources, we derive a(n) _LRAC_ curve. Where this curve declines as output rises, there are _economies of scale_ in production.

10. According to the _survival_ principle, only those firms that evolve to the most efficient size (lowest _ave. cost_ of production) will pass the test of the market place by exhibiting staying power.

STANDARD MULTIPLE CHOICE

THERE IS ONLY ONE BEST ANSWER FOR EACH QUESTION.

B 1. Not among the types of utility created by production is:
   a. form.
   b. substance.
   c. time.
   d. place.
   e. possession.

D 2. The relationships between all possible inputs and the level of a firm's output are summarized in a(n):
   a. input/output matrix.
   b. production possibilities frontier.
   c. total product curve.
   d. production function.
   e. elasticity of supply.

B 3. Short, and long runs are different in the:
   a. lengths of time considered.
   b. range of responses available to changes in profit opportunities.
   c. total amounts of revenues, costs, and profits experienced.
   d. differences between average and marginal productivity.
   e. flexibility of government policymakers.

C 4. Profit opportunities often induce technological advances that increase:
   a. market demand.
   b. the need for central planning.
   c. long run market supplies.
   d. capitalistic exploitation.
   e. population growth rates.

D 5. The total product curve may initially show output increasing at an increasing rate as more labor is hired because of the:
   a. declining quality of the labor force.
   b. principle of comparative advantage.
   c. law of diminishing marginal returns.
   d. increase in marginal physical product.
   e. rapid rate of technological advance.

E 6. If labor is the only variable resource and its marginal physical product falls as more workers are hired::
   a. the law of diminishing marginal returns is at work.
   b. marginal cost is rising.
   c. average cost may still be declining.
   d. average physical product may still be rising.
   e. All of the above.

D 7. The value of an entrepreneur's resources are known as:
   a. explicit costs.
   b. sunk costs.
   c. operating expenses.
   d. implicit costs.
   e. expected profits.

C 8. Costs incurred only when production occurs are known as:
   a. explicit costs.
   b. fixed cost.
   c. variable cost.
   d. technological expenses.
   e. implicit cost.

C 9. The law of diminishing marginal returns is encountered as increasing amounts of labor are hired because:
   a. as production rises, the additional labor hired is less and less skilled.
   b. experienced workers are hired before the less skilled.
   c. each extra worker hired decreases the amounts of land and capital per worker, so the work place becomes more congested and managerial control becomes more difficult.
   d. as more and more is produced, selling it requires cutting prices.
   e. All of the above.

C 10. Which of the following is irrelevant for **rational** decisionmaking?
   a. average variable cost (AVC).
   b. explicit cost.
   c. average fixed cost (AFC).
   d. marginal cost (MC).
   e. implicit cost.

C 11. Which of the following curves can never be "U" shaped?
   a. average variable cost
   b. marginal cost
   c. average fixed cost
   d. average total cost
   e. long run average cost

C 12. Diminishing marginal returns are most compatible with:
   a. economies of scale.
   b. advantages from specialization.
   c. positively-sloped marginal cost curves.
   d. depreciation of the capital stock.
   e. a unionized labor force.

E 13. If average variable costs fall as output grows:
   a. marginal costs must also be declining.
   b. fixed cost must also be declining.
   c. total cost must also be declining.
   d. average cost must be below average variable cost.
   e. marginal costs must be below average variable cost.

AVC
cost ↓
output ↑

B 14. The application to production of the law of equal advantage yields the principle of:
   a. diminishing marginal returns.
   b. equal marginal productivities per dollar.
   c. variable compensation.
   d. comparable worth.
   e. decreasing marginal cost.

A 15. Declines in long run average cost when a firm expands its capacity occur under conditions of:
   a. economies of scale.
   b. decreasing cost industries.
   c. diminishing marginal returns.
   d. diseconomies of scale.
   e. accelerated depreciation schedules.

265

E 16. Least cost production in the long run requires firms to adjust their resource mixes until the relative prices of resources are equal to the relative:
a. prices of outputs.
b. total costs in acquiring each resource.
c. average productivity per resource.
d. economies of scale of production.
e. marginal productivities of the resources.

D 17. When a firm is experiencing diseconomies of scale:
a. larger firms with bigger plants will tend to be more successful.
b. it should increase the amount of labor it hires.
c. it should fire inept executives and get rid of "dead wood."
d. its average cost will decline if it scales down its operations.
e. average cost will be cut by adopting more modern technology.

A 18. The survival principle is questionable because:
a. efficient firms in declining industries may fail while inefficient firms in growing industries prosper.
b. inefficient firms will survive over the long run if their owners are extremely wealthy.
c. efficient firms that take pride in quality may lose out to inefficient firms that put out shoddy products.
d. in the long run, every organization fails and we all die.
e. All of the above.

A 19. If long run average cost rises as the output and the size of the plant grows:
a. diseconomies of scale are present.
b. marginal cost is below long run average cost.
c. fixed costs are increasingly important for decision making.
d. this is an increasing-cost industry.
e. prices and profit expand proportionally.

A 20. The idea that competitive firms enjoy long run success only by building plants of the optimal size is known as the:
a. survival principle.
b. entrepreneurial hero hypothesis.
c. business Darwinism theory.
d. optimal technology axiom.
e. critical mass corollary.

TRUE/FALSE QUESTIONS

__T__ 1. Production entails transforming goods or resources to create utilities of form, place, time, or possession.

__F__ 2. ? Production functions (how outputs change if one input varies) are synonymous with total output curves.

__F__ 3. Marginal cost is the change in the total cost of all output produced by an additional unit of labor.

__F__ 4. The long run average cost (envelope) curve reflects the plant size associated with the minimum average cost of producing each possible level of output. $ATC/\Delta Q$

__F__ 5. Profitable but inefficient firms inevitably fail.

__F__ 6. Accounting costs and profits are better guides than economic costs and profits to good business decisions.

__T__ 7. The law of diminishing marginal returns asserts that if all resources are simultaneously and proportionally increased, a point is inevitably reached where total output diminishes only at an increasing rate.

__F__ 8. Total product curves allow all resources to vary, while production functions assume that only one input changes.

__T__ 9. Hiring additional workers results in changes in the marginal and average productivities of workers primarily because of the changing short run amounts of fixed resources per worker.

__F__ 10. When the marginal physical product of labor is rising, the average physical product of labor is falling; and when the marginal physical product of labor is falling, the average physical product of labor is rising.

__F__ 11. Implicit costs account for most bookkeeping costs that are deducted from revenue to compute a firm's taxable income.

__F__ 12. The average fixed cost curve, a horizontal line, is a major factor in short run business decisionmaking.

__T__ 13. As output is increased, the minimums of the MC, AVC, and ATC curves are encountered in that order.

__T__ 14. Overhead, historical cost, sunk cost, and fixed cost are all roughly synonymous; and differ from direct cost, operating cost, and variable cost, which are also roughly synonymous.

__T__ 15. The total product curve tends to increase at an increasing rate initially, when the advantages of specialization are being realized, but marginal returns eventually begin to diminish.

__T__ 16. The principle of equal marginal productivities per dollar in production theory parallels the principle of equal marginal utilities per dollar from consumer theory.

__T__ 17. Technological advances that are responses to profit opportunities in the long run invariably reduce the minimum points of long run average cost curves.

__T__ 18. The average variable cost (AVC) and average total cost (ATC) curves are intersected at their minimum points from below by the marginal cost (MC) curve.

__F__ 19. Marginal physical productivity curves are direct measures of each worker's contribution to a firm's profits.

__F__ 20. Horizontal summation of the AFC and AVC curves yields the ATC curve.

267

:H QUESTION HAS FROM ZERO TO FOUR CORRECT ANSWERS.

1. :icroeconomics of production theory:
   :actors of production are fixed in the
   :rt run.
   :least one resource is fixed in the long
   :n, but firms can freely either enter or
   leave an industry.
   (c.) short runs and long runs refer to economic
   adjustments rather than to time per se.
   (d.) it is impossible to say what specific
   temporal time period is sufficient for
   firms to reach long-run adjustment.

2. The law of diminishing marginal returns
   suggests that:
   (a.) declining amounts of a fixed resource per
   variable resource eventually causes the
   marginal productivity of the variable
   resource to fall.
   (b.) beyond some point, larger enterprises will
   have higher average costs than smaller
   production units.
   (c.) it is impossible to grow the world's food
   supply in a flower pot.
   (d.) not all influences on production can be
   changed proportionally during any finite
   period.

3. The marginal physical product of labor:
   a. is the change in total cost associated with
   producing an additional unit of output.
   b. can be computed as w/ATC.
   (c.) will shift upward if all labor becomes more
   productive at each possible level of
   input.
   (d.) intersects the average product of labor
   curve from above when the average
   product of labor attains its maximum
   value. $\not{\Delta B}$ $\frac{\Delta Q}{\Delta}$

4. Average fixed cost:
   (a.) varies inversely with output.
   (b.) is the shape of a rectangular hyperbola
   when graphed.
   c. remains unchanged as output decreases.
   (d.) varies directly with total fixed cost.

5. Economies and diseconomies of scale,
   respectively, are:
   a. present when short run average cost falls
   and then rises.
   b. reflections of diminishing returns and
   specialization.
   c. the result of fixing labor and then capital.
   (d.) only realized in the long run.

PROBLEMS

Problem 1

Table 1 summarizes a firm's production and cost data.

Table 1

UNITS OF VARIABLE INPUT (L) Q	Q/L APP_L	$\Delta Q/\Delta L$ MPP_L	w	TFC	$W\Delta L$ TVC	$TFC+TVC$ TC	TFC/Q AFC	TVC/Q AVC	TC/Q ATC	$\frac{\Delta TC}{\Delta Q}$ MC	$\frac{\Delta TVC}{\Delta Q}$
0	0	0	0	$10	$50	0	$50	0	0	0	0
1	5	5	5	10	50	10	60	10	2	12	2
2	15	7.5	10	10	50	20	70	3.33	1.3	4.67	1
3	30	10	15	10	50	30	80	1.67	1	2.67	.67
4	50	12.5	20	10	50	40	90	1	.8	1.8	.5
5	75	15	25	10	50	50	100	.67	.67	1.33	.4
6	95	15.83	20	10	50	60	110	.53	.63	1.16	.5
7	110	15.71	15	10	50	70	120	.45	.64	1.09	.67
8	120	15	10	10	50	80	130	.42	.67	1.08	1
9	125	13.89	5	10	50	90	140	.4	.72	1.12	2
10	125	12.5	1	10	50	100	150	.4	.8	1.2	0

APP_L $\frac{}{Q/L}$ MPP_L $\frac{}{\Delta Q/\Delta L}$ TVC $\frac{}{W \times L}$ TC $\frac{}{TFC+TVC}$ AFC $\frac{}{TFC/Q}$ AVC $\frac{}{TVC/Q}$

ATC $\frac{}{TC/Q}$ MC $\frac{\Delta TC}{\Delta Q}$

a. Which period of production is depicted above? _SR_ Why? _fixed_ .

b. Please fill in the blanks in Table 1.

c. Graph the total product and average and marginal physical product curves in Figure 1.

d. Use Figure 2 to graph the total cost curve, the total variable cost curve, and the total fixed cost curve.

e. Use Figure 3 to graph the average total cost, average variable cost, average fixed cost, and marginal cost curves.

Figure 1

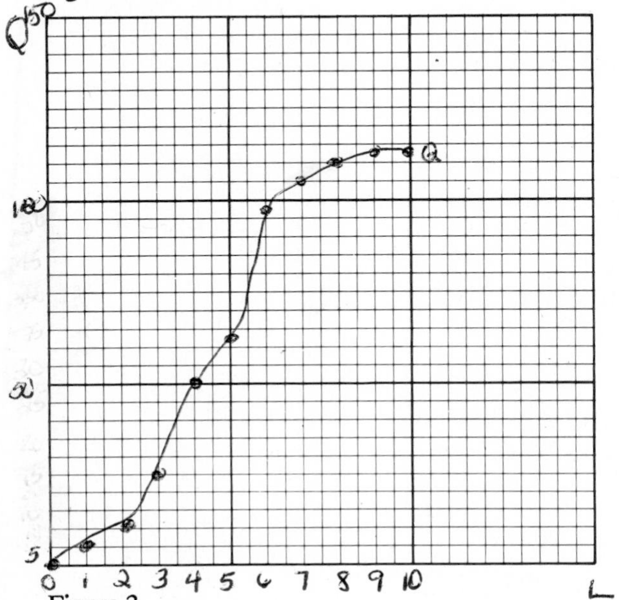

Figure 2

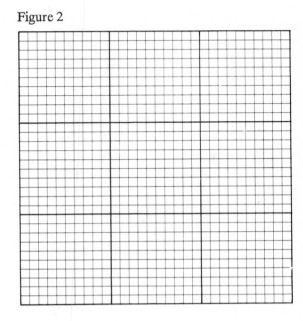

Figure 3

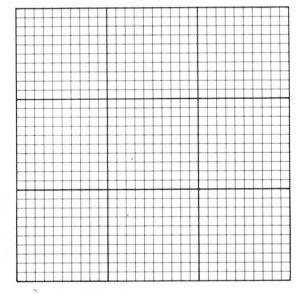

f. Over what input range do marginal returns increase? _____ . remain constant? _____ diminish? _____ .

Problem 2

Table 2 summarizes production and cost relationships for a different product and firm.

Table 2

UNITS OF VARIABLE INPUT (L)	Q	APP_L	MPP_L	w	TFC	TVC	TC	AFC	AVC	ATC	MC
0	0	___	___	$20	$100	___	___	___	___	___	___
1	10	___	___	20	100	___	___	___	___	___	___
2	22	___	___	20	100	___	___	___	___	___	___
3	36	___	___	20	100	___	___	___	___	___	___
4	52	___	___	20	100	___	___	___	___	___	___
5	70	___	___	20	100	___	___	___	___	___	___
6	90	___	___	20	100	___	___	___	___	___	___
7	108	___	___	20	100	___	___	___	___	___	___
8	124	___	___	20	100	___	___	___	___	___	___
9	138	___	___	20	100	___	___	___	___	___	___
10	150	___	___	20	100	___	___	___	___	___	___
11	160	___	___	20	100	___	___	___	___	___	___
12	168	___	___	20	100	___	___	___	___	___	___
13	174	___	___	20	100	___	___	___	___	___	___
14	178	___	___	20	100	___	___	___	___	___	___
15	180	___	___	20	100	___	___	___	___	___	___
16	182	___	___	20	100	___	___	___	___	___	___

a. Complete the blanks in Table 2.

b. Which production period is depicted in the table? _____. Why? _____.

c. Over what range of the variable input does this firm encounter increasing marginal returns? _____; constant marginal returns? _____; diminishing marginal returns? _____.

Problem 3

Use Figure 4 to answer the questions which follow.

a. At output Q_2, average variable cost is ___ H ___?

b. At output Q_1, total variable costs are equal to area 0ABQ_6 ___?

c. At output Q_0, average total costs are ___ G ___?

d. Total cost at output Q_2 is equal to area _____?

e. Total fixed costs are equal to area CFGD ___?

Figure 4

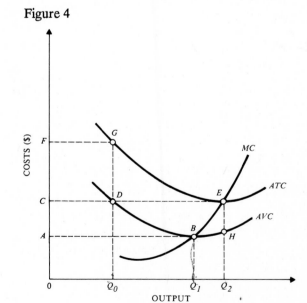

Problem 4

This problem is based on the optional material at the end of Chapter 8. Figure 5 shows an isoquant map with original isocost curve *AB* and new isocost curve *AC*. The firm is assumed to maximize profits and has $500 available to purchase resources.

Figure 5

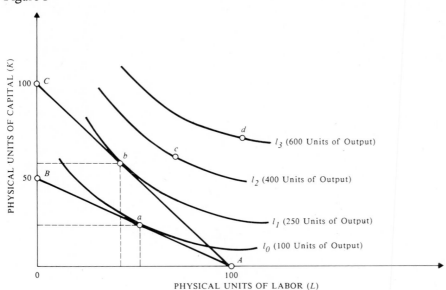

a. What is the original price of capital? _____
How did you compute it? _____

b. What is the original price of labor? _____.
How did you compute it? _____

c. What is the new price of capital? _____. How
did you compute it? _____

d. What is the new price of labor? _____. How
did you compute it? _____

e. The firm is originally in equilibrium at which point?
_____ Why? _____. State the
marginal condition for output maximization or
cost minimization. _____.

f. The new equilibrium point for this firm is at
_____. Why? _____.

g. The isoquant curves are (convex, concave) to the
origin, illustrating the law of (increasing,
diminishing, constant) marginal returns. Explain
what this physical law means.

_____.

h. Write an equation for isocost curve *AB* _____
Write an equation for isocost curve *AC*

_____.

i. What are the relative magnitudes of MPP_K and
MPP_L at point *b*? _____. Why?

_____

j. What are the relative magnitudes of MPP_K and
MPP_L at point *a*? _____. Why?

_____

k. At present, can the firm attain point *c*? _____
Why or why not? _____ What must
change before point *c* becomes attainable?

_____

l. What is the expression for the slope of *AB* in terms
of the money prices for capital and labor?

_____

m. What is the expression for the slope of *AC* in terms
of the money prices for capital and labor?

_____

n. What is the expression for the slope of isoquant I_0
at point *a*? _____

271

ANSWERS

Matching Key Terms and Concepts

SET I

Answer	MIC	ECO
1. f	p. 157	461
2. a	p. 147	451
3. b	p. 141	445
4. g	p. 143	447
5. j	p. 141	445
6. e	p. 140	444
7. h	p. 142	446
8. i	p. 140	444
9. c	p. 141	445
10. d	p. 142	446

SET II

Answer	MIC	ECO
1. h	p. 149	453
2. d	p. 149	453
3. j	p. 143	447
4. f	p. 146	450
5. c	p. 147	451
6. i	p. 149	453
7. e	p. 143	447
8. g	p. 149	453
9. b	p. 144	448
10. a	p. 146	450

SET III

Answer	MIC	ECO
1. i	p. 144	448
2. j	p. 141	445
3. h	p. 154	458
4. b	p. 146	450
5. c	p. 156	460
6. g	p. 146	450
7. d	p. 156	460
8. e	p. 155	459
9. f	p. 158	462
10. a	p. 156	460

Chapter Review (Fill-in Questions)

1. short-run, resource
2. long-run, variable
3. Economic, implicit
4. fixed, variable
5. $\Delta TC/\Delta Q$, $\Delta TVC/\Delta Q$
6. average fixed costs (AFC), rectangular hyperbola
7. diminishing marginal returns, grow
8. decreasing, increasing
9. long run average cost, economies of scale
10. survival, average cost

Standard Multiple Choice

Answer	MIC	ECO
1. b	p. 142	446
2. d	p. 143	447
3. b	p. 142	446
4. c	p. 158	462
5. d	p. 144	448
6. e	p. 144	448
7. d	p. 140	444
8. c	p. 147	451
9. c	p. 144	448
10. c	p. 149	453
11. c	p. 149	453
12. c	p. 144	448
13. e	p. 151	455
14. b	p. 154	458
15. a	p. 156	460
16. e	p. 155	459
17. d	p. 156	460
18. a	p. 157	461
19. a	p. 156	460
20. a	p. 157	461

True/False Questions

Answer	MIC	ECO
1. T	p. 142	446
2. F	p. 143	447
3. F	p. 150	454
4. T	p. 157	461
5. F	p. 141	445
6. F	p. 141	445
7. F	p. 144	448
8. F	p. 144	448
9. T	p. 143	447
10. F	p. 144	448
11. F	p. 141	445
12. F	p. 149	453
13. T	p. 152	456
14. T	p. 146	450
15. T	p. 144	448
16. T	p. 154	458
17. T	p. 158	462
18. T	p. 152	456
19. F	p. 143	447
20. F	p. 149	453

Problem 1

MIC pp. 142-145; *ECO 446-449*

a. Short run; because there are fixed costs.

b. See Table 3.

Table 3

APP_L	MPP_L	TVC	TC	AFC	AVC	ATC	**MC**
- - -	- - -	- - -	$ 50	- - -	- - -	- - -	- - -
5	5	$10	60	$10	$2	$12	$2
7.50	10	20	70	3.33	1.22	4.66	1
10	15	30	80	1.66	1	2.66	0.66
12.50	20	40	90	1	0.80	1.80	0.50
15	25	50	100	0.66	0.66	1.33	0.40
15.83	20	60	110	0.52	0.63	1.15	0.50
15.71	15	70	120	0.63	0.64	1.09	0.66
15	10	80	130	0.41	0.66	1.08	1
13.88	5	90	140	0.40	0.72	1.12	2
12.50	0	100	150	0.40	0.80	1.20	infinity

c. See Figure 6

d. See Figure 7.

Figure 6

Figure 7

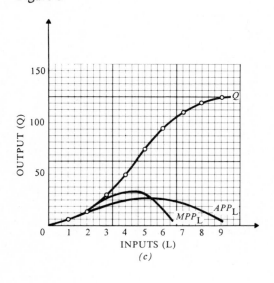

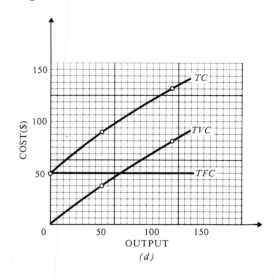

273

e. See Figure 8.

f. 1-5; 5; 5-10.

Figure 8

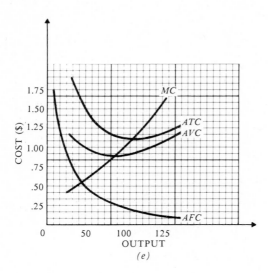

(e)

Problem 2
MIC pp. 142, 150; *ECO 446, 454*

a. See Table 4.

b. short run; fixed costs are included in table.

c. 1-6; 6; 6-16.

Table 4

L	APP$_L$	MPP$_L$	TVC	TC	AFC	AVC	ATC	MC
0	- - -	- - -	0	$100	- - -	- - -	- - -	- - -
1	10	10	$20	120	$10	$2	$12	$2
2	11	12	40	140	4.54	1.81	6.36	1.66
3	12	14	60	160	2.77	1.66	4.44	1.42
4	13	16	80	180	1.92	1.53	3.46	1.25
5	14	18	100	200	1.42	1.42	2.85	1.11
6	15	20	120	220	1.11	1.33	2.44	1
7	15.42	18	140	240	0.92	1.30	2.22	1.11
8	15.50	16	160	260	0.80	1.29	2.09	1.25
9	15.30	14	180	280	0.72	1.30	2.02	1.42
10	15	12	200	300	0.66	1.33	2	1.66
11	14.54	10	220	320	0.62	1.37	2	2
12	14	8	240	340	0.59	1.42	2.02	2.50
13	13.38	6	260	360	0.57	1.49	2.06	3.33
14	12.71	4	280	380	0.56	1.57	2.13	5
15	12	2	300	400	0.55	1.66	2.22	10
16	11.25	0	320	420	0.55	1.77	2.33	infinity

Problem 3
MIC pp. 149-152; *ECO 453-456*

a. Q_2H or $0A$

b. $OABQ_1$

c. GQ_0 or $0F$

d. $OCEQ_2$

e. $CFGD$

Problem 4
MIC pp. 163-167; *ECO 467-471*

a. $10, $500/50

b. $5, $500/100

c. $5, $500/100

d. $5, $500/100

e. a; a dollar spent on each input yields the same output; $MPP_L/P_L = MPP_K/P_K$ or $MPP_L/MPP_K = P_L/P_K$

f. b; a dollar spent on each input yields the same output; $MPP_L/P_L = MPP_K/P_K$ or $MPP_L/MPP_K = P_L/P_K$

g. convex; diminishing; as additional equal units of a variable input are applied to fixed inputs, a point is reached where total output increases at a diminishing rate.

h. $500 = -1/2Q_L + Q_K, $500 = -1Q_L + Q_K$

i. Same; $P_K = P_L$

j. $MPP_K = 2MPP_L, P_K = 2P_L$

k. No; real dollar outlay too small; decrease in input prices or more outlay on inputs.

l. $-P_L/P_K = -$5/$10 = -1/2$

m. $-P_L/P_K = -$10/$10 = -1$

n. $-MPP_L/MPP_K$

CHAPTER TWENTY-THREE
THE COMPETITIVE IDEAL

CHAPTER OBJECTIVES

After you have read and studied this chapter, you should be able to explain the differences between price-taking and price-making, and the differences between competing and competition. You should be able to describe the output decisions of competitive firms and indicate how competitive firms adjust to profit signals in the short and long run. You should know what features of competitive markets make them attractive from the vantage points of efficiency, equity, and prediction. Finally, you should understand the differences between constant cost, increasing costs, and decreasing cost industries.

CHAPTER REVIEW: KEY POINTS

1. Freedom of *entry and exit* is the hallmark of competition. A purely competitive market is comprised of numerous potential buyers and sellers of a homogeneous product, none of whom controls its price. All buyers and sellers are sufficiently small relative to the market so that none is a *price maker*.

2. A competitive buyer faces a perfectly elastic supply curve, while competitive sellers face perfectly elastic demand curves. In competition, all are *price-takers* or *quantity adjusters*.

3. We assume that no firm can adjust output in the *market period*, so total supply is perfectly inelastic. In the *short run (SR)*, existing firms in an industry can vary output, but at least one productive factor is fixed and entry and exit cannot occur. Total supply is at least somewhat elastic. Supply is much more elastic in the long run (LR), because all factors of production are variable and firms may enter or leave the industry.

4. The competitive firm maximizes profits by producing output up to the point where *total revenues minus total costs (TR - TC)* is maximized or *marginal revenue equals marginal cost* (MR = MC). Price must be greater than the minimum of the average variable cost curve, however, which is the *shutdown point*. Because competitive firms face perfectly elastic demands, price (average revenue) and marginal revenue are identical. *Break-even points* are the quantities at which total revenue and total cost are equal.

5. A competitive firm's *short-run supply curve* is its marginal cost curve above the minimum of its average variable costs. Horizontally summing the marginal costs from existing firms yields the *short-run industry supply curve*.

6. Competition erases *economic profits* through entry of new firms in the long run, and economic losses are eradicated by exit from the industry. Thus, competitive firms receive exactly enough revenue over the long run to pay the opportunity costs of resources used and realize only *zero economic profit*.

7. Short-run economic profits are ultimately eliminated because either output will be expanded by both existing and new firms in a competitive industry or increased competition for profitable inputs will drive up resource costs. The long-run adjustments that eliminate short-run losses follow precisely reversed patterns.

8. In the long run, firms are forced by competitive pressures to adopt the most efficient (least costly) plant size and technologies. They operate at output levels where P = MR = SRAC = SRMC = LRAC = LRMC.

For *constant-cost industries*, the minimum LRAC for firms is the same no matter how many firms are in the industry. Costs increase for each firm as firms enter *increasing-cost industries*, and decrease for decreasing-cost industries. Thus, the *long-run industry supply curve* is positively sloped for *increasing-cost industries*, horizontal for *constant-cost industries,* and negatively sloped for *decreasing-cost industries*.

9. A purely competitive market is efficient in the sense that goods are produced at the lowest possible opportunity cost. Every feasible bit of net gain is squeezed from the resources available; marginal social benefits and marginal social costs are equated by competitive forces of supply and demand (MSB = MSC), assuming the absence of externalities. This will be socially optimal and maximize social welfare if the distribution of income is deemed appropriate. A market system does not require that decision making power be vested in a central authority. This permits substantial personal freedom and the absence of coercion.

MSB demand

MATCHING KEY TERMS AND CONCEPTS

SET I

E 1. MR = P F

I 2. market period I

D 3. MC above AVC D

J 4. freedom of entry and exit J

B 5. Long run B

H 6. MSC = MSB H

A 7. MR = MC A

E 8. Increasing cost industry E

G 9. Short run G

C 10. P = miniumum (LRAC) C

a. Profit maximizing condition for all firms, regardless of market structure. MR=MC

b. All aspects of production can be changed, given the technology. LR

c. Long-run equilibrium for competitive industry. P = LRAC

d. A competitive firm's short-run supply curve. MC above AVC

e. Higher industry outputs cause greater resource costs. increasing cost ind.

f. True only of price-taking sellers. MR=P

g. At least one resource is fixed. SR

h. A condition assuring economic efficiency. MSB=MSC

i. When production cannot be altered. market period

j. Assures the absence of long-run economic profits in competitive markets. freedom of exit + entry

1
2
3   15/1

mc = ΔTC/ΔQ

AVC =

ATC = AVC + AFC

28

ATC - AFC = AVC

28 -

ATC   TC/Q

AFC   TFC/Q   20/4

5

277

SET II

H 1. Price maker H   a. Pure quantity adjuster

G 2. Competitive markets G   b. When price equals the minimum of AVC.

A 3. Price taker A   c. As output expands, input costs decline.

D 4. Break-even points D   d. Where price equals AC.

J 5. Constant cost industry J   e. P = MC.

B 6. Shut-down point B   f. An economic cost of doing business.

E 7. Economic efficiency condition E   g. Characterized by a large number of potential buyers and sellers of a homogeneous product.

I 8. Zero economic profits I   h. Any firm with any monopoly power.

F 9. Normal accounting profits F   i. Long-run equilibrium condition for a competitive industry.

C 10. Decreasing cost industry C   j. Minimum AC is not influenced by the number of firms in an industry or by industry output.

CHAPTER REVIEW (FILL-IN QUESTIONS)

1-4. In the short run, all firms maximize profits by maximizing the difference between __TR__ and __TC__ or, equivalently, by producing that level of output at which __MR__ equals __MC__. If MR > MC, the firm increases __profits__ if it increases production slightly; if MR < MC, the firm will __increase__ profits if it reduces output slightly. __Break-even__ points occur where P = ATC. No firm will operate if P < AVC, because its revenues will not cover its variable costs. Where P = minimum AVC is known as the __Shut-down__ point.

5. In the long run, economic profits are eliminated either because __costs__ rise or __prices__ fall, while losses have opposite effects.

6-7. When the level of output or the number of firms in an industry have no influence on costs, the long-run industry supply curve is __horizontal__ and the industry produces under conditions of __constant cost__. If the average cost of output rises as industry output grows, we have a(n) __increasing cost__ industry. A(n) __increasing cost__ industry experiences falling costs of production as it grows.

8-10. Social welfare is maximized if the __distribution__ is deemed proper, and the marginal social benefit (P = MSB) equals the marginal social cost (MC = MSC). In addition to the efficiency and equity of the competitive marketplace, its advocates point to the __decentralized__ decision making which minimizes the coercion associated with other forms of decision making. However, the market may fail because of __monopoly__ power, inequity in the distribution of __income__, __externality__, or __instability__ in the absence of governmental macroeconomic policies.

STANDARD MULTIPLE CHOICE

THERE IS ONLY ONE "BEST" ANSWER FOR EACH QUESTION.

B 1. In the long run for a purely competitive firm:
  a. P = FC = TC = MC = MR = AC.
  b. P = AR = MR = SRMC = SRAC = LRMC = LRAC.
  c. economic profits are possible for especially effective managers.
  d. pure economic losses may be imposed on inefficient firms.
  e. all of the above.

E 2. The competitive firm's short-run supply curve is:
  a. the amount it produced previously, adjusted for growth.
  b. its marginal cost curve over the entire range of possible prices.
  c. the amount of output that assures zero economic profits.
  d. the upward sloping portion of its average total cost curve.
  e. the positively sloped MC curve above the AVC curve.

D 3. The economist who first specified the conditions for the long-run equilibrium of a competitive industry was:
  a. Auguste Cournot
  b. Leon Walras
  c. Vilfredo Pareto
  d. Alfred Marshall *LR equilibrium*
  e. John Stuart Mill

D 4. Which of the following markets is most compatible with the requirements for a purely competitive industry?
  a. steel.
  b. comic books.
  c. sugar-coated cereal.
  d. stocks and bonds, once issued.
  e. gasoline.

C 5. If average costs rise as an industry grows, it is a(n):
  a. economies of scale industry.
  b. diseconomies of scale industry.
  c. increasing cost industry.
  d. decreasing cost industry.
  e. constant cost industry.

6. The most widely accepted description of economic efficiency was first specified by:
  a. Alfred Marshall.
  b. Adam Smith.
  c. Leon Walras.
  d. Louis Pasteur.
  e. Vilfredo Pareto. *efficiency*

7. Modern general equilibrium analysis was founded by:
  a. Leon Walras.
  b. Adam Smith.
  c. Alfred Marshall.
  d. John Maynard Keynes.
  e. Thorstein Veblen.

C 8. Competition for the resources that generate economic profits may lead to:
  a. increased output prices for complementary goods.
  b. losses of economic efficiency.
  c. higher production costs.
  d. a lack of competition.
  e. price-making behavior.

B 9. The demand curve facing a competitive seller is:
  a. negatively sloped.
  b. horizontal at the market price.
  c. vertical at the market quantity.
  d. 1/n, where n is the number of firms in the industry.
  e. upward sloping.

A 10. Which of the following does NOT characterize a competitive market?
   a. substantial barriers to entry and exit.
   b. many small buyers.
   c. many small sellers.
   d. a homogeneous product.
   e. an absence of nonprice competition.

C 11. Rising economic profits in a competitive market do NOT precipitate:
   a. expansions of existing firms. —
   b. entry by new firms. —
   c. pressures for price hikes.
   d. pressures for increases in the costs of specialized resources.
   e. forces that ultimately will eliminate such profits.

B 12. If the competitive price is insufficient to cover average costs, firms should:
   a. definitely shut down as soon as possible.
   b. continue to operate where P = MC if P > AVC.
   c. adopt new technologies.
   d. cut back and eliminate their overhead.
   e. operate as long as price covers all fixed costs.

A 13. Economic profits:
   a. cannot exist in the long run in a competitive market structure.
   b. are the same as normal accounting profits.
   c. do not include the opportunity cost of the entrepreneur.
   d. exist whenever total cost exceeds total revenue.
   e. are always present when marginal revenue exceeds marginal cost.

E 14. The critical feature of a competitive market is that:
   a. many firms produce the same goods.
   b. there are many buyers of the good at the current price.
   c. all transactors have perfect information and free mobility.
   d. many potential buyers and sellers are free to enter or exit.
   e. all of the above.

D 15. Moving towards greater efficiency would require:
   a. expanding output and lowering price if MC > MSB.
   b. lowering both price and output when positive externalities exist.
   c. more efficient firms to enter industries where losses prevail.
   d. lower industry output and higher prices if existing firms experience losses.
   e. all of the above.

TRUE/FALSE QUESTIONS

F 1. A profit seeking firm will shut down if it cannot cover all short run costs of production.

T 2. A firm receives zero economic profits when total revenue equals total cost at the current output level. TR = TC

E 3. The demand curve confronting a purely competitive firm is downward sloping.

F 4. The demand curve confronting a purely competitive industry is perfectly price inelastic.

F 5. The short run supply curve of a competitive firm is the upward-sloping portion of its average variable cost curve.

E 6. Firms in a purely competitive industry compete principally by differentiating the goods they produce.

T 7. Competitive markets tend to be efficient and seem more equitable than solutions yielded by alternative market forms.

T 8. The results of competitive markets are yardsticks by which all other market structures are judged.

F 9. Freedom of entry and exit are unimportant in maintaining the competitive market over time.

T 10. In computing economic profits, the opportunity cost of capital must be considered part of long run average total cost.

T 11. In competition, all desired entry and exit will have occurred only when profits have returned to normal (zero).

T 12. Any industry's response to changes in its demand depends in part on the length of the adjustment period considered.

T 13. In a competitive market, the dynamics of entry and exit will drive normal profits to zero in the long run.

T 14. Competitive firms in long run equilibria produce where P equals minimum LRAC.

T 15. In a competitive market, rational producers employ productive inputs up to the point where the marginal cost of production just equals the price of the good.

T 16. In the long-run period, quantity changes will always be greater and price changes will be smaller for a given change in demand than market or short-run periods of production.

T 17. Most U.S. industries are characterized by increasing per unit costs of production in the long-run period of production.

F 18. The domestic petroleum industry is an excellent example of a constant cost industry.

T 19. In a constant cost industry, as entry occurs, costs of production are the same for new entrants as for established firms.

T 20. The market forces that cause costs to increase in an industry in which most firms reap economic profits also cause decreases in costs when most of the firms incur economic losses.

UNLIMITED MULTIPLE CHOICE

CAUTION: EACH QUESTION HAS FROM ZERO TO FOUR CORRECT ANSWERS.

___ 1. The demand curve for a perfectly competitive firm:
  a. is a horizontal line.
  b. is downward sloping.
  c. is perfectly price elastic.
  d. reflects the firm's inability to influence the market price of the good.

___ 2. Marginal revenue:
  a. is the extra revenue generated by additional units of output.
  b. equals a change in total revenue divided by a change in input.
  c. is synonymous with marginal cost for a perfectly competitive firm.
  d. is almost synonymous with price to a perfectly competitive firm.

$$\frac{\Delta TR}{\Delta Q}$$

3. The short-run supply curves of competitive firms are:
   a. horizontal lines.
   b. the portions of the firms' marginal cost curves that lie above their average fixed cost curves.
   c. the full ranges of the firms' marginal cost curves.
   d. summed horizontally to derive the industry supply curve.

4. Perfectly competitive firms:
   a. are price makers.
   b. are quantity adjusters, but not price adjusters.
   c. are free to enter or to leave an industry in the long run.
   d. attempt to minimize economic losses by locating the rate of output at which marginal revenue exceeds marginal cost by the greatest amount.

5. Economy-wide economic efficiency requires that:
   a. consumer desires be satisfied at the lowest possible opportunity cost.
   b. the value of output is maximized, given input constraints.
   c. input expenditures or opportunity costs are minimized for each form of output.
   d. when firms produce a given quantity of output, its value relative to the other outputs foregone will be at the lowest possible value.

6. The competitive market system:
   a. allocates inputs and outputs in an optimal manner if the income distribution is judged fair and if there are no externalities.
   b. is unanimously regarded as rather cold-hearted in its allocation process.
   c. maximizes society's net welfare regardless of the prevailing income distribution.
   d. assuming no externalities, results in the production of output at the point where MSB = MSC in each output market.

7. Long-run equilibrium for the purely competitive firm:
   a. occurs where the firm's demand curve is tangent to its long-run average cost curve.
   b. means that the firm reaps only normal accounting profits.
   c. requires revenue to just equal the value of resources used.
   d. occurs where the firm's marginal revenue curve is tangent to the long-run average cost curve.

8. Efficiency in a competitive economy requires that:
   a. only positive externalities exist in consumption and production.
   b. production or consumption activities have no effects on anyone except through the market prices of goods or productive inputs.
   c. anything that benefits a consumer benefits society by a similar amount.
   d. the prevailing distribution of income is judged fair by society.

9. The purely competitive industry's supply curve:
   a. has a price elasticity of roughly zero in the market period.
   b. is fairly price inelastic in the long-run period of production.
   c. in the long run graphically represents the relationship that exists between price and the maximum amount of output that an industry is willing to offer after all entry and exit has occurred.
   d. in the short run is derived by horizontally summing the short-run supply curves of the firms comprising the industry.

10. The long-run supply curve for a(n):
    a. increasing cost industry is vertical.
    b. constant cost industry is downward sloping.
    c. decreasing cost industry is a horizontal line.
    d. constant cost industry is a vertical line.

PROBLEMS

Problem 1

Table 1 summarizes revenue and cost data for a profit maximizing competitive firm. Use this information to answer the following questions.

Table 1

UNITS OF VARIABLE INPUT	(q)	(P_N)	(P_Q)	(TR)	(AR)	(MR)	(TC)	(TFC)	(TVC)	(ATC)	(AVC)	(AFC)	(MC)
0	0	$20	$2	—	—	—	—	$150	—	—	—	—	
1	5	20	2	—	—	—	—						
2	15	20	2	—	—	—	—						
3	30	20	2	—	—	—	—						
4	50	20	2	—	—	—	—						
5	75	20	2	—	—	—	—						
6	95	20	2	—	—	—	—						
7	110	20	2	—	—	—	—						
8	120	20	2	—	—	—	—						
9	125	20	2	—	—	—	—						
10	125	20	2	—	—	—	—						

(q)	=	Units of Output
(P_N)	=	Variable Input Price
(P_Q)	=	Output Price
(TR)	=	Total Revenue
(AR)	=	Average Revenue
✓(MR)	=	Marginal Revenue

✓(TC)	=	Total Cost
✓(TFC)	=	Total Fixed Cost
✓(TVC)	=	Total Variable Cost
✓(ATC)	=	Average Total Cost
✓(AVC)	=	Average Variable Cost
✓(AFC)	=	Average Fixed Cost
✓(MC)	=	Marginal Cost

a. Complete the table.

b. At what output does the firm maximize profit or minimize losses _____?

c. Use Figure 1 to graph the average revenue, the marginal revenue, the average total cost, the average variable cost, the average fixed cost, and the marginal cost curves. At which rate of output is the firm either maximizing economic profits or minimizing economic losses? _____ Explain _____

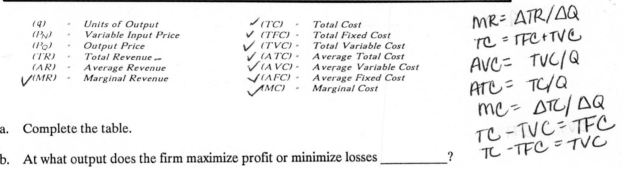

$TC = ATC \times Q$

$AFC = TFC/Q$

$MR = \Delta TR/\Delta Q$
$TC = TFC + TVC$
$AVC = TVC/Q$
$ATC = TC/Q$
$MC = \Delta TC/\Delta Q$
$TC - TVC = TFC$
$TC - TFC = TVC$

Figure 1

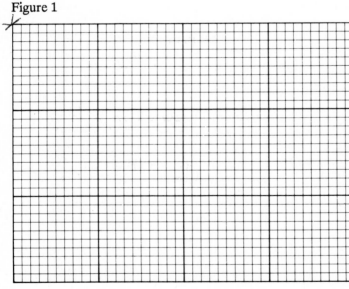

$MR = \dfrac{\Delta TR}{\Delta Q}$

$\boxed{MR \times \Delta Q = \Delta TR}$

$Q \times P = T$

$MR = \dfrac{\Delta TC}{\Delta Q} \quad \dfrac{\Delta TVC}{\Delta Q}$

$ATC = \dfrac{TC}{Q}$

$TC = TVC + TFC$

$AVC = \dfrac{TVC}{Q}$

$MC = \dfrac{\Delta TC}{\Delta Q}$

$TC = TFC + TVC$
$TC - TVC = TFC$

Problem 2

Figure 2 contains revenue and cost curves for two different firms producing in the same competitive industry. Use this information to answer the following true/false questions.

Figure 2

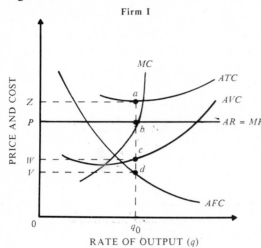

MR = P

TR = P × Q

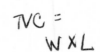

TVC = W × L

TFC = TVC +

TC = TFC + TVC

F a. At output q_0, Firm I fails to minimize its losses.

F b. At output q_0, Firm II earns only normal profits.

T c. Both firms are perfectly competitive in nature.

T d. Both firms are operating in the short-run.

F e. Firm I incurs economic losses equal to area *PZab*.

T f. Firm II earns economic profits equal to area *ZPab*.

F g. Total revenue received by Firm I equals area *0Zaq_0*.

___ h. Firm II incurs fixed cost equal to rectangle *WZbc*.

T i. Firm I incurs total variable cost equal to area *0Wcq_0*.

___ j. Firm I incurs fixed cost equal to area *0Vdq_0*.

T k. Firm I faces a demand curve with infinite price elasticity.

T l. The demand curve confronting Firm II is perfectly price elastic.

___ m. Firm I incurs total cost equal to area *0Pbq_0*.

___ n. Firm II incurs total cost equal to area *0Zbq_0*.

284

Problem 3

Figure 3 shows revenue and cost curves for two firms. Use this information to answer the following true/false questions.

Figure 3

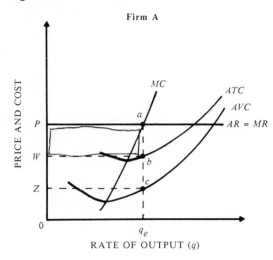

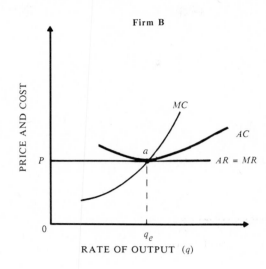

T a. Firm B is a price taker.

F b. Firm A is a price maker.

F c. Both firms are operating in the long run.

T d. Only short run data are shown for both firms.

F e. Firm B is earning economic profits.

F f. Firm A incurs economic losses equal to area *WPab*.

F g. At output q_e, firm A maximizes profits, which equal area *WPab*.

F h. Firm B is not profit-maximizing.

T i. Firm A is not producing output efficiently.

F j. Firm B is not producing output efficiently.

? F k. Firm A will be able to earn long run economic profits.

___ l. Firm A is incurring only variable costs of production.

___ m. Firm B incurs both fixed and variable costs of production.

T n. Firm A's total revenue equals area $0Paq_e$.

___ o. Fixed costs for firm A are equal to area $0Zcq_e$.

___ p. Total fixed costs for firm B are equal to area $0Paq_e$.

Problem 4

Figure 4 depicts the market supply and demand curves for a given commodity. Assume the market is competitive and generates no externalities, and that society is indifferent about questions of income distribution. Use this information to answer the following true/false questions.

Figure 4

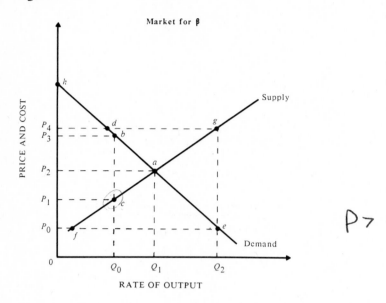

__I__ a. The demand curve is a marginal social benefits curve.

__F__ b. The supply curve is not related in any way to the marginal social costs incurred in producing this product.

__F__ c. Economic efficiency occurs at point b.

__I__ d. Total social benefits equal social costs at point a.

__F__ e. The dollar value that society places on the Q_0th unit of the good is greater than its opportunity cost.

__T__ f. The net welfare of the consumers who purchase the good is maximized at point a.

__F__ g. The dollar value that society places on the Q_2th unit is greater than its opportunity cost of production.

__I__ h. The dollar value that society ascribes to the Q_1th unit is equal to its opportunity cost of production.

____ i. The marginal social cost of producing the Q_2th unit is equal to the marginal private cost of producing it.

____ j. The dollar value that society places upon the first Q_1 units of the good is equal to area $OhaQ_1$.

____ k. The optimal rate of output from society's point of view exceeds Q_0.

____ l. The optimal rate of output from society's point of view is less than Q_2.

Problem 5

Pictured in Figure 5 are two equilibrium situations that confront the same competitive firm. Use this information to answer the following True/False questions.

Figure 5

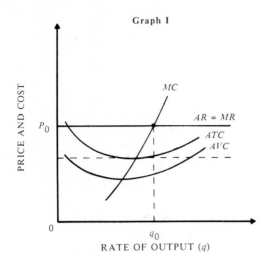

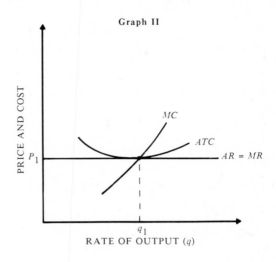

___ a. Graph I depicts a short-run equilibrium for the firm.

___ b. Graph II depicts the long-run equilibrium situation for the firm.

___ c. The firm earns pure profits at output q_0 in Graph I.

___ d. Costs have remained the same, despite the expansion of the industry, depicted in Graph II.

___ e. Free entry has caused the price in Graph II to be considerably lower than the price that the firm charged in Graph I.

___ f. Graph II illustrates a situation where the firm must still worry about the potential threat of further entry by new firms.

___ g. Graph II shows that the firm is incurring both fixed and variable costs.

___ h. Graph II suggests that price adjustment was achieved through an increase in the industry's supply curve.

___ i. Graph I shows that the firm confronts diminishing marginal returns to the variable input.

___ j. In the long-run situation depicted in Graph II all but one factor of production is variable.

Problem 6

Figure 6 includes total cost and total revenue curves for a firm. After studying the figure answer the questions.

a. What type of market does this show?
_____ Why?
_____

b. Is this a short run or long run analysis?
_____ Why?
_____

c. What is the firm's fixed cost of the firm in this problem? _____

d. What is the price of the good in this problem?
_____

e. What are this firm's break-even levels of output?
_____

f. What is the approximate profit maximizing level of output and what is the level of profit?
_____

Figure 6

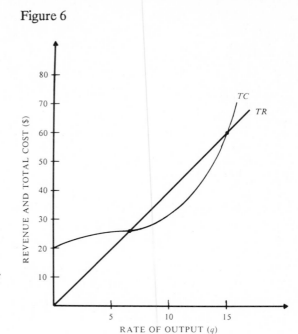

Problem 7

Use Figure 7 to draw two graphs side by side. In the graph on the left side, illustrate a competitive firm with economic profits. In the graph on the right side, illustrate a competitive market. Use the subscript 0 to label all of the initial positions. Graphically illustrate how purely competitive processes erode economic profits. Use the subscript 1 to label all the new equilibrium positions.

Figure 7

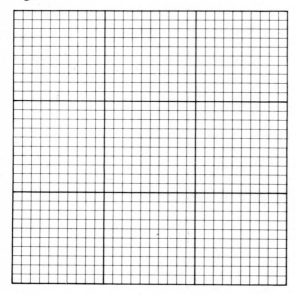

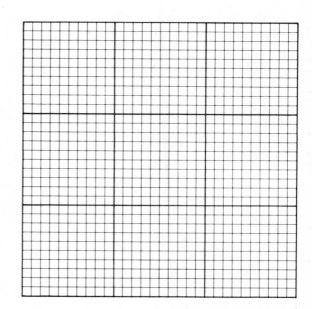

ANSWERS

Matching Key Terms and Concepts

SET I

Answer	MIC	*ECO*
1. f	p. 177	*481*
2. i	p. 172	*476*
3. d	p. 182	*486*
4. j	p. 171	*475*
5. b	p. 172	*476*
6. h	p. 191	*495*
7. a	p. 177	*481*
8. e	p. 198	*502*
9. g	p. 172	*476*
10. c	p. 190	*494*

SET II

Answer	MIC	*ECO*
1. h	p. 169	*473*
2. g	p. 170	*474*
3. a	p. 170	*474*
4. d	p. 179	*483*
5. j	p. 188	*492*
6. b	p. 181	*485*
7. e	p. 191	*495*
8. i	p. 184	*488*
9. f	p. 184	*488*
10. c	p. 190	*494*

Chapter Review (Fill-in Questions)

1. total revenue, total costs
2. marginal revenue, marginal costs
3. profits, increase
4. Break-even, shut down
5. costs, prices
6. horizontal, constant cost
7. increasing cost, decreasing cost
8. income distribution, decentralized
9. monopoly, income
10. externalities, instability

Standard Multiple Choice

Answer	MIC	*ECO*
1. b	p. 190	*494*
2. e	p. 182	*486*
3. d	p. 176	*480*
4. d	p. 171	*475*
5. c	p. 198	*502*
6. e	p. 192	*496*
7. a	p. 192	*496*
8. c	p. 198	*502*
9. b	p. 172	*476*
10. a	p. 170	*474*
11. c	p. 183	*487*
12. b	p. 180	*484*
13. a	p. 184	*488*
14. e	p. 170	*474*
15. d	p. 191	*495*

True/False Questions

Answer	MIC	*ECO*
1. F	p. 180	*484*
2. T	p. 184	*488*
3. F	p. 172	*476*
4. F	p. 172	*476*
5. F	p. 182	*486*
6. F	p. 170	*474*
7. T	p. 191	*495*
8. T	p. 191	*495*
9. F	p. 187	*491*
10. T	p. 184	*488*
11. T	p. 187	*491*
12. T	p. 187	*491*
13. T	p. 190	*494*
14. T	p. 190	*494*
15. T	p. 178	*482*
16. T	p. 187	*491*
17. T	p. 189	*493*
18. F	p. 188	*492*
19. T	p. 188	*492*
20. T	p. 184	*488*

Unlimited Multiple Choice

Answer	MIC	*ECO*
1. acd	p. 172	*476*
2. ad	p. 175	*479*
3. d	p. 182	*486*
4. bc	p. 170	*474*
5. abc	p. 191	*495*
6. abd	p. 191	*495*
7. abcd	p. 187	*491*
8. bc	p. 191	*495*
9. acd	p. 182	*486*
10. none	p. 189	*493*

Problem 1
MIC pp. 174-181; *ECO 478-485*

a. See Table 2.

Table 2

UNITS OF VARIABLE INPUT	(q)	(P_N)	(P_Q)	(TR)	(AR)	(MR)	(TC)	(TFC)	(TVC)	(ATC)	(AVC)	(AFC)	(MC)
0	0	$20	$2	$ 0	$2	$2	$150	$150	$ 0	- - -	- - -	- - -	- - -
1	5	$20	2	10	2	2	170	150	20	$34.00	$4.00	$30.00	$4.00
2	15	20	2	30	2	2	190	150	40	12.66	2.66	10.00	2.00
3	30	20	2	60	2	2	210	150	60	7.00	2.00	5.00	1.33
4	50	20	2	100	2	2	230	150	80	4.60	1.60	3.00	1.00
5	75	20	2	150	2	2	250	150	100	3.33	1.33	2.00	0.80
6	95	20	2	190	2	2	270	150	120	2.84	1.26	1.58	1.00
7	110	20	2	220	2	2	290	150	140	2.63	1.27	1.36	1.33
8	120	20	2	240	2	2	310	150	160	2.58	1.33	1.25	2.00
9	125	20	2	250	2	2	330	150	180	2.64	1.44	1.20	4.00
10	125	20	2	250	2	2	350	150	200	2.80	1.60	1.20	infinity

(q)	=	Units of Output	(TR)	= Total Revenue
(P_N)	=	Variable Input Price	(AR)	= Average Revenue
(P_Q)	=	Output Price	(MR)	= Marginal Revenue
(TC)	=	Total Cost	(ATC)	= Average Total Cost
(TFC)	=	Total Fixed Cost	(AVC)	= Average Variable Cost
(TVC)	=	Total Variable Cost	(AFC)	= Average Fixed Cost
			(MC)	= Marginal Cost

b. between 110 and 120 units.

c. See Figure 8, 110 or 120 units, at that output MR = MC.

Figure 8

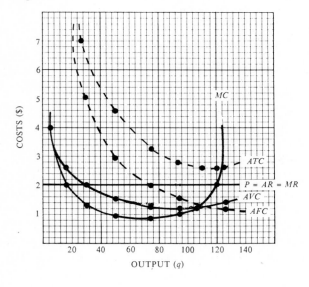

Problem 2	Probelm 3
MIC pp. 174-181	MIC 170-191
ECO pp. 478-485	*ECO 474-495*
a. F	a. T
b. F	b. F
c. T	c. F
d. T	d. F
e. T	e F
f. T	f. F
g. F	g. T
h. T	h. F
i. T	i. F
j. T	j. F
k. T	k. F
l. T	l. F
m. F	m. F
n. T	n. T
	o. F
	p. F

Problem 4
MIC p. 191; *ECO 495*

a. T
b. F
c. F
d. F
e. T
f. T
g. F
h. T
i. T
j. T
k. T
l. T

Problem 5
MIC pp. 178-187; *ECO 482-491*

a. T
b. T
c. T
d. T
e. T
f. F
g. F
h. T
i. T
j. F

Problem 6
MIC p. 175; *ECO 479*

a. This is a perfectly competitive market because price is constant to the firm (total revenue is a straight line).

b. This is a short run analysis because there are fixed costs (when output = 0, total costs = $20)..

c. $20 (when $Q = 0$, $TC = \$20$).

d. $4 (when $Q = 5$, $TR = \$20$, thus $P = TR/Q = \$20/5 = \$4$).

e. 7, 15 (break-even occurs where $TR = TC$).

f. The profit maximizing quantity is approximately 11. Total revenue minus total cost = profit; $45 - $35 = $10.

Problem 7
MIC pp. 183-186; *ECO 487-490*

See Figure 9. On the top panel, the firm initially earns economic profits with output q_0. Since entry is unrestricted in competitive markets, other firms desire to earn a share of the industry's economic profits causing industry supply to increase to S_1. As entry and increased supplies drive price to P_1, economic profits are eliminated.

Figure 9

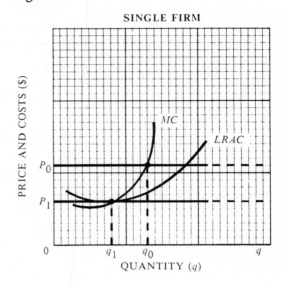

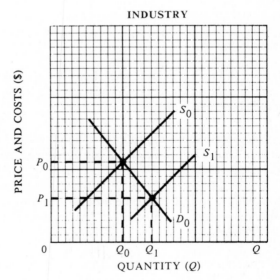

CHAPTER TWENTY-FOUR
MONOPOLY

CHAPTER OBJECTIVES

After you have read and studied this chapter, you should be able to describe pricing and output decisions by firms with monopoly power; discuss barriers to entry that may permit a monopolist to realize long-run economic profits; explain the effects of price discrimination and describe why inefficiency and inequity may be problems if monopoly power is widespread.

CHAPTER REVIEW: KEY POINTS

1. An unregulated *monopoly* controls the output and price of a good for which there are no close substitutes.

2. Few monopolies are unregulated, but all firms with any ability to control prices have *monopoly power.* Models of pure monopoly provide insights into the behavior of the many firms with this power.

3. Monopoly power is maintained through *barriers to entry.* Barriers may be *artificial,* such as government patents or licenses, excessive model changes, and so on. Other entry barriers may be *"natural"*--the result of extreme economies of scale, where average costs decline over a large range of output. A natural monopoly emerges if market demand falls within such ranges.

4. A nondiscriminating monopolist's *marginal revenue* is less than its price. Marginal revenue equals the price the monopolist receives from the sale of the additional unit minus the revenue lost because prices must be reduced on all other units sold. The marginal revenue curve is below the demand curve when monopoly power is present..

5. The demand for a good is elastic when output is below the quantity where marginal revenue is zero. Demand is unitarily elastic when marginal revenue is zero. Demand is inelastic for outputs above the point where marginal revenue is zero.

6. A monopolist maximizes profit (or minimizes loss) by selling that output where marginal revenue equals marginal cost. The price charged corresponds to the maximum price from the demand curve at this MR = MC output level.

7. Monopolists' profit-maximizing (or loss-minimizing) levels of output do not normally occur at the minimum points on average cost curves. This level of output can either be less or more than the minimum average cost output.

8. If a monopolist is able to maintain its monopoly position in the long run, then pricing, output, and economic profit will reflect variations in demand. A monopolist may also choose inefficient, but comfortable, policies.

9. *Price discrimination* entails sales of essentially the same good at different prices when these differences are not justified by variations in costs. Price discrimination occurs in airline fares, theater ticket prices, charges for medical and dental services, and in many other areas.

10. Effective price discrimination requires a firm to have some monopoly power and the ability to separate customers into groups with different price elasticities of demand for the good. Further, it must prevent *arbitrage*--the selling of the good to high-price customers by low-price customers.

11. *Price discrimination* boosts a firm's total profit. *Perfect* price discrimination allows a firm to reap as profit all the consumer surplus that could be derived from the product.

12. A nondiscriminating monopoly is less economically efficient from society's point of view than are competitive industries. A monopolist typically produces less than if the industry were purely competitive and sells at a higher price. Price discrimination may reduce this inefficiency but it intensifies questions about equity in the distribution of income.

MATCHING KEY TERMS AND CONCEPTS

C 1. Price discrimination

H 2. Natural monopoly

I 3. Licensing

E 4. Total revenue maximization

F 5. Marginal revenue

G 6. P > MC, so MSB > MSC

J 7. Consumer surplus

A 8. Arbitrage

B 9. High fixed costs, low variable costs

D 10. Necessary for monopolization

a. Risklessly buying low in one market, selling high in another.

b. Typical of a natural barrier to entry.

c. Charging different prices not justified by cost differences.

d. A lack of close substitutes for the firm's output.

e. MR = 0; price elasticity = 1.

f. Less than price for a non-discriminating monopolist.

g. Proof that non-discriminating monopoly is inefficient.

h. When economies of scale for a single firm persist across the full range of market demand. *cost ↓ output ↑*

i. An example of a legal barrier to entry.

j. Eliminated by perfect price discrimination.

CHAPTER REVIEW (FILL-IN QUESTIONS

1. A firm has a *monopoly* in a market if it controls production of a product for which there are no *substitutes*.

2-3. The profit maximizing output occurs where $MR = MC$, which is always in the *elastic* range of demand as long as marginal costs are positive. Firms with monopoly power are not certain to be profitable, because *costs* may be too high relative to *demand*.

4. A *nat. monopoly* occurs when demand is sufficiently small relative to *ec. of scale* that only one firm can best serve the market.

5-6. An unregulated monopolist may increase its profits through _discrimination_ which means that different prices are charged for identical goods and there are no differences in production costs. Successful price discrimination requires that the market must be _subdivided_ into at least two groups, and the group charged the lower price must be prevented from selling to the group charged the higher price, a practice known as _arbitrage_. Perfect price discrimination occurs when the full value of _cons. surplus_ is appropriated by a seller who charges all the traffic will bear for every unit of its output.

7-9. Competitive markets meet the condition that _P = MC_, which is necessary for economic efficiency. Nondiscriminating monopolists do not because _P > MC_ in equilibrium, which means that the marginal social _benefit_ of a monopolized good exceeds its marginal social _cost_. Price discrimination may enhance economic efficiency because the price charged for the _last_ unit of the good will equal _MC_.

10. Even if only one (or two) firms are presently in a market, they may be forced to act as if they were in _competition_ if a potent threat of entry exists, according to the _survival_ hypothesis.

STANDARD MULTIPLE CHOICE

THERE IS A SINGLE "BEST" ANSWER TO EACH QUESTION.

___ 1. Unlike a purely competitive firm, a monopolist:
   a. can select a price and sell as much as it desires.
   b. equates marginal revenue and marginal cost to maximize profits.
   c. can produce any desired amount and charge as much as it desires.
   d. can choose a profit-maximizing price and output combination from the market demand curve.
   e. faces a perfectly elastic demand curve.

___ 2. A monopoly with huge fixed costs but no variable costs will maximize profits where:
   a. the price elasticity of demand equals zero.
   b. marginal revenue is maximized.
   c. MR = MC = 0.
   d. average revenue is maximized.
   e. total costs are minimized.

___ 3. Suppose a monopolist can sell 10 units for $10.00 each, but selling 11 units forces a reduction in price to $9.95. Marginal revenue is:
   a. $10.00.
   b. $9.95.
   c. $9.45.
   d. $9.40.
   e. $109.95

___ 4. Patents are examples of:
   a. legal economies of substitution.
   b. legal barriers to entry.
   c. natural barriers to entry.
   d. natural economies of complementarity.
   e. illegal marginal diseconomies.

___ 5. An example of a natural monopoly is:
   a. OPEC, the international oil cartel.
   b. United States Steel Corporation.
   c. General Electric.
   d. the *New York Times*.
   e. the local telephone company.

___ 6. The economist who first specified the MR = MC rule for profit maximization was:
   a. Adam Smith.
   b. A. A. Cournot.
   c. Leon Walras.
   d. Alfred Marshall.
   e. Karl Marx.

___ 7. Price discrimination means:
   a. charging different prices for identical goods.
   b. paying wages according to race or sex rather than productivity.
   c. exploiting the working masses by charging the highest single price possible.
   d. eliminating all costs so that only pure profits are realized.
   e. all of the above.

$$MR = \frac{\Delta TR}{\Delta Q}$$

A 8. Compared to the outcome of a purely competitive market, a nondiscriminating monopolist tends to:
    a. produce less and charges more.
    b. maximize total profits wherever possible.
    c. set price in the inelastic range of the demand curve.
    d. confront a demand curve where P = MR.
    e. produce more and charge more.

9. Most markets in the American economy are:
    a. purely competitive.
    b. primarily unregulated monopolies.
    c. mixtures of monopolistic and competitive elements.
    d. regulated monopolies.
    e. governed by the decisions of union leaders.

10. A nondiscriminating monopolist chooses an economically inefficient level of output because:
    a. the difference between MR and MC is maximized.
    b. P > ATC, so MSB > MSC when MR = MC.
    c. all consumer surplus is appropriated.
    d. P > MR = MC, so MSB > MSC when MR = MC.
    e. too much is charged for too much production.

11. Regardless of the number of firms in an industry, complete freedom to enter or leave in the long run makes a market:
    a. purely competitive.
    b. more highly concentrated.
    c. innovative.
    d. capital intensive.
    e. contestable.

12. All consumer surplus is absorbed into profit by:
    a. pure monopoly power.
    b. perfect price discrimination.
    c. firms that maximize MR - MC
    d. monopolistic expropriation.
    e. profit maximization.

TRUE/FALSE QUESTIONS

T 1. Monopolists produce and sell extra output if MR > MC.

F 2. Profit-maximizing monopolists will continue to produce in the long-run even if they incur economic losses.

T 3. Monopolists equate the marginal social cost of production with the marginal social benefits to consumers.
                                      MSC > MSB

T 4. Natural monopolies are usually government regulated.

F 5. All price discrimination is illegal.

F 6. Barriers to entry ensure profits to all monopolists.

F 7. Restrictions on entry ensure monopolization.

F 8. Natural barriers to entry are government-sanctioned.

F 9. In long-run equilibrium, the profit-maximizing monopolist produces output where marginal revenue is maximized.
                     P > MR

F 10. Monopolists invariably earn super-normal profits in the long run.

UNLIMITED MULTIPLE CHOICE

CAUTION: EACH QUESTION HAS FROM ZERO TO FOUR CORRECT ANSWERS.

___ 1. A monopoly:
- (a.) may reap economic profits in the long run.
- (b.) may incur economic losses in the long run.
- c. produces a rate of output at which marginal social benefits exceed marginal social costs, assuming no price discrimination.
- (d.) may be able to produce output at lower average costs than would its perfectly competitive counterpart.

___ 2. Perfect price discrimination:
- a. involves charging all customers the same prices for units of output.
- (b.) results in the seller appropriating all consumer surplus.
- (c.) involves charging different prices that may not reflect different costs of production.
- d. cannot actually be practiced because the information that firms need to determine all the prices willingly paid by each customer is too costly to acquire.

___ 3. Demand curves facing nondiscriminating monopolists:
- (a) are identical to the demand curves for their industries.
- (b) are downward sloping..
- (c.) are also their average revenue curves.
- (d.) fall more slowly than do their marginal revenue curves.

___ 4. If the same cost conditions confront both a non- discriminating monopoly and firms in a purely competitive industry:
- (a.) the monopoly will produce less output than the total of all firms in the competitive industry.
- (b.) both types of firms may be able to reap economic profits in the short-run.
- c. both types of firms will charge prices equal to marginal revenue.
- (d.) both types of firms will produce where marginal revenue equals marginal cost.

___ 5. Barriers to entry:
- a. are unimportant in preventing entry into an industry.
- (b.) may make it extremely difficult for new firms to enter an industry.
- (c.) aid existing firms in realizing economic profits.
- (d.) may be natural, illegal, or even created by law.

PROBLEMS

Problem 1

Table 1 lists the demand schedule that confronts a particular monopolist. Use this information to answer the following questions.

$\dfrac{TR}{Q}$ ~~ATC~~

$\dfrac{\Delta TR}{\Delta Q}$

Table 1

PRICE	UNITS OF OUTPUT	TOTAL REVENUE	AVERAGE REVENUE	MARGINAL REVENUE
20	0	0	0	0
18	2	36	18	18
16	4	64	16	
14	6	84	14	
12	8	96	12	
10	10	100	10	
8	12	96	8	
6	14	84	6	
4	16	64	4	
2	18	36	2	
0	20	0	0	

a. Complete Table 1.

b. Graph the monopolist's demand and marginal revenue curves in Figure 1. Once the figure is complete, break the demand schedule into three ranges of price elasticity.

6/14

Figure 1

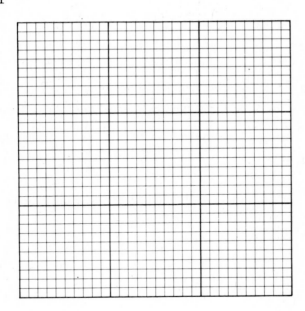

c. What is the relationship between MR and the three ranges of elasticity you noted? _____

_____

d. Compare the monopolist's marginal revenue curve with that of a competitive firm. What causes the differences in their slopes? _____

Problem 2

Use the information about the revenues and costs for two different monopolists graphed in Figure 2 to answer the following true/false questions.

Figure 2

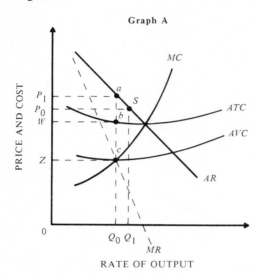

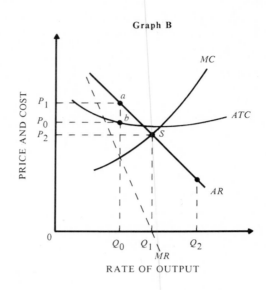

___ a. Graph A depicts a monopoly that has made all profit maximizing, long run adjustments.

___ b. Graph B shows a monopoly producing in the short run.

___ c. In Graph A, point S lies in the inelastic range of the monopolist's demand curve.

___ d. In Graph B, point a lies in the elastic range of the monopolist's demand curve.

___ e. In Graph B, total revenue is maximized at point S.

___ f. The monopoly in Graph A maximizes profit by producing Q_0 units of output per time period.

___ g. In Graph A, the profit-maximizing price is P_o.

___ h. The monopoly in Graph B can maximize its total sales revenue by producing Q_1 units of output per time period, selling each unit at a price of P_2.

___ i. The monopoly in Graph A can earn maximum profits equal to WP_1ab.

___ j. In Graph B, marginal revenue is negative and demand is inelastic at Q_2 units of output.

___ k. In Graph B, point S lies in the elastic range of the monopolist's demand curve.

___ l. In Graph A, the monopolist can maximize total sales (revenues) by producing Q_0 units of output per time period.

___ m. Total fixed costs for the monopolist in Graph A equal area $OWbQo$.

___ n. If the monopolist in Graph B attempts to maximize sales revenues it suffers economic losses.

298

Problem 3

Pictured in Figure 3 are the revenue and cost curves of two different firms. Use this information to answer the following questions.

Figure 3

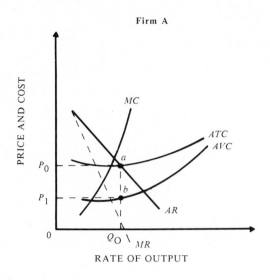

Firm A

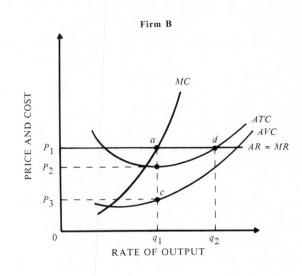

Firm B

___ a. Firm A has monopoly power.

___ b. Firm B is a price maker.

___ c. Firm A is a price taker.

___ d. Firm B perceives the price of output as a given.

___ e. Firm A is operating in the short-run period of production.

___ f. Firm B is operating in the long-run period of production.

___ g. At output Q_0, firm A is profit maximizing.

___ h. At output q_1, firm B maximizes its potential total revenues.

___ i. Firm B is a competitive firm.

___ j. If firm B produces output q_2 it would suffer an economic loss.

___ k. Total fixed costs for firm B equal area $0P_3cq_1$.

___ l. Firm B can earn economic profits of up to P_2P_1ab.

___ m. Output q_1 for firm B represents a point in the inelastic range of the demand curve.

___ n. To earn economic profits, firm A should produce less than Q_0.

Problem 4

The demand schedules in Table 2 are for two separate markets facing a particular monopolist. Assume that ATC = MC = a constant $4 per unit. Use this information to answer the following questions.

Table 2

PRICE	QUANTITY DEMANDED IN MARKET A	QUANTITY DEMANDED IN MARKET B
$10	10	0
9	20	2
8	30	4
7	40	8
6	50	16
5	60	32
4	70	64
3	80	100
2	90	200
1	100	400
0	110	1000

a. Assume that arbitrage initially prevents price discrimination. In Figure 4, draw the total market demand, marginal revenue and marginal cost curves facing this nondiscriminating monopolist.

Figure 4

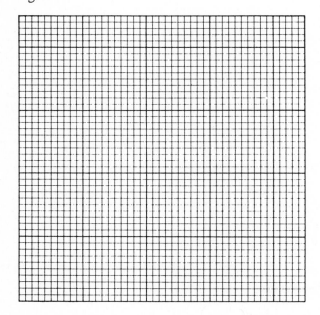

b. What will be the profit maximizing output, price, and total profit based on the assumptions in Question a?

_____

c. Now assume the monopolist gains the ability to prevent arbitrage, segments the market, and implements a price discrimination policy. Use Figure 5 to diagram that demands and marginal revenues for the two markets.

Figure 5

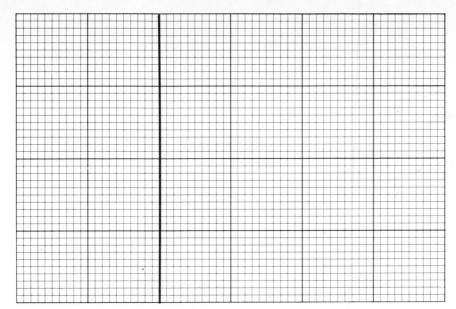

d. What will be the profit maximizing output, price, and total profit in each market based on the assumption in Question c? _____

e. How much more profit is realized through price discrimination? _____

Problem 5

Assume a firm with the cost and revenue structures shown in Table 3:

Table 3

(Q)	(TVC)	(TC)	(ATC)	(MC)	(Px)	(TR)	(MR)
0	0	150	- - -	- - -	$200	0	- - -
1	110	- - -	- - -	110	175	- - -	- - -
2	- - -	320	- - -	- - -	- - -	300	- - -
3	- - -	366	- - -	- - -	135	- - -	- - -
4	250	- - -	- - -	- - -	- - -	480	- - -
5	- - -	445	- - -	- - -	105	- - -	- - -
6	360	- - -	- - -	- - -	90	- - -	- - -

a. Complete the cost and revenue structure in Table 3.

b. What are the fixed costs of this firm?_____

c. What is the profit maximizing position for this firm? $P =$ ___ , $Q =$ ___ .

d. Is this a long-run equilibrium for an industry with free entry and exit?_____ Why or why not? _____

e. Is the demand for the firm's product elastic or inelastic over the range of prices described above? _____

f. What is the profit or loss at the equilibrium position? _____

g. Is this firm producing at lowest possible ATC?_____

h. Is this firm in a purely competitive market?_____ Why or why not?_____

Problem 6

The relationship between elasticity and total revenue is an important one when discussing product market structures. Review the demand data below

P	Q
$7	2
$5	6
$3	10
$1	14

a. Use Figure 6 to draw three separate graphs (A, B, C) illustrating the change in total revenue as price decreases from $7 to $5, $5 to $3, and $3 to $1.

Figure 6

Graph A

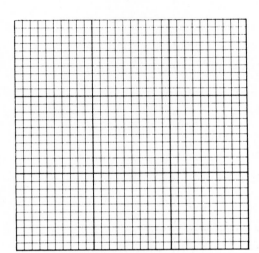

Graph B

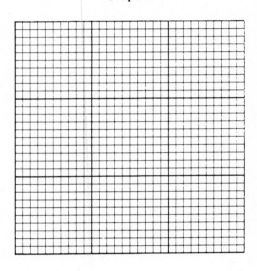

Graph C

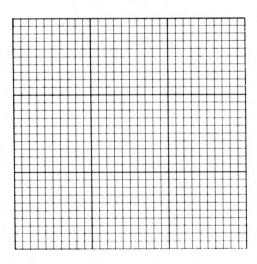

b. What is happening to total revenue as price falls in Graph A? _____ Graph B? _____ Graph C? _____

c. Calculate the price elasticity of demand for each price change. _____

ANSWERS

Matching Key Terms and Concepts

Answer	MIC	*ECO*
1. c	p. 209	*513*
2. h	p. 207	*511*
3. i	p. 207	*511*
4. e	p. 202	*506*
5. f	p. 203	*507*
6. g	p. 213	*517*
7. j	p. 214	*518*
8. a	p. 210	*514*
9. b	p. 207	*511*
10. d	p. 200	*504*

Chapter Review (Fill-in Questions)

1. monopoly, close substitutes
2. MR = MC, elastic
3. production costs, demand
4. natural monopoly, economies of scale
5. price discrimination, separable
6. Arbitrage, consumer surplus
7. P = MC, P > MC
8. benefit, cost
9. last, marginal cost
10. competition, contestable markets

Standard Multiple Choice

Answer	MIC	*ECO*
1. d	p. 200	*504*
2. c	p. 203	*507*
3. c	p. 201	*505*
4. b	p. 207	*511*
5. e	p. 207	*511*
6. b	p. 199	*503*
7. a	p. 209	*513*
8. a	p. 200	*504*
9. c	p. 198	*502*
10. d	p. 213	*517*
11. e	p. 208	*512*
12. b	p. 210	*517*

True/False Questions

Answer	MIC	*ECO*
1. T	p. 203	*507*
2. F	p. 205	*509*
3. F	p. 213	*517*
4. T	p. 207	*511*
5. F	p. 208	*512*
6. F	p. 207	*511*
7. F	p. 207	*511*
8. F	p. 207	*511*
9. F	p. 205	*509*
10. F	p. 205	*509*

Unlimited Multiple Choice

Answer	MIC	*ECO*
1. acd	p. 200, 205, 213	*504, 509, 517*
2. bcd	p. 210	*514*
3. abcd	p. 200-202	*504-506*
4. abd	p. 200-204	*504-508*
5. bcd	p. 205-207	*509-511*

Problem 1
MIC pp. 201-202; *ECO 505-506*

a. See Table 4

Table 4

(Q)	(TR)	(AR)	(MR)
0	0	-	-
2	$ 36	$18	$ 18
4	64	16	14
6	84	14	10
8	96	12	6
10	100	10	2
12	96	8	- 2
14	84	6	- 6
16	64	4	-10
18	36	2	-14
20	0	0	-18

b.   See Figure 7.

Figure 7

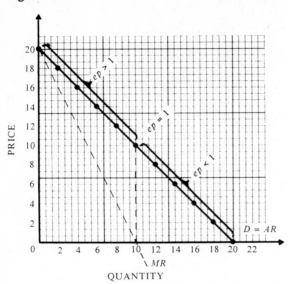

QUANTITY

c.   If MR > 0, ep > 1; if MR = 0, ep = 1; if MR < 0, ep < 1.

d.   The monopolist faces a downward sloping demand curve.

Problem 2
MIC pp. 200-205; *ECO 504-509*

a.   F
b.   F
c.   F
d.   T
e.   T
f.   T
g.   F
h.   T
i.   T
j.   T
k.   F
l.   F
m.   F
n.   T

Problem 3
MIC pp. 200-205; *ECO 504-509*

a.   T
b.   F
c.   F
d.   T
e.   T
f.   F
g.   F
h.   F
i.   T
j.   F
k.   F
l.   T
m.   F
n.   T

Problem 4
MIC pp. 200-205, 208-212; *ECO 504-509, 512-516*

a.   See Figure 8.

Figure 8

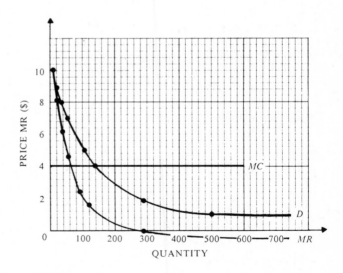

QUANTITY

b.   Q = 48, P = $7, profit = TR - TC = $336 - (48 x 4)
     = 336 - 192 = $144.

c. See Table 5 and Figure 9

Table 5

Market A

P	Q	TR	ΔTR	ΔQ	$MR = \frac{\Delta TR}{\Delta Q}$
10	10	100	100	10	10.0
9	20	180	80	10	8.0
8	30	240	60	10	6.0
7	40	280	40	10	4.0
6	50	300	20	10	2.0
5	60	300	0	10	0
4	70	280	- 20	10	- 2.0
3	80	240	- 40	10	- 4.0
2	90	180	- 60	10	- 6.0
1	100	100	- 80	10	- 8.0
0	110	0	-100	10	-10.0

Market B

P	Q	TR	ΔTR	ΔQ	$MR = \frac{\Delta TR}{\Delta Q}$
10	0	0	0	0	0
9	2	18	18	2	9.0
8	4	32	14	2	7.0
7	8	56	24	4	6.0
6	16	96	40	8	5.0
5	32	160	64	16	4.0
4	64	256	96	32	3.0
3	100	300	44	36	1.22
2	200	400	100	100	1.00
1	400	400	0	200	0
0	1000	0	-400	600	-0.66

Figure 9

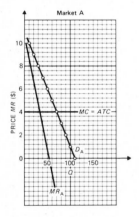

Market A

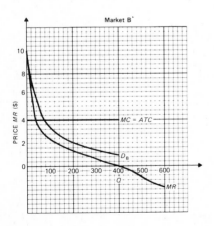

Market B

d. Market A: P_A = 7; Q_A = 40; profit = TR_A - TC_A
= 280 - 160 = $120.

Market B: P_B = 5; Q_B = 32; profit = TR_B - TC_B
= 160 - 128 = $32.

e. Total profit--discriminating monopolist = 120 +
32 = $152; for nondiscriminating monopolist =
$144 difference = $8.

Problem 5
MIC pp. 200-205, 208-212; *ECO 504-509, 512-516*

a. See Table 6.

b. $150

c. P = 105 (120), Q = 5 (4)

d. No, there are economic profits present.

Table 6

(Q)	(TVC)	(TC)	(ATC)	(MC)	(Px)	(TR)	(MR)
0	0	150	- - -	0	$200	0	- - -
1	110	260	260	110	175	175	175
2	170	320	160	60	150	300	125
3	216	366	122	41	135	405	105
4	250	400	100	34	120	480	75
5	295	445	89	45	105	525	45
6	360	510	85	65	90	540	15

e. elastic

f. $80 (TR = $525, TC = $445, $525 - $445 = $80)

g. No (A firm with monopoly power will not
necessarily produce at lowest possible ATC)

h. No, because the firm faces a downward sloping
demand curve.

Problem 6
MIC pp. 200-205, 208-212; *ECO 504-509, 512-516*

a. See Figure 10.

b. increasing, constant, decreasing

c. Ep = 3., Ep = 1, Ep = .33

Figure 10

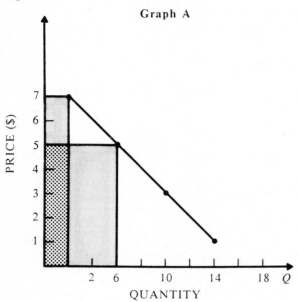

Graph A

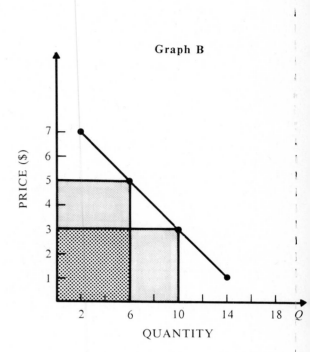

Graph B

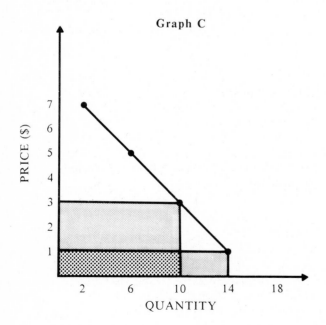

Graph C

CHAPTER TWENTY-FIVE
MONOPOLISTIC COMPETITION AND OLIGOPOLY

CHAPTER OBJECTIVES

[handwritten: 1) many suppliers 2) differentiated product 3) easy entry/exit]

After you have read and studied this chapter, you should be able to describe the similarities and differences between competitive and monopoly markets, and the range of markets between these extremes; describe the salient features of monopolistically competitive markets in the short and long run; discuss the features of the kinked demand and limit-pricing oligopoly models; explain how product differentiation and interdependencies among firms may influence the prices charged and the amounts produced; and discuss the long-term prospects for cartels such as OPEC.

CHAPTER REVIEW: KEY POINTS

1. Most U. S. markets fit neither the purely competitive nor the monopoly molds. Most industries are *monopolistically competitive* or *oligopolistic*.

2. *Product differentiation* refers to differences that consumers perceive in goods that are close substitutes. These differences can be real or imagined. They are created by such things as advertising and promotion and/or by differences in the actual goods. Product differentiation is intended to expand the demand for a firm's output and make demand less elastic.

3. *Monopolistic competition* occurs when entry into an industry is easy and there are large numbers of suppliers of slightly differentiated products. Demands for a pure competitor's products are perfectly elastic (horizontal at the market price), but the demands facing monopolistic competitors are negatively-sloped but still highly elastic.

4. Monopolistically competitive firms produce and sell levels of output that equate marginal revenue and marginal cost. The price is then determined by demand. This is similar to pure monopoly, but the level of short-run profits derived from monopoly power is generally lower, given that numerous other firms sell close substitutes.

5. Entry is relatively easy in monopolistic competition, so accounting profits are reduced to normal levels (zero economic profits) in the long run. However, equilibrium output will be less and prices will be higher under monopolistic competition than in purely competitive markets. Higher prices and lower levels of output are the costs of product differentiation.

6. An *oligopoly* is an industry comprised of a few sellers who recognize their mutual interdependence. Competitive strategies by one firm in the industry will normally be countered by the other sellers.

7. Economies of scale are one of several reasons for oligopoly. Some goods require substantial plant and equipment so that efficient production requires servicing a considerable portion of the total industry demand. Mergers also facilitate the creation of oligopolies by joining competitors into single firms. Finally, oligopolies may exist because of legal or other artificial barriers to entry that deter new firms from entering the industry.

9. There are hundreds of oligopoly pricing models, but they break down into two major categories: *collusive* and *noncollusive*. The *kinked demand curve model* assumes that if one firm raises its prices, other firms will ignore the increase, while other firms in the industry will match any price cuts. The result is a demand curve for the firm that is kinked at the current equilibrium price. This irregularity leads to a discontinuity (gap) in the marginal revenue curve. Consequently, changes in costs may not lead to changes in prices. This theory forecasts "sticky" prices in oligopolistic industries, but price stickiness is not confirmed empirically. Kinked demand curve models also fail to explain how the original equilibrium price is established, how prices change, or how entry by new rivals is deterred.

10. *Limit pricing* is a model of how oligopolists maintain market power by deterring entry. Oligopolists may establish a low price, making it unprofitable for new firms to enter the industry. Existing firms then accept lower short-run profits to preserve economic profits over the long run.

11. A *cartel* is an effort by firms in an industry to collude, setting prices and limiting output for all its members. Cartels must be concentrated in the hands of a few firms that control significant proportions of an industry's output. The product needs to be reasonably homogeneous, since agreements regarding heterogeneous products would be complex and difficult to enforce.

12. Cartels try to *maximize joint profits* and then allocate territories or industry output quotas. The stability of any cartel is threatened by the profitability associated with undetected price cuts, or "cheating"; by potential new entrants who seek to share in profits; and by adverse legal action. Collusion is illegal in most markets in the United States.

13. *Game theory* is an attempt to model strategic behavior. It requires pairing each possible option open to each participant with the options available to other participants, and then ascertaining the most likely sets of options.

14. Industry output tends to be less and prices tend to be higher under oligopoly than in pure- or monopolistic competition. Relative to market demands, economies of scale tend to be more significant for natural monopolies than for oligopolies, larger for oligopolies than for monopolistic competitors, and more significant for monopolistic competitors than for pure competitors. Some economists argue that monopoly profits for large firms are necessary to finance extensive research and development activities and facilitate technological advance. The evidence does not confirm this hypothesis.

MATCHING KEY TERMS AND CONCEPTS

SET I

___ 1. Production quotas

___ 2. Limit pricing

___ 3. Kinked demand curves

___ 4. Merger

___ 5. Oligopoly

_I_ 6. Monopolistic competition

_J_ 7. Product differentiation

___ 8. Cartels

___ 9. Territories

___ 10. Incentives to cheat

a. Sacrificing some short-run profits to keep new competitors from entering.

b. Cartel output limits to boost prices.

c. A market with only a few, large, interdependent firms.

d. A technique used to split and share a market.

e. Attempts to joint-profit maximize.

f. Why cartels tend to be unstable.

g. Raise prices, competitors do nothing; lower prices, competitors follow.

h. One means of eliminating competitors.

i. Many firms, heterogeneous products.

j. Attempts to increase demand and make it less price elastic.

SET II

___ 1. Collusion

___ 2. Pure oligopoly

_G_ 3. Informative advertising

___ 4. OPEC

_H_ 5. Zero economic profits

___ 6. Impure oligopoly

___ 7. Concentration ratio

_B_ 8. Persuasive advertising

___ 9. Conscious mutual interdependence

___ 10. Sticky prices

a. Consequence of kinked demand curves.

b. Attempts to hold or secure a market share; inefficient.

c. When a few firms produce close substitutes.

d. Example of a successful cartel.

e. A few firms producing homogeneous products.

f. Conspiratorial price and output setting; usually illegal.

g. Reduces transactions costs; efficient.

h. Long-run equilibrium for monopolistic competitors.

i. The shares of total sales by 4 (or 8) biggest firms.

j. Uniquely true of oligopolies.

CHAPTER REVIEW (FILL-IN QUESTIONS)

1-2. Firms in a(n) _____ oligopoly produce identical products, while _____ oligopolies are comprised of firms whose outputs are differentiated. Except for pure competition, all market structures confront each firm with a negatively-sloped demand curve so that, in the absence of price discrimination, the _____ curve lies below the _____ curve.

3-4. Small numbers of firms that base their decisions on what their competitors will do are in _____ markets. The degree of market concentration is important and is commonly measured by a _____, which is the percentage of sales controlled by the top _____ dominant firms in an industry. The theory of _____ markets, however, suggests that the number of firms presently in a market is less important than is the threat of entry in response to profit opportunities.

5-8. Oligopolies are caused by substantial _____ or other barriers to entry, or are formed through _____. The _____ curve model presumes that each firm fears that its competitors will match any price cuts, but will _____ any price increases. This kink in the demand curve leaves a gap in the _____ curve, so that changes in marginal cost may not change the price charged. This model was developed to explain the _____ once thought to characterize oligopoly, but which are indiscernible from the evidence. Among the many other theories of oligopoly is the _____ model, which assumes that existing firms leave so little of the market demand available for potential new entrants to serve that new rivals would be unable to overcome the _____, given current technology.

9. A _____ is a collusive oligopoly that usually operates internationally in an attempt to maximize the _____ of its members, just as if it were a monopoly. Because cheating is potentially so profitable for cartel members, cartels tend to be unstable unless controlled, at least in part, by governmental actions.

10. Regardless of their precise form, all non-discriminating market structures that are not _____ tend to be economically inefficient because each firm equates marginal revenue to marginal cost, and marginal revenue curves lie below the demand (average revenue) curves the firms confront. Hence, _____, and the marginal social benefit (MSB) of additional production will be greater than its marginal social cost (MSC). The existence of any monopoly power causes output to be restricted below the socially optimal level, and the price charged to be greater than would be the case under pure competition.

STANDARD MULTIPLE CHOICE

THERE IS A SINGLE BEST ANSWER FOR THESE QUESTIONS

___ 1. Monopolistically and purely competitive markets have in common:
  a. differentiated products.
  b. many potential buyers and sellers.
  c. that horizontal demand curves face each firm.
  d. homogeneous products.
  e. conscious interdependence in decisionmaking.

___ 2. Informative advertising:
  a. reduces transactions cost, and hence, is efficient.
  b. decreases supplies because of its cost.
  c. decreases demands for resource inputs.
  d. is less desirable than persuasive advertising.
  e. all of the above.

3. Sticky prices in oligopoly markets are:
   a. predicted by the kinked demand curve model.
   b. confirmed by the evidence.
   c. more common than in other market structures.
   d. explained by limit-pricing models.
   e. all of the above.

4. In the long run:
   a. purely competitive firms make zero economic profits.
   b. monopolistically competitive firms make zero economic profits.
   c. persistent barriers to entry may make economic profits possible.
   d. oligopolists and monopolists whose markets are not contestable may realize economic profits.
   e. all of the above. ⟵ *(circled)*

5. Existing firms may preclude entry by absorbing so much of the market demand that potential entrants, confronted by substantial economies of scale, would find entering the market to be a losing proposition according to the theory of:
   a. cartelization.
   b. kinked demand curves.
   c. limit pricing.
   d. monopolistic competition.
   e. price leadership.

6. Marginal revenue is not below the market price from the perspectives of:
   a. monopolistic competitors.
   b. monopolists.
   c. cartel members.
   d. pure oligopolists.
   e. pure competitors.

7. If your competitors will follow any of your price cuts, but will ignore any price hikes, your firm:
   a. faces cutthroat competition.
   b. faces a kinked demand curve.
   c. is the price leader of an oligopoly.
   d. must be the most efficient firm in the industry.
   e. must be one of the industry's marginal firms.

8. The theory of monopolistic competition was developed by:
   a. Joan Robinson.
   b. E.A.G. Robinson.
   c. Joseph Schumpeter.
   d. Edward Chamberlin. ⟵ *(circled)*
   e. Zeppo Marx.

9. The economist who developed a general theory of imperfect competition and first separated average revenue (demand) curves from marginal revenue curves was:
   a. Edward Chamberlin.
   b. A. A. Cournot.
   c. Joan Robinson. ⟵ *(circled)*
   d. Joseph Schumpeter.
   e. Friedrich Engels.

10. Which of the following products has never been cartelized?
   a. oil.
   b. bananas.
   c. sugar
   d. wheat.
   e. coffee.

11. A member of a cartel would be most likely to increase its profits by:
   a. undercutting the prices of other cartel members, as long as it did not get caught.
   b. setting its price above that of other cartel members.
   c. pursuing an aggressive nonprice promotions policy.
   d. restricting its output below the cartel-set production quota in order to drive the price up.
   e. insisting that the cartel continually raise the price it charges.

12. Defenders of the efficiency of monopolistic competition insist that:
   a. consumers benefit greatly from product differentiation. ⟵ *(circled)*
   b. the inefficiency of pure competition exceeds that of pure monopoly.
   c. pure competition leads to unstable cutthroat competition.
   d. diseconomies of scale are so substantial that differentiation is inevitable.
   e. all of the above.

production ↑
prices ↑

311

13. The idea that the number of firms currently in an industry is far less important in determining its pricing and output than is the ease of entry or exit over the long run is known as the:
    a. limit pricing doctrine.
    b. kinked demand curve model.
    c. incentive for cartel-cheating hypothesis.
    d. theory of pure competition.
    e. contestable markets hypothesis.

TRUE/FALSE QUESTIONS

___ 1. The costs of product differentiation account for the cost structures of monopolistically competitive firms being higher than for competitive firms.

___ 2. Decisionmaking by firms in oligopolistic industries depends heavily on the expected reactions of other firms to any changes in prices or outputs.

___ 3. The sparseness of evidence of price collusion in the U.S. raises serious questions about collusive limit-pricing models.

___ 4. Monopolistically competitive or oligopolistic industries tend to produce lower rates of output and to charge higher prices than purely competitive industries.

___ 5. When economies of scale are such that only a firm of considerable size, relative to the market, is able to produce output efficiently, the market naturally gravitates toward the competitive mold.

___ 6. A monopolistically competitive industry is made up of firms that behave in a consciously interdependent manner.

___ 7. Impure oligopolies are characterized by product differentiation.

___ 8. Desires for increased monopoly power probably have been behind the creation of most oligopolies.

___ 9. Cartels tend to be unstable without governmental controls.

___ 10. When economics of scale are significant, there is a tendency to slash prices during periods of slack demand in order to spread overhead costs over greater amounts of output.

UNLIMITED MULTIPLE CHOICE

CAUTION: EACH QUESTION HAS FROM ZERO TO FOUR CORRECT ANSWERS!

___ 1. In the long run, monopolistically competitive firms:
   a. produce at the lowest possible per unit cost.
   b. find that entry and exit are relatively easy.
   c. face numerous competitors, all being small relative to the size of the market.
   d. produce a homogeneous commodity.

___ 2. Product differentiation:
   a. only exists in the mind of the consumer.
   b. is frequently used by firms to shift the demand curves for their commodities upward and to the right.
   c. causes the price elasticity of demand to decrease.
   d. is often used as a means by which firms can exert influences over the prices of their outputs.

___ 3. An oligopoly:
   a. is any industry comprised of fewer than ten firms.
   b. produces homogeneous outputs.
   c. is an industry into which entry is relatively easy.
   d. can be created by economies of scale, by mergers, or by substantial barriers to entry.

___ 4. According to the kinked demand curve theory of oligopolistic pricing behavior:
   a. changes in the cost structure of the oligopolist rapidly change the price of output.
   b. marginal cost can change without changes in the price of output.
   c. it is impossible for the price charged by oligopolists to remain rigid in the face of changes in cost.
   d. firms consider the reactions of their competitors whenever a price change is contemplated.

___ 5. Cartels:
   a. are illegal in most instances in the U.S.
   b. normally entail overt collusion on the parts of member firms.
   c. try to joint-profit maximize, meaning that they try to behave as a monopoly would in setting prices and production.
   d. operate primarily in international markets for manufactured goods.

PROBLEMS

Problem 1

Graphed below are the revenue and cost curves for two monopolistically competitive firms. Use this information to answer the following true/false questions.

Figure 1

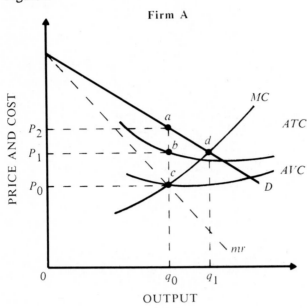

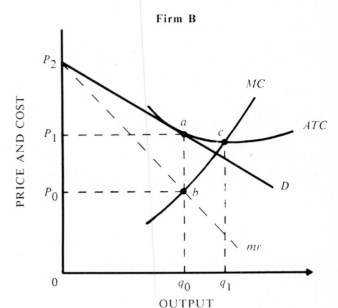

_____ a. Firm B is operating in the long-run period of production.

_____ b. Firm A can maximize total revenue by producing q_1 units of output.

_____ c. Firm A is producing in the long-run period of production.

_____ d. Firm A is incurring an economic loss.

_____ e. Point a lies in elastic range of Firm A's demand curve.

_____ f. Point d lies in the elastic range of Firm B's demand curve.

_____ g. Firm B would maximize society's net benefits by producing q_1 units of output.

_____ h. Firm B is allocating productive inputs efficiently from society's point of view when producing q_0 units of output.

_____ i. Firm A maximizes profit by producing q_1 units of output.

_____ j. Both firms are plagued by excess capacity.

_____ k. Firm A will always earn economic profits, regardless of the period of production.

_____ l. At output q_0, Firm B is producing output at the point where total revenue equals total cost.

_____ m. Total profits to Firm A are represented by area $P_0 P_2 ac$.

_____ n. Total profits to Firm B are represented by area $P_0 P_1 ab$.

_____ o. Total fixed costs for Firm A are represented by area $P_0 P_1 bc$.

_____ p. Total variable costs for Firm A are equal to area $0 P_0 c q_0$.

314

Problem 2

Illustrated below are the revenue and cost curves for four different profit maximizing firms. Use this information to answer the following true/false questions.

Figure 2

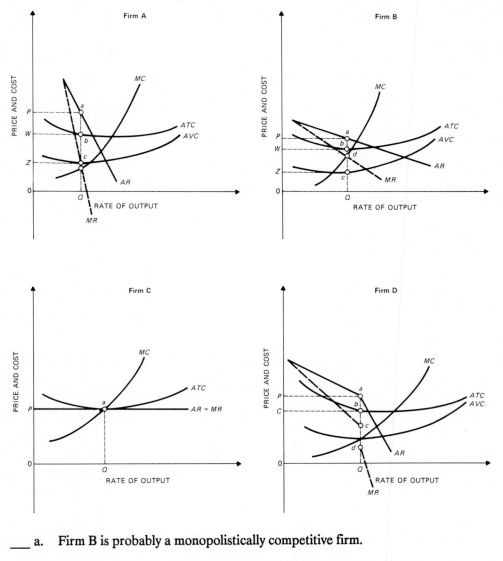

___ a. Firm B is probably a monopolistically competitive firm.

___ b. Firm C is producing in the short-run period of production.

___ c. Firm D is earning economic profits in the short-run period of production.

___ d. Firm A is a monopolist.

___ e. Firm D is earning normal profits which are equal to the area of rectangle *CPab*.

___ f. Firm C is pricing at a point along its demand curve that has a price elasticity of one.

___ g. Firm D is a monopolistically competitive firm.

___ h. Firm D will always be compelled to pass forward to the consumer any increases in the costs of production in the form of higher prices.

___ i. Firm A is a sales maximizer.

___ j. Firm B is incurring total variable costs which are equal to the area of rectangle *zwbc*.

___ k. Firm A incurs total fixed costs equal to *zwbc*.

___ l. Firm C is a purely competitive firm.

___ m. Firm A is maximizing the net benefits received by society.

___ n. Firm B is producing output at the lowest possible opportunity cost from society's point of view.

___ o. Firm B can earn economic profits in the long-run period of production.

___ p. Firm B can reap economic profits in the short-run period of production.

Problem 3

Using your knowledge of monopolistically competitive markets and cost curves:

a. In graph "A" illustrate a firm that is suffering economic losses.

b. In graph "B" illustrate the long run solution for a firm in this industry.

c. What has caused the change in the firm's profit picture from A to B? _____
_____
_____

Figure 3

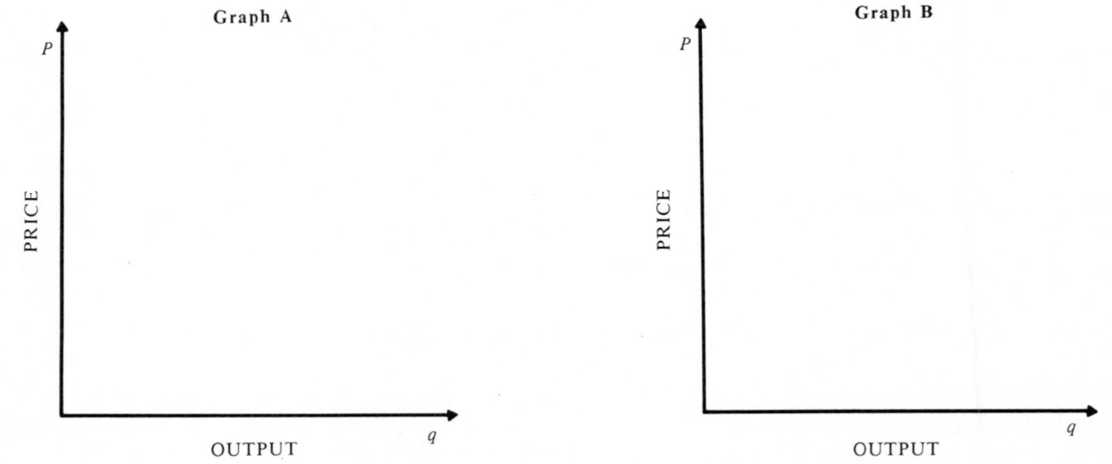

Graph A

Graph B

P

PRICE

OUTPUT   q

P

PRICE

OUTPUT   q

Problem 4

The following graph depicts a firm in a particular oligopoly market model.

Figure 4

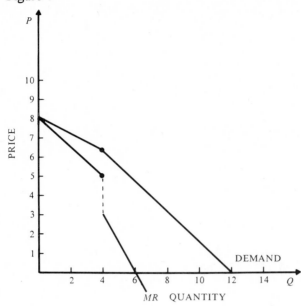

a. What market model does this graph represent? _____

b. Assume that marginal cost is constant at $3.50. What is the price and quantity of output for this firm?
    _____

c. If the marginal cost increases to $5.00, what are the new equilibrium price and quantity?
    _____

d. Over what range of quantities is the firm concerned with its own demand curve? _____ Over what range
    is the firm concerned with the market demand curve? _____

e. At what level of output is the industry's price elasticity of demand unitary? _____

ANSWERS

Matching Key Terms and Concepts

SET I

Answer	MIC	ECO
1. b	p. 231	535
2. a	p. 230	534
3. g	p. 227	531
4. h	p. 226	530
5. c	p. 218	522
6. i	p. 219	523
7. j	p. 219	523
8. e	p. 231	535
9. d	p. 231	535
10. f	p. 231	535

SET II

Answer	MIC	ECO
1. f	p. 228	532
2. e	p. 224	528
3. g	p. 221	525
4. d	p. 231	535
5. h	p. 223	527
6. c	p. 224	528
7. i	p. 224	528
8. b	p. 221	525
9. j	p. 224	528
10. a	p. 227	531

Chapter Review (Fill-in Questions)

1. pure, impure
2. marginal revenue, demand
3. oligopoly, concentration ratio
4. four or eight, contestable
5. economies of scale, mergers
6. kinked demand, ignore
7. marginal revenue, sticky prices
8. limit price, economies of scale
9. cartel, joint profits
10. contestable, P > MC

Standard Multiple Choice

Answer	MIC	ECO
1. b	p. 222	526
2. a	p. 221	525
3. a	p. 227	531
4. e	p. 223	527
5. c	p. 230	534
6. e	p. 223	527
7. b	p. 227	531
8. d	p. 220	524
9. c	p. 220	524
10. d	p. 231	535
11. a	p. 232	536
12. a	p. 223	527
13. e	p. 222	526

True/False Questions

Answer	MIC	ECO
1. T	p. 223	527
2. T	p. 224	528
3. T	p. 231	535
4. T	p. 223	527
5. F	p. 224	528
6. F	p. 222	526
7. T	p. 224	528
8. T	p. 224	528
9. T	p. 232	536
10. T	p. 227	531

Unlimited Multiple Choice

Answer	MIC	ECO
1. bc	p. 223	527
2. bd	p. 219	523
3. d	p. 224	528
4. bd	p. 227	531
5. abc	p. 231	535

Problem 1
MIC pp. 222-223; *ECO 526-527*

a. T
b. F
c. F
d. F
e. T
f. T
g. F
h. F
i. F
j. T
k. F
l. T
m. F
n. F
o. T
p. T

Problem 2
MIC pp. 222-227; *ECO 526-531*

a. T
b. F
c. T
d. T
e. F
f. F
g. F
h. F
i. F
j. F
k. T
l. T
m. F
n. F
o. F
p. T

Problem 3
MIC pp. 222-223; *ECO 526-527*

a. See figure 5.
b. See figure 5.
c. As illustrated, the monopolistically competitive firm survives because other firms exit the industry. As these firms leave, the individual firm's demand (d') increases until it no longer incurs economic losses. Another way to approach this problem is to assume the firm's demand does not increase but its average total costs are reduced because it no longer has to advertise as much with fewer competitors. In reality, some combination of the two approaches is probably accurate.

Figure 5

Graph A

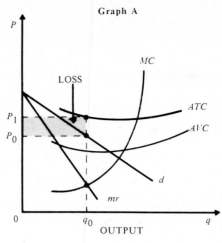

Graph B

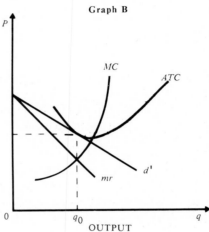

Problem 4
MIC p. 227; *ECO 531*

a. kinked demand curve model

b. P = $6.50, q = 4

c. P = $6.50, q = 4

d. q = 0-4, q = 4-6

e. q = 6

319

CHAPTER TWENTY-SIX

ANTITRUST POLICY: REDUCING MONOPOLY POWER

CHAPTER OBJECTIVES

After you have read and studied this chapter you should be able to differentiate between the various types of mergers and discuss the different "waves" that have occurred in this country's history. You should know the various antitrust acts and what roll they played in shaping the past merger waves. Lastly, you should have an ideal of what is presently considered permissible and forbidden under the current antitrust laws, and what the future of antitrust legislation and monopoly power might look like.

CHAPTER REVIEW: KEY POINTS

1. *Monopoly power* exists whenever a firm can set the price of its output. (Monopoly power and monopoly are not synonymous.) As monopoly power grows, the gap between price (P) and marginal cost (MC) widens. The *Lerner index of monopoly power* (LMP) uses this fact to measure monopoly power as (P - MC)/P. However, estimating MC with accounting data is difficult, and using average costs as a proxy for MC may overstate monopoly power.

2. Market concentration ratios provide some evidence of monopolization or oligopolistic power. *Concentration ratios* are the percentages of total sales, output, or employment in an industry controlled by a small number of the largest firms in the industry. Concentration ratios for the Big 4, Big 8, Big 20, and Big 50 are computed for many industries.

3. Major difficulties are encountered in defining an industry. The existence of *close consumption substitutes* is one consideration; the ease with which potential competitors might enter an industry (*contestability*) is another. The Department of Commerce lumps firms into Standard Industrial Classifications (SICs) to try to solve this problem, but with only mixed success.

4. The *Herfindahl-Hirschman Index* (HHI) is the sum of squared market shares (Si^2). Squaring places more emphasis on big firms. The Justice Department now uses the HHI as a guide to the permissibility of mergers.

5. *Concentration* varies substantially between industries. Nearly 100 percent of all cigarettes produced and sold in the United States are produced by fewer than eight companies, and the eight largest printing companies produce about one-tenth of all printing. However, roughly 70 percent of all manufacturing assets are controlled by the 200 largest American corporations. The numbers on industrial concentration grew dramatically from 1890 to 1929, but have only crept up slowly since.

6. Big firms might be justified by enormous capital requirements or substantial economies of scale. In those instances, proper public policy may take the form of regulation (dealt with in the next chapter). The major thrust of public policy where no such justifications for bigness exist has been to encourage competition through *antitrust actions*. The current level of concentration is testimony to the apparent failure of this policy.

7. One reason for merger is to increase the scope of a firm's operations so that economies of scale in information, marketing, advertising, production, or financial management may be exploited. A second reason, which is far more important for public policy, is that merger may eliminate business rivals and facilitate increases in economic concentration and monopoly power. Increases in monopoly power that result from merger may be reflected rapidly in higher prices for the merged companies' stock. This creates *promotional profit* for current stockholders.

8. The first major wave of mergers in the United States lasted roughly from 1890 until 1914, and was dominated by *horizontal mergers*.

9. Most horizontal mergers were outlawed with the passage of the *Clayton Antitrust Act*, so a wave of *vertical* mergers, lasting from 1914 until the 1929 Stock Market Crash resulted in further economic concentration. Vertical mergers unite suppliers of raw materials or intermediate goods with processors or other firms further along the production chain.

10 Merger activity died during the Great Depression, but revived in the mid-1950s. Since most vertical mergers were prohibited by the Celler-Kefauver Antimerger Act, companies that were very dissimilar were merged into *conglomerates*. Merger activities slowed down during the 1970s but re-emerged strongly during the 1980s.

11. The Big Five Antitrust Laws are summarized in Table 4 of the text.

12. Agricultural cooperatives, athletic organizations, labor unions, export trade associations, and regulated industries are largely exempt from antitrust action.

13. In applying the *Sherman Antitrust Act,* the Court has historically taken two different approaches. The rule of reason approach prohibits bad monopolies and permits reasonable restraints on trade, while the *per se doctrine* forbids all monopolies regardless of conduct.

14. Merger policy is now based on various factors, but if the post-merger HHI exceeds 1,800, the Department of Justice is likely to challenge the merger.

MATCHING KEY TERMS AND CONCEPTS

SET I

A 1. Sherman Antitrust Act

I 2. The Clayton Act *or correct bargain*

E 3. Market concentration ratio

F 4. Lerner index

G 5. Conscious parallelism

J 6. Celler-Kefauver Act *stocks of a comp*

H 7. Herfindahl index

B 8. Webb-Pomerene Act *export org*

D 9. Robinson-Patman Act *price dis*

C 10. Federal Trade Commission

a. Originally was used to break up union activity. *Sherman Anti-trust*

b. Largely exempts export organizations from antitrust actions. *Webb-Pomerene Act*

c. Investigates and challenges unfair methods of competition used by firms. *FTC*

d. Amended Section 2 of the Clayton Act to limit price discrimination even further. *Robinson-Patman*

e. The percent of total industry sales, employment, assets, value-added, or output accounted for by the largest 4, 8, or 20 firms in an industry. *concentration ratio*

f. One measure of the monopoly power exercised by a single firm. *Lerner index*

g. Doctrine dealing with the identical behavior of oligopoly firms. *Conscious parallelism*

h. Weights biggest firms disproportionately heavily in estimating concentrations of market power. *Herfindahl index*

i. Exempted collective bargaining from antitrust litigation. *Clayton Act*

j. Made it illegal for a firm to acquire the stock or assets of a competitor. *Celler-Kefauver*

C 1. "Rule of reason" approach

I 2. Horizontal merger

G 3. Promotional profits

D 4. Conglomerate merger

H 5. Trusts

E 6. The *per se* approach

A 7. Divestiture

J 8. Monopoly power

B 9. SIC codes

F 10. Vertical merger

a. Breaking up a firm convicted of Sherman Act violations.

b. Categorize firms by their markets.

c. "Good" trusts were not in violation of the Sherman Act.

d. Acquiring a firm with no intermediate or competitive products.

e. Certain contracts are so restrictive of competition that they are automatically held to be illegal.

f. Acquiring a firm that supplies intermediate products or buys output.

g. Increases in the values of the stocks of merged firms.

h. Cartel-like combinations of related firms.

i. Acquiring a directly competitive firm.

j. Having control over price.

CHAPTER REVIEW (FILL-IN QUESTIONS)

1-2. The degree of monopoly power can be estimated by; __mkt. concentration ratio__, which measure the percentages of sales, assets, or employees of the top __4-8__ firms in an industry; by the Lerner Index of Monopoly Power, which is computed as __$\frac{P-MC}{P}$__; or by the __Hirfandahl__ index, which is computed as Si^2. __Hirschman__

3-7. __Mergers__ have been a major source of the rapid growth in the __concent.__ of specific industries between 1895 and 1930, and of the slow, but continuing concentration of control of industrial capacity since then. The first wave, __Horizontal__ mergers, consisted of absorption of direct competitors and lasted from roughly 1895 until 1914, when the __Clayton Anti__ Act was passed. The second wave, __vertical__ mergers, began soon after World War I and peaked in 1929, declining until roughly 1935. The __Celler-Kefauver__ Act of 1950 channeled the third wave of mergers, which has lasted from roughly the early 1950s until today, into a __conglomerate__ pattern. Why do firms seek merger? The organizers of mergers hope that __promotional__ profits will be realized from gains in the prices of the stocks of the companies involved. These profits are largest when some __comp.__ is eliminated and __monopoly power__ is enhanced.

8-9. The defenders of concentration argue that huge firms are required in many __capital intensive__ industries, that there are cost savings when firms are __vertically__ integrated, and that size is needed to cope with regulation. Moreover, they argue that the __turnover__ among the top 200 or top 500 largest firms are evidence of substantial competition. When economies of scale seem obvious, the government has used __regulation__ to offset the absence antitrust litigation.

10. Under the early __rule of reason__ approach, good monopolies were held to be legal, but the more recent __per se__ approach holds certain actions automatically to be violations of antitrust laws, regardless of whether they are the actions of "good" trusts or bad ones.

STANDARD MULTIPLE CHOICE

THERE IS A SINGLE "BEST" ANSWER TO EACH OF THE FOLLOWING QUESTIONS.

C 1. The type of merger that creates the greatest threat of increased monopoly power is:
   a. conglomerate.
   b. vertical.
   c. horizontal.
   d. diagonal.
   e. marital.

B 2. Firms that control all aspects of production for some form of output from raw materials to retail sales are:
   a. multinational conglomerates.
   b. vertically-integrated firms.
   c. trusts.
   d. horizontally-integrated multinationals.
   e. laterally infiladed mountebanks.

 A 3. Which of the following arguments best supports the validity of the Lerner Index of Monopoly Power ?
   B
   a. industries in which four or fewer firms dominate sales are very monopolistic.
   b. monopoly power is reflected in a relatively great differences between price and marginal cost.
   c. oligopolies tend to exercise far more monopoly power than do firms in a monopolistically competitive industry.
   d. conscious parallelism of action is evidence of monopoly power.
   e. brand proliferation is incompatible with competition; it signifies monopoly power.

D 4. Joint-profit maximization is NOT compatible:
   a. with shared monopoly.
   b. with a successful cartel.
   c. with a collusive agreement.
   d. with a monopolistically competitive market structure.
   e. within and between General Motors' various divisions (Chevrolet, Pontiac, Oldsmobile, Buick, Cadillac, etc.)

A 5. "Good" trusts were long exempt from antitrust action under the:
   a. *per se* approach.
   b. Webb-Pomerene doctrine.
   c. Clay-Liston decision.
   d. acceptable behavior guideline.
   e. rule of reason approach.

C 6. Export associations are exempted from antitrust actions by the:
   a. Celler-Kefauver Anti-Merger Act.
   b. Trade Adjustment Assistance Act of 1921.
   c. Webb-Pomerene Act.
   d. Federal Trade Act (1914).
   e. Hawley Smoot Act.

E 7. Which of the following is largely exempt from antitrust action because of court decisions rather than because of explicit legislation?
   B
   a. agricultural cooperatives.
   b. amateur and professional sports organizations.
   c. labor unions and collective bargaining.
   d. export associations.
   e. regulated industries.

A 8. Defenders of large firms in highly concentrated industries may reasonably argue that:
   a. some industries have huge capital requirements for each firm.
   b. some firms must be large because of substantial diseconomies of scale.
   c. decreasing cost industries are always concentrated.
   d. increasing cost industries are necessarily concentrated.
   e. large firms in all industries are always more efficient than small firms.

D 9. The antitrust act most vulnerable to the charge that it protects competitors rather than competition is the:
   a. Sherman Act.
   b. Clayton Act.
   c. Federal Trade Commission Act.
   d. Robinson-Patman Act.
   e. Celler-Kefauver Anti-Merger Act.

A 10. Which of the following industries has NOT become noticeably more competitive in the past two decades?
   a. wheat farming.
   b. reproduction equipment (xeroxing, etc.)
   c. automobiles.
   d. electronics (TV's, stereos, etc.).
   e. computers.

B 11. Recent guidelines to prohibit mergers rely on the:
   a. Lerner index of Monopoly Power (LMP).
   b. Herfindahl index.
   c. occurrence of brand proliferation.
   d. concentration ratios over sales for the four largest firms.
   e. need to have several big firms in industries that historically have had a few dominant firms and many small ones.

D 12. Although growing concentration within most industries has almost ceased in the past few decades:
   a. the evidence suggests that market forces and not antitrust actions have been largely responsible.
   b. income and wealth appear to be increasingly concentrated in the hands of the top 1/2 percent of the population.
   c. the ownership of total manufacturing assets in the U.S. continues to be ever more concentrated within the largest two hundred or so corporations, perhaps because of conglomerate mergers.
   d. major industries like computers, reproducing (copying) equipment, steel, and automobiles continue to grow ever more monopolistic.
   e. the LMP index suggests that monopoly power is increasingly exercised.

TRUE/FALSE QUESTIONS

T 1. Monopoly power does not necessarily imply a monopoly.

T 2. Economic theory suggests that as monopoly power increases, the difference between price and marginal cost increases.

T 3. The U.S. economy has experienced three major merger movements during the past century.

T 4. Market concentration within most industries has not increased significantly in the past decade.

F 5. Among the most capital intensive industries in the U.S. are public utilities, petroleum, communications, and transportation.

T 6. Public policy generally presumes that monopoly power is socially undesirable.

F 7. Sports organizations have consistently been involved in antitrust actions.

T 8. According to the doctrine of conscious parallelism, the court could infer conspiracy from parallel action displayed by the firms comprising an oligopoly; this approach is not used anymore.

F 9. The top one hundred firms in the U.S. economy have consistently held nearly half of all manufacturing assets in the past three decades.

T 10. In the 1940s, the U.S. Supreme Court replaced its "Rule of Reason" with the "*per se*" approach to antitrust policy.

T 11. A pure monopoly generates a Herfindahl index of 10,000.

T 12. Divestiture is a common result of antitrust prosecution.

UNLIMITED MULTIPLE CHOICE

CAUTION: EACH QUESTION HAS FROM ZERO TO FOUR CORRECT RESPONSES!

___ 1. The Sherman Antitrust Act:
  (a.) was enacted in 1890.
  (b.) was originally used to break up unions.
  c. clearly specified illegal activities.
  (d.) makes the attempt to monopolize illegal.

___ 2. The Clayton Act:
  (a.) prohibited certain forms of price discrimination.
  b. was enacted in 1936.
  c. created the Federal Trade Commission.
  d. outlawed buying competitors' assets.

___ 3. The Lerner index (LMP):
  a. cannot assume a value of zero.
  (b.) measures a firm's monopoly power.
  (c.) is a difficult measure to use because of problems in estimating marginal cost.
  (d.) assumes larger positive values as a firm's monopoly power grows.

___ 4. The Celler-Kefauver Act:
  (a.) was enacted in 1950.
  (b.) eliminated most horizontal and vertical mergers involving large corporations.
  (c.) made it illegal for a firm to acquire the stock or assets of a competitor.
  (d.) made merger in a particular industry more difficult if there was a noticeable trend toward greater concentration.

___ 5. The Herfindahl index:
  a. was enacted in 1936.
  b. estimates permissible price discrimination, based on differences in production costs.
  (c.) weights the biggest firms extra heavily in generating a number that summarizes market concentration.
  (d.) is used by the Justice Department as a guide for challenges of proposed mergers.

PROBLEM

Assume an eight firm industry with the following information.

FIRM	Sales (Millions)	% of Market
A	$9	45
B	5	25
C	3	15
D	2	10
Others	1	5

Also assume that all the firms have identical price/marginal cost relationships at equilibrium. The price of the good is $6., the marginal cost is $5.

a. What is the four firm concentration ratio? _____ the eight firm concentration ratio? _____

b. What is the LMP for a firm in this industry? ____

c. What is the Herfindahl index for this industry? (For simplicity consider "Others" as one firm") _____

d. Does the LMP seem unusual given the Herfindahl index and the concentration ratio? _____

e. What might be causing this apparent anomaly?
_____
_____
_____

f. If firm B and C merge what happens to the Herfindahl index? _____ the concentration ratios? _____ the Lerner index? _____

g. Generally speaking, would the Federal government allow this merger to occur under current antitrust laws? _____

ANSWERS

Matching Key Terms and Concepts

SET I

Answer	MIC	ECO
1. a	p. 247	551
2. i	p. 248	552
3. e	p. 240	544
4. f	p. 240	544
5. g	p. 252	556
6. j	p. 249	553
7. h	p. 243	547
8. b	p. 251	555
9. d	p. 249	553
10. c	p. 248	552

SET II

Answer	MIC	ECO
1. c	p. 251	555
2. i	p. 245	549
3. g	p. 244	548
4. d	p. 246	550
5. h	p. 244	548
6. e	p. 251	555
7. a	p. 247	551
8. j	p. 239	543
9. b	p. 242	546
10. f	p. 246	550

Chapter Review (Fill-in Questions)

1. concentration ratios, 4, 8, or 20
2. (P - MC)/P, Herfindahl
3. Mergers, concentration
4. horizontal, Clayton Antitrust
5. vertical, Celler-Kefauver
6. conglomerate, promotional
7. competition, monopoly power
8. capital intensive, vertically
9. turnover, regulation
10. rule of reason, per se

Standard Multiple Choice

Answer	MIC	ECO
1. c	p. 245	549
2. b	p. 246	550
3. b	p. 240	544
4. d	p. 244	548
5. e	p. 251	555
6. c	p. 251	555
7. b	p. 250	554
8. a	p. 241	545

9. d	p. 249	553
10. a	p. 242	546
11. b	p. 253	557
12. c	p. 241	545

True/false Questions

Answer	MIC	ECO
1. T	p. 239	543
2. T	p. 240	544
3. T	p. 244	548
4. T	p. 240	544
5. T	p. 242	546
6. T	p. 247	551
7. F	p. 250	554
8. T	p. 252	556
9. T	p. 240	544
10. T	p. 251	555
11. T	p. 243	547
12. F	p. 247	551

Unlimited Multiple Choice

Answer	MIC	ECO
1. abd	p. 247	551
2. a	p. 248	552
3. bcd	p. 240	544
4. abcd	p. 249	553
5. cd	p. 243	547

Problem

a. four firms = 95%, eight firms = 100%

b. LMP = .167

c. HHI = 3,000

d. LMP seems low given high concentration ratio and Herfindahl index.

e. One possibility is that the firms are limit-pricing to deter entry into the industry.

f. The HHI increases to 3,750 for the industry. The concentration ratios and the LMP index remain unchanged.

g. The HHI for the B/C combination would be 1,600 which is right on the decision line under the current regulatory climate.

CHAPTER TWENTY-SEVEN
THE ROLE OF GOVERNMENT REGULATION

CHAPTER OBJECTIVES

After you have read and studied this chapter, you should be able to broadly describe the extent and growth of economic regulation; offer some explanations for the growth of regulation, discuss the effects of economic regulation on business efficiency and on the ranges of choices available to consumers; and discuss the concept of block-pricing and how it yields efficient results.

CHAPTER REVIEW: KEY POINTS

1. The *public interest* theory of regulation focuses on some possible failures of the price system, including poor information, fraud, externalities, and monopoly power. Laissez-faire markets will not provide the socially optimal quantity of a product with externalities, so direct regulation is commonly used in an attempt to protect the public interest.

2. A *natural monopoly* involves substantial economies of scale, rendering direct competition impractical. Society has turned to regulation to prevent natural monopolies from reaping enormous profits and to move them towards socially efficient levels of output. The public interest may be served by requiring the firm to use *block pricing,* which uses price discrimination both to achieve efficiency and to equate total revenues from sales of the service with total costs of production, including a normal accounting profit.

3. The *industry interest* view of regulation expressed by George Stigler suggests that industries can gain from regulation, and therefore "demand" regulation from the government. As Stigler has noted, the state can, and often does, change the profitability of an industry through four main mechanisms: (a) direct taxes or subsidies, (b) restrictions on entry, (c) impacts on an industry's complementary or substitute products, and (d) direct price-fixing policies.

4. Stigler views the government as the supplier of regulatory services to various industries. The costs of obtaining favorable regulation include campaign contributions and lobbying expenses.

5. The bulk of regulatory agencies in this country were created during three decades. The first great surge occurred during the 1930s, when policymakers attempted to buffer the violent swings in the business cycle on our economic system. Well over half of all regulatory agencies, however, came into existence in the 1960s and 1970s. It is not obvious why regulation increased so dramatically during a period of relative prosperity and high economic growth.

6. The law of product liability has evolved from an approach of *caveat emptor*--"Let the buyer beware"--to one of *caveat venditor*--"Let the seller beware." Direct mandates or prohibition of some transactions are also increasingly common. For example, new cars are required to have specific safety equipment; some new drugs are banned. *Caveat emptor* is most appropriate when both producers and consumers have roughly equal access to knowledge about the product. Today, however, producers commonly have considerably more information about complex products than do consumers. It would be prohibitively costly for consumers to detect design and manufacturing flaws in most goods. In addition, modern corporations may use their massive financial and market power to manipulate consumers. Advertising claims are difficult for consumers to verify. Thus, government regulation is seen by many as the only practical solution to the problem of misrepresentation.

7. Opponents of *consumer protection* regulations argue that unregulated competition will force producers to respond to consumer needs, albeit imperfectly. Those individuals who want safer products will pay for them, and those willing to incur more risk will not. Furthermore, opponents argue that the poor are hurt most by consumer protection, which removes inferior but cheaper products from the market. For many of the poor, consumption opportunities are limited already, and removing the inferior (usually cheaper) products from the market may force them out of the market entirely.

8. Regulating public utilities is considerably more difficult than simple theory would suggest. Major problems arise in determining the *rate base*, a *"fair" rate of return*, and allowable costs. Regulatory agencies face a difficult task in balancing the interests of consumers and utility investors.

9. Regulation is increasingly attacked as misguided and "nit-picky." Various deregulation schemes have been implemented in the 1980s. The next decade will probably bring continued reappraisal of the government's role as regulator, but whether this will translate into further reductions in regulation is highly speculative.

MATCHING KEY TERMS AND CONCEPTS

B 1. Occupational licensing

A 2. Rate structure

D 3. Deregulation

C 4. Block-pricing

H 5. Rate base

I 6. Public-interest theory of regulation

E 7. *Caveat emptor*

F 8. Industry-interest theory

J 9. Natural monopoly

G 10. *Caveat venditor*

a. A schedule of price/quantity combinations set by a regulatory commission.

b. Barriers to entry that enhance some workers' incomes.

c. Economic efficiency can be enhanced with this form of price discrimination on utility rates.

d. A movement most notable in the transportation and financial industries.

e. Let the buyer beware.

f. Firms demand regulation and government supplies it.

g. Let the seller beware.

h. Investment that determines the net returns allowed utilities.

i. Regulation can correct for failures of the market system.

j. Charge too much and produce too little if unregulated.

OPTIONAL MATCHING

Match these regulatory agencies with the areas they regulate.

___ 1. EPA   a. Aviation

___ 2. FDA   b. Discrimination in employment

___ 3. NRC   c. Environmental quality

___ 4. FPC   d. Radio and TV broadcasting

___ 5. FCC   e. Interstate electric power transmission

___ 6. FRS/FDIC   f. Home mortgages

___ 7. OSHA   g. Safety of consumer products

___ 8. FHA   h. Edibles and pharmaceuticals

___ 9. ICC   i. Collective bargaining

___10. FTC   j. Stock and bond issues

___11. EEOC   k. Nuclear power (formerly AEC)

___12. FAA/CAB   l. Saving and loan associations

___13. CPSC   m. Federally chartered banks

___14. SEC   n. The suitability of work environments

___15. NLRB   o. Trains, trucks, and pipelines

___16. FHLB/FSLIC   p. The fairness of business practices

___17. CFTC   q. Mine safety

___18. FMC   r. Highway safety

___19. ERISA   s. Range lands

___20. W&HA   t. Oceanic shipping

___21. DOE   u. Minimum wages, overtime

___22. BLM   v. Federal contracts

___23. OFCC   w. Civil rights, other than employment

___24. CRC   x. Energy allocations

___25. MESA   y. Pension plans

___26. NHTSA   z. Commodities trading

CHAPTER REVIEW (FILL-IN QUESTIONS)

1-8. The two peak decades for adopting new government regulations were the ___*30s*___ and
___*70s*___ ; with well over half of all regulatory agencies being created since 1960. Some observers
see the increasing ___*complexity*___ of society as requiring greater regulation; others perceive government
as following an evolutionary process in its relations with business from ___*promoter*___ to
___*regulator*___ to ___*guarantor*___ . But why is business regulated? One explanation, the
___*public-int.*___ theory of regulation, focuses on such imperfections in particular markets as
___*monopoly*___ power, production ___*externalities*___ that cause ___*pollution*___ of the environment,
or imperfect ___*info*___ on the part of consumers. A challenge to this view is the _____ theory. This
theory suggests that regulations are shaped to the interests of regulated firms. Because the government can
___*restrict*___ the entry of potential competitors, can ___*subsidize*___ an industry or give it special tax
breaks, can influence the costs of ___*resources*___ or ___*substitute*___ goods, or can impose price floors
or ceilings, industry finds it worthwhile to lobby to secure regulations that are helpful to existing firms in an
industry. This explanation accounts for regulatory boards that are captives of the regulated industries, and
for the pervasiveness of regulation in industries in which economies of scale, externalities, or inadequate
information are insignificant.

9-10. In a world with ideal regulators and regulations, the rate structures of natural monopolies would be set to
yield only normal, or ___*fair*___ rates of return on investment. Because efficiency requires that the
price of the marginal good (MSB) would just equal its marginal cost, some form of ___*p. disc.*___ such
as ___*block pricing*___ would be required for those industries in which the ___*marginal cost*___ of a single firm
declined across the full range of market output.

STANDARD MULTIPLE CHOICE

THERE IS ONLY ONE "BEST" ANSWER FOR EACH QUESTION.

A 1. The public-interest theory of regulation is
LEAST compatible with:
- a. limiting consumer access to only top
quality merchandise.
- b. limiting natural monopolies to a fair return
on investment.
- c. limiting pollutants emitted as
manufacturing by-products.
- d. requiring labels describing the
characteristics of products.
- e. mandating automobile accessories to
improve pedestrian safety.

D 2. The product characteristics LEAST likely to
cause regulation would be:
- a. something considered essential to
consumers.
- b. something physically hooked up to many
properties.
- c. product homogeneity.
- d. relative stability of demand, supply, and
price.
- e. infrequent but expensive purchases by
typical consumers.

D 3. The full costs of a natural monopoly can be
covered in an economically efficient manner
if the rate structure uses:
- a. uniform average cost pricing.
- b. uniform marginal cost pricing.
- c. uniform average variable cost pricing.
- d. block-pricing.
- e. none of the above.

C 4. NOT among the major mechanisms by which
government can benefit business is:
- **B** a. restriction of entry into an industry.
- b. placing price ceilings on an industry's
products.
- c. placing price floors under an industry's
output.
- d. direct subsidies or tax breaks.
- e. subsidies for complements or taxes on
substitute goods.

fluctuations
essential
hooked up

A 5. The doctrine of *caveat emptor* is most easily justified when:
   a. products are standardized, low priced, and frequently purchased.
   b. product technology is extremely complex.
   c. the government has better information than either producers or consumers.
   d. producers have better information than consumers.
   e. products are heterogeneous, expensive, and infrequently purchased.

E 6. The doctrine of *caveat venditor* (seller liability) seems most appropriate when:
   a. private researchers (e.g., Consumers Union) evaluate products.
   b. firms comply with truth in labeling laws.
   c. the government publishes extensive information on the product.
   d. a consumer misuses a product and is injured.
   e. product quality is assured by the manufacturer, but not delivered.

C 7. Deregulation has most obviously enhanced efficiency in:
   a. pharmaceutical research and development.
   b. agriculture.
   c. airlines ticket prices.
   d. the practice of medicine.
   e. education.

E 8. The economist primarily responsible for formulating and advancing the industry-interest theory of regulation is:
   a. Karl Marx.
   b. Henry David Thoreau.
   c. Milton Friedman.
   d. Paul Samuelson.
   e. George Stigler.

D 9. Consumer protection regulations impose costs that are borne most heavily by:
   a. managers of regulated industries, who are denied exploitative profits.
   b. the wealthy, who face much higher prices for luxury goods.
   c. workers, who become less productive as standardization results in losses of jobs due to automation.
   d. the poor, as inferior, but cheaper, goods are removed from the market.
   e. the middle class, who inevitably pay the price for government errors.

B 10. According to the industry-interest theory, the gains from government regulation favoring an industry:
   a. generally result in increased economic efficiency nationwide.
   b. are secured through expensive lobbying and similar activities.
   c. are offset by consumers' gains from lower utility rates.
   d. increase the risks to a firm of being in the industry.
   e. arise only from special tax advantages or subsidies.

TRUE/FALSE QUESTIONS

T 1. By forcing a natural monopoly to charge a price for its marginal output which is only equal to marginal cost, the government can structure incentives for the firm to produce the socially optimal rate of output.

T 2. Rate structures normally permit regulated public utilities to earn a normal return (profit).

F 3. It is impossible for regulated public utilities to earn economic profits in the short-run period of production.

T 4. A "fair" rate structure only permits a regulated firm to earn normal profits.

T 5. Uniform (constant) utility rates are socially optimal if they are set equal to average cost.

E 6. The concept of *caveat emptor* implicitly assumes that both consumers and producers possess a similar level of knowledge concerning the safety and effectiveness of a product.

T 7. According to the proponents of consumer protection regulation, today's consumers have very few ways to verify the advertising claims of business firms short of the purchase and consumption of the goods that are advertised.

T 8. Occupational licensing improves the economic conditions of those who are licensed.

T 9. Externalities exist whenever some production or consumption activity confers either costs or benefits on a party not monetarily involved in the market activity or transaction.

T 10. Opponents argue that consumer protection regulation tends to destroy product diversity.

UNLIMITED MULTIPLE CHOICE

CAUTION: EACH QUESTION HAS FROM ZERO TO FOUR CORRECT RESPONSES!!

___ 1. Industry-interest views of regulation suggest:
  a. externalities generated by production may justify governmental regulations.
  b. natural monopolies should be replaced by perfect competition.
  c. regulation should stimulate production that involves huge positive externalities.
  d. consumers benefit immensely when lower prices are facilitated by economies of scale in production.

___ 2. An efficient rate structure based on block-pricing:
  a. permits a well managed regulated firm to earn normal (zero economic) profits.
  b. enables the continued existence of the regulated firm.
  c. is synonymous with a uniform socially optimal price.
  d. permits a regulated firm to earn long run economic profits.

___ 3. Proponents of consumer protection laws believe that:
  a. regulation diminishes economic freedom by reducing the range of goods available.
  b. safety devices that are required by law do not noticeably diminish the number of accidents.
  c. regulation of some consumer products provides consumers with nearly costless information about some goods.
  d. regulation of consumer products decreases fraudulent advertising.

___ 4. According to the opponents of consumer protection regulation:
  a. governmental regulation of consumer products decreases the variety of products offered to consumers.
  b. governmental regulation of consumer products reduces the real purchasing power of lower income families.
  c. competition forces business firms to respond to consumer needs; governmental regulation of business to protect the welfare of consumers is unnecessary.
  d. governmental regulation of consumer products decreases the welfare of the consuming public.

___ 5. Government regulation of business is likely in those industries that produce goods:
  a. considered vital to consumers.
  b. the demands for which experience frequent and sizable fluctuations.
  c. that are homogeneous.
  d. that are attached directly to the property of consumers.

PROBLEMS

Problem 1

Use the information about revenues and costs contained in the graph below to answer the following true/false questions.

Figure 1

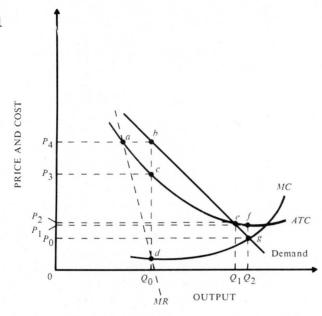

___ a. The market structure graphically depicted is a natural monopoly.

___ b. If this firm was not regulated, it would sell Q_2 units of output at a price of P_1.

___ c. Proper regulation of this firm would result in production of Q_0 units of output.

___ d. The firm could break even (earn zero economic profits) by selling Q_1 units of output at a price of P_2 per unit.

___ e. The socially optimal output is Q_1.

___ f. This firm can cover its costs and produce a socially optimal level of output through an appropriate "block-pricing" rate structure.

___ g. If the firm was regulated and forced to produce the socially optimal output the firm would earn a fair return equal to area P_0gfP_1.

___ h. If it could not price discriminate but were left to its own devices, this firm would earn economic profits equal to area P_3cbP_4.

___ i. The natural monopoly policy dilemma is illustrated by this figure.

___ j. The socially optimal output is Q_2.

___ k. Consumers would be better off if this was a competitive industry.

___ l Output Q_1 is not the socially optimal output because the cost of the resources used to produce the last unit of output exceeds the benefits to society from that last unit.

Problem 2

Use the information in the graph below to answer the following questions.

Figure 2

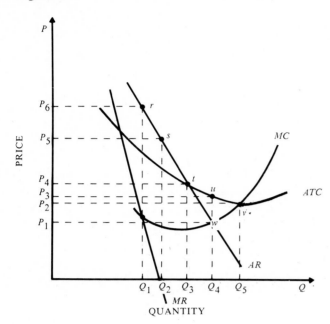

a.   As illustrated this firm exhibits _____.

b.   If this profit maximizing firm is NOT regulated the price would be _____; and the quantity _____.

c.   If the firm preferred to maximize total revenue as opposed to profits the price would be _____; and the quantity _____.

d.   If the firm were regulated under the efficiency criteria of P = MC, then the firm would produce at a uniform price _____; and quantity _____. This would entail a loss to the firm of _____.

e.   If the firm were regulated and allowed to have price equal to average cost, then the price would be _____; and the quantity _____. The problem with this approach is that from an efficiency standpoint _____.

f.   If these were the cost curves of a purely competitive firm what would the equilibrium price _____; and quantity _____ be. Is this a fair comparison? _____.

g.   What regulatory pricing tool did you learn from the text to deal with situations such as the one pictured?_____.

Problem 3

A hypothetical supply and demand relationship for Seattle taxis is pictured below. Assume that this is the part of the market that benefitted from deregulation. Answer the following questions based on the graph.

Figure 3

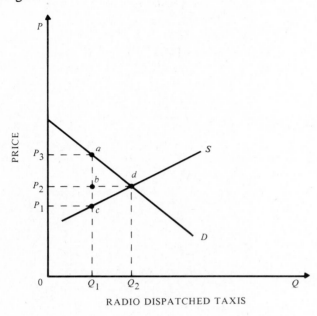

RADIO DISPATCHED TAXIS

a. If this market was not regulated the free market equilibrium price is _____; and quantity _____. In this situation the industry earns _____ economic profits in the long run.

b. If the market for radio dispatched taxis were regulated and the quantity restricted to $Q1$, then the price would rise to _____. If the average cost at Q_1 equals P_2, then there would be economic profits of _____ shared by firms in the industry.

c. As can be seen in your text, industries that are regulated often gain profits from restricted entry into the industry. Our case illustrates just that point. The license to own and operate a taxi earns economic profit. What might you expect to happen to the value of a taxi license after deregulation?

_____

_____

d. In a market such as the taxi market, that overtly seems purely competitive, why might regulation have occurred in the first place? _____

_____

ANSWERS

Matching Key Terms and Concepts

Answer	MIC	*ECO*
1. b	p. 272	*576*
2. a	p. 268	*572*
3. d	p. 275	*579*
4. c	p. 268	*572*
5. h	p. 268	*572*
6. i	p. 264	*568*
7. e	p. 273	*577*
8. f	p. 266	*570*
9. j	p. 266	*570*
10. g	p. 273	*577*

Optional Matching
MIC p. 263; *ECO 567*

Answer
- 1. c
- 2. h
- 3. k
- 4. e
- 5. d
- 6. m
- 7. n
- 8. f
- 9. o
- 10. p
- 11. b
- 12. a
- 13. g
- 14. j
- 15. i
- 16. l
- 17. z
- 18. t
- 19. y
- 20. u
- 21. x
- 22. s
- 23. v
- 24. w
- 25. q
- 26. r

Chapter Review (Fill-in Questions)

1. 1930s, 1970s
2. complexity, promoter
3. regulator, guarantor
4. public-interest, monopoly
5. externalities, pollution
6. information, industry-interest
7. restrict, subsidize
8. resources, complements or substitutes
9. fair, price discrimination
10. block-pricing, marginal or average cost

Standard Multiple Choice

Answer	MIC	*ECO*
1. a	p. 266	*570*
2. d	p. 269	*573*
3. d	p. 268	*572*
4. b	p. 270	*574*
5. a	p. 273	*577*
6. e	p. 273	*577*
7. c	p. 275	*579*
8. e	p. 265	*569*
9. d	p. 274	*578*
10. b	p. 266	*570*

True/False Questions

Answer	MIC	*ECO*
1. T	p. 266	*570*
2. T	p. 268	*572*
3. F	p. 267	*571*
4. T	p. 268	*572*
5. F	p. 268	*572*
6. T	p. 273	*577*
7. T	p. 273	*577*
8. T	p. 272	*576*
9. T	p. 268	*572*
10. T	p. 274	*578*

Unlimited Multiple Choice

Answer	MIC	*ECO*
1. none	p. 266	*570*
2. ab	p. 267	*571*
3. cd	p. 273	*577*
4. abcd	p. 274	*578*
5. abcd	p. 269	*573*

Problem 1
MIC pp. 266-268; *ECO 570-572*

a. T
b. F
c. F
d. T
e. F
f. T
g. F
h. T
i. T
j. T
k. F
l. F

Problem 2
MIC pp. 266-268; *ECO 570-572*

a. monopoly power and decreasing costs (economies of scale).
b. P_6; Q_1.
c. P_5; Q_2.
d. P_1; Q_4. P_1P_3uw.
e. P_4; Q_3. P is greater than MC which violates our efficiency criteria.
f. P_2; Q_5. This is not fair because the whole crux of the problem is that the firm has large economies of scale and therefore is a natural monopoly.
g. block-pricing

Problem 3
MIC p. 276; *ECO 580*

a. P_2; Q_2. no or zero
b. P_3. P_2P_3ab.
c. The license value was largely based on the economic profit. If the economic profit is gone we can assume that most, if not all, of the license value will deteriorate.
d. Quality of service (safety) was also a reason for regulation.

   As is indicated in the airport taxi market, cutthroat competition may indeed erode the quality of service.

CHAPTER TWENTY-EIGHT
WAGES AND EMPLOYMENT IN
COMPETITIVE LABOR MARKETS

CHAPTER OBJECTIVES

After you have read and studied this chapter, you should be able to describe a competitive firm's demand for labor in competitive labor markets; the accumulation of human capital and its effect on the demand for labor; the determinants of labor supplies and the influences on labor force participation rates; equilibrium in a competitive labor market; and the effects of applying minimum wage laws or the doctrine of comparable worth in a competitive labor market.

CHAPTER REVIEW: KEY POINTS

Prod. tech. used
Amounts of other factors employed
Demand for the product

1. The demand for any resource is related to the: (a) amounts of other factors employed, (b) production technology used, and (c) demand for the product. Because the demand for labor (or any factor) hinges on the demand for final products, it is a *derived demand*.

MRP = VMP in pure comp.

2. *Marginal revenue product* (MRP) is the firm's revenues generated by hiring the marginal unit of some input. In pure competition, this is the same as VMP. Labor (or any factor) will be employed up to the point where the additional revenue competitive firms receive (*value of the marginal product,* or VMP) just equals the cost of an additional unit of the resource (*marginal factor cost*, or MFC). In competitive labor markets, the marginal factor cost (MFC) equals the *wage rate* (w), so pure competition in all markets means that VMP = MRP = MFC = w.

3. Increases (decreases) in the demand for the product, in labor productivity, or in the amounts of other resources used will normally increase (decrease) the VMP and demand for labor. Technological changes may either increase or decrease labor demands. Automation is the replacement of workers by new technologies.

4. The *elasticity of demand for labor* is directly related to the: (a) *elasticity of demand for the final product,* (b) *labor's share of total costs* represented by the wage bill, (c) ease of factor substitution, and (d) time for adjustment. *TIME FOR ADJUSTMENT* *ELASTICITY OF D for final product* *EASE OF FACTOR SUB* *LABOR'S SHARE OF TC*

5. The supply of labor depends on: (a) wage rates and structures, (b) labor force participation, (c) the number of hours people are willing to work, and (d) the education, training, and skills of workers.

6. Workers experience both *income* and *substitution effects* when wage rates change. Increased wages cause labor to substitute work for leisure because work expands consumption opportunities and leisure is more costly. However, higher wages mean that for a given amount of labor effort, workers will earn more income, and, if leisure is a normal good, they will want to consume more leisure and work less. If the substitution effect is larger than the income effect, supplies are positively sloped. Backward-bending labor supplies result when income effects dominate substitution effects.

7. While the individual's labor supply curve may be backward bending, the supply of labor to any industry will always be positively sloped. Industry supplies and demands for labor establish the *equilibrium wage* as each firm hires additional units of labor until the value of the marginal product equals the market wage rate.

8. Competitive demand curves for labor represent the marginal benefits society receives from additional employment, and supply curves reflect the marginal cost to society of using those resources. Employing labor to the point where $D_L = S_L$ is efficient because society's benefits from additional employment equals its costs. More or less employment than where $D_L = S_L$ yields inefficient resource allocations since society gets more (or less) than it desires in an opportunity cost sense.

9. Labor quality improves through investments in *human capital* that include formal education and on-the-job training. Education benefits both the individual and society at large. Training is classified as either general or specific: *General training* enhances a worker's productivity equally for many firms, while *specific training* only increases the worker's productivity for the current employer.

10. Turnover and quit rates are negatively related to the levels of specific training workers have received and to the wage premiums paid them. Firms that invest heavily in their employees have strong incentives to retain them and do so: (a) by paying higher wages than other firms will offer, and (b) through special rules based on seniority or pension provisions that reward longevity with the firm.

11. *Minimum-wage laws* intensify the unemployment of unskilled workers (especially teenagers) and may foster discrimination. Widespread implementation of a *comparable worth* doctrine would require bureaucratic comparisons of jobs to determine wages, and might stimulate disemployment of many workers in the competitive occupations into which women have historically been channeled.

MATCHING KEY TERMS AND CONCEPTS

SET I

E 1. marginal revenue product (MRP)

I 2. elasticity of demand for labor

B 3. backward bending labor supply

G 4. resource substitutability

A 5. marginal factor cost (MFC) = wage rate

D 6. implicit labor contract .

C 7. marginal productivity theory

F 8. value of the marginal product (VMP)

J 9. labor force participation rate

H 10. labor-leisure trade-off

a. $\Delta wL/\Delta L$.

b. When income effects dominate substitution effects of wage changes.

c. Your income depends on the productivity of your resources.

d. lower wages in return for increased job security.

e. $\Delta TR/\Delta L$, or $\Delta PQ/\Delta L$.

f. $P \times MPP_L$.

g. If easier, causes the elasticity of demand for resources to grow.

h. Choices that must be made when wage rates change.

i. $\%\Delta L/\%\Delta w$.

j. The percentage of a population that is in the work force.

D 1. automation   a. Equal pay for work requiring equivalent skills and experience.

I 2. credentialism   b. Job skills that are valuable only to the particular firm.

E 3. income effect   c. Resource demands depend on demands for final goods.

J 4. substitution effect   d. When new forms of capital replace workers on a job.

F 5. minimum wage laws   e. Can cause labor supply curves to "bend backward."

B 6. specific training   f. May promote racial discrimination, especially among young workers.

A 7. comparable worth   g. Skills valuable to many firms.

G 8. general training   h. Skills and experience that enhance MRP.

C 9. derived demand   i. Excessive emphasis on formal education.

H 10. human capital   j. Accounts for the normal, positive slope of labor supply curves.

income — sloped back bending

CHAPTER REVIEW (FILL-IN QUESTIONS)

1. The **subst.** effect occurs because wage changes alter the costs of leisure relative to other goods, but there is an offsetting **income** effect due to the changes in people's purchasing power as wage rates change. The individual's supply curve of labor is **positively** sloped if the substitution effect is more powerful than the income effect, and **negative** if the income effect is dominant. Even though individual supplies may be negatively sloped, the supplies of labor to firms or individual industries are invariably positively sloped because higher **wages** attract more **workers**.

4-7. Human capital represents the skills of individuals; training may be either **specific**, in which case workers become more productive only at their current jobs, or **general**, which makes the worker a more productive employee for a number of firms. **Firms** will pay for specific training, but **workers** bear the investment costs for general training in the forms of **wages** that are below the workers' **MRP's**. Once a worker receives specific training, the employer will pay a premium in excess of the workers' MRPs in their next best alternative employments in order to reduce **labor turnover** and realize returns on their investments. Another way to acquire human capital is through formal education, although some critics think that **credentialism** (overemphasis on degrees) is a common failing in employment decisions.

8-10. Minimum wage laws cause **unemployment** among unskilled workers, especially **teens**. Low-skilled workers who manage to retain their jobs and skilled workers who do not have to compete with low-wage workers are the major beneficiaries of these laws. Among the harmful side effects of these laws is that employment discrimination is encouraged because minority groups cannot compete on the basis of wages. Advocates of the doctrine of employment discrimination may be dismayed if it becomes public policy because low wages in work that has been traditional among **women** may be a symptom that supply is large relative to demand. If so, regulations requiring higher **wages** may result in higher **unemployment** among people in these occupations.

STANDARD MULTIPLE CHOICE

EACH QUESTION HAS A SINGLE BEST ANSWER.

C 1. Increases in derived demands are best illustrated by rising:
   a. peanut sales during baseball season.
   b. sales of convertibles during hot summers.
   c. new capital orders during economic booms.
   d. beef prices when cowboys unionize.
   e. teenage unemployment when minimum wage laws rise.

D 2. Marginal productivity theory was primarily developed by:
   a. Thorstein Veblen.
   b. Karl Marx.
   c. Alfred Marshall.
   d. J.B. Clark.
   e. Lorenzo Engels.

E 3. An increase in the competitively-set wage tends to cause:
   a. firms to reduce the amounts of labor hired.
   b. increases in the MRPs of the workers a firm retains.
   c. higher MFCs of labor to competitive firms.
   d. pressure for greater automation in an industry.
   e. All of the above.

B 4. A competitive firm will demand more labor if:
   a. technological changes lead to automation.
   b. the price of the firm's output rises.
   c. more firms enter the industry.
   d. the value of the marginal product is below the wage rate.
   e. workers employed by other firms acquire more specific training.

 5. If labor is a competitive firm's only variable resource:
   a. labor demand will become less elastic as time goes by.
   b. there will be an elastic demand for labor if the product demand is elastic.
   c. wage hikes are easily accommodated if the demand for the firm's output is highly elastic.
   d. rising capital costs will cause workers to lose their jobs.
   e. the money available to pay workers is only the revenue remaining after all fixed costs are paid.

A 6. The percentage of a given population who are either employed or unemployed is known as the:
   a. labor force participation rate.
   b. work-force proportion.
   c. labor supply.
   d. substitution effect dominance rate.
   e. income-leisure loss curve.

D 7. A firm that provides its workers with substantial general training tends to:
   a. pay such individuals premium wages to retain them.
   b. require workers to sign legal contracts of peonage and indenture.
   c. increase worker productivity the most in their current jobs.
   d. pay wages below the market wage during training periods.
   e. Hire only workers with MBAs.

A 8. For most types of labor, the most accurate ranking of labor supplies from <u>most</u> elastic to <u>least</u> elastic is probably:
   a. firm, industry, occupation.
   b. economy, individual, occupation.
   c. firm, economy, occupation.
   d. individual worker, firm, occupation.
   e. economy, firm, individual worker.

342

9. As people acquire more formal education, they tend to:
   a. uniformly earn more at every point over their entire lives.
   b. earn more primarily early during their working lives.
   c. earn more, but primarily later during their working lives.
   d. receive ever higher rates of return from their education.
   e. start work at later ages and retire earlier.

10. Workers will eventually be less productive if:
   a. the amount of physical capital is increased.
   b. they acquire more and more human capital.
   c. they receive more specific training and become more specialized.
   d. the wage rate is increased.
   e. more and more people are put on an assembly line.

11. If the income effect of a wage increase is more powerful than the substitution effect, the:
   a. labor supply curve will be "backward bending."
   b. unemployment rate will rise when people become "welfare cheaters."
   c. labor force participation rate will rise.
   d. firm will hire more workers at higher wages.
   e. value of the marginal product will exceed the wage rate.

12. Since World War II, in the United States, the:
   a. amount of human capital per worker has fallen.
   b. labor force participation rate of women has risen.
   c. supply of labor has consistently grown faster than the demand.
   d. rates of return from advanced education have more than tripled.
   e. All of the above.

13. "Comparable worth" policies would be least likely to cause:
   a. unemployment among women to rise.
   b. employment discrimination by appearance or personality.
   c. greater automation in nursing, teaching, and clerical work.
   d. reduction in the poverty rates of households headed by women.
   e. persistent surpluses of nurses, teachers, and secretaries.

14. Education is too heavily weighted in many employment decisions according to the critics of:
   a. credentialism.
   b. formalism.
   c. nepotism.
   d. plutocracy.
   e. decentralization.

15. Workers who retain their jobs will be more productive after firms adjust to increases in:
   a. competition in an industry.
   b. wages.
   c. technological advances.
   d. capital costs.
   e. government regulation.

16. Technological changes that replace workers with machinery are known as:
   a. homeostasis.
   b. peridontalism.
   c. automation.
   d. featherbedding.
   e. solipsism.

17. A government-supported literacy program provided through an employer of unskilled labor is an example of:
   a. human capital depreciation.
   b. business paternalism.
   c. specific training.
   d. laissez faire economics.
   e. general training.

A 18. A firm's demand for labor would increase if the:
- (a.) price of the output rose.
- b. labor supply shifted to the right.
- c. new technology encouraged automation.
- d. wage rate fell.
- e. market became more competitive.

C 19. Competitive equilibria in competitive labor markets require:
- a. P = MR = AVC.
- b. VMP - P is maximized.
- c. VMP = MRP = MFC = w.
- d. output is at a break-even level.
- e. MPP = P.

D 20. The elasticity of the demand for labor tends to increase as there are increases in the:
- a. amount of capital used in a production process.
- b. rate of automation in an industry.
- c. difficulty in substituting among different resources.
- (d.) share of wages in total production costs.
- e. participation rates of women in the labor force.

TRUE/FALSE QUESTIONS

T 1. In a competitive labor market, the marginal factor cost of labor (MFC) to a firm is the same as the wage rate.

F 2. Competitive firms will hire workers where MPP = w.

F 3. Technological advances always raise the demand for labor.

T 4. Output per worker typically rises when the capital to labor ratio is increased.

T 5. Firms tend to bear the cost of specific training in hopes of returns, even though such investments are embodied in individual workers.

F 6. The value of the marginal product (VMP) equals the marginal physical product (MPP) times the wage rate (w).   VMP = MPP × P

T 7. The supply of a specific type of labor skill to a particular firm is normally more elastic than to the entire industry.

F 8. General training is normally "paid for" by the trainee.

T 9. If the VMP exceeds the wage rate, the competitive firm gains by hiring more workers.

T 10. Hikes in wage rates may cause the competitive firm's short-run demand for labor to fall as it substitutes capital for labor.

T 11. Minimum wage laws reduce the losses incurred by firms that use race to discriminate when they make employment decisions.

F 12. Minimum wage laws have been very effective in reducing poverty in households headed by unskilled workers.

T 13. Adjustments by employers when wages rise increase the productivity of the workers who retain their jobs.

T 14. Labor productivity tends to rise when workers are provided more land or capital with which to work.

F 15. The productivity gain that occurs when computer operators learn to apply a particular piece of software to their current employer's business is an example of general training.

T 16. Advances in technology that allow easier substitution of capital for labor raise the elasticity of demand for labor and encourage automation.

T 17. Wages can be raised with less loss of employment if the demand for output is highly elastic.

T 18. A clerk who learns the codes to dial to create particular colors or tints on a Sears Paint Mixer gains productivity in the form of specific training.

T 19. Critics of "credentialism" argue that formal education is over-rated as a predictor of a job applicant's productivity.

F 20. A competitive firm can increase its profits by hiring more workers whenever the MRP of labor exceeds the VMP.

UNLIMITED MULTIPLE CHOICE

CAUTION: EACH QUESTION HAS FROM ZERO TO FOUR CORRECT RESPONSES.

1. The MRP of labor is:
   a. synonymous with the MPP of labor.
   b. the additional total revenue attributable to an additional unit of output.
   c. the additional total revenue associated with an extra worker.
   d. computed by dividing the change in total revenue by the total number of laborers.

2. Marginal factor cost: MFC
   a. equals the wage rate for a firm in a competitive labor market.
   b. is synonymous with the marginal cost of output.
   c. is the addition to total cost attributable to an additional unit of output.
   d. is a measure of total factor cost per unit of input.

3. The supply curve of labor for individuals:
   a. slopes upward when the income effect with an increase in the wage rate is less than the substitution effect.
   b. slopes upward whenever the income effect with an increase in the wage rate is greater than the substitution effect.
   c. is vertical where the income effect with an increase in the wage rate just counterbalances the substitution effect.
   d. is derived from individuals' choices about their labor/leisure trade-offs.

4. Human capital:
   a. consists of improvements to human productive capacity.
   b. partially explains differences in the incomes earned by different people.
   c. consists, in part, of increased labor productivity brought about by job training programs.
   d. consists of improvements to raw land brought about by labor.

5. Individual labor force participation is more likely:
   a. the higher are the incomes of other family members.
   b. for female than male family members.
   c. the lower is the education and experience of the individual.
   d. for women 30 to 50 than for women 20 to 30.

Problem 1

Table 1 displays the cost and revenue data used by a competitive firm to decide how much labor to hire and how much output to produce. Assume that Total Fixed Costs (TFC) are $50. Use this information to answer the following questions:

Table 1

PROFIT/ LOSS	(MC)	(TVC)	(L)	(Px)	(MR)	(Qx)	(TR)	(APPL)	(MPPL)	(MRPL)	(ARPL)	(WL)	(MFC)	(TC)
___	___	___	0	$3	___	0	___	___	___	___	___		$15	___
___	___	___	1	$3	___	3	___	___	___	___	___		$15	___
___	___	___	2	$3	___	8	___	___	___	___	___		$15	___
___	___	___	3	$3	___	15	___	___	___	___	___		$15	___
___	___	___	4	$3	___	24	___	___	___	___	___		$15	___
___	___	___	5	$3	___	35	___	___	___	___	___		$15	___
___	___	___	6	$3	___	48	___	___	___	___	___		$15	___
___	___	___	7	$3	___	59	___	___	___	___	___		$15	___
___	___	___	8	$3	___	68	___	___	___	___	___		$15	___
___	___	___	9	$3	___	75	___	___	___	___	___		$15	___
___	___	___	10	$3	___	80	___	___	___	___	___		$15	___
___	___	___	11	$3	___	83	___	___	___	___	___		$15	___
___	___	___	12	$3	___	84	___	___	___	___	___		$15	___

MC	=	Marginal Cost
TVC	=	Total Variable Cost
L	=	Units of Labor
Px	=	Price of Output
MR	=	Marginal Revenue
Qx	=	Total Output
TR	=	Total Revenue

APPL	=	Average Physical Product
MPPL	=	Marginal Physical Product
MRPL	=	Marginal Revenue Product
ARPL	=	Average Revenue Product
WL	=	Price of Labor (wage rate)
MFC	=	Marginal Factor Cost
TC	=	Total Cost

a. Complete the table (remember that Total Fixed Costs are $50).

b. The firm sells its product in what kind of industry? _____ Explain your answer. _____

c. The firm purchases labor in what type of market? _____ Explain your answer.
_____

d. How many units of labor should the firm hire? _____ Why? _____

e. How much of the good should the firm produce and sell? _____ Why? _____

f. Assume the price of labor (wage rate) falls to $9. How many units of labor should the firm hire? ___ Why?
_____

g. Explain why the firm's demand for labor is a derived demand. _____
_____

h. Assume the wage rate rises to over $40. How many units of labor should the firm hire? _____
Why? _____

Problem 2

Figure 1 illustrates the short run supply and demand curves for labor for a competitive firm. Use this information to answer the following true/false questions.

Figure 1

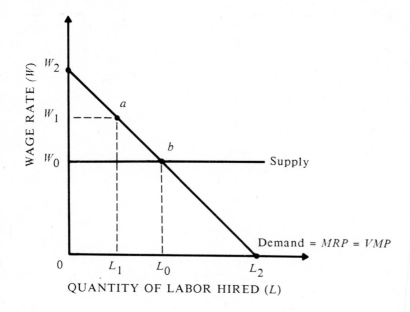

____ a. The firm immediately encounters diminishing marginal returns upon hiring the first several units of labor.

____ b. The firm hires labor in a purely competitive labor market.

____ c. The firm can influence the price of labor.

____ d. The firm will hire L_0 units of labor per time period.

____ e. The dollar value to the firm of the output produced by L_0 units of labor is given by the area of trapezoid $0W_2bL_0$.

____ f. The per unit price of labor is $0W_0$.

____ g. The fixed inputs will share total income that equals the area of triangle W_0W_2b.

____ h. Labor receives an amount of income equal to the area of rectangle $0W_0bL_0$.

____ i. The supply curve of labor is also the average factor cost curve of labor.

____ j. The MFC of the L_1th unit of labor is W_1.

____ k. The marginal physical product of the L_2th unit of labor is roughly zero.

ANSWERS

Matching Key Terms and Concepts

SET I

Answer	MIC	ECO
1. e	p. 283	587
2. i	p. 286	590
3. b	p. 288	592
4. g	p. 286	590
5. a	p. 284	588
6. d	p. 295	599
7. c	p. 284	588
8. f	p. 284	588
9. j	p. 287	591
10. h	p. 288	592

SET II

Answer	MIC	ECO
1. d	p. 285	589
2. i	p. 299	598
3. e	p. 288	592
4. j	p. 288	592
5. f	p. 295	599
6. b	p. 294	598
7. a	p. 299	603
8. g	p. 294	598
9. c	p. 283	587
10. h	p. 291	595

Chapter Review (Fill-in Questions)

1. substitution, income
2. positively, "backward bending"
3. relative wages, workers
4. specific, general
5. Firms, workers
6. wages, MRPs
7. labor turnover, credentialism
8. unemployment, teenagers
9. comparable worth, women
10. wages, unemployment

Standard Multiple Choice

Answer	MIC	ECO
1. c	p. 283	587
2. d	p. 292	596
3. e	p. 297	601
4. b	p. 285	589
5. b	p. 286	590
6. a	p. 287	591
7. d	p. 294	598
8. a	p. 286	590
9. c	p. 293	597
10. e	p. 284	588
11. a	p. 288	592
12. b	p. 287	591
13. d	p. 299	603
14. a	p. 294	598
15. b	p. 290	594
16. c	p. 285	589
17. e	p. 294	598
18. a	p. 285	589
19. c	p. 284	589
20. d	p. 286	590

True/False Questions

Answer	MIC	ECO
1. T	p. 290	594
2. F	p. 284	588
3. F	p. 285	589
4. T	p. 294	598
5. T	p. 294	598
6. F	p. 284	588
7. T	p. 286	590
8. T	p. 294	598
9. T	p. 290	584
10. F	p. 286	590
11. T	p. 297	601
12. F	p. 297	601
13. T	p. 290	594
14. T	p. 284	588
15. F	p. 294	598
16. T	p. 286	590
17. F	p. 286	590
18. T	p. 294	598
19. T	p. 294	598
20. F	p. 284	588

Unlimited Multiple Choice

Answer	MIC	ECO
1. c	p. 283	587
2. a	p. 284	588
3. ad	p. 288	592
4. ac	p. 291	595
5. none	p. 287	591

Problem 1
MIC pp. 283-284, 289-291
ECO 587-588, 593-595

a. See Table 2.

Table 2

PROFIT OR LOSS	(MC)	(TVC)	(L)	(P$_X$)	(MR)	(Q$_X$)	(TR)	(APP$_L$)	(MPP$_L$)	(MRP$_L$)	(ARP$_L$)	(W$_L$)	(MFC)	(TC)
-50	--	0	0	$3	3	0	0	--	--	--	--	$15	15	50
-56	5	15	1	3	3	3	9	3	3	9	9	15	15	65
-56	3	30	2	3	3	8	24	4	5	15	12	15	15	80
-50	2.14	45	3	3	3	15	45	5	7	21	15	15	15	95
-38	1.66	60	4	3	3	24	72	6	9	27	18	15	15	110
-20	1.36	75	5	3	3	35	105	7	11	33	21	15	15	125
+ 4	1.15	90	6	3	3	48	144	8	13	39	24	15	15	140
+22	1.36	105	7	3	3	59	177	8.42	11	33	25.29	15	15	155
+34	1.66	120	8	3	3	68	204	8.50	9	27	25.50	15	15	170
+40	2.14	135	9	3	3	75	225	8.33	7	21	25.00	15	15	185
+40	3	150	10	3	3	80	240	8	5	15	24	15	15	200
+34	5	165	11	3	3	83	249	7.54	3	9	22.64	15	15	215
+22	15	180	12	3	3	84	252	7	1	3	21	15	15	230

b. Purely competitive; product price is a given parameter.

c. Purely competitive; input price (wage rate) is a given.

d. 10; MRP = MFC = $15 and P = MR = MC = $3.

e. 80; MR = MC = $3.

f. 11; MRP = MFC = $9 and P = MR = MC = $3.

g. The demand for labor is derived from the demand for output.

h. None; MFC > ARP for all levels of employment; therefore the firm should shut down.

Problem 2
MIC pp. 289-291; *ECO 593-595*

a. T
b. T
c. F
d. T
e. T
f. T
g. T
h. T
i. T
j. F
k. T

CHAPTER TWENTY-NINE

LABOR MARKETS: MONOPOLY POWER, MONOPSONY POWER, AND LABOR UNIONS

CHAPTER OBJECTIVES

After you have read and studied this chapter you should be able to discuss the effects of a firm's monopoly power and/or monopsony power on wages and hiring; major features of U.S. labor legislation; evolution of the labor union movement; and overall effects of unions on economic performance.

CHAPTER REVIEW: KEY POINTS

1. The *marginal revenue product curve* (*MRP*) for a firm selling in an imperfectly competitive product market will be below the *value of the marginal product of labor* (*VMP*) curve. All firms will hire labor until the marginal revenue product equals the *marginal factor cost* (*MFC*) of labor. Because *MRP* < *VMP* for employees of firms with monopoly power, are paid less than the values of their marginal products. This difference is called *monopolistic exploitation.*

2. A *monopsonist* is the sole buyer of a particular resource or good. Labor monopsonists face an entire market supply of labor and, if all workers are paid equally, their marginal factor cost curve will lie above the labor supply curve. Relative to pure competitors, labor monopsonists pay lower wages and hire fewer workers. In addition, labor will be paid less than the value of its marginal product, a difference referred to as *monopsonistic exploitation.*

3. When competitive conditions prevail in both resource and product markets, the firm hires labor until *VMP* = *MRP* = *MFC* = *w*. When monopoly prevails in the product market but the monopoly firm hires labor under competitive conditions, labor is hired up to the point where *VMP* > *MRP* = *MFC* = *w*. Given a competitive product market and monopsony power in the labor market, a firm will maximize profits by hiring labor until *VMP* = *MRP* = *MFC* > *w*. Finally, when a firm has both monopoly and monopsony power, labor is hired up to the point where *VMP* > *MRP* = *MFC* > *w*. Any difference between *VMP* and *w* represents *exploitation,* a term borrowed from Marxist jargon.

4. A minimum wage legally set above the equilibrium wage in competitive labor markets will raise unemployment. It is possible, but unlikely, that minimum wages might increase employment and wages simultaneously, but only where there is substantial monopsonistic exploitation of unskilled workers and wage discrimination is not practiced, an unlikely combination. A union wage hike might have the same effect. However, the markets where minimum-wage hikes raise existing wages are typically rather competitive. Thus, increased unemployment is the normal result when minimum wages are increased.

5. *Bilateral monopoly,* a very early model of collective bargaining, describes the limits to the wage bargaining process but provides little predictive power. Sir John Hicks's bargaining model predicts both final wage settlements and the duration of strikes.

6. *Labor unions* have typically employed three methods to increase the wages of their members: (a) reductions of the supply of workers to an industry; (b) establishing higher wages and then parceling the available work to members; and (c) policies designed to increase demands for union labor.

7. Unions have traditionally organized into craft or industrial unions. Craft unions were the bulwark of the *American Federation of Labor* (*AFL*); industrial unions comprised the *Congress of Industrial Organizations* (*CIO*). Frequent jurisdictional disputes over which organization would represent particular workers caused the two to merge into the AFL-CIO in 1955.

8. Unions and their leaders use several kinds of agreements with organized firms to protect their prerogatives as sole bargaining agents for workers. *Closed shops* require workers to be union members as a precondition for employment. At the other end of the spectrum, *open shops* permit union and nonunion members to work side by side. This arrangement is quite unsatisfactory to unions since nonmembers receive the benefits of collective bargaining but need not pay union dues. *Union shops* are compromises between closed and open shops. The employer can hire union or nonunion workers, but an employee must join the union within some specified period (usually 30 days) to retain the job. The Taft-Hartley Act of 1947 outlawed the closed shop and permitted individual states to pass right-to-work laws forbidding union shops. In many of these states, *agency shops* have been created to protect unions from free riders. Workers may choose not to belong to the union but must pay dues.

9. Unionism developed in a hostile environment. The Great Depression shifted public policy in favor of collective bargaining. As trade unionism grew, many felt that unions became corrupt and too powerful, and tighter organizing and financial reporting constraints were imposed on labor organizations. The union movement was relatively stable from roughly 1950 until 1980, but has declined as a percentage of the total labor force in the 1980s. The labor force increasingly consists of white-collar workers who are reluctant to join unions.

10. *Wage differentials* between union and nonunion workers average roughly 10-15 percent. Some people blame inflation on excessive union wage demands. Large wage hikes in key industries may set the pattern for other industries. Higher wages may raise unemployment and induce public officials to pursue expansionary macroeconomic policies, further intensifying inflationary pressures. Since organized labor represents less than one-sixth of the work force, it is unlikely that unionism explains much inflation.

11. A small percentage of collective bargaining negotiations end in *strikes*, and most are short. Strikes often impose costs on individuals and firms that are not direct parties to labor negotiations. Strikes may cause shortages, shipping delays, or losses of perishable products.

12. Public sector unions have been growing in recent years. Public employee unions frequently mix politics and collective bargaining to win their demands. Public officials negotiating contracts are seldom those who are responsible for developing government budgets; thus, they may have only weak incentives to resist union wage demands.

MATCHING KEY TERMS AND CONCEPTS

SET I

___ 1. monopsonist

___ 2. the Wagner Act

___ 3. marginal factor cost (MFC)

___ 4. blacklists

___ 5. bilateral monopoly

___ 6. MRP = MFC

___ 7. the Taft-Hartley Act

___ 8. public employees

___ 9. yellow dog contracts

___10. the Clayton Act

a. Guaranteed labor the right to organize unions.

b. Now-outlawed agreements not to join unions.

c. Exempted from the protection of the Wagner Act.

d. Is a price maker as a buyer.

e. Used to prevent union organizers from getting jobs.

f. The equilibrium condition for inputs for all firms.

g. Permits individual states to enact "right-to-work" laws that forbid the closed-shop

h. Lies above the labor supply curve facing a monopsonist.

i. Exempts most union activity from the Sherman Act.

j. One of the earliest models of collective bargaining.

SET II

___ 1. monopolistic exploitation

___ 2. agency shop

___ 3. "right-to-work" laws

___ 4. open shop

___ 5. perfect wage discrimination

___ 6. closed shop

___ 7. Taft-Hartley Act

___ 8. union shop

___ 9. monopsonistic exploitation

___10. minimum wage laws

a. $VMP > MRP = MFC = w$.

b. May eliminate inefficiencies of monopsony power.

c. The closed-shop is illegal.

d. $VMP = MRP = MFC > w$.

e. If monopsony power exists, may cause increases in both wages and employment.

f. All workers eventually must join a union.

g. Only union members may be hired.

h. Employment is not affected by union membership.

i. Dues are paid by nonunion workers.

j. Outlaw the union shop.

CHAPTER REVIEW (FILL-IN QUESTIONS)

1. All firms maximize profits by hiring inputs until their _____ equal their _____.

2. If a firm with monopoly power is a competitive employer, the VMP _____ the MRP, so profit-maximizing equilibrium occurs where _____.

3. _____ is a primitive model of collective bargaining in which a monopsony firm deals with a monopoly union. However, the model only determines the _____ in which wage contracts will fall, not the precise wage rate that will be the outcome of bargaining.

4-8. _____ unions are organized along occupational lines, while _____ unions include all workers in an industry. When employment is denied to everyone not a union member, there is a(n) _____ agreement, which is a violation of the _____. _____ shops, for which a worker must join a union to maintain employment, are legal unless a state has passed a(n) _____. Union membership is irrelevant for employment in a(n) _____, but non-union members still pay dues if a(n) _____ arrangement exists. Because both union and non-union workers get the same benefits, this is one means by which non-union workers are prevented from being _____. Firms deduct union dues from workers' paychecks when contracts include _____ provisions.

9-10. Approximately one American worker in _____ is a union member; this is down from the peak decade of the _____. Consequently, widespread concern about growth in union power is probably misplaced. It is dubious that union wage demands cause substantial _____. In typical years, only _____ percent of all workers are on strike.

STANDARD MULTIPLE CHOICE

EACH QUESTION HAS ONE BEST ANSWER

___ 1. If a firm hires to the point where VMP > MRP = MFC = w:
  a. there is a bilateral monopoly situation.
  b. the firm has monopsony power.
  c. there is monopolistic exploitation of workers.
  d. monopolistic economic profits are necessarily being realized.
  e. wage discrimination is being exercised.

___ 2. The employer least likely to have monopsony power would be:
  a. a secretarial service firm in Chicago.
  b. the police force in Macon, Georgia.
  c. the U.S. Army.
  d. a lumber mill in Greer, Arizona.
  e. the community hospital in Pocatello, Idaho.

___ 3. Unlike competitive employers, firms with monopsony power can:
  a. set any wage they want and hire as many workers as they desire.
  b. produce any amount and charge any price they want for output.
  c. be expected to try to maximize their profits.
  d. always wage discriminate to ensure monopolistic exploitation.
  e. pay workers wages less than MRP.

___ 4. When a firm's wage structure reflects the eagerness of individual employees to work, terms that are most applicable include:
  a. monopsonistic exploitation and wage discrimination.
  b. monopolistic exploitation and separation of ownership and control.
  c. surplus values and hedonistic preferences.
  d. wage peonage and capitalistic defoliation.
  e. third degree price discrimination and labor rent controls.

5. An employer can legally follow a policy of:
   a. wage discrimination based on race or gender.
   b. closed shop agreements with unions.
   c. firing workers because they join unions.
   d. price discrimination based on cost differentials.
   e. telling other firms which job applicants are union sympathizers.

6. Minimum wage laws are most likely to raise equilibrium employment if a firm has been exercising:
   a. monopoly power and price discrimination.
   b. employee selection in markets for unskilled workers.
   c. collective bargaining with an aggressive union.
   d. monopsony power without wage discrimination.
   e. racial discrimination in its hiring practices.

7. When a powerful seller confronts a powerful buyer, there is:
   a. reciprocal exploitation.
   b. bilateral monopoly.
   c. dialectical bargaining.
   d. ancillary reciprocity.
   e. strategic bloc management.

8. Agreements not to join unions were once common requirements for employment. Now outlawed, these are known as:
   a. yellow dog contracts.
   b. blacklist contracts.
   c. exclusionary provisions.
   d. employment screens.
   e. union busters.

9. Industrial unions intend to organize all workers within:
   a. a particular company.
   b. the United States.
   c. a particular skill or craft.
   d. a specific occupation.
   e. a broad industry.

10. The idea that unions are more powerful than ever before is:
    a. supported by the effects of unions on inflationary spirals.
    b. reflected in the growing numbers of violent and costly strikes.
    c. contrary to the fact that union membership is declining.
    d. demonstrated by the growing political influence of unions.
    e. especially true in the cases of middle managers.

11. The least likely result if unions succeed in raising their wages is that:
    a. wages in nonunion sectors will fall.
    b. employment will grow in nonunion sectors.
    c. barriers will be constructed to limit entry into unions.
    d. the share of labor in national income will grow.
    e. nonunion firms will have competitive advantages over union firms.

12. Prior to the AFL-CIO merger in 1955:
    a. the AFL was an alliance of industrial unions.
    b. the CIO was an alliance of craft unions.
    c. strikes over which unions would represent workers were common.
    d. the union movement was restricted to public employees.
    e. the union movement in the U.S. was declining.

13. Strikes tend to be resolved after workers' savings trickle down into a discomfort zone and there is exhaustion of:
    a. public tolerance, causing government to set a fair settlement.
    b. managers and inventories, causing firms to raise their offers.
    c. diminishing returns to union leaders and business agents.
    d. labor force participation by nonunion "scabs."
    e. legal remedies that might correct managerial misbehavior.

___14. The Taft Hartley Act of 1946 made it illegal to have a:
a. right-to-work law passed by a state legislature.
b. conviction for a misdemeanor and serve as a union officer.
c. union for agricultural migrants or government workers.
d. closed shop agreement that prevents hiring nonunion workers.
e. yellow dog contract or a blacklist of potential troublemakers.

___15. Union membership is most prevalent among:
a. white collar workers.
b. supervisors and managers.
c. pink collar clerical workers.
d. young, upwardly mobile, urban professionals.
e. blue collar workers.

___16. The union strategy that probably yields the highest wages for both union members and other workers over the long run is:
a. restricting entry from particular occupations.
b. lobbying for tariffs against imports that compete with union-produced goods.
c. setting rigid rules for firms employing union workers to maximize "feather bedding."
d. facilitating management plans to increase productivity.
e. demanding uniform wage rates with premiums for seniority.

___17. Contracts requiring employment when some workers' jobs have been made obsolete by automation are examples of:
a. blacklisting.
b. featherbedding.
c. check-off provisions.
d. yellow dog contracts.
e. labor-reducing protectionism.

___18. Nonunion members cannot "free-ride" in states with Right-to-Work laws if a company agrees to operate a/an:
a. closed shop.
b. union shop.
c. open shop.
d. agency shop.
e. shoe shop.

___19. If a collective bargaining contract contains a "check-off provision":
a. union workers can be fired if they do not meet production quotas.
b. firms collect union dues by deducting them from paychecks.
c. workers are required to do only tasks in their job descriptions.
d. quality control in a plant is performed by union representatives.
e. seniority creates a first right of refusal for layoffs, so older workers can choose to draw unemployment compensation or work.

___20. Workers who are now allowed to join unions but who still may not legally strike include:
a. civilian federal employees.
b. medical professionals.
c. military personnel.
d. elected state and local officials.
e. television newscasters.

TRUE/FALSE QUESTIONS

___ 1. A labor monopsonist that does not wage discriminate hires fewer workers and pays lower wages than a purely competitive employer.

___ 2. Equilibrium employment falls for all firms when minimum legal wages rise.

___ 3. Firms maximize profits by buying resources until each input's marginal revenue product equals its marginal factor cost.

___ 4. Monopsonists confront perfectly elastic supplies of labor.

___ 5. Values of the marginal product equal the extra revenue that would be generated if a purely competitive seller of output hired extra units of a resource.

___ 6. Bilateral monopoly occurs when two powerful oligopolists share an output market, and is also known as duopoly.

___ 7. Firms can exercise either monopolistic exploitation or monopsonistic exploitation, but not both simultaneously.

___ 8. Wage discrimination cannot occur in equilibrium without monopsonistic exploitation of labor.

___ 9. There are incentives for employees not to share wage information if a firm follows a policy of wage discrimination.

___10. Unions existed in the U.S. before the Civil War.

___11. Yellow dog contracts that require employees to agree not to join unions are still a popular union-busting technique.

___12. The Sherman Antitrust Act was originally used to prosecute unions on the grounds that strikes were "restraints of trade."

___13. Union organizers were forbidden by the Taft Hartley Act to place firms that resisted union objectives on "blacklists" that required current union members to boycott these firms.

___14. Cost-push inflation is often blamed on labor unions because of wage increases negotiated through collective bargaining.

___15. In an average year, approximately 12 percent to 14 percent of the total labor force is involved in strikes.

___16. Strikes typically waste 6 to 10 percent of annual GNP.

___17. The typical gap in wages between comparable union and nonunion workers is roughly one third.

___18. Strikes tend to be settled because firms are eventually pressured to meet all union demands.

___19. Federal workers may all now join unions and strike to ensure that the government collectively bargains in good faith.

___20. Union membership has recently declined to less than 20 percent of the U.S. labor force.

UNLIMITED MULTIPLE CHOICE

CAUTION: EACH QUESTION HAS FROM ZERO TO FOUR CORRECT RESPONSES.

___ 1. The labor union in a given industry can increase its members' wage rates by implementing policies:
   a. with firms in the industry to increase labor productivity.
   b. that decrease the supply of union workers in the industry.
   c. that increase the demand for union labor.
   d. of featherbedding if firms would otherwise have monopoly profits.

___ 2. A profit maximizing monopsonist in the labor market always hires more workers up to the point where the:
   a. value of labor's marginal product equals its marginal factor cost.
   b. marginal revenue product of labor equals its marginal factor cost.
   c. wage rate is the lowest possible proportion of the marginal factor cost of labor.
   d. wage rate just equals labor's marginal factor cost.

___ 3. The bilateral monopoly model:
   a. is one of the most modern theories of collective bargaining.
   b. specifies equilibrium price when one buyer deals with one seller.
   c. is useful in explaining the limits to bargaining between a monopsonistic buyer and a monopolistic seller of labor services.
   d. describes in general terms the boundaries for wage negotiations.

___ 4. A labor monopsonist that cannot wage discriminate to take advantage of different people's willingness to work confronts a:
   a. perfectly wage elastic supply curve of labor.
   b. marginal factor cost of labor that is upward sloping and above the labor supply curve.
   c. positively sloped labor supply curve.
   d. fixed wage that it must pay, but may then hire as many workers as it chooses.

___ 5. A nondiscriminating firm that is both a monopolist in the output market and a monopsonist in the labor market will employ workers until the:
   a. value of labor's marginal product equals its average factor cost.
   b. marginal revenue product of labor equals its average factor cost.
   c. wage rate most greatly exceeds the marginal factor cost of labor.
   d. marginal revenue product of labor is equal to the wage rate.

Problem 1

Table 1 contains data on the wage rate structures for two firms that are in pure competition in different output markets. Use this information to answer the following questions.

Table 1

Firm A					Firm B				
(L)	(W)	Total Labor Cost	Average Labor Cost	(MFC)	(L)	(W)	Total Labor Cost	Average Labor Cost	(MFC)
0	$10	——	——	——	0	$5	——	——	——
1	10	——	——	——	1	5.50	——	——	——
2	10	——	——	——	2	6.00	——	——	——
3	10	——	——	——	3	6.50	——	——	——
4	10	——	——	——	4	7.00	——	——	——
5	10	——	——	——	5	7.50	——	——	——
6	10	——	——	——	6	8.00	——	——	——
7	10	——	——	——	7	8.50	——	——	——
8	10	——	——	——	8	9.00	——	——	——
9	10	——	——	——	9	9.50	——	——	——
10	10	——	——	——	10	10.00	——	——	——

a. Complete Table 1.

b. What type of firm is Firm A in the labor market? _____ Why? _____

c. What type of firm is Firm B in the labor market? _____ Why? _____

d. Plot the average labor resource cost (ARC) and marginal factor cost (MFC) curves for both firms in Figure 1.

Figure 1

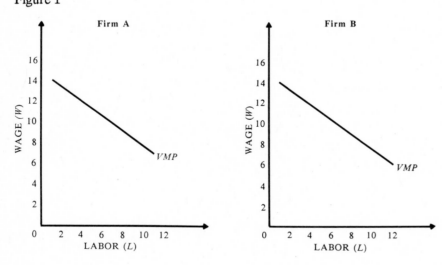

e. Firm A will hire _____ workers at an hourly wage rate of _____.

f. Firm B will hire _____ workers at an hourly wage rate of _____.

g. Total monopsonistic exploitation by Firm B is _____.

Problem 2

Figure 2 shows the revenue and cost curves in different labor markets for two different firms. Use this information to answer the following true/false questions.

Figure 2

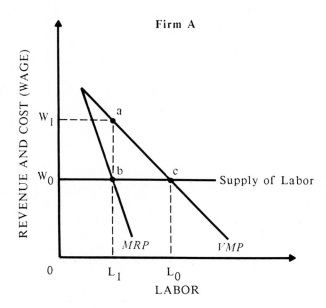

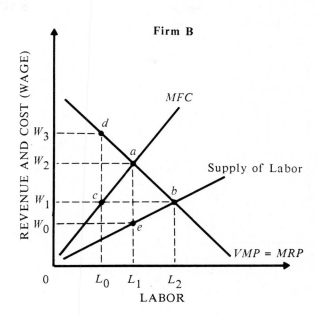

___ a. Firm A is a price maker in the output market.

___ b. Firm A is able to influence the wage rate of the labor service that it purchases.

___ c. Firm B is a competitive seller in the output market.

___ d. Firm B is a price taker in the input market.

___ e. Firm A will hire L_0 workers in equilibrium.

___ f. Firm B will hire L_1 workers in equilibrium.

___ g. In equilibrium, Firm A will pay a wage of W_0.

___ h. In equilibrium, Firm B will pay a wage of W_2.

___ i. The labor supply curve that confronts Firm A is also its marginal factor cost curve of labor.

___ j. The labor supply curve that confronts Firm B is also its average resource (labor) cost.

___ k. For Firm B, the line segment ae represents the degree of monopolistic exploitation per unit of labor.

___ l. For Firm A, the line segment ab represents the degree of monopsonistic exploitation per unit of labor.

Problem 3

Figure 3 depicts the revenue and cost curves of two firms hiring from different labor markets. Use this information to answer the following true/false questions.

Figure 3

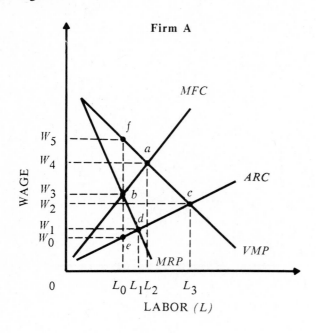

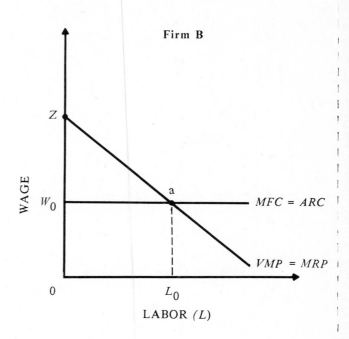

___ a. Firm A is a price taker in the input market.

___ b. Firm A is a price taker in the output market.

___ c. Firm B is a price maker in the output market.

___ d. Firm B is a price maker in the input market.

___ e. Firm A will hire L_0 labor to maximize profits.

___ f. Firm A will pay a wage of $0W_2$ to maximize profits.

___ g. Firm B incurs total labor costs equal to area W_0Za.

___ h. Firm A incurs total labor costs equal to area $0W_0eL_0$.

___ i. Firm A's derived demand for labor is actually the value of the marginal product curve.

___ j. Firm A will hire L_0 workers at a wage of $0W_5$.

___ k. If Firm A hires L_0 workers for a wage of W_0, line segment fb is the degree of monopolistic exploitation and line segment be is the degree of monopsonistic exploitation.

___ l. Firm B pays workers the value of their marginal products and no exploitation of labor results.

ANSWERS

Matching Key Terms and Concepts

SET I

Answer	MIC	ECO
1. d	p. 309	613
2. a	p. 318	622
3. h	p. 310	614
4. e	p. 318	622
5. j	p. 314	618
6. f	p. 310	614
7. g	p. 318	622
8. c	p. 323	627
9. b	p. 318	622
10. i	p. 318	622

SET II

Answer	MIC	ECO
1. a	p. 309	613
2. i	p. 317	621
3. j	p. 317	621
4. h	p. 317	621
5. b	p. 311	615
6. g	p. 317	621
7. c	p. 318	622
8. f	p. 317	627
9. d	p. 310	622
10. e	p. 312	622

Chapter Review (Fill-in Questions)

1. marginal revenue products (MRP), marginal factor costs (MFC)
2. exceeds, VMP > MRP = MFC = W
3. Bilateral monopoly, range
4. Craft, industrial
5. closed shop, Taft-Hartley Act
6. Union, right-to-work law
7. open shop, agency shop
8. free riders, check-off
9. five, 1950s
10. inflation, 2 to 4

Standard Multiple Choice

Answer	MIC	ECO
1. c	p. 309	613
2. a	p. 310	614
3. e	p. 310	614
4. a	p. 310	614
5. d	p. 311	615
6. d	p. 312	616
7. b	p. 314	618
8. a	p. 318	622
9. e	p. 317	621
10. c	p. 322	626
11. d	p. 322	626
12. c	p. 317	621
13. b	p. 316	620
14. d	p. 318	622
15. e	p. 317	621
16. d	p. 319	623
17. b	p. 316	620
18. d	p. 317	621
19. b	p. 318	622
20. a	p. 323	627

True/False Questions

Answer	MIC	ECO
1. T	p. 309	613
2. F	p. 312	616
3. T	p. 308	612
4. F	p. 310	614
5. T	p. 308	612
6. F	p. 314	618
7. F	p. 313	617
8. T	p. 311	615
9. T	p. 311	615
10. T	p. 318	622
11. F	p. 318	622
12. T	p. 318	622
13. F	p. 318	622
14. T	p. 322	626
15. F	p. 322	626
16. F	p. 322	626
17. F	p. 321	625
18. F	p. 322	626
19. F	p. 323	627
20. T	p. 322	626

Unlimited Multiple Choice

Answer	MIC	ECO
1. abcd	p. 315	619
2. b	p. 310	614
3. cd	p. 314	618
4. bc	p. 310	614
5. none	p. 315	619

Problem 1
MIC pp. 308-313; *ECO 612-617*

a. See Table 2.

Table 2

FIRM A					FIRM B				
(L)	(W)	Total Labor Cost	Average Labor Cost	(MFC)	(L)	(W)	Total Labor Cost	Average Labor Cost	(MFC)
0	$10	0	- -	- -	0	$ 5.00	0	- -	- -
1	10	10	10	10	1	5.50	5.50	5.50	5.50
2	10	20	10	10	2	6.00	12.00	6.00	6.50
3	10	30	10	10	3	6.50	19.50	6.50	7.50
4	10	40	10	10	4	7.00	28.00	7.00	8.50
5	10	50	10	10	5	7.50	37.50	7.50	9.50
6	10	60	10	10	6	8.00	48.00	8.00	10.50
7	10	70	10	10	7	8.50	59.50	8.50	11.50
8	10	80	10	10	8	9.00	72.00	9.00	12.50
9	10	90	10	10	9	9.50	85.50	9.50	13.50
10	10	100	10	10	10	10.00	100.00	10.00	14.50

b. Purely competitive; a fixed wage rate faces the firm.

c. The firm has monopsony power; the firm can use its hiring decision to influence the wage rate it pays.

d. See Figure 4.

Figure 4

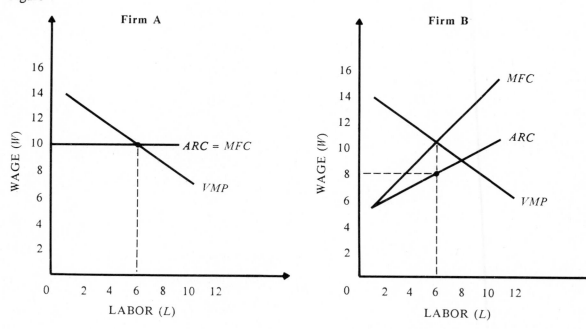

e.   6; $10.

f.   6; $8.

g.   ($10.50 - 8.00) x 6 = $15.00.

Problem 2
MIC pp. 308-313; *ECO 612-617*

a.   T
b.   F
c.   T
d.   F
e.   F
f.   T
g.   T
h.   F
i.   T
j.   T
k.   F
l.   F

Problem 3
MIC pp. 308-313; *ECO 612-617*

a.   F.
b.   F
c.   F
d.   F
e.   T
f.   F
g.   F
h.   T
i.   F
j.   F
k.   T
l.   T

CHAPTER THIRTY

RENT, INTEREST, PROFITS, AND CAPITALIZATION

CHAPTER OBJECTIVES

After you have completed this chapter you should be able to differentiate between rent, interest, and profits, and describe their determinants; and explain the capitalization process through which income streams are translated into wealth.

CHAPTER REVIEW: KEY POINTS

1. *Economic rent* exists whenever resource owners receive more than the minimum required for them to supply given amounts of the resource.

2. Land has a unique economic characteristic--it is fixed in supply. Thus, its supply curve is perfectly inelastic, and all payments for the use of land are pure rent. Land rents vary by location and particular physical characteristics.

3. Land is not the only resource that generates economic rents. Other factors that are supplied at prices above the minimum amounts required to elicit their availability also generate economic rents.

4. "Single taxers" inspired by Henry George propose a 100 percent tax on land rent as a single tax to finance all government spending. They argue that taxing this unearned surplus would not distort the allocation of land, and thus would not hinder economic efficiency. The *single-tax proposal* suffers from: (a) inability to finance the entire public sector, (b) administrative problems in distinguishing land values arising out of improvements made by owners from rent as an unearned surplus, and (c) reduced incentives for landowners to put their land to the best possible uses if rent is taxed away.

5. Economic rent promotes economic efficiency by providing resource owners with incentives to put their assets to the most valuable uses.

6. *Nominal interest* rates are the percentage annual premiums paid for the use of borrowed funds. Interest rates on financial instruments vary according to: (a) risk, (b) maturity, and (c) liquidity. The interest rate normally means the rate on a long-term riskless bond.

7. In the long run, *real* (purchasing power) *interest rates* depend on: (a) premiums required to induce savers to delay consumption, (b) desires for liquidity, and (c) the productivity of capital investments. These factors determine interest rates through the supply and demand for *loanable funds*. Government macroeconomic policies also influence loanable funds markets.

8. *Pure economic profits* are the residual after adjusting accounting profits for the opportunity cost of resources provided by a firm's owners. Profit may arise from *monopoly power,* bearing business *uncertainty,* or *innovation.*

9. Profits channel resources to their most productive uses in a market economy and stimulate progress as entrepreneurs innovate and endure business uncertainty to secure profits. Profits induce efficiency; competitive firms that do not produce at the lowest possible cost will suffer economic losses.

10. *Present values* are the sums of the discounted values of future income that may be expected from owning an asset. The present value of an asset and its price will be identical in equilibrium. If the present value exceeds price, then the asset is a profitable investment because the expected rate of return exceeds the interest rate. *Capitalization* is the process whereby expected future incomes are discounted so that prices gravitate toward present values of assets.

MATCHING KEY TERMS AND CONCEPTS

___ 1. single tax movement

a. Income per period as a percentage of investment.

___ 2. economic rents

b. The prime motivation for innovation.

___ 3. interest rates

c. Income generated for landowners because of reduced transaction costs.

___ 4. rate of return

d. When probabilities are known of realizing certain outcomes.

___ 5. location rents

e. Corporate bonds.

___ 6. capitalization

f. Based on the idea that land rents are unearned surpluses.

___ 7. perpetuity

g. A promise to pay a specified amount annually, forever.

___ 8. economic profit

h. The percentage annual premiums paid to ultimate capital suppliers for the use of money.

___ 9. debt capital

i. Transforming income streams into wealth.

___ 10. risk

j. The area above a resource supply curve but below the market price.

CHAPTER REVIEW (FILL-IN QUESTIONS)

1. _____ is any payment greater than the _____ necessary to secure the social use of a resource.

2. Many resources other than land generate economic rent, which is the area _____ the price line for a resource but above its _____ .

3-8. All _____ can also be considered economic rent since it is an unearned surplus. Pure profits are residuals after all opportunity costs to firms are deducted from their _____. They are signals that society would like _____ resources devoted to a particular type of production. These desires may be frustrated if _____ power is present, but competition generally causes profitable industries to grow until all profits are eliminated. Joseph _____ emphasized profits as incentives for _____, which is another of the functions of profit. Frank Knight emphasized profit as a pure residual after all costs are deducted from revenue. After concluding that risk involves reasonably certain _____ of certain events, Knight reasoned that entrepreneurs could make such adjustments as buying _____ against undesirable events; hence, risk was a cost of doing business. However, totally unpredictable events create _____ as a source of profit according to Knight. Thus, profit is a reward for bearing _____, or for _____ new products or production techniques; it is also a _____ directing the allocation of resources to their most valuable uses.

9. Using revenues expected over time and the interest rate, the _____ of an asset can be computed as _____.

10. In equilibrium, _____ equals price and the _____ equals the interest rate.

STANDARD MULTIPLE CHOICE

EACH QUESTION HAS A SINGLE BEST ANSWER.

___ 1. Land values attributable to the ways particular sites reduce transportation costs are known as:
   a. location rents.
   b. transportation rents.
   c. short-term quasi-rents.
   d. parcel posts.
   e. transaction rents.

___ 2. If you lease a building for five years and quickly achieve profits because it is located conveniently for potential customers:
   a. you could still receive all of the pure profits that could be anticipated if you sold your business with a sublease at the end of the second year.
   b. your rent would probably be raised when the lease ran out.
   c. the owner evidently underestimated the building's location rents.
   d. similar firms probably would soon open for business near you.
   e. all of the above.

___ 3. Owners of resources other than land receive rents that are equal to the area below the:
   a. consumer surplus rectangle generated by price discrimination.
   b. resource price line but above the resource supply curve.
   c. supply curve and out to the quantity of resource sold.
   d. total cost curve but above the total revenue curve.
   e. marginal cost curve but above the average variable cost curve.

___ 4. The main instigator of the single-tax movement was:
   a. British Prime Minister Lloyd George.
   b. John Stuart Mill.
   c. Henry George.
   d. Henry David Thoreau.
   e. David Ricardo.

___ 5. Taxes on pure economic rents:
a. pose especially severe problems for economic efficiency.
b. reduce the incentives to put resources to their best uses.
c. could easily replace all other forms of taxation.
d. have much stronger substitution than income effects.
e. are rapidly shifted forward to users of final products.

___ 6. Economic rents differ most from pure profits in that they are:
a. received by the owners of productive resources.
b. costs to the firm using the resources that generate them, but not to society as a whole.
c. realized only in the short run, but not in the long run.
d. a major cause of cost-push inflation.
e. All of the above.

___ 7. Interest rates on given securities will be lower the:
a. shorter the period to maturity.
b. greater the risk involved.
c. less liquid the asset is.
d. greater the expected rate of inflation.
e. greater is the face value relative to the market price.

___ 8. Market interest rates are least related to the:
a. willingness of people to defer consumption (to save) if they are rewarded for doing so.
b. desires of people for liquidity.
c. marginal productivity of new capital relative to its price.
d. par values of stocks relative to their current prices.
e. current prices of bonds relative to their face values.

___ 9. The monetary premiums paid per period as a percentage of the cost of a financial investment is known as the:
a. real rate of return.
b. nominal rate of interest.
c. rate of capitalization.
d. financial elasticity coefficient.
e. real rate of interest.

___ 10. Owners of corporate stock receive pure economic profit only to the extent that the rates of return realized from owning the stock exceed the:
a. interest rate that would have been generated by other financial investments carrying similar risks.
b. immediate gratification available by not delaying consumption.
c. funds saved by taking advantage of tax loopholes.
d. discount rate offered by exchange rate depreciation.
e. rate of arbitrage available in real estate investments.

___ 11. Economic profits are:
a. signals that society desires more resources in an industry.
b. rewards to successful innovators.
c. capitalized as wealth if they can be expected over time.
d. a residual to a firm's owners for bearing uncertainty.
e. All of the above.

___ 12. According to Frank Knight, unlike uncertainty, risk is:
a. totally unpredictable.
b. a major source of pure economic profits.
c. possible to estimate so that firms can adjust appropriately.
d. impossible to account for when making rational decisions.
e. unimportant to entrepreneurs who seek profits through innovation.

___13. NOT among the personal characteristics of most successful entrepreneurs is an unusual capacity to:
   a. work long hours when you perceive better ways to do things.
   b. take big chances if you think you are right.
   c. recover from disaster when your earlier plans have failed.
   d. see solutions where other people see only problems.
   e. compromise and be a "team player" in a large organization.

___14. When the likelihood of a certain event cannot reasonably be predicted, business decisionmakers are confronted by:
   a. random selection.
   b. uncertainty.
   c. stochastic probability.
   d. moral hazards.
   e. risk.

___15. That profit functions primarily as an incentive for innovation was among the key contributions to economic thought by:
   a. Karl Marx.
   b. Frank Knight.
   c. Joseph Schumpeter.
   d. Adam Smith.
   e. Alfred Marshall.

___16. Securities annually paying specific amounts forever are:
   a. stocks.
   b. perennials.
   c. royalties.
   d. perpetuities.
   e. renewals.

___17. The current worth of an income stream after discounting it by the interest rate is known as the:
   a. present value.
   b. discount rate.
   c. rate of return.
   d. perpetuity.
   e. internal interest rate.

___18. If the rate of return on an asset exceeds the interest rate:
   a. its present value exceeds its price.
   b. the market is moving away from equilibrium.
   c. you should sell the asset as quickly as possible.
   d. economic rent is being realized by the resource supplier.
   e. current purchase of the asset would be unprofitable.

___19. Investment is NOT necessarily in equilibrium if:
   a. after adjusting for risk, liquidity, and time to maturity, all income-producing assets yield the same returns.
   b. all prices exactly equal their corresponding present values.
   c. the average expected rates of return on all investments equal the market rate of interest.
   d. the risks for all investments are equal, regardless of their rates of return.
   e. the market interest rate on loanable funds and the rates of return on existing capital and on new investments are all equal.

___20. If the price of each of these assets is $1,000 and the interest rate is 10 percent, investment is most justified for:
   a. a perpetuity paying $90 annually.
   b. a machine with a 3-year life that is leasable for $1 per day.
   c. an income stream paying $500, $400, and $300, respectively, at the ends of each of the next three years.
   d. a bond paying $1,300 two years from today.
   e. an asset with a rate of return calculated at 8.5 percent.

TRUE/FALSE QUESTIONS

___ 1. The supply of land is perfectly elastic in the long run.

___ 2. Location rents are more important in explaining the high prices of farm land than the prices of land in urban centers.

___ 3. Reductions of transportation costs for customers and resource suppliers are the major sources of location rents.

___ 4. A single tax of 100 percent of land rents would easily generate sufficient revenues to replace all other taxes.

___ 5. Property taxes would influence resource allocations more than would pure land taxes that generated identical tax revenues.

___ 6. Equilibrium investment occurs when total profits are maximized because rates of return exceed interest rates by the largest possible amounts.

___ 7. A corporation that issues stock instead of bonds to raise money for new investments relies on debt capital.

___ 8. New capital formation is enhanced when people increasingly sacrifice liquidity or delay their consumption.

___ 9. The more liquid a financial asset, the greater tends to be its expected rate of return.

___10. Expanded financial investment in an economic sector tends to promote economic investment in that sector.

___11. Capitalists are rewarded with profits, while entrepreneurs are the recipients of interest incomes.

___12. High and widespread industry profits are an indication that society would gain by channeling more resources into an industry.

___13. Frank Knight argued that riskbearing is a surer way than dealing with uncertainty for individuals to gain economic profits.

___14. Inventors are far more important to the dynamic process of capitalism, according to Joseph Schumpeter, than are the business entrepreneurs who merely produce and distribute innovations.

___15. Monopoly profits stimulate long run economic efficiency.

___16. If the rate of return on an asset equals the interest rate, then the price of the asset just equals its present value.

___17. Prices of perpetuities rise when interest rates rise.

___18. Expected economic profits from an asset cannot be capitalized into wealth in the same way as are economic rents.

___19. The present value of an asset exceeds its current price whenever its rate of return exceeds the market rate of interest.

___20. Vigorous competition for profit opportunities cause the expected profits from most investments to be approximately zero.

UNLIMITED MULTIPLE CHOICE

CAUTION: EACH QUESTION HAS FROM ZERO TO FOUR CORRECT RESPONSES!

___ 1. Economic rents are realized whenever resource:
   a. supply curves are perfectly elastic to society as a whole.
   b. payments are the minimums needed to secure current quantities.
   c. coordination by entrepreneurs yields them pure economic profits.
   d. market supplies are less than perfectly elastic.

___ 2. Supplies of loanable funds tend to grow when households:
   a. delay consumption out of current income.
   b. feel more secure and reduce the average liquidity of their assets.
   c. begin to expect higher rates of return on new investments.
   d. seek bigger mortgages because they want to buy bigger houses.

___ 3. The present value of an asset rises when the expected:
   a. interest rate falls.
   b. total fixed income stream is spread over a longer period.
   c. future costs and revenues in each period rise by equal amounts.
   d. number of years rises for which a given annual income is expected.

___ 4. Likely consequences of high rates of economic profit being realized by innovative firms in an industry include:
   a. imitation of successful innovators by other firms.
   b. adoption by other firms of any cost-cutting innovations.
   c. hikes in the incomes of owners of vital resources.
   d. a rise over time in the prices consumers pay.

___ 5. Opportunity costs to the society as a whole include:
   a. pure economic profits.
   b. pure economic rents.
   c. the wages required before people will provide labor services.
   d. interest payments.

Problem 1

Figure 1 shows a market for raw land. Use this information to answer the following true/false questions.

Figure 1

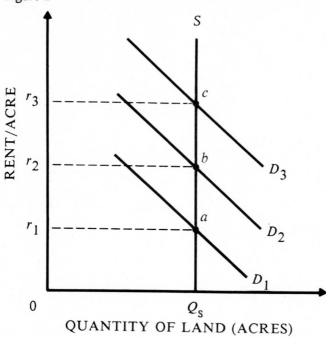

QUANTITY OF LAND (ACRES)

___ a. If the demand for raw land is D_2, total economic rent is equal to area $0r_2bQ_s$.

___ b. As the demand for raw land changes, the economic rent on land varies as well.

___ c. If demand for raw land is D_2 and a tax per acre of ab is imposed, economic rent will rise by area r_1r_2ba.

___ d. If demand for raw land rises from D_2 to D_3 and a tax per acre of bc is imposed simultaneously, net economic rent to the owner stays constant.

___ e. A tax on raw land affects the supply because economic rent is reduced.

Problem 2

Figure 2 depicts the supply and demand curves for the loanable funds market. The equilibrium interest rate is i_e, and i_c denotes a ceiling interest rate imposed by the federal government. Use this information to answer the following true/false questions.

Figure 2

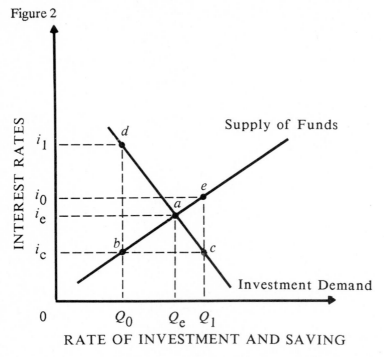

___ a. The demand for loanable funds is negatively sloped in part because of diminishing marginal returns to investment.

___ b. At point a, the expected rate of return on the marginal investment project is equal to the interest rate ceiling established by the government.

___ c. The present value of the Q_0th unit of investment is greater than the present value of the Q_1th unit of investment, assuming that both units bear the same price.

___ d. At interest rate i_c, the quantity demanded is equal to the quantity supplied of loanable funds.

___ e. At point a, the expected rate of return on the Q_eth unit of investment is equal to the interest rate that would be established by the unhindered interaction of supply and demand.

___ f. A shortage of loanable funds exists in the loanable funds market when the interest rate ceiling is i_c.

___ g. Allocative efficiency requires the loanable funds market to be at equilibrium point a.

___ h. Market mechanisms efficiently allocate loanable funds to the investment opportunities yielding the highest rates of return when the interest rate is pegged by the government at i_c.

___ i. The expected rate of return on the Q_0th unit of investment is less than the opportunity cost of the Q_1th unit of investment, expressed in percentage terms.

___ j. Society would realize a net welfare gain if the interest rate were allowed to rise to the equilibrium rate i_e.

Problem 3

Interest rates and asset prices vary inversely. The following examples give you a chance to use discounting to compute present values. The letter R denotes the net revenue in each year; subscripts indicate its time period; and i denotes the market interest rate used to compute discounted present values of the assets. Note: You are computing the present values and demand prices of the assets. Prove that market interest rates and asset prices vary inversely by using different interest rates to recompute one or two examples.

(a)

$i = 10\%$

$R_0 = 0$

$R_1 = 200$

Present discounted value = _____.

(b)

$i = 5\%$

$R_0 = 0$

$R_1 = 200$

Present discounted value = _____.

(c)

$i = 20\%$

$R_0 = 0$

$R_1 = 200$

$R_2 = 400$

$R_3 = 600$

Present discounted value = _____.

(d)

$i = 10\%$

$R_0 = 0$

$R_1 = 200$

$R_2 = 400$

$R_3 = 600$

Present discounted value = _____.

(e)

$i = 5\%$

$R_0 = 0$ $R_3 = 400$

$R_1 = 100$ $R_4 = 500$

$R_2 = 200$ $R_5 = 1,000$

Present discounted value = _____.

(f)

$i = 10\%$

$R_0 = 0$ $R_3 = 400$

$R_1 = 100$ $R_4 = 500$

$R_2 = 200$ $R_5 = 1,000$

Present discounted value = _____.

ANSWERS

Matching Key Terms and Concepts

Answer	MIC	ECO
1. f	p. 335	639
2. j	p. 332	636
3. h	p. 337	641
4. a	p. 343	647
5. c	p. 332	636
6. i	p. 341	645
7. g	p. 343	647
8. b	p. 339	643
9. e	p. 337	641
10. d	p. 340	644

Chapter Review (Fill-in Questions)

1. Economic rent, minimum
2. below, supply curve
3. economic profit, total revenues
4. more, monopoly
5. Schumpeter, innovation
6. probabilities, insurance
7. uncertainty, uncertainty
8. innovating, signal
9. present value, $PV = \sum_{t=1}^{n} \frac{Y_t}{(1 + i)^t}$

10. present value, rate of return

Standard Multiple Choice

Answer	MIC	ECO
1. a	p. 332	636
2. e	p. 333	637
3. b	p. 334	638
4. c	p. 335	639
5. b	p. 336	640
6. b	p. 332	636
7. a	p. 337	641
8. d	p. 337	641
9. b	p. 337	641
10. a	p. 339	643
11. e	p. 339	643
12. c	p. 340	644
13. e	p. 342	646
14. b	p. 341	645
15. c	p. 340	644
16. d	p. 343	647
17. a	p. 343	647
18. a	p. 344	648
19. c	p. 344	648
20. c	p. 343	678

True/False Questions

Answer	MIC	ECO
1. F	p. 332	636
2. F	p. 332	636
3. T	p. 333	637
4. F	p. 336	640
5. T	p. 336	640
6. F	p. 344	648
7. F	p. 337	641
8. T	p. 337	641
9. F	p. 337	641
10. T	p. 341	645
11. F	p. 339	643
12. T	p. 341	645
13. F	p. 340	644
14. F	p. 340	644
15. F	p. 340	644
16. T	p. 344	648
17. F	p. 343	647
18. F	p. 341	645
19. T	p. 344	648
20. T	p. 341	645

Unlimited Multiple Choice

Answer	MIC	ECO
1. cd	p. 334	638
2. ab	p. 337	641
3. ad	p. 343	647
4. abc	p. 341	645
5. cd	p. 336, 339	640, 643

Problem 1
MIC pp. 332-336; ECO 636- 640

a. T
b. T
c. F
d. T
e. F

Problem 2
MIC 337-339, 343-344
ECO 641-643, 647-448

a. T
b. F
c. T
d. F
e. T
f. T
g. T
h. F
i. F
j. T

Problem 3
MIC 343
ECO 647

a. 181.81
b. 190.47
c. 791.65
d. 963. 50
e 1,820.92
f. 1,524.39

CHAPTER THIRTY-ONE

MARKET FAILURES AND PUBLIC MICROECONOMICS

CHAPTER OBJECTIVES

After you have read and studied this chapter, you should be able to describe Musgrave's idealized three-budget framework for government actions in the economic sphere; explain the circumstances under which the market system may misallocate resources, and indicate proper governmental remedies; and critique the efficiency and equity of our tax system and evaluate proposals for its reform.

CHAPTER REVIEW: KEY POINTS

1. Some market solutions may be inefficient; others are inequitable in the minds of many people. It has become conventional to categorize *market failures* as problems of either *allocation, distribution,* or *stabilization*. Attacking problems individually according to this division would permit the use of the best policy tool to solve any problem. Any side effects then may be addressed with appropriate measures. This three-branch distinction is useful for planning, but is tempered by politics in actual budgeting situations.

2. Musgrave's *distribution* branch would secure taxes from those who have "too much", and would provide higher incomes for the needy via a negative income tax of some sort. This budget would be continuously balanced.

3. The *stabilization* branch would run deficits through tax cuts to buffer recessions, and surpluses to dampen inflationary pressures. This would be the only part of the government budget ever out of balance.

4. The *allocation* branch would provide public goods that the market will not provide efficiently because of economies of scale in production or because of nonrivalry and nonexclusion in consumption. *Nonrivalry* means that a good is not used up when any individual enjoys it; a beautiful sunset is an example. *Nonexclusion* means that it is prohibitively expensive to deny access to a good. Note, however, that public provision does not require public production. Private firms often produce goods that government then distributes.

5. A good that is both nonrival and nonexclusive is a *pure public good*. Public goods will be less than optimally provided by the market system, if provided at all, because of attempts to *free ride*. A rival but nonexclusive good embodies *externalities* that often hinders the efficiency of market solutions. Pollution may be the problem if externalities are negative (costly); underproduction may result if externalities are positive (beneficial).

6. The *benefit principle of taxation* suggests that people should pay taxes in proportion to the marginal benefits they receive from a governmentally provided good. Ideally, Musgrave's allocation branch would run a balanced budget based on the benefit principle.

7. The demand for a pure public good is the *vertical summation of individual demand curves* since all can enjoy the good simultaneously, while demands for private goods are summed horizontally. Adequate revenue for optimal quantities of public goods is generated if people pay taxes equal to their marginal benefits multiplied by the amount of public good provided.

8. The *ability-to-pay principle of taxation* requires taxes in proportion to people's income, wealth, or possibly, their consumption. This principle is closely related to the idea that government policies should move the income distribution closer to equality than the market distribution of income.

9. The principle of *horizontal equity* suggests that equals should pay equal taxes; *vertical equity* requires higher taxes on the wealthy than on the poor.

10. If the loss to a taxpayer exceeds the government revenue gained, there is an *excess burden* of taxation. *Neutral taxes* impose only income, not substitution, effects and impose no excess burdens.

11. The *personal income tax* system is nominally progressive, but various loopholes make it somewhat inefficient and inequitable.

12. *Social Security taxes* are the second largest and fastest growing sources of federal revenues. They and other *payroll taxes* may be borne primarily by workers. Moreover, they are regressive, typically declining proportionately as personal income rises.

13. *Sales taxes* are reasonably efficient but, like income taxes, are marred by numerous exemptions. Many *excise taxes* apply to "sin" or "wasteful luxuries." Unless they are based on a benefit principle of taxation (for example, public zoo ticket fees or gasoline taxes), they tend to cause inefficiency and be regressive. (Poor people smoke and drink as much, by volume, as rich people.)

14. The *corporate income tax* discriminates against the corporate form of business and against the goods produced primarily by corporations. In the long run, most of this tax is probably forward-shifted to consumers. Thus, in the minds of most experts, this tax tends to be both inefficient and inequitable.

15. *Property taxes* provide disincentives for improvement and are blamed by some for the deterioration of central cities.

16. *Inheritance* and *gift taxes* have high and progressive rates, but can be avoided because these tax laws are riddled with loopholes.

17. A *value-added tax* (*VAT*) is similar to a sales tax in that it is forward-shifted. VATs only apply to the value added by each firm. VATs, *flat rate taxes*, and progressive *consumption taxes* (not income) have been proposed as replacements for corporate income taxes or Social Security taxes.

MATCHING KEY TERMS AND CONCEPTS

SET I

___ 1. negative externality

___ 2. free-rider problem

___ 3. positive externality

___ 4. nonrival principle

___ 5. shifted forward

___ 6. nonexclusion principle

___ 7. backward shifting

___ 8. transfer payments

___ 9. sales taxes

___10. loopholes

a. Legal clauses that channel too many resources into favored areas.

b. Arises when people can consume a public good at no charge.

c. Too little of the product is produced.

d. Everyone can enjoy specific goods simultaneously.

e. When barring consumption is prohibitively expensive.

f. Litter is an example.

g. Final burden of tax falls on consumer.

h. Percentage taxes on dollar sales.

i. When suppliers of resources bear tax burdens.

j. Primary modes of poverty relief by the distribution branch.

SET II

___ 1. value added taxes (VAT)

___ 2. neutral taxes

___ 3. ability to pay taxation

___ 4. income taxes

___ 5. gift taxes

___ 6. sales taxes

___ 7. benefit taxes

___ 8. excise taxes

___ 9. payroll taxes

___10. corporate income taxes

a. Taxes that do not cause substitution effects.

b. Taxes based on the value of government services to the individual taxpayer.

c. Social security and unemployment compensation taxes are examples.

d. Percentage taxes on the differences between a firm's receipts and its purchases of intermediate goods.

e. Either forward shifted to consumers or backward shifted to capital suppliers.

f. Taxes applied only to specific goods.

g. Typically a percentage of total purchases in dollars.

h. Plug one loophole in inheritance taxation.

i. The 1986 Tax Reform Act attempted to revamp this type of tax.

j. Taxing more as income or wealth rises.

___ 1. vertical equity   a. People with equal incomes should pay equal taxes.

___ 2. excess burden   b. Would run deficits during recessions, surpluses during inflations.

___ 3. stabilization branch   c. Characterized by nonrivalry and nonexclusion.

___ 4. vertical summation   d. Ideally uses benefit principle taxation.

___ 5. distribution branch   e. The difference between government receipts and taxpayer costs.

___ 6. flat rate tax   f. Process by which total demands for public goods are derived.

___ 7. pure public good   g. An ethical criterion for ability to pay taxation.

___ 8. consumption taxes   h. One tax rate without exemptions or deductions.

___ 9. horizontal equity   i. Ideally, only ability to pay taxation is used, with the poor receiving negative tax rates.

___ 10. allocation branch   j. Might be like income taxation, but would allow deductions for saving or investment.

CHAPTER REVIEW (FILL-IN QUESTIONS)

1-5. Pure public goods are both _____ and _____. This poses the problem that voluntary taxes to pay for public goods will be inadequate because people will attempt to be _____ and will not reveal their true demands for public goods. The total demand for a public good is derived through _____ summation of individual demands. If all taxpayers pay taxes equal to their _____ times the amounts of public goods, there will be adequate revenues to secure the _____ amounts of these goods. This is in accord with the _____ principle of taxation, which would be the basis for the balanced budget of Musgrave's _____ branch of government. Major practical problems with this approach cause us to rely heavily on the _____ principle, which suggests that the rich should pay more taxes than the poor, an idea also called _____ equity.

6-7. When the _____ of a tax exceeds the government revenues generated, there is a(n) _____ on taxpayers. Generally, when the direct effect of a tax is only a(n) _____ effect, there is no such "dead weight" social loss, but if _____ effects are direct results, the tax is inefficient.

8. _____ taxes are perhaps the most loophole ridden, but cannot be avoided by simply giving things away because then _____ taxes apply.

9-10. A tax on _____ (the difference between a firm's revenues and its outlays for intermediate goods) is one proposed replacement for several of the more seriously flawed taxes (e.g., social security and corporate income tax levies). The complexity of our income tax system has brought about calls for _____ rate taxation, which would eliminate virtually all "loopholes" and make income taxes _____ instead of progressive. Another recent proposal, aimed at stimulating economic growth, would eliminate most loopholes and would replace income taxation with a progressive tax on _____, so that people would be allowed deductions for saving and investing.

STANDARD MULTIPLE CHOICE

EACH QUESTION HAS ONE BEST ANSWER.

___ 1. The least clear examples of market failures are problems of:
   a. inequities in the distributions of income and wealth.
   b. an unstable price level and high unemployment.
   c. cutthroat competition.
   d. externalities.
   e. nonrivalry and nonexclusion.

___ 2. Nonrivalness and nonexclusiveness characterize:
   a. pure private goods.
   b. goods embodying negative diseconomies.
   c. natural monopolies.
   d. pure public goods.
   e. goods for which there is persistent excess capacity.

___ 3. If a good is nonexclusive, people tend to:
   a. vote to have the maximum possible amount provided by government.
   b. buy the good according to their demand curve and the good's price.
   c. not care if the good generates negative externalities.
   d. try to be "free riders".
   e. have a high benefit/cost ratio from its purchase.

___ 4. Negative externalities, if uncorrected, cause a good to be:
   a. underproduced and overpriced.
   b. overproduced and overpriced.
   c. underproduced and underpriced.
   d. overproduced and underpriced.
   e. underfinanced because of the "free rider" problem.

___ 5. A major reason why "free riders" pose problems is:
   a. nonexclusion.
   b. exclusion.
   c. rivalry.
   d. nonrivalry.
   e. nonneutrality.

___ 6. Musgrave's "Allocation Branch of Government" ideally would:
   a. be financed by the ability to pay principle of taxation.
   b. use only regulation to correct for failures of the market system.
   c. run deficits during recessions and surpluses during inflation.
   d. focus on correcting for problems of merit goods.
   e. run a balanced budget.

___ 7. Tax receipts will be exactly adequate to pay for the optimal amount of a public good if:
   a. taxes levies are equal to people's marginal benefits from it times the number of units of the good.
   b. everyone pays taxes equal to their total benefits from the good.
   c. perfect price discrimination is used to pay for all public goods.
   d. individual demands for the public good are summed horizontally.
   e. voluntary taxes are used to pay for nonexclusive but rival goods.

___ 8. Goods such as hamburgers and french fries are examples of:
   a. rival goods.
   b. nonrival goods.
   c. public goods.
   d. nonexclusive goods.
   e. merit goods.

___ 9. The only budgets ever unbalanced in Musgrave's "Normative Theory of the Public Household" would be the budget(s) of the:
   a. state and local governments.
   b. allocative branch.
   c. civilian branch of the federal government.
   d. stabilization branch.
   e. distribution branch.

379

10. The ability to pay principle requires:
    a. the "haves" to pay more taxes than the "have nots."
    b. progressive taxes.
    c. proportional taxes.
    d. regressive taxes.
    e. neutral taxes.

11. If we ignore loopholes, good examples of progressive taxes are:
    a. statutory taxes.
    b. sales taxes.
    c. social security taxes.
    d. tobacco and liquor taxes.
    e. income and inheritance taxes.

12. If all taxpayers in equivalent circumstances pay identical taxes, there is:
    a. benefit taxation.
    b. ability to pay taxation.
    c. horizontal equity.
    d. vertical equity.
    e. tax neutrality.

13. If a tax causes substitution effects, it generally is a:
    a. transfer tax.
    b. neutral tax.
    c. source of excess burden.
    d. progressive tax.
    e. pro rata tax.

14. Preferential tax treatment for some forms of income are NOT:
    a. violations of vertical and horizontal equity.
    b. known as loopholes.
    c. as beneficial to the wealthy as the rates alone seem to suggest.
    d. sources of inefficiency that hold down the value of real GNP.
    e. mechanisms that distort production away from consumer preferences.

15. A value-added tax is most closely related to a:
    a. progressive income tax.
    b. retail sales tax.
    c. property tax.
    d. gift or inheritance tax.
    e. corporate income tax.

16. Corporate income taxes are popular with politicians, but are not favored by most economists because:
    a. their incidence is uncertain, and may be inequitable.
    b. they reduce production by corporations in the long run.
    c. they are notably nonneutral.
    d. they are economically inefficient.
    e. all of the above.

17. Taxes that are the most completely borne by workers are:
    a. sales taxes.
    b. social security and other payroll taxes.
    c. property taxes.
    d. income taxes.
    e. excise taxes.

18. Inheritance taxes do not provide wealthy people with incentives to:
    a. lobby for loopholes in the American tax system.
    b. invest in their children's educations.
    c. spend more and save less.
    d. structure their wills so that their heirs avoid these taxes.
    e. work harder to amass huge fortunes.

19. Virtually all taxes are nonneutral in that they induce:
    a. changes in behavior intended to avoid tax burdens.
    b. income effects that more than offset their substitution effects.
    c. growth in government relative to private activities.
    d. substantial reductions of labor productivity.
    e. all of the above.

20. Reforms to plug tax loopholes, flatten income tax progressivity, and lower personal and corporate tax rates were features of major legislation in:
    a. 1890.
    b. 1956.
    c. 1966.
    d. 1976.
    e. 1986.

TRUE/FALSE QUESTIONS

___ 1. Most state and local governments rely on income taxes as their primary sources of revenue.

___ 2. Pure public goods are rival but non-exclusive.

___ 3. Spillovers, or externalities, occur when third-party costs or benefits from an activity not are considered by those directly making decisions.

___ 4. The goals of efficiency, equity, and economic stability are only somewhat resolved in a market system.

___ 5. Government policies have little effect on the allocation of resources in the U.S. economy.

___ 6. Pure private goods are both rival and exclusive.

___ 7. A nonexclusive but rival good is typically never used, assuming that the good is provided.

___ 8. Pure competition would efficiently provide most merit goods.

___ 9. Most allocative failures of a market system arise because of monopoly power, externalities, and nonrivalry or nonexclusion.

___10. Externalities are only problems with pure private goods.

___11. A tax is neutral if its total burden exactly equals the amount of tax revenue collected from the tax.

___12. Most taxes directly reduce disposable income and alter the patterns of saving and consumption.

___13. A tax is neutral only if its imposition induces absolutely no changes in economic behavior.

___14. High marginal income tax rates provide incentives for tax evasion.

___15. Tax loopholes tend to be efficient but pose major barriers to equity in the distribution of income.

___16. A progressive consumption tax system is a contradiction in terms because the poor spend larger portions of their incomes than rich people do.

___17. A proportional income tax would also be a flat tax.

___18. U.S. income tax rates are higher on average than income tax rates in Great Britain.

___19. Tax avoidance is legal, but tax evasion is not.

___20. Social Security taxes provide more federal tax revenues than corporate income taxes do.

UNLIMITED MULTIPLE CHOICE

CAUTION: EACH QUESTION HAS FROM ZERO TO FOUR CORRECT RESPONSES.

___ 1. Public goods are:
  a. subject to nonrivalry in consumption.
  b. efficiently produced in private markets.
  c. chosen by individuals who vote with money.
  d. subject to the nonexclusion principle.

___ 2. The free rider problem arises:
  a. in consuming all rival economic goods.
  b. because there are few incentives for people to express their true preferences when goods are nonexclusive.
  c. only in the consumption of private goods.
  d. because public goods are viewed as "free."

___ 3. A neutral tax:
  a. is a tax that does not distort relative prices.
  b. generates no excess burdens.
  c. does not induce substitution effects.
  d. will be, on average, more certain, convenient, and economical than a nonneutral tax.

___ 4. A pure private good is a good that is:
  a. nonrival and nonexclusive.
  b. efficiently provided if markets are competitive.
  c. vertically and horizontally equitable.
  d. rival and exclusive in nature.

___ 5. Markets may fail to provide certain goods efficiently because of:
  a. externalities in their consumption or production.
  b. substantial economies of scale relative to market demand.
  c. public goods problems.
  d. rivalry and exclusion.

Problem 1

Figure 1 depicts supply and demand curves for a particular market. Assume a new per unit tax on the good shifts the supply from S_0 to S_1. Use this information to answer the following questions.

Figure 1

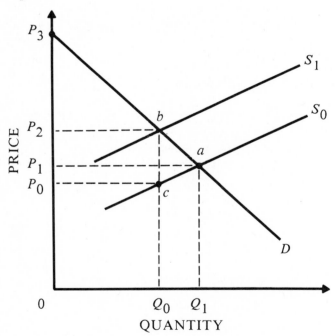

___ a. The amount of the per unit tax is $P_1 - P_0$.

___ b. The per unit tax is equal to line segment bc.

___ c. This per unit tax is neutral.

___ d. The excess burden of this per unit tax is zero.

___ e. Prior to the tax, consumer surplus equaled trapezoid P_1P_2ba.

___ f. After imposition of the tax, consumer surplus equals P_2P_3b.

___ g. The tax causes consumer surplus to decrease by area P_1P_2ba.

___ h. The price of the good rises by the full amount of the tax.

___ i. The excess burden of this tax equals triangle cba.

___ j. The total burden of the tax equals P_0P_2bac.

___ k. The total revenue yielded by the tax equals area P_0P_2bc.

___ l. The economic incidence of the tax falls on both the consumers and producers of this good.

Problem 2

Suppose that your salary is more than $200,000 per year and that you have $1,000,000 to invest. Your federal marginal tax rate is fifty percent on normal investment income.

a. How many extra after-tax dollars will you receive annually if you invest in tax free state and local bonds that yield an 8 percent return annually instead of the taxable 12 percent return you could realize if you bought corporate bonds? _____

b. What return would make you indifferent between income from a tax free investment and the taxable 12 percent return on corporate bonds? _____

c. What will happen to rates of return generally for investments that generate income that receives preferential tax treatment? _____

d. Why? _____

e. What does this example suggest will happen to investment in sectors that have preferential tax treatments relative to possible investments not offering "loopholes"? _____

f. What does this example suggest about whether or not high income investors receive the full advantages of such loopholes? _____

g. The adjustments in this exercise are examples of the _____ costs of government.

ANSWERS

Matching Key Terms and Concepts

SET I

Answer	MIC	ECO
1. f	p. 355	659
2. b	p. 359	663
3. c	p. 355	659
4. d	p. 357	661
5. g	p. 367	671
6. e	p. 357	661
7. i	P. 367	671
8. j	P. 353	657
9. h	P. 367	671
10. a	P. 363	667

SET II

Answer	MIC	ECO
1. d	p. 369	673
2. a	p. 362	666
3. j	p. 360	664
4. i	p. 365	669
5. h	p. 368	672
6. g	p. 367	671
7. b	p. 359	663
8. f	p. 367	671
9. c	p. 366	670
10. e	p. 367	671

SET III

Answer	MIC	ECO
1. g	p. 360	664
2. e	p. 361	665
3. b	p. 353	657
4. f	p. 358	662
5. i	p. 353	657
6. h	p. 369	673
7. c	p. 358	662
8. j	p. 369	673
9. a	p. 360	664
10. d	p. 353	657

Chapter Review (Fill-in Questions)

1. nonrival, nonexclusive
2. free riders, vertical
3. marginal benefits, optimal
4. benefit, allocation
5. ability to pay, vertical
6. total burden, excess burden
7. income, substitution
8. Inheritance, gift
9. value added, flat
10. proportional, consumption

Standard Multiple Choice

Answer	MIC	ECO
1. c	p. 355	659
2. d	p. 358	662
3. d	p. 359	663
4. d	p. 355	659
5. a	p. 359	663
6. e	p. 353	657
7. a	p. 358	662
8. a	p. 356	660
9. d	p. 353	657
10. a	p. 360	664
11. e	p. 368	672
12. c	p. 360	664
13. c	p. 361	665
14. c	p. 364	668
15. b	p. 369	673
16. e	p. 367	671
17. b	p. 366	670
18. e	p. 368	672
19. a	p. 362	666
20. e	p. 365	669

True/False Questions

Answer	MIC	ECO
1. F	p. 367	671
2. F	p. 358	662
3. T	p. 355	659
4. T	p. 352	656
5. F	p. 353	657
6. T	p. 357	661
7. F	p. 357	661
8. F	p. 352	656
9. T	p. 355	659
10. F	p. 355	659
11. T	p. 362	666
12. T	p. 362	666
13. F	p. 362	666
14. T	p. 363	667
15. F	p. 363	667
16. F	p. 369	673
17. T	p. 369	673
18. F	p. 359	663
19. T	p. 363	667
20. T	p. 366	670

Unlimited Multiple Choice

Answer	MIC	*ECO*
1. ad	p. 356	*660*
2. bd	p. 362	*666*
3. abcd	p. 362	*666*
4. bd	p. 357	*661*
5. abc	p. 355	*659*

Problem 1
MIC p. 361; *ECO 665*

   a. F
   b. T
   c. F
   d. F
   e. F
   f. T
   g. T
   h. F
   i. T
   j. T
   k. T
   l. T

Problem 2
MIC p. 364; *ECO 668*

a. $80,000 - ($120,000/2) = $80,000 - 60,000 = $20,000 annually.

b. 6 percent return on the tax free investment. (The marginal tax rate [50 percent] times the taxed rated of return [12 percent] equals the equivalent nontaxed rate of return [6 percent].)

c. Competition will make them fall until the after tax returns are roughly equal.

d. Competition among high income people for the advantages of loopholes will increase the supply of financial capital to sectors receiving preferential tax treatment, reducing their rates of return. These sectors will grow relative to sectors without loopholes.

e. The after-tax rates of return should be roughly equalized.

f. Competition causes the loopholes to yield only small advantages to those who seek to exploit them.

g. indirect

CHAPTER THIRTY-TWO
PUBLIC CHOICE

CHAPTER OBJECTIVES

After you have studied this chapter you should be able to describe the economic effects of various voting systems; behavior underpinning the public policymaking process; and extent of public bureaucracies and their consequences.

CHAPTER REVIEW: KEY POINTS

1. No allocative mechanism works ideally under all circumstances. Just as the market fails in some instances, there are forces within all political systems that prevent government from smoothly reflecting the preferences of the people governed. The application of economic analysis to political behavior is known as *public choice.*

2. The probability that one vote will swing a major election is close to infinitesimal. Because the personal payoffs from voting are small, many people do not vote, nor do most find it personally worthwhile to inform themselves on a broad range of social issues. This is known as *rational political ignorance*, and tends to be more prevalent than the lack of information confronted when people make market decisions.

3. All voting systems are flawed in that economic efficiency may be lost through political decision making. *Majority rule* voting tends to impose losses on those taking minority positions; this is inefficient if their losses exceed the majority's gains. Majority rule may also lead to inconsistent or unstable political choices.

4. A *unanimity* rule ensures that all changes in laws are efficient because everyone must expect to gain before acquiescing to a change. People who are reasonably indifferent about a policy change, however, might require excessive compensation for agreeing to the change from those who stand to gain much from the change. This would make changes in policies a very cumbersome and time-consuming process. Moreover, a unanimity rule assumes that the initial situation is equitable, which may be untrue in some cases.

5. *Point voting* would allow voters to indicate their preferences by allocating votes in proportion to how strongly they felt about some issues relative to others. This system is flawed, however, by the potential for strategic behavior; people might not vote their preferences per se, tending instead to weigh their votes according to how they expected others to vote.

6. Voting is a *lumpy* process; we cannot pick and choose among the political stances taken by the candidates for an office. The market permits us to fine-tune our decisions, but we generally can choose only a single candidate or platform when we vote.

7. Attempts to maximize their chances for election cause candidates and political parties to try to attract the *median voter,* whose vote tends to determine the outcomes of elections. Rational ignorance among voters causes many candidates to avoid taking stands on issues while attempting to project a moderate image. Political competition for the support of the median voter causes candidates and parties to cluster around *middle-of-the-road* positions, and creates pressures for a *two-party system.*

8. *Logrolling* occurs when lawmakers trade votes. This allows legislators to register the intensities of their preferences because they trade votes about which they care little for votes about things which they feel relatively strongly. Logrolling can, however, result in inefficient amounts of *pork barrel legislation*, which occurs when projects that have primarily local benefits are paid for by a broader taxpaying public.

9. *Special interests groups* may be over represented because of low voter turnouts, widespread rational political ignorance, and intense lobbying. However, intensities of preference may be better reflected in political decisions because of this overrepresentation.

10. *Rent-seeking* involves attempts by special interest groups to manipulate government policies for private gain even though the social costs of special laws or regulations would exceed the expected benefits to the interest group that seeks economic rents.

11. The efficiency of most government *bureaucracies* is hard to measure, and the absence of a profit motive reduces incentives for efficiency in the public sector. Managerial salaries and "perqs" are often tied to the numbers of employees supervised and the size of the agency budget, which leads to *empire-building* and further growth of government.

MATCHING KEY TERMS AND CONCEPTS

SET I

___ 1.	median voter model	a.	Tries to explain the popularity of middle-of-the-road policies.
___ 2.	unanimity requirement	b.	The study of *homo economicus* in politics.
___ 3.	political "tie-in" sales	c.	Most protective of existing minority rights; ensures that any policy changes are efficient, but may bar corrections of inequities and promote political "blackmail."
___ 4.	merit good	d.	Deemed desirable by some elite group.
___ 5.	point voting	e.	Lumpy "either-or" choices in voting.
___ 6.	majority rule	f.	Perception that personal costs exceed the personal benefits.
___ 7.	voter "apathy"	g.	Reasonably efficient if there is no strategic voting.
___ 8.	public choice theory	h.	The losses of losers may often exceed the gains to winners.
___ 9.	voting cycle	i.	When some things are just not worth knowing.
___10.	rational ignorance	j.	Voting chains that tend to yield erratic policies inconsistent with the will of the majority.

___ 1.	lobbying	a.	Their aims are facilitated by intense political action.
___ 2.	special interest groups	b.	Exchanges of legislative votes.
___ 3.	two-party system	c.	The employees, rules, and resources of large organizations.
___ 4.	empire building	d.	Local public projects that are funded nationally.
___ 5.	pork barrel	e.	The goal is gains at the expense of the broader society.
___ 6.	bureaucracy	f.	A consequence of majority rule, according to the median voter model.
___ 7.	rent-seeking	g.	Attempts by private parties to sway laws and regulations.
___ 8.	logrolling	h.	Campaigns intended to enlarge the budget of a bureaucracy.

CHAPTER REVIEW (FILL-IN QUESTIONS)

1. The economic study of political behavior is known as _____ analysis, which assumes that people are as _____ in the political arena as they are in their private behavior.

2-3. The _____ model explains why serious candidates often adopt _____ positions and the dominance of the _____ system when a _____ voting system is used.

4-7. Vote trading by legislators is known as _____ and allows them to express the intensity of their preferences, but it also promotes _____ legislation that uses national _____ for projects that primarily generate local _____. The strong preferences of _____ cause them to _____ intensively and be very active politically. Their aims are often expressed as _____ behavior, which attempts to shape laws and regulations beneficial to themselves even though the _____ costs are substantially higher.

8-10. People who work in them know that their personal power and income are linked to their supervision of large numbers of _____ and to their control over big _____. This leads managers in private organizations to try to demonstrate above average _____ potential, which facilitates economic _____. Managers of public agencies, however, tend to try _____ by exaggerating the importance and difficulty of their mission, and economic _____ is encouraged.

STANDARD MULTIPLE CHOICE

THERE IS ONE BEST ANSWER FOR EACH QUESTION.

___ 1. A perception that the personal gains from learning more about politics are less than the expected costs of information leads to:
   a. majority rule voting.
   b. the two-party system.
   c. rational political ignorance.
   d. lumpy "either/or" choices.
   e. political blackmail.

___ 2. Widespread voter apathy may be a symptom that many people:
   a. fail to realize how frequently one vote swings an election.
   b. dislike politicians and are unaffected by political decisions.
   c. view politics as an extremely enjoyable spectator sport.
   d. realize that single votes are unlikely to change election results.
   e. are unconstitutionally deprived of their voting rights.

___ 3. A law requiring all adults to vote would tend to reduce the:
   a. ability of voters to register the intensity of their preferences.
   b. apathy of those who vote.
   c. rational political ignorance of most people.
   d. ability of ambitious bureaucrats to build empires.
   e. red tape in government agencies.

___ 4. The reason why many people do vote is best explained by the:
   a. fact that "every vote counts."
   b. tie-in sales aspects of voting.
   c. slogan, "If you don't vote, you can't complain."
   d. enjoyment some people must receive from voting.
   e. high probability that a single vote will swing a major election.

___ 5. It is most difficult to "fine tune" your decisions to conform with your preferences when you make choices about:
   a. the accessories to add if you buy a new car.
   b. what to buy at the grocery store.
   c. the candidate for whom you will vote.
   d. your major field of study.
   e. where you will live.

___ 6. The personal losses resulting from rational ignorance tend to be lowest when you make choices about:
   a. whom to marry.
   b. how much to cheat on your taxes.
   c. voting.
   d. major financial investments.
   e. career paths and occupations.

___ 7. Majority rules voting will be economically inefficient if:
   a. a minorities lose more than majorities gain from policies.
   b. rich minorities bribe poor majorities to vote a particular way.
   c. special interest groups donate huge campaign contributions.
   d. people are less rational in politics than in business.
   e. many people choose not to vote.

___ 8. The availability of fine gradations of market choices are not matched in the political arena because of:
   a. overrepresentation of special interests.
   b. voter apathy.
   c. strategic behavior by voters.
   d. tie-in sales aspects of voting.
   e. all of the above.

___ 9. An explanation for the dominance of middle-of-the-road political policies is offered by the:
   a. rational ignorance hypothesis.
   b. theory of structural conformity.
   c. lumpiness of "tie-in sales" voting.
   d. iron law of oligarchy.
   e. median voter model.

___10. Voting cycles tend to result if many voters prefer:
  a. pure capitalism to decentralized planning.
  b. either political extreme to middle-of-the-road positions.
  c. special interest laws to the public interest.
  d. complex bureaucracies to inequitable income distributions.
  e. Republicans to Democrats.

___11. "Pork barrel" tends to result from extensive:
  a. empire building.
  b. boon-doggling.
  c. logrolling.
  d. cut-throat competition.
  e. monopolization.

___12. A law allowing individuals to specify the programs to be funded by their fixed personal tax dollars would tend to stimulate:
  a. strategic voting behavior.
  b. increases in logrolling by legislators.
  c. replacement of cash by in-kind transfers.
  d. everyone trying to be a free rider.

___13. Regulated firms that try to manipulate regulation so that it favors them and harms their competitors provide an example of:
  a. pork barrel.
  b. plutocracy.
  c. survivalism.
  d. rent-seeking.
  e. conflict of interests.

___14. Logrolling may improve economic efficiency to the extent that it enables legislators to:
  a. improve their prospects for reelection.
  b. use federal spending to cover local costs.
  c. focus on morality instead of pure politics.
  d. aid rent-seeking by special interest groups.
  e. register the intensities of their preferences.

___15. Efficiently accommodating the strong preferences of minority interest groups can never involve:
  a. rent-seeking.
  b. lobbying.
  c. logrolling.
  d. a unanimity voting rule.
  e. a point voting rule.

___16. Trying to raise your government agency's budget by overstating the importance and difficulty of its mission is known as:
  a. frosting the cake.
  b. empire building.
  c. gilding the lily.
  d. boosterism.
  e. brown nosing.

___17. Employees of large organizations are known as:
  a. agents.
  b. autocrats.
  c. bureaucrats.
  d. nepotists.
  e. boondogglers.

___18. NOT a reason for the relative growth of government is:
  a. empire building.
  b. logrolling.
  c. rent-seeking.
  d. porkbarrel legislation.
  e. taxpayer revolts.

___19. Higher pay and more "perqs" tend to reward bureaucrats who:
  a. supervise more employees and control larger budgets.
  b. support the party in power.
  c. "blow the whistle" when their supervisors make errors.
  d. develop extremely narrow areas of expertise.
  e. accomplish their tasks at minimal costs.

___20. NOT a reasonable explanation for exorbitant government contract costs are cases where contracts are:
  a. awarded before appropriate technology is developed.
  b. monitored by potential employees of contractors.
  c. overspecified by bureaucrats who want to look busy.
  d. for standard items produced by many cutthroat competitors.
  e. awarded before final specifications are known.

TRUE/FALSE QUESTIONS

___ 1. The historical rights of minority interest groups are commonly ignored under a unanimity voting rule.

___ 2. Failure to vote is a symptom of irrationality and apathy.

___ 3. Public choice analysis examines private market failure.

___ 4. Political extremists who want to be elected usually gain votes if they moderate their positions.

___ 5. Two major political parties will often jointly support laws that erect barriers against third parties.

___ 6. Voting cycles often yield choices that are very different from those that would be made under a simple majority rule voting system.

___ 7. Inherent in point voting or unanimity rules are incentives for strategic voting that may not reflect voters' true preferences.

___ 8. Fine tuning your choices is easier in the political arena than in the market system.

___ 9. Most economists and political scientists have concluded that most politicians are inherently wiser than college professors, more ethical than used car dealers, and more competent than journalists.

___ 10. A policy adopted because of rent-seeking that would double the profits of mustard producers would tend to be favored by most of them even if it decreased the standard of living 2 percent for everyone else in the country.

___ 11. Logrolling enables legislators to register the intensity of their preferences, but often yields inefficient pork barrel legislation.

___ 12. Successful lobbying invariably results in economically inefficient policies.

___ 13. Projects that have local benefits but national funding are known as apple dumplings.

___ 14. Rent seeking involves trying to mold laws or regulations to serve the national interest instead of narrow private interests.

___ 15. The general name for relatively small government agencies such as the FBI is "bureau"; such large organizations as the military are known as departments.

___ 16. Rent-seeking is a word used to describe strategies to artificially boost a government agency's budget.

___ 17. Overly precise specifications have driven up the costs of many government contracts.

___ 18. The incomes and "perqs" of bureaucrats tend to be more closely related to their job titles than to the number of people they supervise or the amounts of budget they control.

___ 19. Most experts in virtually every field favor huge federal spending cuts on programs in their areas of expertise.

___ 20. Compulsory education is an example of a merit good.

UNLIMITED MULTIPLE CHOICE

WARNING: EACH QUESTION HAS FROM ZERO TO FOUR CORRECT ANSWERS.

___ 1. "Public choice" focuses on such areas as why:
   a. government is so small relative to the business sector.
   b. many people don't vote.
   c. special interest groups devote resources to lobbying.
   d. capitalism is inequitable relative to socialism.

___ 2. Decision making is based on rational ignorance when choices are made about:
   a. voting in political primaries.
   b. laws passed by the congress and signed by the president.
   c. buying goods at your local shopping mall.
   d. how to treat your relatives.

___ 3. The median voter model offers explanations for why:
   a. the median voter is unlikely to vote.
   b. political extremists have so much influence on public policies.
   c. majority rules voting leads to a two party system.
   d. serious political candidates generally adopt moderate positions.

___ 4. Special interests may be overrepresented because their:
   a. members will often vote based on only one issue.
   b. devotion of many hours to lobbying and campaigning is effective.
   c. concerns are issues that matter little to most other people.
   d. members may donate substantially to political campaigns.

___ 5. Public policies only crudely reflect voter preferences because of:
   a. empire building by ambitious bureaucrats.
   b. successful rent-seeking behavior.
   c. lobbying that results in pork barrel legislation.
   d. vote-seeking candidates who advocate moderate positions.

Problem 1

Table 1 indicates how 300,000 potential voters (110,00 Mugwumps, 100,000 Know Nothings, and 90,000 Goldbugs) rate the other parties' candidates in an election for local dog catcher that must be won by a clear majority. If no one initially receives 50 percent plus 1 vote, a runoff is held between the top two vote getters.

Table 1

# OF VOTERS / RANKING	110,000 MUGWUMPS	100,000 KNOW NOTHINGS	90,000 GOLDBUGS
First Choice	Mugwump	Know Nothing	Goldbug
Second Choice	Know Nothing	Goldbug	Mugwump
Third Choice	Goldbug	Mugwump	Know Nothing

Although everyone votes in the runoff, people differ in their voting patterns on primary election day according to the weather. Instead of voting on snowy primary days, half of the Mugwumps and one-fifth of Know Nothings stay inside next to a warm fire, but all of the Goldbugs ride their dogsleds to the polls. On sunny primary days, the Mugwumps all vote, but half of the Know Nothings and one- fifth of the Goldbugs go golfing instead. On rainy primary days, the Know Nothings all vote, but half of the Goldbugs and one-fifth of the Mugwumps stay home all day and watch soap operas. Fill in Table 2 to show how the weather on primary days affects the final results.

Table 2

ELECTION	POSITION	Party Affiliation of Candidate	WEATHER ON PRIMARY DAY		
		Number of Votes	Sunny	Rainy	Snowy
PRIMARY	FIRST	Party / Votes	___	___	___
	SECOND	Party / Votes	___	___	___
	LAST	Party / Votes	___	___	___
RUNOFF	WINNER	Party / Votes	___	___	___
	LOSER	Party / Votes	___	___	___

Do you believe that such factors as weather, campaign advertising, or the order in which things are voted on frequently affect the outcomes of elections? What does your answer suggest about the consistency of democratic institutions? Can you think of other mechanisms used to make political choices? Are these mechanisms at least as flawed? If so, how are they inferior to representative democracy?

Problem 2

Table 3 projects. Efficiency requires proposals to pass if benefits exceed costs, and lose if costs exceed benefits.

Table 3

PROPOSALS	VOTERS									
	Bruce		Cathy		Debbie		George		Jim	
	Benefits	Costs	Benefits	Costs	Benefits	Costs	Benefits	Costs	Benefits	Costs
Airport	90	100	25	100	50	100	280	100	300	100
Firehouse	60	100	5	100	10	100	50	100	210	100
Garbage Dump	0	100	50	500	180	100	70	100	180	100
Hospital	130	100	110	100	190	100	0	100	90	100
School	120	100	120	100	120	100	60	100	0	100

a. Fill in rows 1-5 of Table 4 to show how these people will cast their ballots under a majority rule.

Table 4

ROW	Proposal	Pass/Fail	Bruce	Cathy	Debbie	George	Jim
		MAJORITY RULE VOTES					
1	Airport						
2	Firehouse						
3	Garbage Dump						
4	Hospital						
5	School						
		IDEAL POINT VOTING					
6	POINTS PER DOLLAR						
7	Airport						
8	Firehouse						
9	Garbage Dump						
10	Hospital						
11	School						
		STRATEGIC POINT VOTING					
12	POINTS PER DOLLAR						
13	Airport						
14	Firehouse						
15	Garbage Dump						
16	Hospital						
17	School						

b. The new airport proposal was ____ (passed/defeated); this voting result was ____ (efficient/inefficient).

c. The new firehouse proposal was _____; this vote was _____.

d. The new garbage dump proposal was _____; this vote was _____.

e. The new hospital proposal was _____; this vote was _____.

f. The new school proposal was _____; this vote was _____.

g. Fill in row 6 to show the points per dollar of potential gain or loss from this set of proposals for each of these voters, assuming that each voter has 1,000 to allocate among these propositions. (Each proposal costs each voter $100. A proposal must yield at least $100 worth of benefits to a voter before it will be favored by that voter. Thus, multiply the individual's absolute deviations of benefits from $100 costs by the points per dollar.) Fill in rows 7-11 to show how these voters ideally would vote if each voter allocates points in proportion to the individual's expected gains or losses on the issues.

h. Are there any inefficient results under point voting? _____

i. Efficient point votes include passage of the _____ and _____.

j. The _____, _____, and _____ proposals were efficiently defeated.

k. Fill in rows 12-17 of Table 4 on the assumption that Cathy convinced Debbie (mistakenly) that the hospital and firehouse proposals would pass and fail, respectively, regardless of their votes, so that these two voters each place all of their point votes on other issues.

l. This strategic voting causes inefficiency because _____

m. Losers from this strategic voting are _____

n. Gainers from this strategic voting are _____

o. Would any proposal pass if unanimity were required and bribes were forbidden? _____ Is this efficient? _____

p. If bribes are permitted under a unanimity rule, what is the structure of feasible bribes that might secure efficiency? _____
_____
_____

ANSWERS

Matching Key Terms and Concepts

SET I

Answer	MIC	ECO
1. a	p. 378	682
2. c	p. 376	680
3. e	p. 378	682
4. d	p. 381	685
5. g	p. 377	681
6. h	p. 375	679
7. f	p. 374	678
8. b	p. 373	677
9. j	p. 376	680
10. i	p. 374	678

SET II

Answer	MIC	ECO
1. g	p. 381	685
2. a	p. 381	685
3. f	p. 379	683
4. h	p. 385	689
5. d	p. 380	684
6. c	p. 383	687
7. e	p. 382	686
8. b	p. 380	684

	MIC	ECO
6. c	p. 374	678
7. a	p. 375	679
8. e	p. 374-381	678-685
9. e	p. 378	682
10. b	p. 376, 378	680, 682
11. c	p. 380	684
12. a	p. 377	681
13. d	p. 382	686
14. e	p. 380	684
15. a	p. 382	686
16. b	p. 385	689
17. c	p. 383	687
18. e	p. 383	687
19. a	p. 385	689
20. d	p. 384	688

Chapter Review (Fill-in Questions)

1. public choice, self interested
2. median voter, moderate or middle-of-the-road
3. two-party, majority rules
4. logrolling, pork barrel
5. funding, benefits
6. special interest groups, lobby
7. rent-seeking, social
8. subordinate employees, budgets
9. profit, efficiency
10. empire building, inefficiency

Standard Multiple Choice

Answer	MIC	ECO
1. c	p. 374	678
2. d	p. 374	678
3. a	p. 374	678
4. d	p. 374	678
5. c	p. 378	682

True/False Questions

Answer	MIC	ECO
1. F	p. 375	679
2. F	p. 374	678
3. F	p. 373	677
4. T	p. 378	682
5. T	p. 380	684
6. T	p. 376	680
7. T	p. 378	682
8. F	p. 375	679
9. F	p. 383	687
10. T	p. 382	686
11. T	p. 380	684
12. F	p. 381	685
13. F	p. 380	684
14. F	p. 382	686
15. F	p. 383	687
16. F	p. 382	686
17. T	p. 384	688
18. F	p. 383	687
19. F	p. 385	689
20. T	p. 381	685

Unlimited Multiple Choice

Answer	MIC	ECO
1. bc	p. 373	677
2. abcd	p. 374	678
3. cd	p. 378	682
4. abcd	p. 381	685
5. abcd	p. 380-383	684-687

Problem 1
MIC p. 376; *ECO 680*

See Table 5

Table 5

	POSITION	Party Affiliation of Candidate	WEATHER ON PRIMARY DAY		
		Number of Votes	Sunny	Rainy	Snowy
PRIMARY	FIRST	$\frac{Party}{Votes}$	Mugwump 110,000	Know Nothing 100,000	Goldbug 90,000
	SECOND	$\frac{Party}{Votes}$	Goldbug 72,000	Mugwump 88,000	Know Nothing 80,000
	LAST	$\frac{Party}{Votes}$	Know Nothing 50,000	Goldbug 45,000	Mugwump 55,000
RUNOFF	WINNER	$\frac{Party}{Votes}$	Goldbug 190,000	Mugwump 200,000	Know Nothing 210,000
	LOSER	$\frac{Party}{Votes}$	Mugwump 110,000	Know Nothing 100,000	Goldbug 90,000

Problem 2
MIC p. 376; *ECO 680*

a.   See Table 6.

Table 6

ROW	Proposal	Pass/Fail	Bruce	Cathy	Debbie	George	Jim
		MAJORITY RULE VOTES					
1	Airport	Fail	No	No	No	Yes	Yes
2	Firehouse	Fail	No	No	No	No	Yes
3	Garbage Dump	Fail	No	No	Yes	No	Yes
4	Hospital	Pass	Yes	Yes	Yes	No	No
5	School	Pass	Yes	Yes	Yes	No	No
		IDEAL POINT VOTING					
6	POINTS PER DOLLAR		5	4	3	2.5	2
7	Airport	Pass	-50	-300	-152	450	400
8	Firehouse	Fail	-200	-380	-273	-125	220
9	Garbage Dump	Fail	-500	-200	242	-75	160
10	Hospital	Pass	150	40	273	-250	-20
11	School	Fail	100	80	60	-100	-200
		STRATEGIC POINT VOTING					
12	POINTS PER DOLLAR		5	6.95	6.67	2.5	2
13	Airport	Fail	-50	-517	-333	450	400
14	Firehouse	Fail	-200	0	0	-125	220
15	Garbage Dump	Fail	-500	-345	534	-75	160
16	Hospital	Fail	150	0	0	-250	-20
17	School	Pass	100	138	133	-100	-200

b. defeated, inefficient

c. defeated, efficient

d. defeated, efficient

e. passed, efficient

f. passed, inefficient

g. See Table 6.

h. no

i. airport, hospital

j. firehouse, garbage, school

k. See Table 6.

l. The airport and hospital proposals are inefficiently defeated and the school proposal is inefficiently passed.

m. Debbie (-$20); George (-$120); Jim (-$90)

n. Cathy (+$85 = +$75 repeal of airport) $10 (repeal of hospital) + $20 (passage of school) [Bruce breaks even ($0)]

o. no, no

p. Table 3 suggests that the airport proposal will pass if George and Jim bribe Bruce, Cathy, and Debbie for their votes. Jim would be willing to give up to $200 and George would be willing to give up to $180 to Bruce (who requires at least $10 for his vote), Cathy (who requires at least $75), and Debbie (who must receive at least $50). Bribes in this range improve efficiency if a unanimous vote is required. Similarly, the hospital proposal will pass if Bruce, Cathy, and Debbie (who, respectively, are willing to contribute $30, $10, and $90 for its passage) offer appropriate payoffs to George (who requires at least $100 for his assent), and Jim (who must be paid at least $10). The other proposals each bear total costs that exceed their benefits and so bribery cannot secure unanimity in these cases.

CHAPTER THIRTY-THREE

EXTERNALITIES AND ENVIRONMENTAL ECONOMICS

CHAPTER OBJECTIVES

After you have read and studied this chapter you should be able to describe how both positive and negative externalities cause inefficiency; the advantages that cause individuals and firms to pollute; and alternative policies to overcome pollution.

CHAPTER REVIEW: KEY POINTS

1. Positive *externalities* occur when an activity confers benefits on external third parties. Too few of such activities are undertaken because decision makers tend to ignore the external benefits.

2. Pollution situations in which damaged third parties are uncompensated, and hence unconsidered, are examples of negative externalities. Negative externalities impose costs on third parties. Too many activities generating negative externalities are undertaken because decision makers weigh the costs imposed on others too lightly.

3. Environmental quality is a public good, and controlling environmental pollution is costly. There are trade-offs between protecting the environment and producing goods that generate pollution, so the *optimal pollution* level generally is not zero.

4. *Pollution abatement* may occur through negotiation, *moral suasion* (jawboning and bad publicity), lawsuits initiated by damaged parties, controls (government ceilings on pollution levels), the use of *effluent charges*, or government subsidies for pollution control. No single solution applies to all situations of negative externalities; they must generally be resolved on a case by case basis.

5. The four stages in the development of property rights are (a) common access nonscarcity, and (b) common access-scarcity/tragedy of the commons, (c) agency restrictions, (d) fee-simple property rights. The term *fee-simple property rights* means that you can do anything you want with your property so long as you do no physical damage to the property of others.

6. Pollution rights might be auctioned and then made transferable. The Environmental Protection Agency initially relied heavily on direct regulation through pollution ceilings, but is increasingly using *property rights* solutions to control environmental deterioration.

7. The *bubble concept* sets a pollution performance standard for a plant. A firm can transfer rights to pollute within or between plants inside the "bubble" as long as the standard is met.

8. The *offset policy* allows new firms that wish to produce in a polluted area to operate if they can induce existing firms to reduce air pollutants to "offset" the newcomer's emissions.

MATCHING KEY TERMS AND CONCEPTS

___ 1. effluent charges

___ 2. internalization

___ 3. fee simple property rights

___ 4. pollution rights

___ 5. regulation

___ 6. moral suasion

___ 7. bubble concept

___ 8. common access

___ 9. abatement subsidies

___ 10. offset policies

a. Social pressure to persuade people or institutions.

b. Payments to a firm for adopting less-polluting technologies.

c. New firms may pollute only if they induce other firms to reduce emissions.

d. Fully considering the effects on others of one's decisions.

e. Limits pollution within an area, but not by specific source.

f. A synonym for nonexclusion.

g. Reduce production and pollution, but lack incentives for cleaner technologies.

h. Rights to use or transfer property as one wishes.

i. Fees per unit of a pollutant.

j. Rights to emit pollution, or to deny emissions.

CHAPTER REVIEW (FILL-IN QUESTIONS)

1-2. The _____ is normally too high and the level of _____ is too low in the case of positive externalities, while the price is too _____ and the level of production is too _____ when such negative externalities as pollutants are generated.

3-5. How far to pursue environmental purity and what techniques to use are controversial issues. Environmental use is rival between competing groups, but it is also _____. If, for example, government requires cleaner air, everyone in the vicinity enjoys the benefits--no one can be _____. Any efficient remedy for problems caused by negative _____ requires _____, and may require correction of problems from either _____ or _____ activities.

6-8. There are tradeoffs between environmental _____ and high standards of _____. As we approach 100 percent purity the marginal social benefits of abatement _____ while the marginal social costs _____. Optimal pollution abatement requires _____ to equal _____.

9-10. Common access resources are available to all on a first-come, first-served basis, and when resources become scarce, _____ results. Assigning rights to pollute has been used by the Environmental Protection Agency under what has become known as the _____ concept. Another approach to stabilize pollution in a given area is to require new firms to _____ their anticipated pollution by inducing other firms to _____ their effluents.

STANDARD MULTIPLE CHOICE

EACH QUESTION HAS ONE BEST ANSWER.

___ 1. Negative (cost) spillovers:
   a. result in too much of a product at too low a price.
   b. are exemplified by air pollution and education.
   c. are exemplified by transportation and immunization.
   d. result in too little of a product at too high a price.
   e. are caused by wastes of taxpayers' dollars.

___ 2. An excise tax newly imposed on a good for which negative externalities are generated in production would tend to cause:
   a. enormous excess burdens relative to tax revenues collected.
   b. unambiguously enhanced economic equity.
   c. greater use of the good to replace its close substitutes.
   d. higher prices and falling production, which may be desirable in such cases.
   e. increased production and consumption.

___ 3. Private decision makers will confront prices that are socially too high and, thus, will pursue too little of an activity relative to a social optimum if the activity generates:
   a. merit goods.
   b. negative externalities.
   c. excess burdens.
   d. cutthroat competition.
   e. positive externalities.

___ 4. Negative externalities are least likely to be created if:
   a. a TV game show host practices smiling in front of a mirror.
   b. your neighbor begins raising pigs in her back yard.
   c. teenagers throw a BYOB party during their parents' vacation.
   d. Ear Throb plays a free high-decibel concert at a local park.
   e. a Soviet nuclear reactor at Chernobyl melts down.

___ 5. Positive externalities are least likely to be created if:
   a. your neighbor cuts her law on a regular basis.
   b. rusty, old, pink garbage trucks are repainted a soothing beige.
   c. the driver of a smoky old gas hog has her car engine rebuilt.
   d. the EPA fires half of its inspectors to save tax dollars.
   e. volunteers remove litter from the roadside of a busy highway.

___ 6. In equilibrium, uncontrolled pollution causes the marginal:
   a. social costs to exceed a good's marginal private costs and benefits.
   b. social benefits from the good to exceed marginal private benefits.
   c. private costs to exceed marginal social benefits.
   d. customers to pay prices that exceed production costs.
   e. customers to pay prices exceeding the value of the good to them.

___ 7. Internalizing all costs that were previously external to a polluting industry and its customers causes:
   a. both output and the cost of the product to rise.
   b. output to fall and the private cost of the product to rise.
   c. the standard of living adjacent to polluting factories to fall.
   d. both output and the price of the product to decline.
   e. output to rise and the price of the product to decline.

___ 8. If more stringent emissions controls are placed on new cars:
a. we will be paying a higher price than currently for clean air.
b. real national output grows by the value of the control equipment.
c. average car mileage per gallon of gasoline is likely to rise.
d. there will be downward pressure on the prices of used cars.
e. all of the above.

___ 9. Fee simple property rights do not include rights to:
a. sell property.
b. make choices reducing the market value of another's property.
c. destroy your own property.
d. physically damage another's property.
e. contract with others to exchange property.

___ 10. If both polluters and pollutees belong to small, easily identified groups:
a. regulation is the best solution to pollution.
b. output taxes create proper incentives to adopt cleaner technology.
c. private bargaining to optimal pollution levels is facilitated.
d. it is very difficult for polluters to internalize externalities.
e. pollution can be eradicated at zero cost.

___ 11. Unlike pure public goods, environmental quality often involves:
a. nonrivalry.
b. nonsatiety.
c. nonexclusion.
d. rivalry.
e. exclusion.

___ 12. Early government campaigns to cut pollution relied most on:
a. direct regulation.
b. effluent charges.
c. private bargaining.
d. the bubble concept.
e. offset policies.

___ 13. A legal requirement that all pollution be reduced to zero:
a. is desirable from the vantage point of increasing social welfare.
b. would efficiently eliminate all forms of production.
c. is incompatible with the standards of living most Americans enjoy.
d. could be enforced inexpensively because of its legal simplicity.
e. would undoubtedly eradicate pollution.

___ 14. The evolution from common access to fee simple property rights suggests that government policies:
a. slowly move toward more economically efficient modes of ownership.
b. yield to pressures for capitalistic environmental exploitation.
c. are controlled by large, polluting, industrial conglomerates.
d. headed in the direction of environmental decay.
e. are backing away from serious commitments to conservation.

___ 15. Private bargaining to resolve externalities tends to be least feasible when there are:
a. many polluters and many people damaged by pollutants.
b. fee simple property rights to govern environmental use.
c. easy measurements of harmful emissions.
d. remote wilderness areas that are being polluted by a few firms.
e. extremely harmful emissions from long-established firms.

___ 16. Pollution rights can be sold by existing polluters under:
a. regulatory standards.
b. effluent charge policies.
c. common access doctrines.
d. offset policies.
e. the Monroe Doctrine.

17. Optimal adjustments when externalities are present involve:
    a. forbidding the activities that generate the externalities.
    b. internalization of all relevant external costs or benefits.
    c. rigid standards that reduce externalities to tolerable levels.
    d. total benefits from abatement that equal total abatement costs.
    e. maximization of the dollar value of marketable production.

18. Eliminating auto emissions in central cities by requiring that people ride horses instead of cars would:
    a. increase our standard of living.
    b. represent adoption of policies advocated by the auto industry.
    c. give Japan even more of a competitive advantage than it now has.
    d. replace one form of pollution with another.
    e. be one effective way to internalize externalities.

19. If the marginal private costs of pollution abatement exceed its marginal social benefits, efficient moves might entail reducing:
    a. pollution until the external effects were negligible.
    b. abatement programs and allowing more pollution.
    c. the adoption of newer and more efficient capital.
    d. national output to conserve more of our natural resources.
    e. domestic production that generates positive externalities.

20. Regulatory standards that limit pollution typically:
    a. impose extremely high penalties for noncompliance.
    b. lack incentives to reduce pollution once the standard is met.
    c. were more important earlier in the history of the EPA.
    d. are applied when pollutants are extremely dangerous and dispersed.
    e. All of the above.

TRUE/FALSE QUESTIONS

1. A negative externality causes the private supply curve to be to the right of society's optimal supply curve.

2. Sexually transmitted diseases from promiscuous contacts are examples of negative externalities if people consider their own likelihood of infection but fail to consider possible dangers to their subsequent partners.

3. Controls over externalities tend to become more formal as increasing numbers of people spread across greater areas are affected.

4. An example of a positive externality occurs when an erratic golfer whose ball is coming towards you yells "FORE".

5. Community projects to beautify neighborhood greenbelts and parks are examples of how positive externalities can be internalized.

6. Developed nations tend to export pollution to less developed countries.

7. Market exchanges occur between economic transactors whenever they expect personal prospects of gains from the exchange.

8. The socially optimal rate of pollution is zero.

9. Moral suasion is among the most effective ways of dealing with the pollution problem.

___10. One politically popular method for reducing environmental damage is direct regulation or prohibition.

___11. Effluent charges to deal with the pollution problem are uniformly relatively easy to administer.

___12. Society's net welfare always attains a maximum value when marginal private benefits are equal to marginal private costs.

___13. Efficiency occurs when competitive firms internalize any external production costs, making consumers of pollution-causing goods pay the marginal social costs of production.

___14. Regulations governing how much firms can pollute are costly to administer and fail to provide firms with incentives to reduce pollution once the firms comply with legal standards.

___15. Market solutions to the pollution problem require sizable government intervention in the marketplace.

___16. Pollution rights are most efficient when bubble charges are bought and sold in a free market.

___17. Increasing automobile emissions standards should increase the amounts of air pollution in most communities.

___18. The evolution from common access to fee simple property rights is the major cause of most current pollution.

___19. Optimal resolution of negative externalities requires reducing the activities that generate them and raising their prices, while positive externalities require increases in the activities that produce them and reductions in their costs to buyers.

___20. Relative to direct regulation effluent charges create more incentives to adopt cleaner technologies.

UNLIMITED MULTIPLE CHOICE

CAUTION: EACH QUESTION HAS FROM ZERO TO FOUR CORRECT RESPONSES.

___1. Externalities:
   a. are one variety of market failure.
   b. arise whenever some aspect of consumption or production affects people not directly involved in the specific activity.
   c. have no impact on the efficiency of resource allocations.
   d. can be cured through internalization.

___2. Allocative efficiency occurs whenever:
   a. marginal private benefits are equal to marginal social costs, assuming that no external effects exist.
   b. scarce resources are used to produce the most valuable output.
   c. all outputs are produced at the lowest opportunity costs.
   d. marginal social benefits are equal to marginal social costs.

___3. Instances of negative externalities include:
   a. the 1986 nuclear accident at Chernobyl in the U.S.S.R.
   b. the slaughtering of whales by Japan and the Soviet Union.
   c. someone's bad breath.
   d. your neighbor's brown lawn during the summer months.

___4. Whenever all marginal social benefits from production equal the relevant marginal social costs:
   a. the costs incurred in producing given outputs are minimized.
   b. society's total production is at its maximum value.
   c. no resource reallocations would improve society's net welfare.
   d. there is both consumption and production efficiency.

5. Imposing a per unit tax on output to reduce pollution:
   a. is a market approach to dealing with pollution.
   b. is more efficient than the imposition of effluent charges.
   c. shifts the firm's supply curve to the left.
   d. may force the consumers and producers of the output to internalize the external costs it generates.

Problem 1

Figure 1 shows the private demand and supply curves in the market for steel. Use this information to answer the following true/false questions.

Figure 1

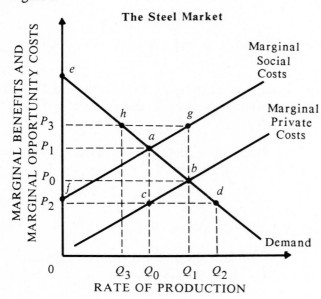

a. The marginal private cost curve reflects only the private costs of steel production.

b. The demand curve reflects the marginal social benefits from consuming extra units of steel.

c. Steel production imposes external costs on society that are not captured in the marginal private cost curve.

d. External cost per unit of steel equals $P_3 - P_0$.

e. Steel output generates negative externalities.

f. The dollar value that society as a whole places upon the Q_1th unit of steel is less than the dollar value of inputs used in its production.

g. The socially optimal rate of production is Q_1.

h. The socially optimal per unit price is P_2.

i. Allocative efficiency is obtained at point b.

j. The net welfare of society would be maximized in this market if the steel industry produced Q_2 units per time period.

k. A tax per unit of steel equal to $P_1 - P_2$ would result in the socially optimal output of steel if no preferable technologies can be substituted.

l. Total tax revenue from such a tax would equal area P_0P_3gb

ANSWERS

Matching Key Terms and Concepts

Answer	MIC	ECO
1. i	p. 397	701
2. d	p. 393	697
3. h	p. 390	694
4. j	p. 399	703
5. g	p. 400	704
6. a	p. 397	701
7. e	p. 402	706
8. f	p. 390	694
9. b	p. 398	702
10. c	p. 402	706

Chapter Review (Fill-in Questions)

1. price, output
2. low, high
3. nonexclusive, excluded
4. externalities, internalization
5. production, consumption
6. quality, production or consumption
7. diminish, rise
8. marginal social benefits, marginal social costs
9. overutilization, "bubble"
10. offset, reduce

Standard Multiple Choice

Answer	MIC	ECO
1. a	p. 392	696
2. d	p. 397	701
3. e	p. 392	696
4. a	p. 392	696
5. d	p. 392	696
6. a	p. 393	697
7. b	p. 393	697
8. a	p. 393	697
9. d	p. 390	694
10. c	p. 399	703
11. d	p. 400	704
12. a	p. 401	705
13. c	p. 394	698
14. a	p. 390	694
15. a	p. 399	703
16. d	p. 402	706
17. b	p. 393	697
18. d	p. 394	698
19. b	p. 395	699
20. e	p. 400-402	704-706

True/False Questions

Answer	MIC	ECO
1. T	p. 393	697
2. T	p. 392	696
3. T	p. 400	704
4. F	p. 391	695
5. T	p. 391	695
6. T	p. 396	700
7. T	p. 399	703
8. F	p. 394	698
9. F	p. 397	701
10. T	p. 400	704
11. F	p. 397	701
12. F	p. 393	697
13. T	p. 393	697
14. T	p. 400	704
15. F	p. 398	702
16. F	p. 399	703
17. F	p. 393	697
18. F	p. 390	694
19. T	p. 391-393	695-697
20. T	p. 397, 400	701, 704

Unlimited Multiple Choice

Answer	MIC	ECO
1. abd	p. 391	695
2. abcd	p. 393	697
3. abcd	p. 392	696
4. bcd	p. 393	697
5. cd	p. 397	701

Problem 1
MIC pp. 393; *ECO 697*

a. T
b. T
c. T
d. T
e. T
f. T
g. F
h. F
i. F
j. F
k. T
l. F

CHAPTER THIRTY-FOUR
THE ECONOMICS OF AGRICULTURE

CHAPTER OBJECTIVES

After you have read and studied this chapter, you should be able to discuss the three factors that have contributed to farmers' problems; traditional farm programs and the concept of parity; and agricultural policies of the past two decades.

CHAPTER REVIEW: KEY POINTS

1. The major problem for farmers is that income from agriculture has been relatively low and erratic for generations. No other sector of the economy has as consistently experienced tremendous productivity growth, so these low incomes are largely market signals that our society desires shifts of resources from agriculture into other forms of economic activity.

2. The demand for all farm products lumped together tends to be relatively price and income inelastic. Thus, much lower prices are required to clear markets when agricultural supplies grow significantly, and the widespread adoption of more productive agricultural technologies tends to drive farmers' revenues down sharply.

3. Farming is our largest industry, and it is among our most competitive. There are strong political pressures for the federal government to support farmers, however, for at least two reasons: (a) many nonfarmers have great empathy for farming as a way of life, and (b) although a small minority, farmers have been active for a century in making their problems known to lawmakers.

4. The strong tendency for people to make decisions at the margin means that there will always be high-cost marginal producers who will be wiped out by slight reversals in the markets where they operate. No policy can prevent this from happening. The principle thrust of agricultural policy has been to restrict farm production to raise prices and farm revenues. These farm programs can be classified into: (a) *Crop restriction programs* (b) *Purchase-loan storage programs* to boost farm prices, and (c) *Purchase-and-resale subsidy programs.*

5. "*Parity pricing*" is based on the notion that the prices of farm products should not change relative to the prices farmers pay. A policy of 100 percent parity would enrich farmers who experience productivity gains and would freeze the incentives for efficient reallocations that are imbedded in relative price changes.

6. Most policies intended to preserve the family farm have largely benefitted large farming operations, many of which are corporate.

MATCHING KEY TERMS AND CONCEPTS

___ 1. Purchase and Resale Subsidy Program

a. one unit of output maintains the same real purchasing power

___ 2. Agriculture & Consumer Protection Act

b. a "heads I win, tails you loose" proposition for the farmer.

___ 3. parity

c. the government sells the commodity on the open market and the farmer receives price support

___ 4. Crop Limitation Program

d. attempts to raise the prices received by farmers.

___ 5. support price

e. reduced the subsidy ceiling to $20,000.

___ 6. Purchase-Loan Price Support Program

f. equivalent to a price floor.

___ 7. allotment rights

g. results from the absence of good substitutes for all farm commodities.

___ 8. Inelastic Demand

h. allows the cultivation of specific crops on a specified amount of land.

___ 9. Restrict production and raise incomes

i. typically a family farmer.

___10. Marginal Farmer

j. the goal of agricultural policy in the U.S.

CHAPTER REVIEW: (FILL-IN QUESTIONS)

1-3. Farmers' woes are largely due to three factors. The first, rapid growth in _____ has lead to a decline in _____ despite increases in farm yields. Low price and income _____ of demand for farm products is a second factor because of the absence of good _____ for farm commodities as a whole. The relative _____ of agriculture resources is a third factor, especially for family farmers who cannot easily _____ their laborers since they are usually family members.

4-8. Agricultural programs have attempted to restrict farm _____ in an effort to raise _____. One program, the _____ attempts to limit _____ in order to drive the price of agricultural commodities upward. Another approach to this program has been to assign _____, which allow farmers to grow specific crops, but only _____ amounts of land can be cultivated. A _____ program allows farmers to store their output and obtain loans equal to a price floor or _____. A program which is more economically efficient is the _____ program. Under this program the farmer is guaranteed a support price and the government sells the commodity to consumers at the _____ price.

9-10.A depreciated dollar and crop failures abroad led to a boom period in the _____ for farmers. The appreciation of the dollar and a reversal of foreign crop failures reduced U.S. agricultural exports in the_____. Farmers problems were further exacerbated during this time by a _____ in land values, and _____ harvests which further depressed agricultural prices.

STANDARD MULTIPLE CHOICE

THERE IS ONLY ONE BEST ANSWER FOR EACH QUESTION.

___ 1. Farm income has been:
   a. relatively stable over the past two centuries.
   b. increasing relative to manufacturing income.
   c. unstable and lower than for non-farmers over the past two centuries.
   d. a great inducement for more people to take up farming.
   e. three to four times greater than non-farm income for the past two centuries.

___ 2. The ratio of Americans who actively farm today is approximately:
   a. 19 in 20
   b. 10 in 20
   c. 30 in 100
   d. 1 in 40
   e. 1 in 100

___ 3. Farmers who are on the verge of "going under" are essentially:
   a. good credit risks
   b. marginal farmers.
   c. corporate farmers.
   d. hydroponic farmers.
   e. tobacco farmers.

___ 4. While farm incomes are typically below non-farm incomes, the average farmer:
   a. is wealthier than the average non-farmer.
   b. is more educated than the average non-farmer.
   c. is happier than the average non-farmer
   d. is better-looking than the average non-farmer.
   e. is more likely to have assets such as stocks and bonds than the average non-farmer.

___ 5. Agricultural productivity has NOT been aided by:
   a. modern machinery.
   b. new strains of seeds.
   c. selective animal breeding.
   d. extensive irrigation.
   e. an expanding labor pool.

___ 6. Agricultural products as a whole are characterized by :
   a. a wide array of substitutes.
   b. elastic demands.
   c. high income elasticities.
   d. inelastic demands.
   e. inelastic supplies.

___ 7. Arguments for aid to farmers include all of the following except:
   a. Farmers are confronted with extraordinary hardships.
   b. Positive spillovers have accrued from productivity gains in agriculture.
   c. Agriculture is highly competitive.
   d. Farmers have been unintentionally hurt by government policies.
   e. Farmers have been prevented from taking up other occupations.

___ 8. Adjusting the prices of agricultural products to the price farmers pay for commodities is know as:
   a. price support.
   b. parity pricing.
   c. stop-gap payments.
   d. allotment rights.
   e. marginal payments.

___ 9. Allotment rights are a subset of the:
   a. Crop Limitation Programs
   b. Purchase-Loan Price-Support Programs.
   c. Purchase and Resale Programs
   d. Agriculture and Consumer Protection Act of 1973.
   e. Food and Agriculture Act of 1977.

___ 10. A Purchase-Loan Price Support Program:
   a. is efficient from society's view point.
   b. results in consumers paying lower prices.
   c. is a no win program for farmers.
   d. results in higher prices paid by the consumer.
   e. decreases tax rates to U.S. citizens.

___11. From a consumer's perspective the most effective agricultural program is the:
a. Crop Limitation Program.
b. Purchase and Resale Program.
c. Purchase -Loan Price-Support Program.
d. Parity-Price Program.
e. Farm Aid Program.

___12. Farm subsidies under traditional programs were paid:
a. only to farmers in the Northeast.
b. to family farmers only.
c. to fewer than one-fifth of all farmers.
d. to needy farmers on the edge of bankruptcy.
e. primarily to wheat and sorghum producers.

___13. A surge in agricultural sales in the 1970s CANNOT be explained by:
a. increased agricultural productivity.
b. the Soviet Unions' purchase of wheat from the U.S.
c. rising demands for livestock.
d. poor agricultural harvests aboard.
e. a sharp depreciation of the dollar.

___14. Agricultural policy in the 1970s was not focused on:
a. reducing inflation from high farm prices.
b. avoiding possible agricultural shortages.
c. overproduction and lower farm incomes.
d. reversing the balance of payments deficit.
e. marketing agricultural products abroad.

___15. One result of the Agriculture and Consumer Protection Act of 1973 was the:
a. establishment of parity prices.
b. imposition of increased crop limitations.
c. concentration of farming profits.
d. guarantee of "substantial" price support.
e. limiting of subsidy payments to individual farmers.

___16. High incomes for farmers in the 1970s led to:
a. increased investments in land and machinery.
b. lobbying for crop limitation programs.
c. to a decrease in proprietors' equity.
d. a decrease in land values.
e. a decline in tractor sales.

___17. All of the following contributed to the farmers' "plight" in the 1980s except:
a. the appreciation of the dollar.
b. previous importers of grain becoming net exporters.
c. the re-establishment of target prices and acreage set-asides.
d. bountiful harvests in most years.
e. the reduction of agricultural exports.

___18. Because the demand for agricultural products is price inelastic, increased agricultural productivity by all wheat farmers will, ceteris paribus:
a. result in a higher price paid by consumers of wheat products.
b. increase the demand for wheat products.
c. decrease wheat farmers' incomes.
d. decrease the supply of wheat available.
e. benefit all wheat farmers.

___19. Tenant farmers are also known as:
a. marginal farmers.
b. share croppers.
c. communal farmers.
d. agronomists.
e. soil managers.

___20. Perhaps the best way to "save" the family farmer would be to implement:
a. price support programs.
b. acreage reduction programs.
c. export subsidies.
d. focused credit markets.
e. broad-based transfer programs.

TRUE/FALSE QUESTIONS

____ 1. There has been an exodus of labor from the farming sector over the past century.

____ 2. Farmers have been fortunate because their incomes have been relatively stable compared to other occupations.

____ 3. Farmers in many areas were left without convenient sources of credit due to a wave of agriculture bank failures in the mid 1980s.

____ 4. A marginal producer/farmer necessarily produces on marginal land.

____ 5. Although farmers' average incomes are less than for non-farmers, the average farmer is wealthier than the average non-farmer.

____ 6. Tenant farmers are also known as marginal farmers.

____ 7. Agricultural products have close substitutes, resulting in elastic demands for agricultural commodities.

____ 8. Productivity growth has been greater in agriculture than in any other major industry.

____ 9. Increased agricultural output by all farmers ensures increased income.

____ 10. Most agricultural products are relatively income inelastic.

____ 11. Farm resources tend to be immobile which further exacerbates farmers' problems.

____ 12. One argument for aiding farmers is that they face extraordinary hardships not faced by other industries.

____ 13. Parity pricing is a recent concept that was introduced by the Agriculture and Consumer Protection Act of 1973.

____ 14. Purchase and Resale Subsidy Programs are more economically efficient than Purchase Loan Price Support Programs.

____ 15. The goal of Crop Limitation Programs is to increase demand and drive up agricultural prices.

____ 16. Purchase-Loan Price Support Programs were no win programs vehemently opposed by farmers.

____ 17. Allotment rights permit a farmer to grown an unlimited amount of one specific crop.

____ 18. Record harvests worldwide and a strong U.S. dollar hurt farmers in the 1970s.

____ 19. Farmers in the 1980s have been able to offset some of their losses because land values have steadily increased.

____ 20. A program of export subsides would probably do the most to help save the family farmer.

UNLIMITED MULTIPLE CHOICE

EACH QUESTION HAS FROM ZERO TO FOUR CORRECT ANSWERS.

___ 1. Factors that have contributed to farmers'
problems include:
a. depreciation of the U.S. dollar.
b. rapid agricultural productivity growth.
c. low price and income elasticities.
d. immobility of agricultural resources.

___ 2. Crop Limitation Programs:
a. are socially efficient.
b. try to restrict output and increase
agricultural prices.
c. encourages intensive cultivation.
d. were widely cheered by farmers.

___ 3. The Agriculture and Consumer Protection Act
of 1973:
a. established parity prices.
b. further limited agricultural production.
c. increased subsidy ceilings.
d. liberated sharecroppers.

___ 4. Purchase and Resale Subsidy Programs:
a. result in consumers paying higher prices.
b. resulted in stockpiling of grains.
c. allowed some farmers to receive huge
subsidies.
d. did away with support prices.

___ 5. The agricultural boom of the 1970s was in part
aided by:
a. the appreciation of the dollar.
b. worldwide crop failures.
c. record Soviet wheat harvests.
d. increased demands for livestock.

413

Problem 1

Use Figure 1 to answer the True/False questions listed below. Demand curve D_0 reflects the private demand for agricultural commodities, while demand curve D_1 reflects private and government demands for agricultural commodities..

Figure 1

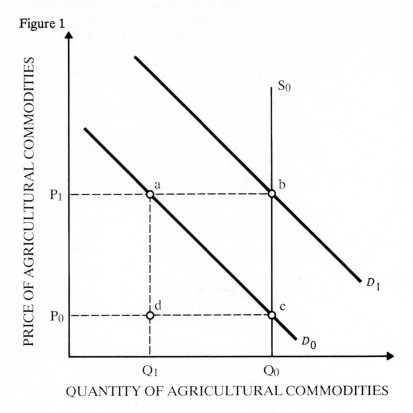

1. _____ Given a market demand curve of D_0, the equilibrium price is equal to P_1.

2. _____ A Purchase Loan Price Support Program undertaken by the government could increase demand from D_0 to D_1.

3. _____ Under a Purchase Loan Price Support Program total payment to farmers would be equal to *abcd*.

4. _____ Under a Purchase Loan and Price Support Program the net social welfare loss is equal to Q_1acQ_0.

5. _____ Consumers benefit from a Purchase Loan Price Support Program because $Q_1 - Q_0$ quantity is now additionally purchased.

6. _____ Under a Purchase and Resale Subsidy Program consumers would pay a price equal to P_0.

7. _____ Total government payments to farmers are equal to P_0P_1bc when a Purchase and Resale Subsidy Program is undertaken.

8. _____ Consumers purchase greater quantities of this good equal to $Q_1 - Q_0$ when a Purchase and Resale Subsidy Program is implemented.

9. _____ The social welfare loss under a Purchase and Resale Subsidy Program is equal to *abc*.

10. _____ The area Q_1dcQ_0 is equal to the "tax" consumers pay under a Purchase and Resale Subsidy Program.

ANSWERS

Matching Key Terms and Concepts

Answer	MIC	*ECO*
1. c	p. 416	*720*
2. e	p. 417	*721*
3. a	p. 413	*717*
4. d	p. 414	*718*
5. f	p. 415	*719*
6. b	p. 415	*719*
7. h	p. 415	*719*
8. g	p. 411	*715*
9. j	p. 413	*717*
10. i	p. 409	*713*

Chapter Review (Fill-in Questions)

1. agricultural productivity, income
2. elasticities, substitutes.
3. immobility, layoff
4. output, prices and incomes.
5. Crop Limitation Program. supply
6. allotment rights, specified.
7. Purchase Loan Price Support, support price.
8. Purchase and Resale Subsidy, equilibrium
9. 1970s, 1980s.
10. decrease, record.

Standard Multiple Choice

Answer	MIC	*ECO*
1. c	p. 408	*712*
2. d	p. 407	*711*
3. b	p. 409	*713*
4. a	p. 410	*714*
5. e	p. 410	*714*
6. d	p. 411	*715*
7. e	p. 413	*717*
8. b	p. 413	*717*
9. a	p. 415	*719*
10. d	p. 415	*719*
11. b	p. 416	*720*
12. c	p. 417	*721*
13. a	p. 417	*721*
14. c	p. 417	*721*
15. e	p. 417	*721*
16. a	p. 418	*722*
17. c	p. 418	*722*
18. c	p. 411	*715*
19. b	p. 410	*714*
20. d	p. 419	*723*

True/False

Answer	MIC	*ECO*
1. T	p. 407	*711*
2. F	p. 408	*712*
3. T	p. 408	*712*
4. F	p. 409	*713*
5. T	p. 410	*714*
6. F	p. 410	*714*
7. F	p. 411	*715*
8. T	p. 410	*714*
9. F	p. 410	*714*
10. T	p. 411	*715*
11. T	p. 412	*716*
12. T	p. 413	*717*
13. F	p. 413	*717*
14. T	p. 416	*720*
15. F	p. 414	*718*
16. F	p. 415	*719*
17. F	p. 415	*719*
18. F	p. 417	*721*
19. F	p. 418	*722*
20. F	p. 419	*723*

Unlimited Multiple Choice

Answer	MIC	*ECO*
1. bcd	p. 410	*714*
2. bc	p. 414	*718*
3. none	p. 417	*721*
4. c	p. 416	*720*
5. bd	p. 417	*721*

Problem 1
MIC pp. 415-416; *ECO 719-720*

1. F
2. T
3. F
4. T
5. F
6. T
7. T
8. F
9. T
10. F

CHAPTER THIRTY-FIVE
REDISTRIBUTION OF INCOME AND WEALTH

CHAPTER OBJECTIVES

After you have completed this chapter you should be able to discuss alternative criteria for distributing income and wealth; critique our current welfare system, describing the problems posed for economic efficiency and social equity; and evaluate proposals for reform of the current "welfare" mess.

CHAPTER REVIEW: KEY POINTS

1. *Lorenz curves* are one way to portray inequality. Lorenz curves for income are graphical representations of the cumulative percentages of income received by given cumulative percentages of families. If the Lorenz curve is a straight-line diagonal, the income distribution is perfectly equal. Deviations from this diagonal reflect inequality in distribution. *shows cum % distribution of income or wealth in a society*

2. Tracing the pretax and retransfer *income distribution* since 1935 gives the appearance of little change, although the share of middle class families has grown. When taxes and transfers are considered, however, the U.S. income distribution has become markedly more equal since the early 1930s.

3. The Social Security Administration has developed income indices that define *poverty lines* for various family sizes, ages, and locations.

4. The causes of *poverty* are many and varied. Relative to middle- or upper-class families, the poor tend to have less education, few earners, and more children. These characteristics of the poor are not necessarily the causes of poverty. *Discrimination* may be an important factor. Persistent discrimination reduces incentives to invest in education and other marketable skills. Discrimination is often cited as the primary reason that a relatively large proportion of black families are in the lower income categories.

5. The major government program to fight poverty is *Aid to Families with Dependent Children (AFDC)*. A floor on family income is established, but as the family earns additional income, reductions of AFDC benefits often pose extreme *disincentives* for work. Given the large number of different programs designed to help the poor, $1 increases in earned income sometimes result in more than $1 of lost benefits.

6. *Negative income tax plans* (*NITs*) have been suggested as solutions to the "welfare mess." Negative income tax proposals provide a floor on income; as additional income is earned, benefits are reduced but by less than the additional income earned. NIT proposals contain two essential elements: a basic floor income and a negative-income-tax rate. Increases in the floor or reductions in the negative tax rate increase the costs of the program. Equity considerations indicate needs for higher floors, while efficiency considerations point to needs for lower negative tax rates. Both goals cannot be satisfied with any one negative income tax plan.

7. Opponents NIT proposals argue that guaranteed income floors will not solve all the problems of the poor. Proponents argue that providing sufficient income will solve the major problems. In general, NIT plans consolidate numerous programs under one administrative roof and might allow either reduced costs or increased benefits.

MATCHING KEY TERMS AND CONCEPTS

SET I

H 1. equality standard

D 2. voluntary poverty

G 3. welfare

B 4. communist ideal

I 5. Lorenz curve

C 6. poverty line

E 7. diminishing marginal utility of income

F 8. economic discrimination

A 9. involuntary poverty

J 10. contribution standard

a. Low income caused by circumstances beyond personal control. *involuntary*

b. "To each according to need." *comm. ideal*

c. Based on the income required to sustain a minimal standard of living. *poverty line*

d. Choosing to be eligible for welfare payments by making a low income. *voluntary*

e. An extra dollar means more to someone poor than to someone rich, according to this hypothesis. *dim. m u of income*

f. Different treatment based on race or sex. *discrimination*

g. Receiving more government benefits, proportionally, than one pays in taxes. *welfare*

h. "To each, equally." *equality*

i. A graph depicting inequality. *Lorenz*

j. "To each according to productivity." *contribution*

break-even level = income floor / NIT

E 1. negative income taxes

G 2. family allowance plans (FAPs)

A 3. "breakeven" level of income

J 4. needs standard

I 5. high marginal tax rates on low income

C 6. personal discrimination

D 7. Aid to Families with Dependent Children

F 8. lowest 20 percent of families by income

H 9. perfect equality

B 10. unemployment compensation

a. (Basic income floor) / (negative income tax rate). *break even level*

b. Encourages erratic employment patterns. *unemployment c.*

c. Causes employment, occupational, and human capital discrimination. *personal d.*

d. A welfare program blamed for severely discouraging work effort and breaking up families. *Fam w/ D kids*

e. A proposal to make income the sole criteria for receiving welfare, which would be cash, not in-kind payments. *NIT's*

f. A definition of poverty making it incurable.

g. An "allowance" is given for minor children, but is absorbed by higher taxes for high income families. *FAP's*

h. A straight-line Lorenz curve. *equality*

i. Severe disincentives for work.

j. Income is distributed according to need. *need st.*

CHAPTER REVIEW (FILL-IN QUESTIONS)

1-3. There is evidence that __wealthier__ people tend to be happier than __poor__ people. Less accepted is the proposition that income itself is subject to the law of __dim marg ret__; that is, that additional dollars mean less the __more__ of them we have. If true, this might provide a justification for redistributing __income__ or __wealth__ from the rich to the poor.

4-5. Pretax __income__ is much more equally distributed than __wealth__, and income appears much more equally distributed, and increasingly so, after adjustments for __taxes__ and __transfer__ payments.

6-7. __employment__ discrimination causes high unemployment rates among those who are discriminated against; __occupational__ discrimination denies them access to certain types of work; __human capital__ discrimination denies them training for remunerative jobs; and __wage__ discrimination occurs when people are paid differently for equivalent labor productivity.

8-10. People are defined as "on welfare" if the __taxes__ they pay are smaller, proportionally, than the __benefits__ they receive from government programs. Welfare programs other than AFDC include __unemploy__ compensation, social security, and such in-kind transfers as food stamps. The welfare "mess" has led to such proposals for reform as the __FAP__, which ensures payments sufficient for minimal standards of living for minor children. The __NIT__ proposal is a suggestion that all welfare programs be replaced with cash transfers based on income alone for families of different sizes. The __marg. income__ rate would always be below one to ensure that work effort was always, at least somewhat, encouraged. *tax*

STANDARD MULTIPLE CHOICE

EACH QUESTION HAS ONE BEST ANSWER.

D 1. The major ethical standard for income distribution that is most compatible with capitalism is the:
   a. traditions standard.
   b. equal distribution standard.
   c. vital necessities standard.
   d. contribution standard.
   e. needs standard.

C 2. The Marxist ideas are most closely related to a(n):
   a. contribution standard based on average productivity.
   b. equality standard.
   c. needs standard.
   d. optimal distribution of inequality.
   e. system of equal opportunity.

C 3. Contribution standards are least compatible with the idea that:
   a. income distribution according to marginal productivity is proper.
   b. markets provide fair measures of contribution.
   c. inequality is proof of inequity.
   d. laissez faire economic policies are usually appropriate.
   e. profits stimulate efficient production and economic growth.

B 4. The U.S. income inequality has NOT been intensified by:
   a. major differences among individuals in inherited wealth.
   b. consistently regressive income taxes and progressive transfers.
   c. economic discrimination based on race or gender.
   d. differences in personal attributes.
   e. differences in luck.

E 5. When comparing income and wealth in the United States:
   a. different distributions reflect economic discrimination precisely.
   b. wealth is a flow variable, while income is a stock variable.
   c. inheritance affects income more than it does wealth differences.
   d. income is much less equally distributed than wealth.
   e. income is more evenly distributed than wealth.

D 6. Roughly what proportion of pretax income is received by the bottom 40 percent of all families?
   a. roughly 2 percent.
   b. roughly 5 percent.
   c. roughly 8 percent.
   d. between 10 percent and 20 percent.
   e. between 20 percent and 30 percent.

B 7. A device that illustrates distributional variance is the:
   a. dispersion/diffusion ratio.
   b. Lorenz curve.
   c. wage/price index.
   d. Murray-Sowell graph.
   e. poverty line.

B 8. Typical age/earnings profiles:
   a. suggest no relationship between age and income.
   b. would cause measured inequality even if all families had identical incomes over their lifetimes.
   c. explain why many families never break out of the trap of poverty.
   d. indicate that, on the average, income rises continuously with age.
   e. indicate that young people earn more, on average, than their middle aged counterparts.

419

C 9. The less equal the distribution of income, the greater the:
   a. level of social stability and harmony.
   b. disincentives for work effort.
   c. area between a Lorenz curve and a 45-degree reference line.
   d. development of the market system in an economy.
   e. All of the above.

C 10. Equality in income distribution is most positively related to the:
   a. area between a Lorenz curve and a 45-degree reference line.
   b. extent of wage, price, and employment discrimination.
   c. level of industrial development in a country.
   d. degree to which the government favors socialist policies.
   e. inheritances passed between generations of wealthy families.

A 11. In the United States, majorities, or near majorities, of those living below the poverty line have:
   a. televisions, automobiles, major appliances, and other amenities possessed only by the wealthy in other countries.
   b. a razor's edge existence, only a few steps above starvation.
   c. no access to government aid of any kind.
   d. impoverishment throughout their lives.
   e. All of the above.

B 12. The proportion of the total U.S. population classified as below the poverty line if only money income is considered:
   a. rises with upturns of the business cycle.
   b. declined from 1960 to 1975, but rose during the 1980s.
   c. has been virtually eliminated by a vigorous "war on poverty".
   d. consistently covers roughly 80 percent of the same people.
   e. is far above that for most of the rest of the world.

D 13. Which of the following is false?
   a. Measured wealth is much less equally distributed than income.
   b. Tax and transfer programs redistribute disposable income more evenly.
   c. Even the most efficient of proposed welfare reforms embody strong disincentives for work.
   d. Most poor people are poor throughout their lives.
   e. Wealth and income are positively correlated.

C 14. Discrimination posing the fewest distributional problems is:
   a. wage discrimination.
   b. human capital discrimination.
   c. price discrimination.
   d. employment discrimination.
   e. occupational discrimination.

C 15. In-kind transfer payments include the:
   a. social security retirement system.
   b. unemployment compensation system.
   c. food stamp program.
   d. Aid for Families with Dependent Children (AFDC) program.
   e. negative income tax proposal.

B 16. Modern advocates of sharp cuts in transfer payments would disagree with the idea that many welfare programs have:
   a. created disincentives for production.
   b. primarily failed because of underfunding.
   c. fostered unhealthy psychological dependency among poor people.
   d. encouraged illegitimacy and broken families.
   e. caused major increases in voluntary poverty.

C 17. A program initiated to help overcome economic discrimination is:
   a. food stamps.
   b. Aid to Families with Dependent Children.
   c. affirmative action.
   d. Family allowance plans.
   e. negative income tax.

A 18. The welfare program most frequently accused of breaking up families is:
  a. Aid for Families with Dependent Children.
  b. unemployment compensation.
  c. Social Security.
  d. Medicare and Medicaid.
  e. negative income taxes.

D 19. A proposed reform that would base welfare payments strictly on family size and income, and which would reduce the inconsistencies and disincentives for work embedded in many current welfare programs, is the:
  a. guaranteed annual income.
  b. strict contribution standard.
  c. consolidated security plan.
  d. negative income tax.
  e. workfare program.   *income sole criteria for aid*

E 20. Under a negative income tax system, as the basic income floor is increased and as the marginal income tax rate of low incomes is reduced:
  a. the disincentive to the poor for earning more income is reduced.
  b. the poor have higher minimal standards of living.
  c. government outlays on welfare payments rise.
  d. a growing proportion of the population is on welfare.
  e. All of the above.

TRUE/FALSE QUESTIONS

F 1. It has been estimated that more than half of the world's people live in hunger.

F 2. It is unarguably equitable when income is distributed to resource suppliers according to their contributions to total output.

T 3. Distribution of income according to contribution is compatible with a capitalistic system.

F 4. There have been only small changes in the pretax distribution of income in the U.S. since 1950.

T 5. Families in the upper income brackets in the U.S. tend to pay higher taxes and receive fewer transfer payments than those in lower income brackets.

F 6. Our income tax system has increased the inequality of income distribution over time.

F 7. Income and wealth are statistically uncorrelated.

T 8. U.S. welfare programs primarily are intended to aid people who have both few assets and only low incomes.

F 9. Dramatic growth of welfare payments in the past thirty years has substantially reduced the proportion of the population living below the poverty line.

T 10. Human capital discrimination is one form of economic discrimination.

F 11. Most Americans have lived below the poverty line for at least one year early in their lives.

F 12. People who live below the poverty line have an average life expectancy of less than thirty years.

F 13. Numerous studies indicate that price discrimination accounts for over 25 percent of all poverty.

T_ 14. Critics of current welfare programs argue that they stimulate broken homes, illegitimacy, voluntary unemployment, the underground economy, and psychological dependency, and that they also destroy incentives to work.

T_ 15. Subsidized housing, education grants, and food stamps are all examples of in-kind payments.

T_ 16. With an income floor of 5,000 and a marginal tax rate of 40%, $12,500 would be the breakeven level of income.

F_ 17. Many European countries are considering adoption of family allowance plans modeled after the one used in the United States.

T_ 18. Critics argue that the view that poor people have been victimized by society actually harms poor people psychologically and makes it more difficult for them to succeed financially.

F_ 19. Several recent studies suggest that involuntary poverty is growing much faster than voluntary poverty.

T_ 20. Negative income tax plans would be more expensive if they have higher implicit marginal tax rates and lower income floors.

UNLIMITED MULTIPLE CHOICE

CAUTION: EACH QUESTION HAS FROM ZERO TO FOUR CORRECT ANSWERS.

___ 1. The contribution standard of distribution suggests that:
   a. resource owners deserve payment for contributions to output.
   b. paying resources for marginal productivity is efficient.
   c. the marginal productivity theory of income distribution is fair.
   d. markets economize on information needed to distribute income.

___ 2. Lorenz curves can be used to graphically illustrate the:
   a. degree of inequality in the income distribution.
   b. distribution of any quantifiable variable across a population.
   c. concentration of wealth in a society.
   d. probabilities that given political parties will win elections.

___ 3. Aid to Families with Dependent Children (AFDC) payments:
   a. are the major government program designed to alleviate poverty.
   b. are an example of an income maintenance program.
   c. provide welfare recipients with strong incentives to work.
   d. fall by roughly 50 cents for each extra dollar recipients earn.

___ 4. The percentage of families who are poor:
   a. rises during economic downswings.
   b. may be decreased through expansionary macroeconomic policies.
   c. may be decreased by increasing the job opportunities and educational opportunities available to the poor.
   d. is negatively related to the extent to which economic discrimination is practiced.

___ 5. Family allowance plans (FAPs):
   a. are common in many European nations.
   b. base payments to all families on the number of minor children.
   c. provide income floors which are then taxed as normal income.
   d. provide payments adequate to clothe and feed each minor child.

Problem 1

Break-even income under a negative income tax plan depends on its implicit marginal tax rate and the income floor. Fill in the blanks for the following problems.

a. A marginal tax rate of 40 percent and an income floor of $4,000 yields a break-even income of _____ .

b. A marginal tax rate of _____ percent and an income floor of $6,000 yields a break-even income of $15,000.

c. A marginal tax rate of 50 percent and an income floor of _____ yields a break-even income of $18,000.

d. A marginal tax rate of 60 percent and an income floor of $8,000 yields a break-even income of _____ .

e. A marginal tax rate of 25 percent and an income floor of $6,000 yields a break-even income of _____ .

ANSWERS

Matching Key Terms and Concepts

SET I

Answer	MIC	ECO
1. h	p. 426	730
2. d	p. 432	736
3. g	p. 436	740
4. b	p. 426	730
5. i	p. 427	731
6. c	p. 430	734
7. e	p. 423	727
8. f	p. 436	740
9. a	p. 432	742
10. j	p. 425	729

SET II

Answer	MIC	ECO
1. e	p. 439	743
2. g	p. 439	743
3. a	p. 439	743
4. j	p. 426	740
5. i	p. 438	742
6. c	p. 436	740
7. d	p. 437	741
8. f	p. 427	731
9. h	p. 428	732
10. b	p. 438	742

Chapter Review (Fill-in Questions)
1. rich (high income), poor (low income)
2. diminishing marginal returns, more
3. wealth, income
4. income, wealth
5. taxes, transfer
6. Employment, occupational
7. human capital, wage
8. taxes, benefits
9. unemployment, family allowance plan (FAP)
10. negative income tax (NIT), marginal income tax

Standard Multiple Choice

Answer	MIC	ECO
1. d	p. 425	729
2. c	p. 426	730
3. c	p. 425	729
4. b	p. 427	731
5. e	p. 428-429	732-733
6. d	p. 427	731
7. b	p. 427	731
8. b	p. 430	
9. c	p. 428	732
10. c	p. 428	732
11. a	p. 430	734
12. b	p. 432	736
13. d	p. 431	735
14. c	p. 436	740
15. c	p. 438	742
16. b	p. 438	742
17. c	p. 436	740
18. a	p. 437	741
19. d	p. 439	743
20. e	p. 439	743

True/False Questions

Answer	MIC	ECO
1. T	p. 423	727
2. F	p. 425	729
3. T	p. 425	729
4. T	p. 427	731
5. T	p. 430	734
6. F	p. 427	731
7. F	p. 429	733
8. T	p. 436	739
9. F	p. 437	741
10. T	p. 436	740
11. F	p. 433	737
12. F	p. 424	728
13. F	p. 436	740
14. T	p. 438	742
15. F	p. 438	742
16. T	p. 439	743
17. F	p. 439	743
18. T	p. 438	742
19. F	p. 432	736
20. F	p. 439	743

Unlimited Multiple Choice

Answer	MIC	ECO
1. abcd	p. 425	729
2. abc	p. 427	731
3. abd	p. 437	741
4. abc	p. 433	737
5. abcd	p. 439	743

Problem 1
MIC p. 439; ECO 743
a. $10,000
b. 40
c. $9,000
d. $13,333
e. $24,000

CHAPTER THIRTY-SIX
INTERNATIONAL TRADE

CHAPTER OBJECTIVES

After you have studied this chapter, you should be able to explain why the gains from free trade generally outweigh any losses from free trade; describe the major influences on the composition of a country's imports and exports; and distinguish valid arguments against free trade from arguments that are invalid or abused.

CHAPTER REVIEW: KEY POINTS

1. International trade is important to people throughout the world. The smaller and less diversified an economy is, the greater is the importance of its international trade.

2. The *law of comparative advantage* suggests that there will be net gains to all trading parties whenever their pretrade relative opportunity costs and price structures differ between goods.

3. A country's *consumption possibilities frontier* (*CPF*) expands beyond its production possibilities frontier (PPF) with the onset of trade, or with the removal of trade restrictions.

4. The *terms of trade* are the prices of exports relative to the costs of imports. An *adverse change* in the terms of trade lowers the country's CPF, while a favorable change in the terms of trade expands it.

5. Gains from trade arise because international transactions (a) provide unique goods that would not otherwise be available, (b) allow highly specialized industries to exploit economies of scale, (c) speeds the spread of technology and facilitates capital accumulation, (d) encourages peaceful international relations, and (e) facilitates specialization according to comparative advantage.

6. Domestic producers of imported goods may suffer short term losses from trade, as do domestic consumers of exported goods. However, their losses are overshadowed by the specialization gains to the consumers of imports and the producers of exports. The gainers could always use parts of their gains to compensate the losers so that, on balance, no one loses. Moreover, uniqueness, scale, dynamic, and political gains from trade make it unlikely that anyone loses from trade in the long run.

7. Even the most valid of the arguments against free trade are substantially overworked. The arguments that are semi-valid include the ideas that: (a) the income redistributions from trade are undesirable; (b) desirable diversity within a narrow economy is hampered by free trade; (c) national defense requires restrictions to avoid dependence on foreign sources, and (more validly) export restrictions to keep certain technologies out of the hands of potential enemies; and (d) major exporters of a commodity can exercise monopolistic power by restricting exports, while important consuming nations can exercise monopsonistic power through import restrictions.

8. Any exercise of international monopoly/monopsony power invites retaliation and causes worldwide economic inefficiency. Those who lose because of *trade restrictions* will lose far more than is gained by the "winners."

9. If trade is to be restricted, *tariffs* are preferable to *quotas* because of the higher tax revenues and the smaller incentives for bribery and corruption.

10. *Trade adjustment assistance* is one way that the gainers from trade might compensate the losers so that all would gain. However, the difficulty of identifying the losers and the failure to fund this program adequately have resulted in mounting pressures for trade restrictions.

MATCHING KEY TERMS AND CONCEPTS

SET I

___ 1. arbitrage

    a. Saving and investment fostered by higher real income and transfers of technology.

___ 2. law of comparative advantage

    b. Special taxes or quantitative limits on imports or exports.

___ 3. terms of trade

    c. Interdependence raises the costs of conflict.

___ 4. specialization gains from trade

    d. (Prices of exports)/(prices of imports).

___ 5. political gains from trade

    e. Riskless profit-taking by buying low and selling high.

___ 6. principle of absolute advantage

    f. Potential gains from trade among countries exist when relative pretrade costs differ.

___ 7. tariffs and quotas

    g. The expansion of a CPF beyond a PPF that occurs with trade because production costs differ between countries.

___ 8. dumping

    h. Arise because some countries lack certain resources.

___ 9. dynamic gains

    i. Selling cheaper abroad than domestically.

___ 10. uniqueness gains

    j. Sell those goods which you produce most, buy those goods which you produce least.

___ 1.	predatory dumping	a.	An overused but legitimate argument against trade that is probably more valid as a restraint on exports than imports.
___ 2.	infant industry protection	b.	Implicitly assumes that trade is a zero-sum game.
___ 3.	diversification	c.	Generally reduced by protectionist policies.
___ 4.	job destruction	d.	Problems better dealt with by other policies, not protection.
___ 5.	balance of payments deficits	e.	Selling below cost to eradicate foreign competitors.
___ 6.	economic power and growth	f.	Policies to protect emerging industries from mature foreign competition.
___ 7.	trade adjustment assistance	g.	This argument against trade may apply in smaller countries but not in large ones.
___ 8.	national defense	h.	Allows gainers from trade to offset hardships on losers.
___ 9.	exercising monopoly/monopsony power	i.	An argument that ignores employment in export industries and assumes that if foreigners don't produce, we will.
___ 10.	exploitation doctrine	j.	Policies that may allow a powerful country to gain, but less than the rest of the world will lose.

CHAPTER REVIEW (FILL-IN QUESTIONS)

1-6. With no trade, a country's sustainable _____ frontier is limited to its _____ frontier. When trade commences, the uniqueness and specialization gains from trade can be illustrated by a shift in the _____, but not the _____. Gainers include sellers of _____ and buyers of _____; losers include buyers of _____ and sellers of _____. However, trade is a _____ sum game, so that the _____ can (at least theoretically) compensate the _____ so that all would _____.

7-8. _____ gains from trade arise because some countries simply do not have certain resources possessed by others. Rising real incomes stimulate saving and investment, a major source of the _____ gains from trade, which also arise through international transfers of _____. Additionally, _____ gains emerge because trade encourages peace due to the interdependencies associated with the higher incomes from trade. The increases in economic welfare that can be realized through international specialization and exchange are qualitatively the same as those that can be achieved through domestic specialization and exchange.

9-10. Problems of undesirable income _____ from trade can be offset by _____ to those who lose from freer trade. Generally, import _____ pose more problems than do import _____ as barriers to trade because of the inherent incentives for corruption and the reduced flexibility of response to changes in demand.

STANDARD MULTIPLE CHOICE

EACH QUESTION HAS A SINGLE BEST ANSWER.

___ 1. Which of the following countries probably gains the most from international trade:
   a. the United States.
   b. the Soviet Union.
   c. Australia.
   d. the United Arab Emirates.
   e. Brazil.

___ 2. The Law of Comparative Advantage was first stated by:
   a. Reverend Thomas Malthus.
   b. David Ricardo.
   c. Adam Smith.
   d. Paul Samuelson.
   e. Alfred Marshall.

___ 3. If, in the absence of trade, an English worker can produce either 4 barrels of wine or 16 shirts weekly, while a Portuguese worker can produce either 10 barrels of wine or 20 shirts weekly:
   a. trade allows wine to exchange for between 2 and 4 shirts.
   b. Portugal has absolute advantages in both wine and shirts.
   c. England will export shirts and import wine when trade commences.
   d. England has a comparative advantage in shirtmaking.
   e. All of the above.

___ 4. When, under normal conditions, trade is expanded, the:
   a. gainers could compensate the losers so that all would gain.
   b. transactions costs of exchange inevitably rise.
   c. owners of capital gain, but workers inevitably lose.
   d. large countries gain far more than the small ones.
   e. PPFs for the trading countries shift inward.

___ 5. Arbitragers ultimately reap only normal profits because of:
   a. comparative advantages disappearing as trade commences.
   b. inevitable governmental regulation limiting profits.
   c. competition that causes prices to differ by transactions costs.
   d. competition for the political rights to receive monopoly profits.
   e. All of the above.

___ 6. When trade between two countries commences, the:
   a. consumption possibilities of both countries expand.
   b. gains from trade are shared by everyone.
   c. value of output must fall in one country if it rises in the other.
   d. gains to one trading party are offset by loses to the other.
   e. country with the highest opportunity costs will benefit the most from trade.

___ 7. If Japan imports American agricultural products and exports cars to the United States, the:
   a. American farmers gain from trade, while Japanese farmers lose.
   b. U.S. automakers may lose from trade, but American car buyers gain.
   c. Japanese carmakers and food buyers both gain from trade.
   d. total gains from trade will almost invariably exceed any losses.
   e. All of the above.

___ 8. When a small country and a large country begin trading, the:
   a. costs of imports will fall most in the large country.
   b. prices of exports will fall most in the large country.
   c. prices of exports will rise most in the large country.
   d. gains from trade tend to be greater in the small country.
   e. large country's capitalists exploit the small country's workers.

___9. NOT a predictable gain from international trade is:
   a. political spinoff gain.
   b. specialization gain.
   c. uniqueness gain.
   d. dynamic gain.
   e. monopoly power enhancement.

___10. An example of a gain from international trade occurs when:
   a. El Salvador imposes an import tariff on Guatemalan cigars.
   b. A Swedish couple drinks Brazilian coffee.
   c. French bakeries make cream cherry pastries.
   d. cheap Taiwanese watches cost Swiss watchmakers their jobs.
   e. a California drought raises the prices of Mexican tomatoes.

___11. A political spinoff gain from trade occurs when:
   a. wars and conflicts are stimulated by rising real incomes.
   b. interdependencies raise the costs of conflicts and so reduce tensions in international relations.
   c. political opponents of free trade impose high tariff barriers.
   d. countries engage in imperialistic wars in the search for markets.
   e. multinational conglomerates exploit cheap foreign labor.

___12. The dynamic gains from free trade include the:
   a. economic growth fostered by exchanges of technologies and the enhanced saving and investment made possible by higher real incomes.
   b. conquest of foreign markets through a predatory dumping policy.
   c. the spread of Christianity and middle-class values that occurs when primitive societies absorb the cultures of advanced nations.
   d. pressure for international peace that arises from independence.
   e. expansions of consumption possibilities frontiers realized strictly because pretrade cost structures differ.

___13. If emerging industries will ultimately be able to produce at lower cost than their mature foreign competitors can, the:
   a. infant industry protection argument is a valid reason for tariff barriers.
   b. consumer losses from protection may be offset so that there are net gains from such policies when prices fall later.
   c. producers will gain more from protection than consumers will lose.
   d. barriers to foreign trade are both inefficient and unnecessary for the industry to grow.
   e. government should impose export taxes on the emerging industries.

___14. Trade barriers imposed in the interest of national security:
   a. are usually valid when used to rationalize import tariffs.
   b. lower the costs of conflict by increasing interdependencies.
   c. probably apply more to restrictions on exports than on imports.
   d. are always inefficient and cause reductions in economic welfare.
   e. raise the costs of conflict by increasing independence.

___15. Arguments against free trade that apply more to small homogeneous countries than to large heterogeneous nations focus on:
   a. infant industries.
   b. job destruction.
   c. national defense.
   d. nationalistic or patriotic appeals.
   e. diversification.

___16. Some people may lose because of competition from foreign sellers or buyers of certain goods, but it is unlikely that the:
   a. specialization gains from trade ever exceed the dynamic losses.
   b. net effect of all trade in all goods is ever harmful to anyone.
   c. forces of competition will not evolve into monopoly power.
   d. trade deficits that harm them can last more than 2 or 3 years.
   e. country where they live will allow such imports to persist.

17. Special programs to assist and retrain people who lose their jobs because of liberalized international trade are known as:
    a. Aid to Families Dependent on Trade (AFDT).
    b. tariffs and quotas.
    c. Trade Adjustment Assistance.
    d. the Job Corps.
    e. reindustrialization insurance.

18. Allowing free competition after imposing tariffs that exactly offset production cost differences would:
    a. erode the potential gains from different comparative advantages.
    b. facilitate efficient diversification in the United States.
    c. be incompatible with self-sufficiency policies.
    d. be the ideal way to protect infant industries.
    e. enable arbitragers to make exorbitant profits.

19. Corruption of the governmental officials in charge of the program is most likely for a(n):
    a. scientific tariff.
    b. import quota.
    c. import tariff.
    d. tariff on exports.
    e. infant industry protection policy.

20. Of the following, the least likely reason for rising protectionist sentiment in the United States is:
    a. external pressure to shift the U.S. economy towards service and away from commodity production.
    b. job losses in senile "smoke-stack" industries because of an influx of cheaper imports.
    c. irritation because some other countries have high barriers against our exports.
    d. wide publicity for record trade and balance of payments deficits.
    e. an increasingly competitive spirit that welcomes the challenge of an international trade war.

TRUE/FALSE QUESTIONS

___ 1. The terms of trade are the prices of exports relative to the costs of imports.

___ 2. Cheap foreign imports tend to increase the problems caused by concentrated monopoly power in an economy.

___ 3. The Trade Adjustment Assistance provisions in federal laws governing international trade were intended to provide retraining and financial assistance for workers displaced because of liberalized international trade.

___ 4. When imports threaten the survival of an industry, the marketplace is signaling that the industry is extremely efficient.

___ 5. Import restrictions tend to preserve inefficient industries and to retard the growth of efficient industries.

___ 6. Predatory dumping of an industry's exports is a strategy to drive foreign competitors out of their domestic markets.

___ 7. The specialization gains from trade are positively related to differences in pretrade relative costs of production.

___ 8. Imports add to Aggregate Demand.

___ 9. The gains from trade tend to be smallest for the citizens of small, highly specialized countries.

___ 10. Economic efficiency requires all activities to be accomplished at their lowest possible opportunity costs.

___ 11. Trade will occur whenever one of the trading parties has an expectation of gain.

___12. The dynamic, political, and uniqueness losses common from free trade are normally offset by specialization gains from trade.

___13. Standards of living in the United States, more than in most countries, depend heavily on international trade.

___14. The infant industry argument for trade barriers applies very well to protection of the U.S. steel, auto, and textile industries.

___15. Dynamic gains from trade are generated by transfers of technology and the additional saving and investment made possible by higher real income.

___16. Interdependence that is stimulated by trade raises the cost of conflict between nations and is an incentive for world peace.

___17. Import quotas tend to be less flexible than tariffs in allowing adjustments to changes in demand.

___18. High trade barriers that make countries independent of foreign suppliers are more compatible with capitalism than socialism.

___19. Imports tend to raise prices and cause inflation.

___20. The overall long run effects of international trade are almost universally beneficial, although some people may be harmed in the short run by competition from foreign buyers or sellers of particular goods.

UNLIMITED MULTIPLE CHOICE

CAUTION: EACH QUESTION HAS FROM ZERO TO FOUR CORRECT ANSWERS!

___1. The consumption possibility frontier:
a. is a graphical representation of the sustainable consumption possibilities confronting a given economic system.
b. is the same as the production possibility frontier in the absence of international trade.
c. confronting a country shifts inward as a result of the country's engaging in international trade.
d. will be a straight line for a pretrade situation characterized by constant opportunity costs.

___2. Arbitrage:
a. moves relative prices toward equality in all markets.
b. can occur whenever differentials in relative prices exceed transaction costs between two markets for a good.
c. raises demand in the lower-price market, driving up its price, and raises supply in the higher-price market, driving down its price.
d. is the process of buying at a higher price in one market and selling at a lower price in another market, where both prices are known to the arbitrager and the price differential exceeds transaction costs.

___ 3. When two countries engage in international trade:
   a. the equilibrium price in the international market will exceed the original price of the good in the importing country.
   b. there are increases in the domestic production of the good being exported.
   c. there are decreases in the domestic production of the good being imported.
   d. consumers of the traded good in the exporting country pay a higher price for the good than they paid prior to trade.

___ 4. When international trade occurs:
   a. the net gains are usually positive.
   b. those who own resources that are relatively scarce worldwide realize gains exceeding any short run losses incurred by those whose resources are relatively abundant worldwide.
   c. gross losses generally exceed any gains to the participants.
   d. the prices of domestic inputs that are abundant worldwide fall, while the prices of inputs that are relatively scarce worldwide rise.

___ 5. According to the infant industry argument for the imposition of tariffs:
   a. developing domestic industries must be protected from more efficient foreign competitors.
   b. industries in their infancy are compelled to charge higher prices because of higher per unit costs of production, and, as a result, more mature foreign competitors would have an unfair price advantage over unprotected infant industries.
   c. tariffs generate much needed tax revenue which can be meted out to poor families with many infants.
   d. mature industries need to be protected from foreign competitors in order to prevent regression into the senile infant stage.

Problem 1

Table 1 indicates the numbers of roller skates and blue jeans that the United States and the Soviet Union can produce in 10 days, given their respective resources. Assume that opportunity costs increase rapidly, and that the final terms of trade fall midway between pretrade costs.

Table 1

	U.S.	U.S.S.R.	PRETRADE COSTS	POSTTRADE COSTS
Roller Skates	80	60	US _____	US _____
Blue Jeans	40	10	USSR _____	USSR _____

a. Can beneficial trade occur?_____ Why?_____
   Who would gain? _____ Why?_____

b. What principle explaining international trade is illustrated above? _____

c. Define this principle. _____

d. What are the pretrade relative prices of roller skates to jeans in the U.S.? ____ In the Soviet Union?_____

e. If international trade commences, the U.S. will produce _____ (roller skates, blue jeans, both), exporting _____ and importing _____.

432

f. If trade commences, the Soviet Union will produce _____ (roller skates, blue jeans, both); it will export _____ and import _____.

g. Assume that the international terms of trade are such that the gains from trade are evenly divided between both countries. The terms of trade will be roughly _____ (roller skates to jeans)

h. Use Panel A of Figure 1 to draw a production possibility frontier for the U.S. How is it shaped? Why? Draw the pretrade and posttrade U.S. consumption possibilities frontiers. Now use Panel B to do the same for the Soviet Union, emphasizing the relevant differences. What are they? _____

Figure 1

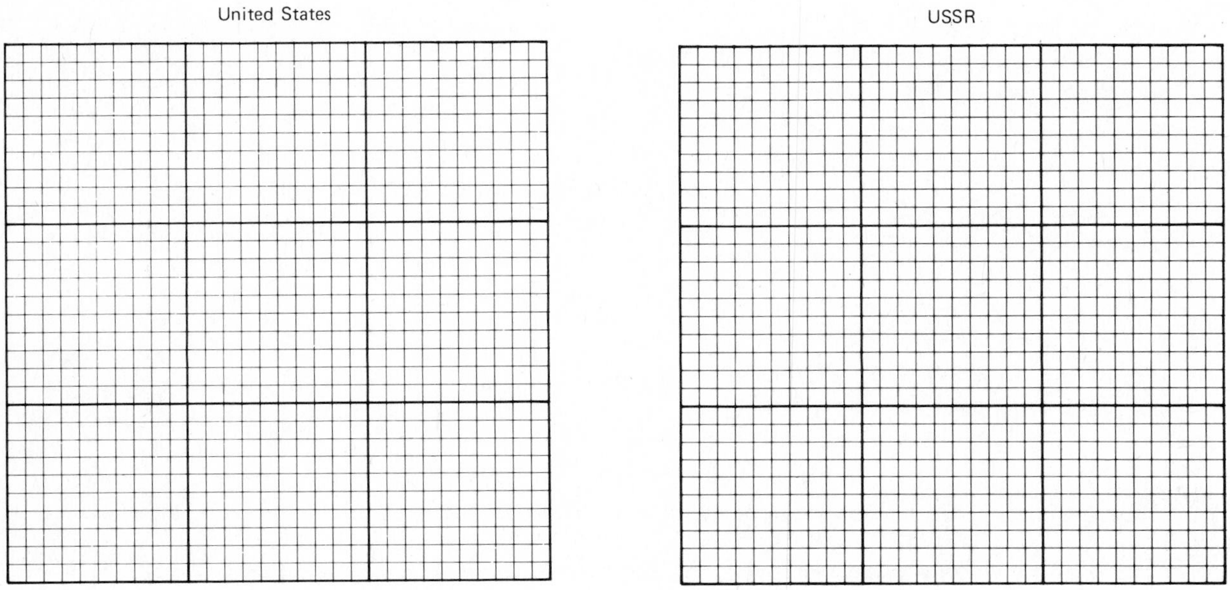

United States

USSR

Problem 2

Figure 2 depicts production possibilities curves for Countries Alpha and Beta. The international terms of trade are given by the lines *TT*; points *x* show consumption and production without international trade; points *y* indicate production combination with international trade; points *z* denote consumption combinations of these goods with international trade. Use this information to answer the following true/false questions.

Figure 2

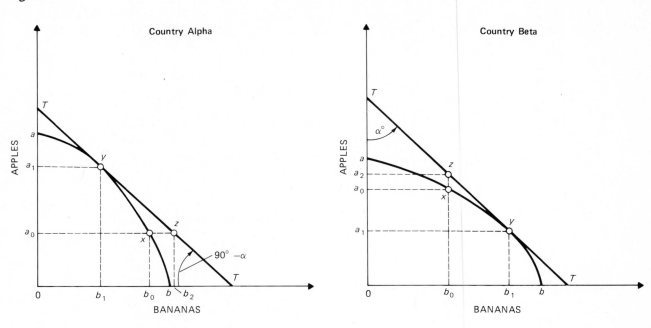

___ a. Both countries confront constant opportunity costs in the production of both apples and bananas.

___ b. The slopes of the PPF's (ab's) at points *x* are consistent with the relative pretrade costs.

___ c. Once international trade commences, country Alpha will produce only apples, while country Beta will produce only bananas.

___ d. In pretrade isolation, curves *ab* represent the consumption possibility frontiers confronting each country.

___ e. The pretrade relative costs are the same in both countries.

___ f. Free international trade can enable people in both countries to consume along higher consumption possibility frontiers.

___ g. Trade cannot yield any net benefits in this example.

___ h. Once international trade commences, country Alpha will choose to produce both commodities.

___ i. Country Alpha will export bananas and import apples.

___ j. Country Beta will export apples and import bananas.

___ k. Before trade, it is cheaper to produce bananas in country Alpha than in country Beta.

___ l. The same international terms of trade confront both countries.

ANSWERS

Matching Key Terms and Concepts

SET I

Answer	MIC	ECO	MAC
1. e	p. 450	754	408
2. f	p. 449	753	407
3. d	p. 450	754	408
4. g	p. 452	756	410
5. c	p. 452	756	410
6. j	p. 449	753	407
7. b	p. 462	764	418
8. i	p. 458	762	416
9. a	p. 452	756	410
10. h	p. 451	755	409

SET II

Answer	MIC	ECO	MAC
1. e	p. 458	762	416
2. f	p. 458	762	416
3. g	p. 461	765	417
4. i	p. 459	763	417
5. d	p. 459	763	417
6. c	p. 464	768	422
7. h	p. 456	760	414
8. a	p. 462	766	420
9. j	p. 461	765	419
10. b	p. 457	761	415

Chapter Review (Fill-in Questions)

1. consumption possibilities, production possibilities
2. CPF, PPF
3. exports, imports
4. exports, imports
5. positive, gainers
6. losers, gain
7. Uniqueness, dynamic
8. technology, political
9. redistributions, trade adjustment assistance
10. quotas, tariffs

Standard Multiple Choice

Answer	MIC	ECO	MAC
1. d	p. 447	751	405
2. b	p. 449	753	407
3. e	p. 450	754	408
4. a	p. 452	756	410
5. c	p. 450	754	408
6. a	p. 453	757	411
7. e	p. 456	760	414
8. d	p. 448	752	406
9. e	p. 452	756	410
10. b	p. 456	760	414
11. b	p. 452	756	410
12. a	p. 452	756	410
13. d	p. 458	762	416
14. c	p. 462	766	420
15. e	p. 461	765	419
16. b	p. 452	756	410
17. c	p. 456	760	414
18. a	p. 462	766	420
19. b	p. 462	766	420
20. e	p. 459	763	417

True/False Questions

Answer	MIC	ECO	MAC
1. T	p. 450	754	408
2. F	p. 461	765	419
3. T	p. 456	760	414
4. F	p. 459	763	417
5. T	p. 459	763	417
6. T	p. 458	762	416
7. T	p. 450	754	408
8. F	p. 447	751	405
9. F	p. 448	752	406
10. T	p. 450	754	408
11. F	p. 450	754	408
12. F	p. 452	756	410
13. F	p. 447	751	411
14. F	p. 458	762	416
15. T	p. 452	756	410
16. T	p. 452	756	410
17. T	p. 462	766	420
18. F	p. 462	766	420
19. F	p. 454	758	412
20. T	p. 452	756	410

Unlimited Multiple Choice

Answer	MIC	ECO	MAC
1. abd	p. 453	757	411
2. abc	p. 450	754	408
3. bcd	p. 454	758	412
4. abd	p. 454	758	412
5. ab	p. 458	762	416

Problem 1
MIC 449-453; *ECO 753-757*; **MAC 407-411**

a. Yes; differences in pretrade costs. Gainers are American jean makers and roller skate buyers and Soviet jean buyers and skate makers.

b. Both absolute and comparative advantage.

c. Gains from trade exist when pretrade costs differ.

d. 1/2; 1/6.

e. Both/jeans/roller skates.

f. Both/roller skates/jeans.

g. 1/3.

h. See Figure 3; PPF for U.S. is concave to the origin reflecting increasing opportunity costs; PPF of U.S.S.R. is also concave but skewed towards skates.

Problem 2
MIC 449-453; *ECO 753-757*; **MAC 407-411**

a. F
b. T
c. F
d. T
e. F
f. T
g. F
h. T
i. F
j. F
k. F
l. T

Figure 3

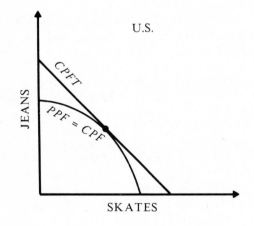

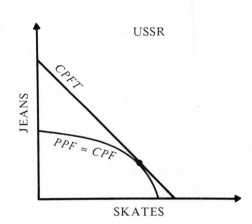

CHAPTER THIRTY-SEVEN
INTERNATIONAL FINANCE

CHAPTER OBJECTIVES

After you have studied this chapter, you should be able to discuss the advantages and disadvantages of fixed and flexible systems of international payments; the problems encountered when currency flows or exchange controls are used to maintain exchange rates at nonequilibrium values; explain the persistence of U.S. balance of payments deficits; and describe some possible reasons for the decline of the dollar from a position of undisputed primacy as the world's medium of exchange.

CHAPTER REVIEW: KEY POINTS

1. Since we have no world currency, we must establish the value of each national currency in terms of all others. The exchange rate is the value of one currency in terms of another.

2. Balance of payments accounts record the flows of money into and out of a country and provide information about trade relationships among countries.

3. Flexible, or floating, systems of exchange rates permit the values of currencies to be set by market forces. If a country experiences a balance of payments surplus (deficit) under such a system, it is an indication that the country's citizens or government (foreigners) desire foreign (domestic) currencies.

4. A fixed exchange rate system imposes price ceilings and floors on currencies, often resulting in persistent disequilibria in balances of payments.

5. Explanations for the decline of the dollar in the 1970s range from relative inflation to expectations of continued inflation and payments deficits to federal budget deficits to the emergence of other strong international currencies to the cartelization of oil to too rapid monetary growth. Opposite trends then strengthened the dollar until 1985. Each of these explanations bears the germ of truth, but none alone is adequate to explain the dance of the dollar.

MATCHING KEY TERMS AND CONCEPTS

SET I

___ 1. "dirty" float

___ 2. gold standard

___ 3. balance of trade

___ 4. exchange rates

___ 5. appreciation

___ 6. fixed exchange rates

___ 7. depreciation

___ 8. foreign exchange

___ 9. balance of payments

___ 10. flexible exchange rates

a. Most exchange rates are set by international agreement.

b. Exports minus imports.

c. When the value of one currency rises relative to others.

d. Currencies' relative prices of currencies are set by market forces.

e. Foreign exchange inflows minus funds outflows.

f. Foreign currencies, collectively.

g. Flows of funds between countries directly change money supplies and lead to macroeconomic adjustments.

h. Government intervention in a flexible exchange system.

i. The prices of currencies relative to one another

j. When a currency's value falls relative to others.

___ 1. devaluation

a. Decline of the fixed value of one currency versus others.

___ 2. dollar surplus

b. Goverments allocate the foreign exchange available to pay for imports.

___ 3. relative inflation

c. A currency that is widely held internationally for transaction, precautionary, and asset reasons.

___ 4. international portfolio adjustments

d. Potential losses to exporters who agree to accept importers' currency, or to importers who must pay in exporters' currency.

___ 5. oil imports

e. _____ of continued inflation lead to depreciation.

___ 6. exchange controls

f. A classic explanation of currency depreciation.

___ 7. international supply of dollars

g. "Mirrors" the U.S. demand for foreign exchange.

___ 8. exchange risk

h. Replacing the dollar as the asset of a central bank with some other strong currency.

___ 9. key currency

i. Caused substantial increases in the international supplies of dollars in the 1970s.

___10. expectations

j. Identical with a shortage of foreign exchange.

CHAPTER REVIEW (FILL-IN QUESTIONS)

1-2. The value of one currency in terms of another is known as its _____. A country's exports minus its imports is its _____; its inflows of funds minus its outflows is its _____. Currencies received from sales of exports are known as _____.

3-4. Under a(n) _____ exchange rate system, such as the _____ standard, payments deficits can be met by borrowing or drawing down previously accrued _____, or by _____ controls, under which government allocates the foreign currencies that are available.

5-7. One problem with flexible exchange rates is that international transactions create exchange _____; if the contract specifies payment in the _____ currency, exchange rate depreciation of that currency will cause the _____ to receive less than expected, while the importer will be forced to pay more than expected if the currency of the _____ is specified and the exchange rate of that currency appreciates. These problems can be finessed, however, if the traders negotiate a contract in either currency and then "buy insurance" against _____ by dealing in the _____ market for foreign exchange.

8-10. In the past half century, the United States has persistently run _____ in its balance of payments. This has been possible because, internationally, the dollar has been a _____ currency. Foreigners have demanded dollars to facilitate transactions, even when American traders are not involved. Our relative political and economic stability have also caused foreigners to demand dollars for _____ and _____ reasons. The ability of the FED to issue "international money" has allowed Americans to reap _____ because of the huge difference between the _____ of dollars and their value in exchange.

STANDARD MULTIPLE CHOICE

EACH QUESTION HAS A SINGLE BEST ANSWER.

_____ 1. A country that exports more than it imports experiences a:
- a. balance of payments surplus.
- b. deficit in its national budget.
- c. balance of trade deficit.
- d. deficit in its balance of payments.
- e. balance of trade surplus.

_____ 2. The major reason for Americans to demand foreign money is to:
- a. add to collections of rare stamps and coins.
- b. pay for imports or foreign investments.
- c. profit from seignorage by printing dollars.
- d. finance tourist visits to foreign countries.
- e. avoid U.S. income tax liabilities.

_____ 3. Americans demand foreign currencies by:
- a. exporting capital goods.
- b. supplying dollars.
- c. running balance of trade surpluses.
- d. creating shortages of U.S. currency.
- e. following inflationary policies.

_____ 4. A gold standard is an example of a:
- a. fixed exchange rate system.
- b. nondiscretionary "pegged" currency.
- c. flexible exchange rate system.
- d. "dirty float."
- e. "crawling peg" automatic stabilizer.

_____ 5. Stocks of foreign currencies that have been received to cover international payments are:
- a. gold coins and bullion.
- b. foreign exchange.
- c. international seignorage.
- d. bills of lading.
- e. international transfer payments.

_____ 6. A currency's value as measured by a foreign currency is known as the:
- a. exchange rate.
- b. terms of trade.
- c. reciprocal value.
- d. counter price.
- e. par value.

_____ 7. Currency revaluation under a gold standard would parallel:
- a. depreciation under a silver standard.
- b. appreciation under a flexible exchange rates.
- c. devaluation under fixed exchange rates.
- d. recycling under an ecological system.
- e. repricing costs in an inflationary system.

_____ 8. A balance of payments surplus could result from:
- a. international surpluses of the country's currency.
- b. falling imports and rising exports.
- c. contractionary policies by its trading partners.
- d. shifting from a fixed to a floating exchange rate system.
- e. overseas investments by domestic firms.

_____ 9. Reversal of a payments deficit if all countries were on a gold standard might entail:
- a. revaluation of the country's currency relative to other currencies.
- b. depreciation of the currency through normal market processes.
- c. contractionary macroeconomic adjustments.
- d. discoveries of new gold supplies in the deficit country.
- e. decreasing Aggregate Demands in surplus countries.

_____ 10. If American balance of payments deficits indicate disequilibrium, the markets for currencies of countries experiencing balance of payments surpluses are characterized by:
- a. shortages.
- b. surpluses.
- c. unusual scarcity.
- d. overproduction.
- e. excessive supply.

11. Appreciation will eliminate a balance of payments surplus most rapidly when:
    a. foreign demands for a country's exports and domestic demands for imports are both extremely inelastic.
    b. foreign demands for exports and domestic demands for imports are both elastic.
    c. domestic exchange controls are rigid.
    d. inflows of foreign exchange are used to pay for all foreign purchases.
    e. none of the above.

12. An American balance of payments deficit would be reduced by:
    a. increased U.S. foreign aid programs.
    b. increased imports by consumers.
    c. greater levels of foreign investment by American corporations.
    d. lower prices for imported goods that are elastically demanded by U.S. consumers.
    e. greater foreign purchases of the bonds of American corporations.

13. A substantial increase in the national income of a country will:
    a. cause a balance of payments surplus under a fixed exchange rate system.
    b. generate pressure for the country's currency to be revalued upward.
    c. cause its exports to increase dramatically.
    d. cause devaluation under a flexible exchange rate system.
    e. create pressure for the depreciation of the exchange rate of its currency.

14. Since 1946, relative to the U.S. balance of payments, our balance of trade has:
    a. far more often been in deficit.
    b. balanced or been in surplus quite often.
    c. consistently been in deficit.
    d. consistently experienced larger deficits.
    e. None of the above.

15. The dollar's position as a key international currency has:
    a. allowed Americans to gain through seignorage by issuing international money.
    b. been a major reason for loss of U.S. power and prestige.
    c. stimulated growth of federal deficits.
    d. driven our balance of trade into persistent surpluses.
    e. dampened economic growth internationally.

16. A hike in international oil prices will cause the dollar to fall more under a flexible exchange rate system if:
    a. foreigners believe that the FED will accommodate these hikes with expansionary monetary policies.
    b. our demands for imports and foreign demands for our exports are both quite inelastic.
    c. foreigners quickly lose faith in the dollar when its exchange rate falls even slightly.
    d. other countries with strong currencies are less dependent on imported oil.
    e. All of the above.

17. Which of the following has not been offered seriously as an explanation for the 1970s decline of the dollar?
    a. OPEC petroleum price hikes.
    b. expectations of continued relative inflation in the United States.
    c. rapid increases in the price of gold.
    d. overly expansionary U.S. monetary policy.
    e. the increasing stability and acceptability of other currencies.

18. Until roughly 1970, foreign central bankers could exchange:
    a. $35 to the U.S. Treasury for an ounce of gold.
    b. deficits in their balance of payments for U.S. Treasury bonds.
    c. international loans at a fixed interest rate at the World Bank.
    d. surpluses for silver certificates issued by the International Monetary Fund.
    e. trade surpluses for United Nations payments.

___19. If exporters' currency appreciates, exchange risk losses could be imposed on:
   a. importers who insisted on paying in their own currency.
   b. exporters who insisted on being paid in their own currency.
   c. arbitragers who exploited price differentials between markets.
   d. importers who agreed to pay in the exporters' currency.
   e. speculators who had bought the exporters' currency earlier.

___20. Consistent U.S. balance of payments deficits are partially explained by:
   a. demands in unstable countries for economically stable currencies.
   b. desires by foreign governments to bolster growth by stimulating exports.
   c. habits developed when the dollar was the only currency convertible to gold, permitting the United States to become the world's money producer.
   d. greater foreign demands for dollars than for American goods.
   e. All of the above.

TRUE/FALSE QUESTIONS

___ 1. The exchange rate is the value of a currency in terms of itself.

___ 2. If the dollar value of imports exceeds the dollar value of exports, there is a deficit in our balance of trade.

___ 3. An international gold standard would be an example of a fixed exchange rate system.

___ 4. Under a flexible exchange rate system currencies' relative values are largely determined by markets.

___ 5. An international gold standard was established by the United Nations at the end of World War I.

___ 6. Foreigners demand dollars primarily because this enables them to import U.S. goods or invest in the United States.

___ 7. Unlike other prices, exchange rates seldom change under a system of flexible exchange rates.

___ 8. As is true of markets for virtually all goods, flexible exchange rate systems tend to drive the prices of all currencies to the equilibrium rates at which supply and demand intersect.

___ 9. "Dirty floats" tend to hamper flexible exchange rates so that they change less than they otherwise might.

___10. Exchange controls create pressures for government corruption and black markets for foreign currencies.

___11. Governments can more independently conduct macroeconomic policies under a flexible than under a fixed exchange rate system.

___12. Between the end of World War II and 1971, the U.S. dollar was the only major world currency that consistently was backed by gold, at least for purposes of international trade.

___13. The international acceptability of the U.S. dollar has been the major reason that the U.S. has been able to run large and persistent deficits between 1951 and the present.

___14. There is a growing perception internationally that, more than anywhere else, the U.S. has a long-term commitment to highly deflationary policies.

___15. In 1985, almost all of the dollars held by OPEC countries were exchanged for other currencies.

___16. International transactions demands for dollars arise because exporters in many countries view dollars as less prone to exchange risk than the currencies of their customers.

____17. International demands for dollars have enabled the United States to offset persistent payments deficits with trade surpluses.

____18. Other countries have been far more successful than the United States in reaping seignorage from international financial markets.

____19. Foreign loans by U.S. organizations have accounted for most of the recent surpluses in U.S. balances of payments.

____20. A "dirty float" occurs when foreign central banks buy dollars from international money markets and store the dollars in their vaults.

UNLIMITED MULTIPLE CHOICE

CAUTION: EACH QUESTION HAS FROM ZERO TO FOUR CORRECT RESPONSES.

____1. Balance of payments:
   a. deficits occur when a country's receipts of money from foreigners exceed its payments of money to foreigners.
   b. accounts use double-entry bookkeeping.
   c. record financial flows among countries that trade internationally.
   d. surpluses occur when a country's receipts of money from foreigners exceed its payments of money to foreigners.

____2. If there is a fixed exchange rate system and a country's currency is characterized by a:
   a. surplus, then its balance of payments tends to be in surplus.
   b. shortage, then its balance of payments tends to be in surplus.
   c. lower demand by foreigners than it has demand for foreign exchange, then there is an international surplus of its currency.
   d. greater demand by foreigners than it has demand for foreign exchange, then there is an international shortage of its currency.

____3. Fixed exchange rates:
   a. respond more quickly than do flexible exchange rates to changes in relative supplies and demands for currencies.
   b. pose no special problems as long as exchange rates reflect the relative supplies and demands for currencies.
   c. distort the true values of all currencies.
   d. cause no problems as long as their values are the same as the values that would exist under flexible exchange rates.

____4. The United States has been able to run balance of payments deficits fairly consistently for almost four decades because dollars:
   a. are widely used as an international medium of exchange.
   b. have been viewed as "insurance" in politically unstable countries.
   c. have been supported at artificially high exchange rates by West Germany, Japan, etc., to boost U.S. demands for their exports (or, perhaps, to indirectly pay for U.S. provision of national defense).
   d. create volatility in the exchange rates of monkey currencies.

___ 5. An increased American preference for
Japanese goods:
    a. will manifest itself in a decreased
American demand for the yen.
    b. will manifest itself in an increased
American supply of dollars in foreign
exchange markets.
    c. means that American importers of
Japanese goods may be forced to pay
higher dollar prices.
    d. implies a depreciation of the yen in terms
of the dollar.

PROBLEM 1

Use Figure 1, which depicts markets for the U.S. dollar and the British pound, to answer the following questions.

Figure 1

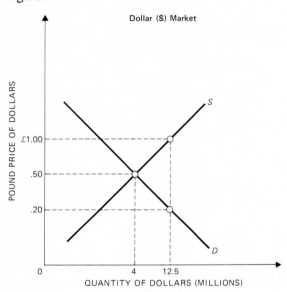

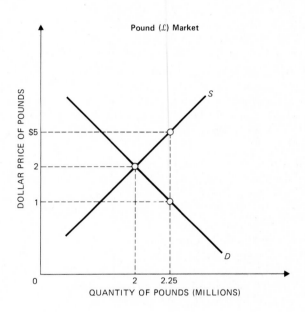

a. What is the equilibrium exchange rate of the dollar? _____

b. What is the equilibrium exchange rate of the pound? _____

c. What is the per unit (pound) price of a dollar? _____

d. What is the per unit price of a U.S. dollar? _____

e. Explain why the U.S. demand for British pounds is downward sloping. _____

f. Explain why the British supply of pounds is upward sloping. _____

g. Suppose Americans purchase British goods valued at $2 million. Americans demand _____ British pounds
in equilibrium and supply _____ dollars.

h. Assume the British manifest an increased preference for U.S. goods. Which curves will shift and why? _____ What happens to the British pound? _____ What happens to the dollar? _____ What happens to the pound price of American exports to Britain? _____ What happens to the dollar price of U.S. imports from Britain? _____

i. Assume that the new equilibrium exchange rate is $1 = 1 pound. What is the equilibrium exchange rate of the dollar? _____ Suppose that Britain purchases U.S. goods whose value is $2.5 million. This implies a British demand for dollars of _____ and a British supply of _____.

j. Return to the original equilibrium exchange rate; that is, $.50 = 1 pound. If the exchange rate is pegged artificially high at $1 = 1 pound, what situation would prevail in the U.S. balance of payments? _____ Why? _____

PROBLEM 2

The balance of payments accounts for the country of Sata is listed below.

Table 1

Sata Balance of Payments for 1992 (millions of suntories)

	Receipts	Payments	Balance
Current Account			
1. Merchandise Exports	+220		
2. Merchandise Imports		-328	
Trade Balance			____
3. Net Investment Income	____		
4. Net Services		-1	
5. Net Unilateral Transfers		-11	
Current Account Balance			-102
Capital Account			
6. Capital Outflows		____	
7. Capital Inflows	+93		
8. Statistical Discrepancy	+36		
Official Reserve Transactions Balance			+6
Method of Financing			
9. Increase in Sata Official Reserve Assets		-9	
10. Increase in Foreign Official Assets	____		
Total Financing of Surplus			-6

a. Fill in the missing entries.

b. The trade balance is equal to _____. This indicates a trade (surplus/deficit).

c. The sum of numbers 1 through 10 equals _____. Is this is coincidence? _____

d. The statistical discrepancy accounts for what kinds of transactions? _____

ANSWERS

Matching Key Terms and Concepts

SET I

Answer	ECO	MAC
1. h	p. 784	p. 438
2. g	p. 775	p. 429
3. b	p. 772	p. 426
4. i	p. 774	p. 428
5. c	p. 774	p. 428
6. a	p. 783	p. 437
7. j	p. 775	p. 429
8. f	p. 775	p. 429
9. e	p. 772	p. 426
10. d	p. 779	p. 433

SET II

Answer	ECO	MAC
1. a	p. 775	p. 429
2. j	p. 779	p. 433
3. f	p. 787	p. 441
4. h	p. 787	p. 441
5. i	p. 788	p. 442
6. b	p. 782	p. 436
7. g	p. 776	p. 430
8. d	p. 780	p. 434
9. c	p. 785	p. 439
10. e	p. 787	p. 441

Chapter Review (fill-in Questions)

1. exchange rate, balance of trade
2. balance of payments, foreign exchange
3. fixed, gold
4. foreign exchange, exchange
5. risk, importer's
6. exporter, exporter
7. exchange risk, forward
8. deficits, key
9. precautionary, asset
10. seignorage, production costs

Standard Multiple Choice

Answer	ECO	MAC
1. e	p. 772	p. 426
2. b	p. 776	p. 430
3. b	p. 776	p. 430
4. a	p. 775	p. 429
5. b	p. 775	p. 429
6. a	p. 774	p. 428
7. b	p. 775	p. 429
8. b	p. 772	p. 426
9. c	p. 781	p. 435
10. a	p. 778	p. 432
11. b	p. 775	p. 429
12. e	p. 772	p. 426
13. e	p. 777	p. 431
14. b	p. 777	p. 431
15. a	p. 772	p. 426
16. e	p. 788	p. 442
17. c	p. 788	p. 442
18. a	p. 785	p. 439
19. d	p. 780	p. 434
20. e	p. 785	p. 439

True/false Questions

Answer	ECO	MAC
1. F	p. 774	p. 428
2. T	p. 772	p. 426
3. T	p. 775	p. 429
4. T	p. 779	p. 433
5. F	p. 783	p. 437
6. F	p. 785	p. 439
7. F	p. 779	p. 433
8. T	p. 779	p. 433
9. T	p. 784	p. 438
10. T	p. 782	p. 436
11. T	p. 781	p. 435
12. T	p. 785	p. 439
13. T	p. 785	p. 439
14. F	p. 781	p. 435
15. F	p. 788	p. 442
16. T	p. 788	p. 442
17. F	p. 785	p. 439
18. F	p. 785	p. 439
19. F	p. 788	p. 442
20. T	p. 784	p. 438

Unlimited Multiple Choice

Answer	ECO	MAC
1. bcd	p. 772	p. 426
2. bd	p. 776-777	p. 430-431
3. bd	p. 783	p. 437
4. abc	p. 784-785	p. 438-439
5. bc	p. 776-777	p. 430-431

Problem 1
ECO pp. 774-778; MAC 428-432

a. .50
b. $2
c. .50
d. $2
e. law of demand; refer to text
f. law of supply; refer to text
g. 1 million; $2 million
h. demand for dollars increases and the supply of pounds increases; depreciates; appreciates; increases; decreases.
i. 1 pound; $2.5 million; L 2.5 million
j. surplus; shortage of dollars due to exchange rate imbalance.

Problem 2
ECO pp. 772-773; MAC 426-427

a. See Table 2

Table 2

Sata Balance of Payments for 1992 (millions of suntories)

	Receipts	Payments	Balance
Current Account			
1. Merchandise Exports	+220		
2. Merchandise Imports		-328	
Trade Balance			**-108**
3. Net Investment Income	**+18**		
4. Net Services		-1	
5. Net Unilateral Transfers		-11	
Current Account Balance			-102
Capital Account			
6. Capital Outflows		**-21**	
7. Capital Inflows	+93		
8. Statistical Discrepancy	+36		
Official Reserve Transactions Balance			+6
Method of Financing			
9. Increase in Sata Official Reserve Assets		-9	
10. Increase in Foreign Official Assets	**+3**		
Total Financing of Surplus			-6

b. -108; deficit
c. 0; no
d. Transactions not easily accounted (illegal and small transactions).

447

CHAPTER THIRTY-EIGHT

CAPITALISM AND ITS ALTERNATIVES

CHAPTER OBJECTIVES

After you have read and studied this chapter you should be able to discuss why capitalism attracts its advocates and repulses its critics; some difficulties faced by central planners, and how planners try to cope with the absence of market mechanisms; and how systems of production and distribution differ in alternative economic systems.

CHAPTER REVIEW: KEY POINTS

1. *Libertarianism* is a philosophy that rejects almost all but the simplest government activities. It strongly advocates laissez faire capitalism.

2. *Anarchy* is the absence of government. *Syndicalism* is a system in which an industry's workers own the means of production, which are controlled by democratically elected worker councils. Syndicates are effectively trade unions that own their industries.

3. Socialism entails eliminating private ownership of nonhuman productive resources, which would be owned collectively.

4. *Marxism* is based on *dialectical materialism,* which suggests that the course of human history is determined by clashes between an economic *thesis* and its *antithesis* that yield a *synthesis,* or progression, for human life.

5. Marxism postulates conflicts between economic classes that emerge from the theft by capitalists of *surplus values,* which are the excesses of production over subsistence wages. These surplus values are translated into accumulations of capital.

6. Marx predicted (a) growing wretchedness and unemployment of the working class, (b) ever-greater concentrations of capital, (c) declining rates of profit, (d) explosive business cycles, (e) increasingly aggressive imperialistic policies, and (f) bloody revolutions as capitalist economies reached full maturity. In most respects, except for the (now slowing) concentration of capital, these predictions seem erroneous.

7. The Soviet Union and the People's Republic of China have used *central planning* extensively, and have managed very high growth rates in their command economies by forcing consumption down in order to raise social saving and investment. These economies have been plagued with inefficiency; great loss of freedom has been just one cost of their rapid economic development. China and the USSR both seem increasingly willing to let market forces operate now that pragmatic new leaders are at the helm.

8. *Indicative planning* is used in France to coordinate the activities of industries, unions, and government. Although not as bureaucratic as Soviet central planning, government has used strong legal and economic sanctions to ensure compliance with its plans.

9. Northern European nations such as Sweden have extensive welfare programs financed by heavy tax rates. However, industry is largely in private hands, and labor productivity is as high as anywhere in the world.

10. *Worker management* of industry has been used in Yugoslavia, which has rejected Soviet-style central planning in favor of indicative planning. The results of this experiment in syndicalism have been mixed, but have attracted attention.

11. Perhaps the most radical criticisms of capitalism and all economies based on material production assume that the proper solution to scarcity is to curtail our material wants and to simplify the economy as much as possible, even if it requires large losses of production. Somewhat less radical critics argue that there are *limits to growth,* and that we must all learn to live with less.

MATCHING KEY TERMS AND CONCEPTS

SET I

___ 1. embodied labor

a. Targets for industrial production are a major planning mechanism.

___ 2. labor theory of value

b. The value of any commodity is proportional to the labor time socially necessary for its production.

___ 3. libertarianism

c. All commodities and capital, according to Marxist theory.

___ 4. indicative planning

d. Is determined by demand.

___ 5. dialectical materialism

e. Resolutions of economic inconsistencies govern historical changes.

___ 6. Christian socialism

f. The difference between wages and the value of output.

___ 7. Fabian socialism

g. Only heavy industry would be nationalized under this system.

___ 8. "socially necessary" labor

h. Emphasizes the dignity of labor and advocates labor unions.

___ 9. surplus value

i. Government should be eliminated completely because it is inherently evil.

___10. anarchism

j. Government should only protect property rights and enforce contracts.

SET II

___ 1.	Buddhist economics	a.	Nowhere; or visionary idealism.
___ 2.	laissez faire	b.	The view that physical and chemical interactions between things determine all of history.
___ 3.	limits to growth	c.	Our current consumption levels are unsustainable.
___ 4.	class warfare	d.	Workers own and manage their industries.
___ 5.	materialism	e.	Government should follow "hands off" policies.
___ 6.	syndicalism	f.	Hallmark of a command economy.
___ 7.	utopian	g.	A fundamental for any market system.
___ 8.	central planning	h.	Capitalist ownership, but distribution is primarily social.
___ 9.	property rights	i.	A symptom of capitalism's contradictions according to Marxists.
___ 10.	welfare state	j.	Materialism and industrialization demean human beings.

SET III

(Note: Each country corresponds best to only one attribute.)

___ 1.	Great Britain	a.	Welfare state
___ 2.	Soviet Union	b.	Indicative planning
___ 3.	Yugoslavia since Tito	c.	"New Man"
___ 4.	China under Mao	d.	Worker management
___ 5.	France since World War II	e.	Command economy par excellence.
___ 6.	Twentieth Century Sweden	f.	Hotbed of alternative economic theories
___ 7.	United States	g.	The most capitalistic of modern economies.

CHAPTER REVIEW (FILL-IN) QUESTIONS

1-2. An early American syndicalist movement was the _____, whose members were known as "_____." Many American firms have _____ plans that are somewhat syndicalist in nature, while unions push for worker participation in managerial _____.

3-5. Revolutionary socialism is epitomized by _____, whose greatest prophet was _____. Aided by _____, a factory owner, he developed _____, a theory of historical change. According to this theory, capitalism is plagued by _____ because of _____ between the interests of capitalists and workers.

6-9. _____ has been the most determined of communist nations to accomplish a rapid "withering away" of the state, and its industries are _____ by worker committees. It follows an _____ scheme of coordination much like that used in _____. Of all capitalist nations, _____ has the highest average tax burden, which it imposes to finance its activities as the epitome of the modern _____. Most heavy industry in _____ has been nationalized, but this hot house of economic theories has been plagued by stagnation because, unlike many socialist countries, it has not successfully stimulated modernization through substantial _____.

10. Some critics of both capitalism and Marxism focus on what they see as excessive materialism, and argue for the simple life. The most notable of these critics either follow the premises of Mohandas Gandhi, whose thought has been characterized as _____, or argue that there are _____ because finite and exhaustible resources are being depleted. Both of these schools of thought oppose substantial industrialization and would scale down the level of economic activity throughout the world.

STANDARD MULTIPLE CHOICE

EACH QUESTIONS HAS ONE BEST ANSWER

___ 1. The economic perspective views broadly defined legal rights as determining the:
   a. structure of property rights.
   b. fairness and morality of particular activities.
   c. amount by which capitalists can exploit workers.
   d. rate of economic growth and development.
   e. types of technologies used in production.

___ 2. Which of the following is not a school of Socialism:
   a. Utopian Socialism.
   b. Fabian Socialism.
   c. Christian Socialism.
   d. Dialectical Socialism.
   e. Revolutionary Socialism.

___ 3. Which of the following is least compatible with the idea of private property rights?
   a. libertarianism.
   b. anarchism.
   c. laissez-faire policies.
   d. syndicalism.
   e. capitalism.

___ 4. The "wobblies" were:
   a. the group responsible for nationalizing British heavy industry.
   b. in favor of collective bargaining and profit sharing.
   c. Russian liberals who were overthrown by V.I. Lenin's Bolsheviks.
   d. instrumental in establishing Yugoslavian worker committees.
   e. an early group of violent radicals who sought to take over American industry.

___5. The idea that government should act as trustee over most property resources, which would be owned collectively by everyone in society, is the central thread running through:
  a. radicalism.
  b. pacifism.
  c. classicism.
  d. socialism.
  e. liberalism.

___6. The idea that workers should jointly own the industries they work in, with control through "workers' councils" is known as:
  a. libertarianism.
  b. syndicalism.
  c. anarchism.
  d. sovietism.
  e. Cuba libre.

___7. The virtues of work and unionization are most central to:
  a. Utopian socialism.
  b. Christian socialism.
  c. Marxist socialism.
  d. Fabian socialism.
  e. Fourier communes.

___8. The English Labour Party evolved most directly from:
  a. Utopian socialism.
  b. anarcho-syndicalism.
  c. Fabian socialism.
  d. Marxist-Leninism.
  e. Christian socialism.

___9. A blend of Christian socialism and revolutionary Marxism yielded the movement known as:
  a. Islamic Jihad.
  b. liberation theology.
  c. Red Cross.
  d. dialectical mysticism.
  e. secular humanism.

___10. Marx's chief collaborator and best friend was the industrialist:
  a. Sir Thomas More.
  b. Robert Owen.
  c. Friedrich Engels.
  d. Prince Kropotkin.
  e. William Godfrey.

___11. Dialectical interactions of thesis and antithesis lead to:
  a. psychokinesis.
  b. photosynthesis.
  c. hypothesis.
  d. synthesis.
  e. dissertation.

___12. Marxists refer to working class people as the :
  a. proletariat.
  b. petit bourgeoisie.
  c. plebians.
  d. protagonists.
  e. producers.

___13. A partially accurate Marxist prediction was:
  a. persistent declines in the average rate of profit.
  b. cyclically increasing rates of unemployment.
  c. explosive business cycles.
  d. worker revolutions sweeping advanced industrial societies first.
  e. growth in industrial concentration, although that trend has abated.

___14. Marxist jargon views all interest, rent, and profit as:
  a. surplus values.
  b. exploitation indicators.
  c. concentration indicators.
  d. dialectical materials.
  e. economic dialectics.

15. The labor theory of value:
    a. was thoroughly refuted by Adam Smith.
    b. is totally wrong according to Marxist theory.
    c. was once widely accepted by almost all Keynesians.
    d. asserts that value is directly proportional to the socially necessary labor that commodities embody.
    e. All of the above.

16. A modern Marxist might rebut a libertarian argument by asserting that freedom under capitalism:
    a. allows excessive unemployment and inflation.
    b. is enjoyed only by rich people; allowing miserable poor people to starve is not true freedom.
    c. is less important than the social injustice of capitalism.
    d. may be enjoyed by many Americans, but it is bought through exploitation of the sweat of poor workers in Third World countries.
    e. All of the above.

17. In the early 1980s, the country that was most rapidly replacing rigid central planning with market incentives was:
    a. India under Gandhi.
    b. the Soviet Union under Gorbachev.
    c. Sweden under Premier Olaf Palme.
    d. China under Deng Tsiao-Peng.
    e. France under Mitterand.

18. The most complete system of central planning is in:
    a. Yugoslavia.
    b. England.
    c. the Soviet Union.
    d. France.
    e. Sweden.

19. The society most intent on molding human nature away from individualistic greed was:
    a. Yugoslavia under Tito.
    b. China under Mao Tse-tung.
    c. France under DeGaulle.
    d. The Soviet Union under Stalin.
    e. Sweden under King Gustav V.

20. The idea that "small is beautiful" is least consistent with:
    a. Limits to Growth.
    b. central planning.
    c. E.F. Schumacher.
    d. Mahatma Gandhi
    e. antimaterialism.

TRUE/FALSE QUESTIONS

___ 1. Most property rights are limited by certain legal restrictions.

___ 2. Property rights and most legal rights are almost synonymous to many economists.

___ 3. Philosophical anarchists insist that laws are unnecessary for social harmony if people will merely cooperate.

___ 4. Syndicalists are only surpassed by anarchists in their dislike of formal hierarchies, and believe that governments everywhere should be overthrown.

___ 5. Socialism is an economic system characterized by the social ownership of all resources and goods and services.

___ 6. According to the labor theory of value, the value of any commodity is exactly proportional to the amount of socially necessary embodied labor time absorbed in its production.

___ 7. Among the specific reforms advocated by utopian socialists, free public education and safer working conditions have been adopted in most mixed economies.

___ 8. The French Labour Party is a direct descendant of Fabian socialism.

___ 9. The labor theory of value is an elaborate supply and demand approach to the determination of relative prices.

___ 10. Christian socialism was blended with revolutionary Marxism by South American priests and transformed into the evangelical metaphysics movement.

___ 11. The Marxist model of capitalism assumes that workers consume virtually all of their incomes.

___ 12. Dialectical materialism suggests that most events (theses) embody contradictions that generate their opposites (antitheses), and that conflicts between thesis and antithesis yield progress in the form of a synthesis.

___ 13. Marxists perceive capitalism as inherently stable.

___ 14. Karl Marx predicted that Russia would continually follow imperialistic policies into the foreseeable future.

___ 15. Prices and wages in the Soviet Union are determined primarily by market forces.

___ 16. Roberto Michels' "Iron Law of Oligarchy" does a reasonable job of explaining successive Soviet leaders over the past 60 years.

___ 17. China has recently been moving away from soviet-styled decentralized socialism to a more rigid central planning system.

___ 18. Economic growth in England has accelerated since it nationalized its heavy industry and freed its colonies.

___ 19. Taxes and payments into an elaborate welfare system absorb roughly half of Swedish national income.

___ 20. "Buddhist economics" rejects industrialization and emphasizes learning to live comfortably with less.

UNLIMITED MULTIPLE CHOICE

CAUTION: EACH QUESTION HAS FROM ZERO TO FOUR CORRECT RESPONSES.

___ 1. Anarchists believe that:
   a. government is inherently good.
   b. cooperation can foster social harmony and make laws unnecessary.
   c. social ownership of property is crucial for human welfare.
   d. private property rights conflict with basic human rights.

___ 2. Dialectical materialism:
   a. is a theory of history developed by Karl Marx.
   b. explains human history in terms of resolutions of contradictions that emerge in the economic fabric of society over time.
   c. explains historical change in terms of the interactions that occur between thesis and antithesis in the material world.
   d. is Marx's attempt to identify the roots of historical change.

___ 3. The labor theory of value suggests that:
   a. the value of any good is proportional to the labor time socially necessary for its production.
   b. supply basically determines relative prices.
   c. demand is important only by specifying which labor is "socially necessary."
   d. commodity values are proportional only to the direct labor time socially necessary for their production.

___ 4. Libertarians believe that:
   a. any form of coercion is unethical or immoral.
   b. individual freedom is the most important goal for any society.
   c. the economic problem is best solved by central planning.
   d. all nonhuman resources should be owned collectively.

___ 5. Syndicalists tend to believe that:
   a. industries should be reorganized into syndicates.
   b. government is inherently good.
   c. capital should be owned collectively by an industry's workers.
   d. workers can overthrow capitalism by staging nationwide strikes.

ANSWERS

Matching Key Terms and Concepts

SET I

Answer	MIC	ECO	MAC
1. c	p. 473	797	441
2. b	p. 473	797	441
3. j	p. 468	792	436
4. a	p. 479	803	447
5. e	p. 471	795	439
6. h	p. 470	794	438
7. g	p. 470	794	438
8. d	p. 473	797	441
9. f	p. 473	797	441
10. i	p. 468	792	436

SET II

Answer	MIC	ECO	MAC
1. j	p. 481	805	449
2. e	p. 481	805	449
3. c	p. 468	795	436
4. i	p. 471	795	439
5. b	p. 471	795	439
6. d	p. 469	793	437
7. a	p. 470	794	438
8. f	p. 475	799	443
9. g	p. 468	792	436
10. h	p. 479	803	447

SET III

Answer	MIC	ECO	MAC
1. f	p. 480	804	448
2. e	p. 476	800	444
3. d	p. 479	803	447
4. c	p. 478	802	446
5. b	p. 479	803	447
6. a	p. 479	803	447
7. g	p. 468	792	436

Chapter Review (Fill-in Questions)

1. Industrial Workers of the World (IWW), wobblies
2. profit-sharing, decisions
3. Marxism/Communism, Karl Marx
4. Friedrich Engels, dialectical materialism
5. contradictions, class conflicts
6. Yugoslavia, managed
7. indicative planning, France
8. Sweden, welfare state
9. England, forced saving and investment
10. Buddhist economics, limits to growth

Standard Multiple Choice

Answer	MIC	ECO	MAC
1. a	p. 468	792	436
2. d	p. 470	794	438
3. d	p. 469	793	437
4. e	p. 469	793	437
5. d	p. 469	793	437
6. b	p. 469	793	437
7. b	p. 470	794	438
8. c	p. 470	794	438
9. b	p. 471	795	439
10. c	p. 472	796	440
11. d	p. 473	797	441
12. a	p. 473	797	441
13. e	p. 474	798	442
14. a	p. 473	797	441
15. d	p. 473	797	441
16. e	p. 473	797	441
17. d	p. 478	802	446
18. c	p. 476	800	444
19. b	p. 478	802	446
20. b	p. 481	805	449

True/False Questions

Answer	MIC	ECO	MAC
1. T	p. 468	792	436
2. T	p. 468	792	436
3. T	p. 468	792	436
4. T	p. 469	793	437
5. F	p. 469	793	437
6. F	p. 473	797	441
7. T	p. 470	794	438
8. F	p. 470	794	438
9. F	p. 473	797	441
10. F	p. 471	795	439
11. T	p. 473	797	441
12. T	p. 471	795	439
13. F	p. 473	797	441
14. T	p. 474	798	442
15. F	p. 476	800	442
16. T	p. 477	801	445
17. F	p. 478	802	446
18. F	p. 480	804	448
19. T	p. 479	803	447
20. T	p. 481	805	449

Unlimited Multiple Choice

Answer	MIC	ECO	MAC
1. bd	p. 468	792	436
2. abcd	p. 471	795	439
3. abc	p. 473	797	441
4. ab	p. 468	792	436
5. acd	p. 469	793	437